W9-CFQ-426

FRANCE

THE BRITANNICA GUIDE TO COUNTRIES OF THE EUROPEAN UNION

FRANCE

EDITED BY MICHAEL RAY, ASSISTANT EDITOR, GEOGRAPHY

Britannica®
Educational Publishing

IN ASSOCIATION WITH

ROSEN
EDUCATIONAL SERVICES

Published in 2014 by Britannica Educational Publishing
(a trademark of Encyclopædia Britannica, Inc.)
in association with Rosen Educational Services, LLC
29 East 21st Street, New York, NY 10010.

First Edition

Britannica Educational Publishing
J.E. Luebering: Director, Core Reference Group
Adam Augustyn: Assistant Manager, Core Reference Group
Marilyn L. Barton: Senior Coordinator, Production Control
Steven Bosco: Director, Editorial Technologies
Lisa S. Braucher: Senior Producer and Data Editor
Yvette Charboneau: Senior Copy Editor
Kathy Nakamura: Manager, Media Acquisition
Edited by: Michael Ray, Assistant Editor, Geography

Rosen Educational Services
Nicholas Croce: Editor
Nelson Sá: Art Director
Cindy Reiman: Photography Manager
Amy Feinberg: Photo Researcher
Brian Garvey: Designer, Cover Design
Introduction by Alexandra Hanson-Harding

Library of Congress Cataloging-in-Publication Data

France/edited by Michael Ray.—First edition.
    pages cm.—(The Britannica guide to countries of the European Union)
"In association with Britannica Educational Publishing, Rosen Educational Services."
Includes bibliographical references and index.
ISBN 978-1-61530-964-1 (library binding)
1. France—Juvenile literature. 2. European Union—France—Juvenile literature.
I. Ray, Michael (Michael J.), 1973-
DC17.F656 2013
944—dc23
                                                            2012045605

Manufactured in the United States of America

CONTENTS

8

21

26

38

49

62

71

76

108

163

198

209

263

293

305

Great Britain

Lille

Arniens

Le Havre

Paris

Brest

Rennes

Le Mans

Nantes

Tours

France

Bastia

Limages

Clermont
Ferrand

Ajaccio

Sa
Et

Bordeaux

Nimes

Montpellier

Toulouse

Spain

Perpignan

Andorra

Holland

um

Germany

uxembourg

Metz

Nancy

Strasbourg

Mulhouse

on

Switzerland

enoble

Italy

Monaco

Nice

le

Toulon

"Liberty, Equality, Fraternity"–this concept has been a part of the French identity since the Revolutionary era of the late 18th century. Although it was but one of the mottoes to emerge from this period, it has proved to be the most enduring. Some Revolutionary phrases were discarded due to their association with one political faction or another. The rousing ultimatum "Liberty, equality, or death!" fell into disuse after the excesses of the Reign of Terror led tens of thousands into the embrace of Madame Guillotine.

"Liberty, Equality, Fraternity" does present some problems when accepted as a whole, however. Can the three concepts, in fact, exist simultaneously? If all are truly equal, has not the liberty to excel been constrained? When the revolutions of 1848 reached France, Roman Catholic priests promoted the notion of "a fraternity in Christ," adding a religious dimension that would prove to be at odds with an avowedly secular state. This was, after all, a nation that had previously attempted to abolish religion from the public sphere by replacing the Gregorian calendar with a "republican" one. Months were renamed, weeks were reconstructed as ten-day "decades," and all traces of Christian holidays were removed. Nonetheless, the motto has received official sanction from numerous French governments, most recently in 1958, when the constitution of the Fifth Republic declared it to be "the maxim of the Republic."

It is ironic then, that so much of French history has been driven by individuals, rather than mass movements. The Revolution itself—perhaps the defining moment in French history—began as an uprising within the nobility before descending into factionalism and, ultimately, dictatorial rule. Even the sansculotte, a highly influential group of working-class, radical revolutionaries who distinguished themselves by eschewing the culotte (knee breeches) common to bourgeois and aristocratic fashion, fell under the sway of journalist Jacques-René Hébert. When Hébert overplayed his hand in the lethal political games that typified the Reign of Terror, he was executed and the sansculotte were effectively sidelined for the remainder of the Revolutionary period. Such were the fortunes of the Revolution; the line between political power and the grave was a blurry one, and often subject to the whims of the architect of the Terror, Maximilien de Robespierre.

Robespierre is probably the best-known figure of the Revolutionary era, but opinions about his character remain divided more than two centuries after his death. Was he a bloody-handed dictator, or merely a patriot who was carried too far by the popular spirit that he had tried to embody? Like other major figures of the Revolution, such as Hébert and Georges Danton, Robespierre was a product of the bourgeoisie. The son of a lawyer, he followed in his father's footsteps and proved to be a gifted student of law and philosophy. He established a reputation as a champion of the poor and working classes at a young age, and he was an outspoken critic of the monarchy. In 1789 Robespierre was elected to serve in the Estates-General, an assembly of clergy, nobles, and commoners that had not met in 175 years. At the time of his election, Robespierre was 30 years old. He would not live to see 37.

Traditionally, the Estates-General had only been called at times of political or financial crisis, and the situation in 1789 certainly had a share of both. Louis XVI was an ineffectual ruler, a far cry from Louis XIV, who had virtually provided the template for the enlightened absolute monarch. The French state was also bleeding cash as a result of the American Revolution. Participation in the war had boosted Louis XVI's prestige, but it further drained an already ailing French treasury. Thus, having failed to support

financial reformers within his own cabinet, Louis XVI was compelled to summon the Estates in an attempt to shore up his weakening regime. In reality, the action would prove to be the beginning of the end of the monarchy.

The Estates-General soon fell to infighting, as the Third Estate (the commoners, including Robespierre) declared themselves to be an independent body called the National Assembly. Rumors of a plot to disperse the Assembly buzzed in the streets of Paris, and Louis XVI had, in fact, called troops to the city for just such an undertaking. It was against this background that a Parisian mob stormed the Bastille on July 14, 1789. In the face of a popular uprising in the capital, Louis XVI capitulated and the National Assembly was allowed to proceed. The result was the Declaration of the Rights of Man and of the Citizen, a document promulgated in August 1789 that served as a summary of French Enlightenment thought.

The Declaration's first article read: "Men are born and remain free and equal in rights. Social distinctions may be based only on considerations of the common good." This statement was a stark rebuke of the system of courtly ranks and privileges that characterized the ancient regime, so it is not surprising that Louis XVI would refuse to endorse the document. The tension between the king and the National Assembly persisted until early October 1789, when a mob descended on Versailles and compelled the royal family to relocate to Paris. Revolutionary politics became a national craze, with newspapers and social clubs celebrating the spirit of the age. The new administration of the National Assembly attempted to further the goals of the Declaration, notably those of its second article, which guaranteed the rights to "Liberty, Property, Safety and Resistance to Oppression." Of course, the French treasury was still virtually empty, so the right to property was nudged aside as the Assembly nationalized the lands belonging to the Roman Catholic Church in November 1789. This property, which amounted to roughly ten percent of the land in France, was placed at the disposal of the state. Publicly issued bonds called assignats were issued against its value to finance the national debt. Although the former church lands eventually passed to the bourgeoisie and the peasantry, the number of assignats in circulation had tripled by September 1790, and inflation, as well as declining public confidence in their value, caused the Revolution's de facto currency to depreciate.

The government that the Assembly envisioned was essentially a constitutional monarchy, and statesmen such as the comte de Mirabeau endeavored to reconcile the forces of revolution with the ancien regime, but Louis's attempt to flee the country in June 1791 put to rest any thoughts of shared power. Louis was apprehended at Varennes and returned to the capital. Whatever remaining prestige might have been attached to the crown was now lost, and the long term prospects for the monarchy—and for Louis himself—grew increasingly dim. Moderates and royalists clashed with radicals over the course of the Revolution, as émigrés (French aristocrats who had fled the country in the early days of the Revolution) plotted against the Revolutionary government from outside its borders. The Jacobin Club, one of the most prominent political societies to emerge from the Revolution, underwent a schism in the wake of Louis's attempted escape, and conservative members, rejecting a proposal to replace the king, split from the group. Among those who remained with the Jacobins was Robespierre, and the character of the former soon came to reflect that of the latter.

As the pace of the Revolution accelerated, resistance from counterrevolutionary forces both at home and abroad strengthened, and the Revolutionary response grew more extreme. Émigrés who failed to return to France by January 1792 were condemned to death in absentia as traitors, and the following month, their property was confiscated by the state. In April of that year France declared war on Austria, the native country of Louis XVI's queen, Marie-Antoinette. Louis approved of the move, as he believed that his survival hinged on liberation by a foreign army or the rise of reactionary elements as a response to a foreign threat. Jacques-Pierre Brissot, a leader of the bourgeois Girondin faction, agitated for war as a means of exporting the Revolution to other countries and neutralizing the émigré threat once and for all. The Austrian army, bolstered by Prussian troops and forces mustered by the émigrés, advanced quickly on Paris, and residents of the capital reacted with a mixture of panic and fierce nationalism. As volunteers rushed to the front in an attempt to stem the advancing Austro-Prussian tide, Paris mobs betrayed a hint of the Terror that was to come. On August 10, 1792, an armed crowd stormed and occupied the Tuileries Palace, the Paris residence where Louis had been kept under house arrest since his attempted flight the previous year. The Legislative Assembly, the successor to the National Assembly, suspended the rule of the king and Robespierre, who had advocated against both the monarchy and the war with Austria, saw his popularity soar.

The political stock of other Jacobins increased dramatically in the wake of the insurrection against the king. Georges Danton was widely credited with the successful overthrow of the monarchy, although his exact role in the affair remains somewhat murky. Jacobin journalist Jean-Paul Marat incited the Paris crowds to further action with nationalistic polemics that raised the specter of threats from within. The mobs responded by attacking the political prisoners held in Paris's jails, fearing that they were plotting against the Revolution. Some 1,200 members of the nobility and the clergy were killed in the space of five days in September 1792. Some were hacked down in the streets while they were being transferred between jails. Many were executed after show trials conducted by the mob found them guilty of crimes against the Revolution. Accounts of the massacres

were publicized abroad, to the shock and horror of readers. The London Times inflated the death toll by a factor of ten and recounted a tale of "trunkless heads and mangled bodies" paraded through the streets of Paris in the name of victory and justice. The indictment by the Times concluded, "Read this ye Englishmen, with attention, and ardently pray that your happy Constitution may never be outraged by the despotic tyranny of Equalization." Robespierre did not take part directly in the overthrow of the king or the violence that followed, but he absolved the participants of any guilt in the matters. Having received Robespierre's endorsement, the mob responded in kind. Parisians elected him to lead the city's delegation to the National Convention, the successor to the Legislative Assembly.

Moderate and radical forces contested for dominance in the National Convention in a battle that would determine the course of the Revolution. Although staunch proponents of republican principles, the Girondin faction resisted the centralization of power in Paris and opposed the proto-Marxist price controls advocated by radicals such as the sansculotte. The Montagnard faction, composed of Jacobins and closely associated with Paris, championed the causes of the lower classes. The first major clash between the two forces concerned the fate of Louis XVI, and Robespierre rallied the Montagnards with calls for the king's death. Some among the Girondins counseled restraint, and this fueled suspicions of lingering royalist sentiment among the moderates. Louis's execution in January 1793 signaled the decline of the Girondins, a descent that accelerated in subsequent months. The British joined the fight against the Revolutionary army, and the war turned against the French, as prices continued to rise in the capital. Robespierre, emboldened by his role in the death of the king, laid the blame for these events on the Girondins, and in May 1793, he called for a popular insurrection to support his campaign against them. The Girondins were purged, and the Committee of Public Safety, an organ that had been created to oversee French domestic and foreign policy, came to occupy a central place in the power structure of the Revolution.

Danton, who had been the guiding force within the Committee, was set aside in July 1793, as Robespierre and the Jacobins came to dominate the body. Throughout the summer of 1793, France was a cauldron of unrest. Food shortages in Paris caused prices to skyrocket and counterrevolutionary uprisings gained strength in the countryside, as tens of thousands took up arms in the Vendée. Robespierre dealt with the former by introducing the Maximum, a price control on food, while the latter he fought with the Reign of Terror. Having earlier decided that the Revolution could only survive if it were guided by "one single will," Robespierre exercised dictatorial power over the Committee and, thus, over France itself. Through mass conscription, the Revolutionary army was able to put over a million men under

arms, and the Terror truly began to live up to its name as the enemies of the Revolution—both real and imagined—were arrested. The spirit of the Terror was best captured by Louis de Saint-Just, a Committee member whose militant zeal exceeded Robespierre's, when he said, "We must not only punish traitors, but all people who are not enthusiastic." Such was the case in 1794, when Robespierre led attacks against Hébert (who wished to accelerate the pace of the Revolution) and Danton (who wished to slow it), and dozens of their followers were led to the guillotine. In all, over 300,000 people were arrested during the Reign of Terror and 17,000 were executed, with countless others dying in prison.

One of the last victims of the Terror was its creator. On June 10, 1794, the Law of 22 Prairial was passed, which stripped accused prisoners of the right to counsel or witness testimony. In the 49 days that followed the passage of the law, almost 1,400 people were executed. As French armies experienced success abroad, the French people grew weary of the increasingly harsh measures employed by Robespierre and the Committee. In spite of his spirited oratorical defenses, the National Convention rose up in revolt against Robespierre and his fall was swift and violent. He was arrested on July 27, 1794, and he was executed the following day. The result was a succession of elections, coups, and plots that culminated in the rise of Napoleon Bonaparte, who had his own opinions about the Revolutionary notions of liberty, equality, and fraternity.

CHAPTER 1

LAND

France is among the globe's oldest countries, the product of an alliance of duchies and principalities under a single ruler in the Middle Ages. Today, as in that era, central authority is vested in the state, even though a measure of autonomy has been granted to the country's 21 *régions* in recent decades. The French people look to the state as the primary guardian of liberty, and the state in turn provides a generous program of amenities for its citizens, from free education to health care and pension plans.

Historically and culturally among the most important countries in the Western world, France has also played a highly significant role in international affairs, with former colonies in every corner of the globe. Bounded by the Atlantic Ocean and the Mediterranean Sea, the Alps and the Pyrenees, France has long provided a geographic, economic, and linguistic bridge joining northern and southern Europe. It is one of Europe's most important agricultural producers and a leading industrial power.

France lies near the western end of the great Eurasian landmass, largely between latitudes 42° and 51° N. Roughly hexagonal in outline, its continental territory is bordered on the northeast by Belgium and Luxembourg, on the east by Germany, Switzerland, and Italy, on the south by the Mediterranean Sea, Spain, and Andorra, on the west by the Bay of Biscay, and on the northwest by the English Channel (La Manche). To the north, France faces

Château Gaillard, a 12th-century castle, overlook the Seine River in the Normandy region of norther France. © Pierre Belzeaux/Photo Researchers

Encyclopædia Britannica, Inc.

southeastern England across the narrow Strait of Dover (Pas de Calais). Monaco is an independent enclave on the south coast, while the island of Corsica in the Mediterranean is treated as an integral part of the country.

RELIEF

The French landscape, for the most part, is composed of relatively low-lying plains, plateaus, and older mountain blocks, or massifs. This pattern clearly predominates over that of the younger, high ranges, such as the Alps and the Pyrenees. The diversity of the land is typical of Continental Europe.

Three main geologic regions are distinguishable: the skeletal remains of ancient mountains that make up the Hercynian massifs; the northern and western plains; and the higher young fold mountains in the south and southeast, including the Alps and the Pyrenees, with their attendant narrow plains. Much of the detailed relief can be attributed geologically to the varying differences in the resistance of rocks to erosion. A great deal of the present landscape detail is due to glaciation during the Pleistocene Epoch (about 2,600,000 to 11,700 years ago). France lay outside the range of the great ice sheets that descended upon the northern part of Europe, so the direct sculpting of the land by ice was restricted to the Alps, the Pyrenees, the Vosges, Corsica, and the highest summits of the Massif Central. Just outside these glacial areas, in what are known as periglacial lands, repeated freezing and thawing of unprotected surfaces modified slopes by the movement of waste sheets (formed of shattered bedrock), producing very much the landscape that exists today. Pleistocene periglacial action generated the sheets of the fine windblown limon, or loess, that is the basis of the most fertile lowland soils, and it possibly also created the Landes, a sandy plain in southwestern France. The development of river terraces (flat, raised surfaces alongside valleys) was another characteristic of periglacial action.

THE HERCYNIAN MASSIFS

The physical structure of France is dominated by a group of ancient mountains in the shape of a gigantic V, the sides of which form the two branches of Hercynian folding that took place between 345 and 225 million years ago. The eastern branch comprises the Ardennes, the Vosges, and the eastern part of the Massif Central, while the Hercynian massifs to the west comprise the western part of the Massif Central and the Massif Armoricain.

These highlands are composed of resistant metamorphic, crystalline, and sedimentary rocks from the Paleozoic Era (about 540 to 250 million years ago), the last including coal deposits. They share the common characteristic of repeated planation, or flattening. Some variety is provided by subsequent deformation and faulting, such as in the ridge-and-valley areas of the Massif Armoricain, where upland surfaces are deeply carved by valleys in dramatic fashion.

THE ARDENNES

The Ardennes massif is an extension, from Belgium into France, of the great Rhine Uplands, characterized by rocks of slate and quartz from the Paleozoic Era. Differential erosion of Paleozoic rocks has produced long ridges alternating with open valleys crossed by the Sambre and Meuse rivers.

THE VOSGES

The Alpine earth movements produced a great upswelling along the line of the present upper Rhine, leaving the Vosges with steep eastern slopes that descend to a rift valley containing the plains of Alsace and Baden; on the west the upland descends rather gently into the scarplands of Lorraine. The Vosges reaches its maximum elevation in the south, near the Alps, where crystalline rocks are exposed; the highest summits are called ballons, and the highest is the Ballon de Guebwiller (Mount Guebwiller), with an elevation of 4,669 feet (1,423 metres). To the north the Vosges massif dips beneath a cover of forested sandstone from the Triassic Period (about 250 to 200 million years ago).

THE MASSIF CENTRAL

The vast plateau of the Massif Central covers about 33,000 square miles (86,000 square km), or some one-sixth of the area

Cinder cones of the Chaîne des Puys in the Massif Central, France. Christian Kempf from TSW—CLICK/Chicago

of the country. The Massif Central borders the Rhône-Saône valley on the east, the Languedoc lowlands on the south, the Aquitaine Basin on the southwest, and the Paris Basin on the north. The planation that occurred following the creation of the Hercynian belt removed the ancient mountain chains, but the block was uplifted under the impact of the Alpine mountain-building movements, with a steep descent on the east and southeast, nearest the Alps, and a gentle decline under the later sediments of the Aquitaine Basin to the west and the Paris Basin to the north. Much of the western massif, notably Limousin, consists of monotonous erosion surfaces. The centre and eastern parts of the massif were much fractured in the course of the Alpine movements, leaving behind upthrust blocks, of which the most conspicuous is the Morvan, the forested bastion of the northeastern corner of the massif. Downfaulted basins filled with sediments from Paleogene and Neogene times (i.e., about 65 to 2.6 million years ago), such as the Limagne near the city of Clermont-Ferrand in south-central France, were also formed. Faulting was associated with volcanic activity, which in the central part of the region formed the vast and complex structures of the massifs of Cantal and Monts Dore, where the Sancy Hill (Puy de Sancy), at 6,184 feet (1,885 metres), is the highest summit of the Massif Central. Farther west, on the fringe of the Limagne, is the extraordinary Chaîne des Puys, whose numerous cinder cones were formed only about 10,000 years ago and still retain the newness of their craters, lava flows, and other volcanic features.

Numerous mineral springs, such as those at Vichy in the central Auvergne region, are a relic of volcanic activity.

The eastern and southern portions of the massif, from the Morvan through the Cévennes to the final southwestern termination of the massif in the Noire Mountains (Montagne Noire), are marked by a series of hill masses that overlook the lowlands of the Rhône-Saône river valley and the région of Languedoc-Roussillon; at least one of these uplands, Beaujolais, has become famous for the grapevines grown at its foot. Between the hill masses lie infolded coal deposits at locations such as Alès, Decazeville, Saint-Étienne, and Blanzy (Le Creusot) that are of more historical than contemporary importance. To the southwest the rocks of the massif are overlain by a great thickness of limestones (causses) from the Jurassic Period (about 200 to 145 million years ago). Lacking in surface water and little populated, this portion of the massif is crossed by rivers that trench dramatic gorges, notably that of the Tarn. Extensive cave systems bear remains of prehistoric art, such as that of Pêche-Merle in the Lot valley and the Lascaux Grotto in the Vézère valley.

THE MASSIF ARMORICAIN

The Massif Armoricain is contained mostly within the région of Brittany (Bretagne), a peninsula washed by the Bay of Biscay on the south and the English Channel on the north. The massif continues beyond Brittany eastward and across the Loire to the south. It is much lower than the other

Hercynian massif; its highest point, the Mont des Avaloirs, on the eastern edge of the massif, attains an elevation of 1,368 feet (417 metres). Alternating bands of Paleozoic sediments and granitic rocks give the massif a generally east-west grain, particularly expressed in the headlands and bays of its rugged coast.

THE GREAT LOWLANDS

The northern and western plains, which together constitute the great lowlands, can be subdivided into five distinct regions: the Paris Basin, the Flanders Plain, the Alsace Plain, the Loire plains, and the Aquitaine Basin.

THE PARIS BASIN

Between the Ardennes, the Vosges, the Massif Central, and the Massif Armoricain lie the sedimentary beds that make up the Paris Basin. Alternating beds of limestones, sands, and clays dip toward the central Paris Basin, their outcrops forming concentric patterns. Especially to the east, erosion has left the more resistant rocks, usually limestones, with a steep, outward-facing scarp edge and a gentler slope toward the centre of the basin. The central Paris Basin is filled by rocks from the Paleogene and Neogene periods, mostly limestones, that form the level plateaus of regions such as Beauce, Brie, Île-de-France, Valois, and Soissonnais. This area is mostly covered with windblown limon, which is the basis of an excellent loamy soil. The limestone levels overlap in sandwich formation. Eroded remnants of higher formations have been left behind as isolated hills called buttes, perhaps the most famous of which is in Paris—the Butte de Montmartre, on which is one of the city's most famous districts. Sandy areas adjoining the limestone formations bear forests, such as the Forest of Fontainebleau, southwest of Paris. In the east, in the regions of Lorraine and Burgundy, are Triassic and Jurassic rocks; among the scarps the Moselle Hills are noted for their minette, low-grade iron ore. In the extreme southeast the Jurassic limestone Plateau de Langres forms the watershed between the Seine and Rhône-Saône river systems; it is crossed by major routes linking Paris with the south. The eastern basin includes the chalk country of Champagne and the Argonne massif. In the western part of the Paris Basin, scarps in the Jurassic and Cretaceous rocks of Normandy are not prominent. The chalk plateau is trenched by the lower Seine in a course marked by spectacular meanders and river cliffs. The plateau surfaces are frequently mantled by clay-with-flints and other residual deposits, producing heavy soils with much forest, grassland, and orchard cultivation. Farther north the wide chalk plateaus of Picardy and Artois are generally covered with limon, which provides for a rich agriculture; many stretches of magnificent white chalk cliffs line the English Channel coast.

THE FLANDERS PLAIN

In the extreme north the French boundary includes a small part of the Anglo-Belgian basin. Coastal sand dunes protect the reclaimed marshes of French Flanders from invasion by the sea.

THE ALSACE PLAIN

East of the Paris Basin is the Alsace Plain, bordered by the Vosges on the west, the Saône basin on the southwest, the Jura Mountains on the south, the Rhine River on the east, and Germany on the north. The terrace and foothills bordering the Rhine are covered with soil-enriching limon. Alluvial fans, which are laid down by tributaries emerging from the Vosges, and much of the floodplain of the Rhine and its major tributary, the Ill River, are forested. The Sundgau region of the Alsace Plain, which lies between the Jura and the Ill River above Mulhouse, is another great alluvial fan overlaying impermeable clays, which hold up numerous lakes. The Rhine River and its tributaries continue to deposit thick sediments on the floodplain. The river is canalized, to the considerable detriment of the water table on both sides.

THE LOIRE PLAINS

Toward the southwest the Paris Basin opens on a group of plains that follow the Loire valley. The hills of this area, such as the limestone plateaus of the Touraine region and the crystalline plateaus of the Anjou and Vendée areas, are cut by the broad valleys of the Loire and its tributaries. The middle Loire valley, which varies in width from about 3 to 6 miles (about 5 to 10 km), is famous for its châteaus and its scenic beauty.

THE AQUITAINE BASIN

The Loire countryside links with the Aquitaine Basin of southwestern France through the gap known as the Gate of Poitou. The Aquitaine Basin is much smaller than the Paris Basin, and, while it is bounded in the south by the Pyrenees, in the northeast it runs into the low foothills of the Massif Central. The slopes of both the Pyrenees and the Massif Central decline toward the central valley of the Garonne River. The Aquitaine Basin lacks the clearly marked concentric relief of the Paris Basin. In the north it has limestone and marl plateaus cut by the fertile river valleys emerging from the Massif Central. The southern low plateaus were mostly filled by a mass of rather ill-defined Paleogene and Neogene sands and gravel called the molasse, stripped off the rising Pyrenees. The foot of the central Pyrenees is marked by a remarkable series of confluent alluvial fans forming the Lannemezan Plateau. The Landes, an area lying between the Garonne and Adour rivers to the west, has a surface that consists of fine sand underlain by impermeable iron pan, or bedrock. The area, once covered by heath and marshes, is now reclaimed and planted with maritime pine. South of the wide, deep Gironde estuary, the Bay of Biscay coast is lined by enormous sand dunes, behind which are shallow lagoons.

The château of Villandry, built in 1532, and its formal gardens in the Loire valley just east of Tours, France. © Rob Palmer from TSW—CLICK/Chicago

THE YOUNGER MOUNTAINS AND ADJACENT PLAINS

France's third principal geologic region includes the Pyrennes, Jura Mountains, and the Alps. Located in southern and southeastern France, they are among the best-known and most beautiful mountains in the world. In addition to these relatively younger mountain chains, the region also includes the narrow plains that adjoin the ranges.

PYRENEES, JURA, AND ALPS

The Pyrenees, whose foothills shelter the picturesque Basque countryside, constitute the most ancient of the more recently formed mountains in France. They stretch for more than 280 miles (450 km), making a natural barrier between France and Spain. Their formation, which began in the Mesozoic Era (about 250 to 65 million years ago), continued in the Paleogene and Neogene periods and perhaps even in the beginning of the Quaternary Period (i.e., from about 2.6 million years ago). The central and highest part of the barrier is composed of a series of parallel chains with only a few, difficult-to-reach passes that have sheer drops at each end. A section of the mountain chain centring on Mont Perdu (Spanish: Monte Perdido) was named a UNESCO World Heritage site in 1997.

The Jura Mountains, extending into Switzerland, are composed of folded limestone. The northeastern part of the Jura, which has the most pronounced folding, is in Switzerland. The highest point, however, is Mount Neige (5,636 feet [1,718 metres]), in France.

The French Alps are only a part of the great chain that extends across Europe, but they include its highest point, Mont Blanc (15,771 feet [4,807 metres]). These majestic mountains were formed in a series of foldings during Paleogene and Neogene times. They include the two greatest regions of permanent snow and glaciers in Europe. The northern Alps are relatively easy to cross because of the numerous valleys created by the movement of glaciers. The relief of the southern Alps is much less orderly, and the valleys, which were not affected by glaciation, form narrow and winding gorges. Like the Pyrenees, the Alps form

a natural barrier, dropping sharply down to the Po River plain in Italy.

THE SOUTHERN PLAINS

Between these young mountains and the ancient Massif Central is a series of plains, including those of the Saône and the Rhône rivers, which extend southward to the great triangular delta of the Rhône on the Mediterranean coast. Its seaward face, the Camargue region, comprises a series of lakes, marshes, and sand spits and includes one of Europe's important wetland nature reserves. West of the Rhône delta the Languedoc coastal plain is broad and rather featureless; behind its sand-spit coast are several formerly mosquito-ridden lagoons, now part of a resort complex. At the southwestern end the foothills of the Pyrenees reach to the rocky coast of the Roussillon region. East of the Rhône delta the lowlands are more fragmentary; in the Côte d'Azur region the Alpine foothills and the ancient Maures and Esterel massifs reach to the Mediterranean, forming the coves, capes, and harbours of the country's most famous tourist and retirement area, the French Riviera. Corsica is also highly regarded for its natural scenery. A number of the island's peaks reach over 6,500 feet, and parts of it are under wild forest or covered with undergrowth called maquis.

DRAINAGE

The river systems of France are determined by a major divide in the far eastern part

The Mediterranean-washed pebble beach at Nice on the French Riviera. © Nedra Westwater/ Black Star

of the country, running from the southern end of the Vosges down the eastern and southeastern edge of the Massif Central to the Noire Mountains, the southwestern promontory of the massif. This divide is broken by occasional cols (depressions) and lowland corridors, notably the Langres Plateau, across the Jurassic outer rim of the Paris Basin. Along the divide originate most of the rivers of the larger, western part of the country, including the Seine and the Loire. Other major rivers include the Garonne, originating in the Pyrenees, and the Rhône and the Rhine, originating in the Alps.

THE SEINE SYSTEM

The main river of the Paris Basin, the Seine, 485 miles (780 km) in length, is joined upstream on the left bank by its tributary the Yonne, on the right bank south of Paris by the Marne, and north of the city by the Oise. While the Seine has a regular flow throughout the year, there may be flooding in the spring and, occasionally more

The Seine River along the Île Saint-Louis, Paris.
© Dana Hyde/Photo Researchers

severely, during the customary fall-winter peak of lowland rivers. Efforts have been made to reduce flooding on the Seine and its tributaries by the building of reservoirs. A number of islands dot the Seine along its meandering, generally westward course across the central Paris Basin and through the capital city itself. One of these, the Île de la Cité, forms the very heart of the city of Paris. Eventually the river enters the English Channel at Le Havre.

THE LOIRE SYSTEM

The Loire, the longest French river, flows for 634 miles (1,020 km) and drains the widest area (45,000 square miles [117,000 square km]). It is an extremely irregular river, with an outflow eight times greater in December and January than in August and September. Rising in the Massif Central on Mount Gerbier-de-Jonc, it flows northward over impervious terrain, with many gorgelike sections. Near Nevers it is joined by the Allier, another river of the massif. Within the Paris Basin the Loire continues to flow northward, as if to join the Seine system, but then takes a wide bend to the west to enter the Atlantic past Nantes and Saint-Nazaire. The Loire is artificially joined to the Seine by several canals. The river's torrential flow, a hindrance to navigation, covers its floodplain with sand and gravel, which has commercial importance. The river is also a source of cooling water for a chain of atomic power stations near its course, which has raised concerns among environmentalists, as have various dam projects along the river. UNESCO designated the valley, between Sully-sur-Loire and Chalonnes, a World Heritage site in 2000.

THE GARONNE SYSTEM

The Garonne, in the southwest, flows through the centre of the Aquitaine Basin. It is the shortest of the main French rivers, with a length of 357 miles (575 km), and it drains only 21,600 square miles (56,000 square km). Its outflow is irregular, with high waters in winter (due to the oceanic rainfall) and in spring, when the snow melts, but with meagre flows in summer and autumn. Its source is in the central Pyrenees in the Aran (Joyeuse) Valley in

Spain, and its main tributaries, the Tarn, the Aveyron, the Lot, and the Dordogne, originate in the Massif Central. With the exception of the Gironde estuary, which is formed by the confluence of the Garonne and the Dordogne and is fully penetrated by the sea, the whole network is generally useless for navigation and is filled with powerful, rapid, and dangerous currents.

THE RHÔNE SYSTEM

In eastern France the direction of the main rivers is predominantly north-south through the Alpine furrow. The Rhône is the great river of the southeast. Rising in the Alps, it passes through Lake Geneva (Lac Léman) to enter France, which has 324 miles (521 km) of its total length of 505 miles (813 km). At Lyon it receives its major tributary, the Saône. The regime of the Rhône is complex. Near Lyon the Rhône and its important Isère and Drôme tributaries, draining from the Alps, have a marked late spring–early summer peak caused by the melting of snow and ice. While this peak is generally characteristic of the river as a whole, it is considerably modified by the contribution of the Saône, of the Durance, and of some tributaries in the Mediterranean south as a result of the fall-winter rainfall peak. Thus, the powerful Rhône has a remarkably ample flow in all seasons. The course of the river and the local water tables have been much modified by a series of dams to generate power and to permit navigation to Lyon. The Rhône also supplies cooling water to a series of atomic power stations. West

of the Rhône the Bas Rhône–Languedoc canal, constructed after World War II to provide irrigation, has proved to be an essential element in the remarkable urban and industrial development of Languedoc. East of the Rhône the Canal de Provence taps the unpolluted waters of a Rhône tributary, the Durance, supplying Aix-en-Provence, Marseille, Toulon, and the coast of Provence with drinking water and providing impetus for urban expansion. At its delta, beginning about 25 miles (40 km) from the Mediterranean, the Rhône and its channels deposit significant amounts of alluvium to form the Camargue region.

THE RHINE SYSTEM

The Rhine forms the eastern boundary of France for some 118 miles (190 km). In this section its course is dominated by the melting of snow and ice from Alpine headstreams, giving it a pronounced late spring–summer peak and often generally low water in autumn. The Ill, which joins the Rhine at Strasbourg, drains southern Alsace. The Rhine valley has been considerably modified by the construction on the French side of the lateral Grand Canal d'Alsace, for power generation and navigation. The eastern Paris Basin is drained by two tributaries, the Moselle, partly canalized, and the Meuse; the former reaches the Rhine by way of Luxembourg and Germany, and the latter, as the Maas (Dutch), reaches the Rhine delta at the North Sea by way of Belgium and the Netherlands.

THE SMALLER RIVERS AND THE LAKES

North of the Artois ridge, a number of small rivers flow into the Escaut (Flemish and Dutch: Schelde) to reach its North Sea estuary through Belgium. The Somme rises in northwestern France and flows a short distance into the English Channel, and in the southwest the Charente, rising in the western Limousin plateau, and the Adour, rising in the central Pyrenees, flow into the Atlantic.

The French hydrographic system also includes a number of natural lakes of different origin. There are the lakes in depressions carved out by glaciation at the western periphery of the Alps, such as the lakes of Annecy and Bourget, the latter being the largest natural lake entirely within France. Others occur on the surfaces of ancient massifs and include the lakes of the Vosges. Some lakes are caused by structural faults and are lodged in narrow valleys, as are the Jura lakes. There are also lakes of volcanic origin, such as those in the Massif Central (crater lakes and lakes ponded behind lava flows), and regions scattered with lagoons or ponds, either created by coastal phenomena, as on the Landes (Atlantic) and Languedoc (Mediterranean) coasts, or caused by impervious terrain and poor local drainage, as in the Sologne plain. Major artificial lakes include the Serre-Ponçon reservoir, on the Durance River in the Alps, and the Sarrans and Bort-les-Orgues reservoirs, both in the Massif Central.

SOILS

On a broad, general scale, virtually the whole of France can be classified in the zone of brown forest soils, or brown earths. These soils, which develop under deciduous forest cover in temperate climatic conditions, are of excellent agricultural value. Some climate-related variation can be detected within the French brown earth group; in the high-rainfall and somewhat cool conditions of northwestern France, carbonates and other minerals tend to be leached downward, producing a degraded brown earth soil of higher acidity and lesser fertility; locally this may approach the nature of the north European podzol. The brown earth zone gives way southward to the zone of Mediterranean soils, which in France cover only a limited area. They are developed from decalcified clays with a coarse sand admixture and are typically red in colour because of the upward migration of iron oxides during the warm, dry summers. These soils can be quite fertile.

Over large areas of France, soils have developed not directly from the disintegrated bedrock but from the waste sheets created by periglacial action. These may provide a particularly favourable soil material; most notable is the windblown limon that mantles the Paleogene and Neogene limestone plateaus of the central Paris Basin and the chalk beds to the northwest, the basis of the finest arable soils of France. The quality of the soils depends heavily upon the origin of their waste sheets; sand spreads derived from the granites of the Hercynian massifs, for example, provide only poor soils. The bedrock, however, is not without influence. Soils developed over clays are likely to be heavy and wet, although not necessarily infertile, as in the Jurassic clay and chalk vales of the eastern Paris Basin. Limestone and chalk enrich soils with lime, which is generally favourable, but there is a marked north-south contrast. The limestone areas of southern France tend to be swept almost bare of soil by erosion; the soil then collects in valleys and hollows. The soils of the higher mountains are naturally stony and unfavourable.

Finally, human action is an extremely important factor in soil quality. As soon as the original forest was cleared, some modification of the soil was inevitable. Generally, farmers through the ages have maintained or improved soil quality by draining and manuring; especially noteworthy were the activities of Flemish peasants who virtually created their soil out of a marshy wilderness. Not all human intervention has been as successful, however. For example, the degradation of brown earths under heath in western France is not a natural feature but the product of human clearance and grazing practices. Large-scale arable cultivation with no use of animal manure is leading in places to soil degradation and soil erosion.

CLIMATE

The climate of France is generally favourable to cultivation. Most of France lies in the southern part of the temperate zone, although the subtropical zone encompasses its southern fringe. All of France is considered to be under the effect of oceanic influences, moderated by the North Atlantic Drift on the west and the Mediterranean Sea on the south. Average annual temperatures decline to the north, with Nice on the Côte d'Azure at 59 °F (15 °C) and Lille on the northern border at 50 °F (10 °C). Rainfall is brought mainly by westerly winds from the Atlantic and is characterized by cyclonic depressions. Annual precipitation is more than 50 inches (1,270 mm) at higher elevations in western and northwestern France, in the western Pyrenees, in the Massif Central, and in the Alps and the Jura. In winter eastern France especially may come under the influence of the continental high-pressure system, which brings extremely cold conditions and temperature inversions over the cities, during which cold air is trapped below warmer air, with consequent fogs and urban pollution. The climate of France, then, can be discussed according to three major climatic zones—oceanic, continental, and Mediterranean, with some variation in the Aquitaine Basin and in the mountains.

THE OCEANIC REGION

The pure oceanic climate prevails in the northwest, especially in Brittany. It is characterized by its low annual temperature variation, with Brest having an average temperature in January of 43 °F (6 °C) and in July of 61 °F (16 °C); by its extreme humidity and moderate rainfall (35 inches

[890 mm] of rain falling through the year), accompanied by cloudiness and haze; by the frequency and sometimes the violence of the west winds that blow almost constantly; and by large variations in the weather, which can change several times a day. This oceanic climate is somewhat modified toward the north, where the winters are cooler, and toward the south, where, in the Aquitaine Basin, the winters are mild and the summers warmer. There is also less rainfall, although at Toulouse great summer storms are quite frequent.

THE CONTINENTAL REGION

The plains of the northeast are particularly affected by a continental climate. The city of Strasbourg has the greatest temperature range in France. Winter is cold, with an average of 83 days of frost and with snow cover for several weeks, although the weather is often sunny. In summer, storms cause maximum precipitation in the region in June and July, although total rainfall is comparatively light.

The climate of the Paris Basin is somewhere between the oceanic and the continental. The average yearly temperature is 53 °F (11 °C) in Paris. In addition, the relatively light annual rainfall (23 inches [58 cm]) follows a pattern of moderately heavy rain in spring and early summer and autumn, as in the oceanic countries, but the maximum amount of rain falls in summer, with storms of the continental type. In summer, spray irrigation is needed for crops in the continental climatic region and the Paris Basin.

THE MEDITERRANEAN REGION

In the southeast the Mediterranean climate extends over the coastal plains and penetrates the valley of the lower Rhône River as far as the Montélimar area. It affects the southern Alps, the southeastern slopes of the Cévennes and the Noire Mountains (in the Massif Central), and the eastern Pyrenees. The latitude and the proximity of the warm Mediterranean Sea contribute to mild winters, with an average temperature of 47 °F (8 °C) in January at Nice and with only a few days of frost. Precipitation is heavy and tends to fall in sudden downpours, especially in the autumn and spring, whereas summer is nearly completely dry for at least three months. In coastal Languedoc-Roussillon, annual rainfall totals can be as low as 17 to 20 inches (430 to 500 mm). It is a unique area because of its clear skies and the regularity of fine weather. This area is also subject to the violent north winds called the mistral, which are peculiar to southern France. The winds are caused by high-pressure areas from central France that move toward the low-pressure areas of the Gulf of Genoa. Permanent irrigation systems are characteristic of the Mediterranean lowlands.

The Aquitaine Basin is intermediate between the oceanic and the Mediterranean climates. Winters tend toward the oceanic type, but springs and summers are warm, although less arid than in the Mediterranean zone.

The mountains have varied climates. West-facing slopes in the Pyrenees have some of the highest precipitation

THE RIVIERA

View of the harbour at Cannes, France. © Adam & Chelsey Parrott-Sheffer

The Riviera includes the Mediterranean coastland between Cannes, France, and La Spezia, Italy. The French section comprises part of the Côte d'Azur (which extends farther west), while the Italian section is known to the west and east of Genoa as the Riviera di Ponente and the Riviera di Levante, respectively. Sheltered to the north by the Maritime Alps and Ligurian Apennines, the district has exceptionally mild winters and brilliant, hot summers, with much sunshine throughout the year. Rain falls on only about 60 days a year, and the coast rarely has snow. Many delicate plants, including the pomegranate, agave, mimosa, and some types of palm, flourish. Flowers are grown out of season in large quantities for export to northern markets. The favourable climate, the grandeur of the rugged coastal scenery, and the attractions of the sea have for long drawn the leisured rich, especially during winter. The resident population is extremely dense and is increased by the tourists.

The popularity of Cannes dates from 1834, when Lord Brougham, avoiding a cholera epidemic in Nice, stayed there instead and set the fashion by returning regularly for the next 30 years. Modern transport has increased the influx of tourists; luxury villas and hotels are mixed with resort facilities of a more popular kind. Monte-Carlo, in the tiny principality of Monaco, offers additional attractions for expensive living. From west to east the main centres of the

The beach at Cannes, France. © Adam & Chelsey Parrott-Sheffer

coastal urban development are Cannes, Juan-les-Pins, Antibes, Nice, Monte-Carlo, Menton (all in France), Bordighera, San Remo, Imperia, Alassio, Genoa, Santa Margherita, Rapallo, Sestri Levante, and Levanto (all in Italy). Land speculation and the power of private interests make planned or limited development for the public good very difficult. A three-tiered system of scenic motor roads (called the Corniches) runs between Nice and the Italian frontier at Menton. The highest is Grande Corniche, constructed by Napoleon I, emperor of France, to replace the Roman road; it passes the picturesque village of La Turbie and overlooks Monaco from a height of more than 1,400 feet (427 metres). The lowest is Corniche, built in the 19th century by a prince of Monaco, which connects the coastal resorts. The middle road, opened in 1939, was created for the tourist industry and passes by the perched village of Èze. A railway passes through numerous tunnels in the projecting limestone headlands.

The allure of the region has attracted more than tourists and the wealthy. Businesses have developed a large cluster of high-technology research and development facilities at Sophia Antipolis, just a few miles northeast of Cannes.

figures in France. Snow cover stays from December to the end of April above 3,000 feet (900 metres) and is perpetual above 9,000 feet (2,700 metres) in the Alps and 10,000 feet (3,000 metres) in the Pyrenees. Locally, the contrast between the sunny south-facing valley slopes (adrets) and the shaded north-facing slopes (ubacs) can be of great importance for land use and settlement, while some intermontane basins can have quite advantageous climates as opposed to that of the surrounding peaks and plateaus.

PLANT AND ANIMAL LIFE

Vegetation is closely related to climate, so that in France it is not surprising that there are two major but unequal divisions: the Holarctic province and the smaller Mediterranean province. Most of France lies within the Holarctic biogeographic vegetational region, characterized by northern species, and it can be divided into three parts. A large area of western France makes up one part. It lies north of the Charente River and includes most of the Paris Basin. There the natural vegetation is characterized by oak (now largely cleared for cultivation), chestnut, pine, and beech in uplands that receive more than 23.6 inches (600 mm) of annual rainfall. Heathland is also common, as a predominantly man-made feature (created by forest clearance, burning, and grazing). Broom, gorse, heather, and bracken are found. South of the Charente, the Aquitaine Basin has a mixture of heath and gorse on the plateaus and several varieties of oak, cypress, poplar, and willow in the valleys. On the causses of the Massif Central and on other limestone plateaus, broom, heath, lavender, and juniper appear among the bare rocks. The vegetation of eastern France, constituting a second part of the Holarctic division, is of a more central European type, with trees such as Norway maple, beech, pedunculate oak, and larch; hornbeam is often present as a shrub layer under oak. The various high mountain zones form a third Holarctic part; with cloudy and wet conditions, they have beech woods at lower elevations, giving way upward to fir, mountain pine, and larch but with much planted spruce. Above the tree line are high mountain pastures, now increasingly abandoned, with only stunted trees but resplendent with flowers in spring and early summer.

The second major vegetation division of the country lies within the Mediterranean climatic zone and provides a sharp contrast with the plant life elsewhere in France. The pronounced summer drought of this zone causes bulbous plants to die off in summer and encourages xerophytic plants that retard water loss by means of spiny, woolly, or glossy leaves; these include the evergreen oak, the cork oak, and all the heathers, cistuses, and lavenders. Umbrella, or stone, pine and introduced cypress dominate the landscape. The predominant plant life of the plateaus of Roussillon is the maquis, comprising dense thickets of drought-resistant shrubs, characterized in spring by the colourful flowers of the cistuses, broom, and tree heather; in most areas this is a form that has developed after human destruction of the evergreen forest. A large part of Provence's hottest and driest terrain is covered by a rock heath known as garigue. This region is a principal domain of the vineyard, but lemon and orange trees grow there also. At elevations of about 2,600 feet (790 metres), as in the Cévennes, deciduous forest appears, mainly in the form of the sweet chestnut. At elevations of 4,500 feet (1,370 metres) this gives way to a sub-alpine coniferous forest of fir and pine.

Forest covers 58,000 square miles of France (15,000,000 hectares), which is more than a quarter of its territory. Most forests are on the upland massifs of the Ardennes and Vosges and within the Jura, Alps, and Pyrenees mountain chains, but extensive lowland forests grow on areas of poor soil, such as that of the Sologne plain south of the Loire River. The planted forest of maritime pine covering about 3,680 square miles (953,000 hectares) in the Landes of southwestern France is said to be the most extensive in western Europe. Increasingly, forests are less a source of wood and more a recreational amenity, especially those on the fringe of large urban agglomerations, such as Fontainebleau and others of the Île-de-France region.

The fauna of France is relatively typical of western European countries. Among the larger mammals are red deer, roe deer, and wild boar, which are still hunted; the fallow deer is rather rare. In the high Alps are the rare chamoix and the reintroduced ibex. Hares, rabbits, and various types of rodents are found both in the forests and in the fields. Carnivores include the fox, the genet, and the rare wildcat. Among endangered species are the badger, the otter, the beaver, the tortoise, the marmot of the Alps, and the brown bear and the lynx of the Pyrenees. Seals have almost entirely disappeared from the French coasts. While French bird life is in general similar to that of its neighbours, southern France is at the northern edge of the range of African migrants, and such birds as the flamingo, the Egyptian vulture, the black-winged stilt, the bee-eater, and the roller have habitats in southern France.

CHAPTER 2

PEOPLE

The French are, paradoxically, strongly conscious of belonging to a single nation, but they hardly constitute a unified ethnic group by any scientific gauge. Before the official discovery of the Americas at the end of the 15th century, France, located on the western extremity of the Old World, was regarded for centuries by Europeans as being near the edge of the known world. Generations of different migrants traveling by way of the Mediterranean from the Middle East and Africa and through Europe from Central Asia and the Nordic lands settled permanently in France, forming a variegated grouping, almost like a series of geologic strata, since they were unable to migrate any farther. Perhaps the oldest reflection of these migrations is furnished by the Basque people, who live in an isolated area west of the Pyrenees in both Spain and France, who speak a language unrelated to other European languages, and whose origin remains unclear. The Celtic tribes, known to the Romans as Gauls, spread from central Europe in the period 500 BCE–500 CE to provide France with a major component of its population, especially in the centre and west. At the fall of the Roman Empire, there was a powerful penetration of Germanic (Teutonic) peoples, especially in northern and eastern France. The incursion of the Norsemen (Vikings) brought further Germanic influence. In addition to these many migrations, France was, over the centuries, the field of numerous battles and of prolonged occupations before becoming, in the 19th and especially in the 20th century, the prime recipient of foreign immigration into Europe, adding still other mixtures to the ethnic melting pot.

Basque peoples of Saint-Etienne-de-Baigorry. © Photononstop/SuperStock

LANGUAGES

French is the national language, spoken and taught everywhere. Brogues and dialects are widespread in rural areas, however, and many people tend to conserve their regional linguistic customs either through tradition or through a voluntary and deliberate return to a specific regional dialect. This tendency is strongest in the frontier areas of France. In the eastern and northern part of the country, Alsatian and Flemish (Dutch) are Germanic languages; in the south, Occitan (Provençal or Languedoc), Corsican, and Catalan show the influence of Latin. Breton is a Celtic language related to languages spoken in some western parts of the British Isles (notably Wales), and Basque is a language isolate. Following the introduction of universal primary education during the Third Republic in 1872, the use of regional languages was rigorously repressed in the interest of national unity, and pupils using them were punished. More recently, in

FRENCH LANGUAGE AND THE FRENCH ACADEMY

The French language is spoken in France, Belgium, and Switzerland; in Canada (principally Quebec) and northern New England; and in many other countries and regions formerly or currently governed by France. It is an official language of more than 25 countries. Written materials in French date from the Strasbourg Oaths of 842.

The standard for French is based on the dialect of Paris, called Francien, which has been the official standard language since the mid-16th century. Francien has largely replaced other regional dialects of French spoken in northern and central France; these dialects made up the so-called *langue d'oïl* (the term is based on the French use of the word *oïl,* modern *oui,* for "yes"). Standard French has also greatly reduced the use of the Occitan language of southern France (the so-called *langue d'oc,* from Provençal *oc* for "yes"). Occitan's major dialect, Provençal, was a widely used medieval literary language. Regional dialects of French survive for the most part only in uneducated rural speech, although thePicard–Walloon dialect of northern France and the Norman dialect of western France gave strong competition to Francien in medieval times, and Walloon is still spoken in Belgium. Other dialects are Orléanais, Bourbonnais, Champenois, Lorrain, Bourguignon, Franc-Comtois, Gallo, Angevin, Maine, Poitevin, Saintongeais, and Angoumois.

French phonology is characterized by great changes in the sounds of words as compared to their Latin parent forms as well as to cognates in the other Romance languages. For example, Latin *securum* "sure, secure" became Spanish *seguro* but French *sûr;* Latin *vōcem* "voice" became Spanish *voz* but French *voix,* pronounced *vwa.*

French grammar, like that of the other Romance languages, has been greatly simplified from that of Latin. Nouns are not declined for case. Formerly, they were marked for plural by the addition of *-s* or *-es,* but the ending, though retained in spelling, has generally been lost in speech. Masculine and feminine gender are distinguished but are usually marked not in the noun but rather in the accompanying article or adjective. Plural marking in spoken French is often similarly distinguished. The verb in French is conjugated for three persons, singular and plural, but again, although distinguished in spelling, several of these forms are pronounced identically. French has verb forms for indicative, imperative, and subjunctive moods; preterite, imperfect, present, future, and conditional, and a variety of perfect and progressive tenses; and passive and reflexive constructions.

The French Academy (Académie Française) was created to maintain standards of literary taste and to establish French literary language, and it remains the final arbiter on matters of French vocabulary and grammar. Established by the French first minister Cardinal de Richelieu in 1634 and incorporated in 1635, and existing, except for an interruption during the era of the French Revolution, to the present day. Its membership is limited to 40. Though it has often acted as a conservative body, opposed to innovations in literary content and form, its membership has included most of the great names of French literature—e.g., Pierre Corneille, Jean Racine, Voltaire, the Viscount de Chateaubriand, Victor Hugo, Joseph-Ernest Renan, and Henri Bergson. Among numerous European literary academies, it has consistently retained the highest prestige over the longest period of time.

reaction to the rise in regional sentiment, these languages have been introduced in a number of schools and universities, primarily because some of them, such as Occitan, Basque, and Breton, have maintained a literary tradition. Recent immigration has introduced various non-European languages, notably Arabic.

RELIGION

About three-fifths of the French people belong to the Roman Catholic Church. Only a minority, however, regularly participate in religious worship; practice is greatest among the middle classes. The northwest (Brittany-Vendée), the east (Lorraine, Vosges, Alsace, Jura, Lyonnais, and the northern Alps), the north (Flanders), the Basque Country, and the region south of the Massif Central have a higher percentage of practicing Roman Catholics than the rest of the country. Recruitment of priests has become more difficult, even though the church, historically autonomous, is very progressive and ecumenical.

Reflecting the presence of immigrants from North Africa, Algeria, and Morocco, France has one of Europe's largest Muslim populations: almost 5,000,000 Muslims, a sizable percentage of them living in and around Marseille in southeastern France, as well as in Paris and Lyon. Protestants, who number 700,000, belong to several different denominations. They are numerous in Alsace, in the northern Jura, in the southeastern Massif Central, and in the central Atlantic region.

There are more than 700,000 adherents of Judaism, concentrated in Greater Paris, Marseille, and Alsace and the large eastern towns. In addition to the religious groups, there also are several societies of freethinkers, of which the most famous is the French Masonry. Large numbers, however, especially among the working classes and young population, profess no religious belief.

In the early 21st century the government approved a number of measures that reflected both France's dedication to being a secular state, a principle known as *laïcité*, as well as the ambivalence and, in some cases, hostility felt by some French toward the country's large Muslim population. In 2004 the government banned Muslim head scarves and other religious symbols in state schools. Additional controversial legislation passed in 2010 prohibited face-concealing garments— i.e., veils that fully covered a woman's face—in public places.

RURAL LANDSCAPE AND SETTLEMENT

Centuries of human adaptation of the various environments of France have produced varied patterns of rural landscape. Scholars have traditionally made an initial contrast between areas of enclosed land (*bocage*), usually associated with zones of high rainfall and heavy soils, and areas of open-field land (*campagne*), generally associated with level and well-drained plains and plateaus. Two other patterns have evolved in the Mediterranean region and in the mountains.

BOCAGE

In its classic form, *bocage* is found in Brittany, where small fields are surrounded by drainage ditches and high earthen banks, from which grow impenetrable hedges arching over narrow sunken lanes. Similarly enclosed land is found elsewhere, however, notably on the northern, western, and southern fringes of the Paris Basin, such as in Normandy, as well as in the western and northern parts of the Massif Central, parts of Aquitaine, and the Pyrenean region. At higher levels hedges may be replaced by stone walls. Settlement mostly takes the form of hamlets and isolated farms.

OPEN-FIELD

The greatest extent of open-field land is found in the Paris Basin and in northern and eastern France, but there are pockets

Fields of lavender in Provence, France. © Digital Vision/Getty Images

of it elsewhere. The landscape typically lacks hedges or fences; instead, the bewildering pattern of small strips and blocks of land is defined by small boundary stones. The land of one farmer may be dispersed in parcels scattered over a wide area. The land is predominantly arable, and the farmsteads are traditionally grouped into villages, which may be irregularly clustered or, as in Lorraine, linear in form.

MEDITERRANEAN

The generally block-shaped Mediterranean lowland parcels normally are not enclosed or are enclosed only by rough stone banks. However, in areas where delicate crops would be exposed to wind damage, there are screens of willows and tall reeds. Hillsides are frequently terraced, although much of this land type has been abandoned except in areas of intensive cultivation, such as the flower-growing region around Grasse. A very large farmhouse built on three floors is characteristic of wine-growing and sheep-raising regions, such as Provence. Rural population was formerly often clustered at high elevations, both for defense and in order to be above the malarial plains. In modern times there has been a move to more convenient lowland locations.

MOUNTAIN

In the high mountains and especially in the Alps, there is the contrast between the *adrets*, the sunny and cultivated valley slopes, and the *ubacs*, the cold and humid slopes covered with forests. The variety of vegetation on the slopes of the mountains is remarkable. Cultivated fields and grasslands are found in the depths of the valleys, followed in ascending order by orchards on the first sunny embankments, then forests, Alpine pastures, bare rocks, and, finally, permanent snow. A unique aspect of the mountain environment is that Alpine villages of the lower valley sides were often combined with *chalets* (*burons* in the Massif Central), temporary dwellings used by those tending flocks on summer pastures above the tree line.

POSTWAR TRANSFORMATION

After World War II the French government instituted a program of consolidation, whereby the scattered parcels of individual farmers were grouped into larger blocks that would accommodate heavier, mechanized cultivation. Initially progress was greatest in the open-field areas, particularly the Paris Basin, where there were few physical obstacles to the process. Subsequent extension to *bocage* areas had more severe consequences for landscape values and ecology, as hedges, sunken lanes, and ponds disappeared in favour of a new open landscape. At the same time, the vast numbers of people abandoning agricultural pursuits enormously changed the nature of rural settlement. Particularly in the more attractive areas, abandoned farms were purchased as second homes or for retirement. Where alternative employment was available, rural people stayed and became commuters, transforming barns and stables for other uses, such as garages. On the fringes of the expanding city regions, new houses and housing subdivisions for urban commuters were built in the villages, markedly changing their character.

URBAN SETTLEMENT

The primacy of Paris as the predominant urban centre of France is well known. After World War II the French government had an ambivalent attitude toward the development of the urban structure. On the one hand there was the desire to see Paris emerge as the effective capital of Europe, and on the other there was the policy of creating "métropoles d'equilibre," through which cities such as Lille, Bordeaux, and Marseille would become growth poles of regional development. Even more evident was the unplanned urbanization of small and medium-size towns related to spontaneous industrial decentralization from

The Old Port of Marseille, France. © Digital Vision/Getty Images

Paris, such as that along the Loire valley, or to retirement migration, such as that along the coastlands of southern France.

DEMOGRAPHIC TRENDS

In 1801 France was the most populous nation in Europe, containing about one-sixth of the continent's inhabitants. By 1936 the French population had increased by 50 percent, but in the same period the number of people in Italy and Germany had nearly trebled, and in the United Kingdom and the Netherlands the population had nearly quadrupled. The marked difference in population growth between France and some of its neighbours up to the 1940s was attributed to a falling birth rate. At the same time, the mortality rate in France began its decline somewhat later than in other advanced European countries, not falling until the close of the 19th century. The birth rate was particularly affected by the practice of French peasants who deliberately limited their families in order to reduce the effect of a Napoleonic law that required the splitting of the family holdings among all heirs. Other factors may have included the rise of bourgeois individualism following the French Revolution of 1789, the decline of Roman Catholic observance (especially among the political left), and the lack of economic opportunity in the interwar years. Population growth was, of course, adversely affected by wars, including the wars of the Revolution; the wars of the First Empire; the Franco-German War (1870–71); World War I (1914–18), which cost France more than 1,500,000 lives; and World War II (1939–45), which reduced the population by 600,000.

The deficit in national growth was so drastic by 1938 that France began to give monetary and other material benefits to families with children. The policy appears to have been effective, because a rise in the birth rate occurred even during the difficult years of Nazi occupation and Vichy France, culminating in the postwar baby boom years, when soldiers and prisoners returned to a climate of economic optimism. The relative youth and high fertility of immigrants also contributed to the upsurge in the birth rate, which was coupled with a decline in mortality rates, attributable to improved public health facilities and social welfare programs.

In the second half of the 20th century, the high birth rate slowed, and about 1974 it fell into a sharp decline, eventually reaching a point insufficient for the long-term maintenance of the population. Since midcentury, because of a corresponding decline in the death rate, the rate of natural increase (balance of births against deaths) has remained positive, though in decline. By the early 21st century France had an average population increase of roughly 300,000 people each year. These changes were not exceptional to France; the same postwar pattern was largely paralleled in neighbouring countries. A number of factors combined to reduce the birth rate, among them the introduction of the contraceptive pill and the new preference for smaller families.

EMIGRATION

Unlike many of its neighbours, France has never been a major source of international migrants. In the 17th century, because of religious persecution, France lost more than 400,000 Huguenot refugees—often highly skilled—mainly to Prussia, England, Holland, and America. The same century saw the beginning of emigration; relatively small numbers of emigrants settled at first in North America, notably in eastern Canada (Quebec) and in Louisiana, in certain parts of Latin America that are still *départements* of France (Martinique, Guadeloupe, and French Guiana), and later in various countries of Africa and Asia that were parts of France's colonial domain. Since decolonialization, whether forced or voluntary, many have returned to France, but others have remained overseas, either in business or in programs of technical and cultural cooperation in most of the former French territories, notably in Africa. Small numbers of French, especially from Brittany and Normandy, continue to relocate to Canada, and a number of Basques go to Argentina.

IMMIGRATION

Intermittently, at least since about 1830 and rather steadily from 1850, there has been a substantial flow of immigrant population into France. France had the reputation into the early 20th century of being the European country most open to immigrants, including political refugees, but this reputation changed in the late 20th century, when opposition rose to continued immigration from Africa. At this time also the countries of the European Union became generally more resistant to the admission of persons claiming political asylum. Most immigration conforms to the economic needs of the host country and tends to be particularly concentrated either in periods of economic growth or after devastating wars. Between 1850 and 1914 about 4.3 million foreigners entered France, and between World Wars I and II nearly 3 million, or 6 percent of the population, came as immigrants. Up to the end of World War I, immigration was free and spontaneous; most of the immigrants came from neighbouring countries, such as Italy, Spain, Belgium, and Switzerland, and they were quickly assimilated into the national population. The slaughter of young men and the devastation of World War I stimulated the government to draw more widely from the reservoirs of foreign manpower. The Italians came in greatest numbers (35 percent), followed by the Poles (20 percent), the Spanish (15 percent), the Belgians (10 percent), and a smaller number of people from central or eastern European countries.

In the years of economic expansion after World War II, when there was an acute labour shortage, immigration again reached a high level. In the first two postwar decades, immigration contributed about 40 percent to the growth of the French population. Although immigration flattened out after 1974, natural increase dropped, so that immigration continued to contribute significantly to population growth. In the early 21st century, there were almost 4 million foreigners resident in France, amounting to some 6 percent of the population, a proportion that had remained constant since 1975. Neighbouring countries such as Portugal, Italy, and Spain continued to be significant contributors, but recent immigrant streams came from North Africa, notably Algeria (an integral part of France until 1962) and the former protectorates of Morocco and Tunisia. Peoples from French or former French territories in Central Africa, Asia, and the Americas provided an additional source of immigrants.

As the numbers of immigrants grew, so did incidents of racial discrimination in housing and employment, as well as social activism among immigrant groups. Initially, immigrants from Africa and the Americas were predominantly males, living in low-standard housing and working in undesirable, low-skilled occupations. As families were progressively reconstituted, immigrants continued to work in jobs that Frenchmen were reluctant to accept. With the beginning of an economic downturn in 1974, though, French workers began to reclaim some of the jobs held by immigrants, and the government began to restrict immigration. Adding to the job competition were approximately one million persons with French citizenship, the so-called *pieds-noirs* (literally "black feet"), who were repatriated from territories in North Africa decolonized in 1962–64. The policy of restricting immigration remains in force, with the result that in the early 21st century the net annual increase of population from legal immigration averaged little more than 50,000 people. With the enactment in 1999 of the Amsterdam Treaty in France, many issues of immigration became shared by participating members of the European Union.

POPULATION STRUCTURE

The aging of the population is common to western Europe, but because of low birth rates it has been observable in France since the beginning of the 19th century. In the early 21st century, more than one-fifth of French citizens were at least 60 years old. The tendency for the proportion of the elderly population to increase also reflects medical advances, which have produced a longer expectation of life. The age structure of the population is of considerable social and economic importance. The steady increase in the proportion of the aged puts an increasing strain on the working population to provide pensions, medical and social services, and retirement housing. The increase in births between 1944 and the mid-1970s, however, brought its own problems, notably the need to rush through a school-building program, followed by the creation of new universities. But this demographically young population also stimulated the economy by creating a greater demand for consumer goods and housing.

Another important aspect of population structure is the proportion of men to women, in society as a whole and in the various age groups. As in most western European countries, women outnumber men in French society and particularly in the older age groups, which is the result of two factors: the wars, which caused the death of a large number of men, and the natural inequality of life expectancy for men and women. A French woman at birth has one of the highest life expectancies in the world (85 years), while a man's is much lower (78 years), although still relatively high when compared with the world in general. The ratio of men to women in employment is another measure of population structure, and in the late 20th century women steadily increased their share of the job market.

POPULATION DISTRIBUTION

Particularly low population densities are characteristic of the mountain regions, such as the Massif Central, the southern Alps, the Pyrenees, and Corsica, but are also reflected in some lowland rural areas, such as the eastern and southern Paris Basin and large parts of Aquitaine. Four of France's least-populated régions—Corsica, Limousin, Franche-Comté, and Auvergne—have one-sixteenth of the national population in about one-eighth of the area. By contrast, the four most populated French régions—Île-de-France (Paris region), Rhône-Alpes, Provence–Alpes–Côte d'Azur, and Nord–Pas-de-Calais—have more than two-fifths of the French population in less than one-fifth of the area. Other high-density areas are the industrial cities of Lorraine; isolated large cities, such as Toulouse; and certain small-farm areas, such as coastal Brittany, Flanders, Alsace, and the Limagne basin of Auvergne.

Until about the mid-19th century, rural and urban populations both increased; thereafter there was a marked depopulation of the more remote, mostly mountainous, rural areas and a swing to urban growth. In the space of a century, from the 1860s to the 1960s, rural population decreased by more than one-third, though since that time the decline has slowed, and the rural population in the early 21st century numbered roughly 10 million. There were still as many rural as urban inhabitants even up to the period between the two World Wars, but by 2010 almost 85 percent of the population was urban. Postwar rural depopulation was associated with the exodus of labour following the modernization of French agriculture. At the time, rural areas were left with an aging population and low birth rates as the young departed to the cities, especially to the growing industrial régions of Nord–Pas-de-Calais, Lorraine, and Île-de-France.

The massive postwar movement from rural areas to the cities was supplemented by immigration, which also focused on urban areas where employment was available. Because immigrants to the cities tended to be young adults of childbearing age, city dwellers multiplied. Urban population growth in the 30 years after World War II was estimated to be at least 16 million persons. Subsequent urban growth was due in part to expanding city limits and was characterized by urban sprawl, accelerated redistribution from city centres to suburban outskirts, though some rebalancing toward the centre has occurred in recent years.

From about 1975, migratory flows were greatly modified, the most immediate cause being economic. The older industrial régions, such as Nord–Pas-de-Calais and Lorraine, were in decline and had become regions of out-migration. The most dynamic migratory flow was experienced in the deindustrialized Île-de-France région; students and young workers flocked to the greater Paris area, while pensioners retired to the coasts. Growth subsequently switched to the south, to the coastlands of Languedoc and of Provence–Alpes–Côte d'Azur; to the west, in the Atlantic régions of Poitou-Charentes and Pays de la Loire; and to the southwest, in the Midi-Pyrénées and Aquitaine régions. These shifts reflect a combination of economic decentralization, retirement migration, sunbelt industrialization, changing residential preferences, and expanding tourism. Population increase has also been strong on the southern and western fringes of the Paris Basin, favoured for industrial decentralization from the Île-de-France région.

Since World War II, urban growth in France has been accompanied by marked suburbanization. This trend was initiated much earlier in Paris, a densely built-up city that leveled off at a maximum population of about 2.8 million in the period 1911–54 and declined thereafter. Proportionately the decline set in much earlier: in 1876 the city of Paris had 60 percent of the population of what was to become the Île-de-France *région*; in 1921, 51 percent; in 1954, 39 percent; and in 2008, 19 percent. The century after 1850 witnessed the rise of the industrialized inner suburbs (the *petite couronne*) outside the walls of the city. There maximum population was reached in the 1970s, followed by a decline associated with a marked degree of deindustrialization. Since the 1980s, population growth has been concentrated in the outer Paris suburbs (*grande couronne*), which by 2008 accounted for 44 percent of the total population of the

Île-de-France *région*, compared with 37 percent in the declining inner suburbs.

In the first half of the 20th century, suburban growth, where it did occur, was not the result of middle-class suburbanization, as it was in the United States and the United Kingdom. It was the working class and the lower middle classes that moved out, while higher-income groups endeavoured to maintain a foothold in central Paris. In the postwar period, however, suburbanization took increasingly middle-class forms, with the building up of satellite low-density subdivisions known as "new villages." Similar postwar suburbanization occurred in cities such as Marseille, Lyon, Lille, and Bordeaux.

Increasingly, the most rapid population growth is relegated to small towns and nominally rural communes on the expanding fringes of the city regions. This dispersal of population is associated with an increasing length of daily commuter movements, with all their human disadvantages, as well as other problems of urban sprawl. Vacation travel, very popular among the French, involves the movement of crowds of people during the peak seasons, particularly during school vacations and in August, when many people take their paid holiday and leave the city. Transport facilities and popular vacation spots become saturated, especially the coastal areas and mountains.

CHAPTER 3

ECONOMY

F rance is one of the major economic powers of the world, ranking along with such countries as the United States, Japan, Germany, Italy, and the United Kingdom. Its financial position reflects an extended period of unprecedented growth that lasted for much of the postwar period until the mid-1970s; frequently this period was referred to as the *trente glorieuses* ("thirty years of glory"). Between 1960 and 1973 alone, the increase in gross domestic product (GDP) averaged nearly 6 percent each year. In the aftermath of the oil crises of the 1970s, growth rates were moderated considerably and unemployment rose substantially. By the end of the 1980s, however, strong expansion was again evident. This trend continued, although at a more modest rate, into the 21st century.

During the same postwar period, the structure of the economy was altered significantly. While in the 1950s agriculture and industry were the dominant sectors, tertiary (largely service and administrative) activities have since become the principal employer and generator of national wealth. Similarly, while it was once the heavily urbanized and industrialized regions of northern and northeastern France that were developing most rapidly, in the 1980s these areas began losing jobs and population. Contemporary growth has switched to regions that lie in the south and, to a lesser degree, the west of France.

Despite the dominance of the private sector, the tradition of a mixed economy in France is well established. Successive governments have intervened to protect or promote different types of economic activity, as has been clearly reflected in the country's national plans and nationalized industries. In the decades following World War II, the French economy was guided by a succession of national plans, each covering a span of approximately four to five years and designed to indicate rather than impose growth targets and development strategies.

The public sector in France first assumed importance in the post-World War II transition period of 1944–46 with a series of nationalizations that included major banks such as the National Bank of Paris (Banque Nationale de Paris; BNP) and Crédit Lyonnais, large industrial companies such as Renault, and public services such as gas and electricity. Little change took place after that until 1982, when the then Socialist government introduced an extensive program of nationalization. As a result, the enlarged public sector contained more than one-fifth of industrial employment, and more than four-fifths of credit facilities were controlled by state-owned banking or financial institutions. Since that period successive right-wing and, more recently, left-of-centre governments have returned most enterprises to the private sector; state ownership is primarily concentrated in transport, defense, and broadcasting.

Postwar economic growth has been accompanied by a substantial rise in living standards, reflected in the increasing number of families that own their home (about half), a reduction in the workweek (fixed at 35 hours), and the increase of vacation days taken each year by the French people. Another indicator of improved living standards is the growth of ownership of various household and consumer goods, particularly such items as automobiles and computers. Over time, however, consumption patterns have altered significantly. As incomes have risen, proportionately less has been spent on food and clothing and more on items such as housing, transportation, health, and leisure. Workers' incomes are taxed at a high to moderate rate, and indirect taxation in the form of a value-added tax (VAT) is relatively high. Overall, taxes and social security contributions levied on employers and employees in France are higher than in many other European countries.

AGRICULTURE, FORESTRY, AND FISHING

France's extensive land area—of which more than half is arable or pastoral land and another quarter is wooded—presents broad opportunities for agriculture and forestry. The country's varied relief and soils and contrasting climatic zones further enhance this potential. Rainfall is plentiful throughout most of France, so water supply is not generally a problem. An ample fish supply in the Atlantic Ocean and Mediterranean Sea provides an additional resource.

Agriculture employs relatively few people—about 3 percent of the labour force—and makes only a small contribution to GDP—about 2 percent. Yet France is the EU's leading agricultural nation, accounting for more than one-fifth of the total value of output, and alone is responsible for more than one-third of the EU's production of oilseeds, cereals, and wine. France also is a major world exporter of agricultural commodities, and approximately one-eighth of the total value of the country's visible exports is related to agriculture and associated food and drink products.

France has a usable agricultural area of nearly 74 million acres (30 million hectares), more than three-fifths of which is used for arable farming (requiring plowing or tillage), followed by permanent grassland (about one-third) and permanent crops such as vines and orchards (about one-twentieth). Areas in which arable farming is dominant lie mostly in the northern and western regions of the country, centred on the Paris Basin. Permanent grassland is common in upland and mountainous areas such as the Massif Central, the Alps, and the Vosges, although it is also a notable feature of the western région of Basse-Normandie. Conversely, the major areas devoted to permanent cultivation lie in Mediterranean regions.

GRAINS

More than half of the country's arable land is used for cereals, which together provide about one-sixth of the total value of agricultural output. Wheat and corn (maize) are the main grains, with other cereals, such as barley and oats, becoming progressively less important. There are few areas of the country where cereals are not grown, although the bulk of production originates in the Paris Basin and southwestern France, where both natural conditions and (in the former case) proximity to markets favour such activity. A considerable area (about one-seventh of the agricultural area), predominantly in western France, is also given over to forage crops, although the acreage has been shrinking since the early 1980s as dairy herds have been reduced in accordance with EU guidelines. In contrast, there has been a substantial increase in oilseed output; the area under cultivation has quadrupled since the early 1980s and now approaches one-tenth of agricultural land.

FRUITS AND WINE MAKING

Vines, fruits, and vegetables cover only a limited area but represent more than one-fourth of the total value of agricultural output. France is probably more famous for its wines than any other country in the world. Viticulture and wine making are concentrated principally in Languedoc-Roussillon and in the Bordeaux area, but production also occurs in Provence, Alsace, the Rhône and Loire valleys, Poitou-Charentes, and the Champagne region. There has been a marked fall in the production of vin ordinaire, a trend related to EU policy, which favours an increase in the output of quality wines. Fruit production (mainly of apples, pears, and peaches) is largely concentrated in

Harvesting grapes in a vineyard at Ay, near Épernay in the Champagne region of France. © Serraillier—Rapho/Photo Researchers

DAIRYING AND LIVESTOCK

Cattle raising occurs in most areas of the country (except in Mediterranean regions), especially in the more humid regions of western France. Animal-related production accounts for more than one-third of the total value of agricultural output. In general, herds remain small, although concentration into larger units is increasing. Overall, however, the number of cattle has been falling since the early 1980s, largely as a result of EU milk quotas. These have adversely affected major production areas such as Auvergne, Brittany, Basse-Normandie, Pays de la Loire, Rhône-Alpes, Lorraine, Nord–Pas-de-Calais, and Franche-Comté. One result has been an increasing orientation toward beef rather than dairy breeds, notably in the area of the Massif Central. The raising of pigs and poultry, frequently by intensive methods, makes up more than one-tenth of the value of agricultural output. Production is concentrated in the régions of Brittany and Pays de la Loire, encouraged originally by the availability of by-products from the dairy industry for use as feed. Sheep raising is less important. Flocks graze principally in southern France on the western and southern fringes of the Massif Central, in the western Pyrenees, and in the southern Alps.

AGRIBUSINESS

Agriculture has changed in other ways. Farm structures have been modified

the Rhône and Garonne valleys and in the Mediterranean region. Vegetables are also grown in the lower Rhône and Mediterranean areas, but a large part of output comes from western France (Brittany) and the southwest and the northern régions of Nord–Pas-de-Calais and Picardy, where sugar beets and potatoes are produced.

CHAMPAGNE

Champagne is a classic sparkling wine named for the site of its origin and exclusive production, the traditional region of Champagne in northeastern France. The term champagne is also applied generically, with restrictions, outside France, to many white or rosé wines that are characterized by effervescence. In the United States, sparkling wines made in a similar manner are designated first by place of origin, as in New York state champagne. Similar wines from Spain and elsewhere are often called "champagne-style."

The region that produces champagne includes certain parishes in the *départements* of Marne, Aisne, Seine-et-Marne, Aube, and Haute-Marne. The best champagne comes from vineyards along the Marne River from Château-Thierry eastward to Épernay and on the plain from Épernay stretching north to Reims, which is dominated by a hill called the Montagne de Reims. Champagne is made from only three grapes: pinot and meunier, both black, and chardonnay, white. Characteristic of champagne is a crisp, flinty taste, sometimes ascribed to the chalky soil. A small amount made from green grapes only is called *blanc des blancs*. Pink champagne is made by adding a little red wine, or by leaving the crushed grapes in contact with their skins for a time.

Champagne is initially fermented in stainless steel vats, after which the wine is blended. If the year has been excellent, only wines of that year are used and the product is vintage champagne; if not, a blend with wines of different years will be made, improving and strengthening the wine and producing a nonvintage champagne. After blending, a mixture of wine, sugar, and yeast is added to the wine before it is transferred to pressure tanks or to strong, dark bottles for a second fermentation that yields carbon dioxide and effervescence. This second fermentation is completed after a few weeks or months. Wine thus fermented in tanks is then transferred to another tank, where it is chilled, sweetened, and bottled. Wine in bottles is left to mature; during this period the bottles are shaken daily and gradually turned and tipped until they are upside down and the impurities (sediment) have settled onto the bottom of the cork. This procedure, called riddling, or *remuage,* has been largely mechanized since the 1970s. When the wine is mature and ready for the market, the deposits are removed in a process called *dégorgement.* In this process, the cork is carefully pried off, allowing the internal pressure in the bottle to shoot the sediment out; this is sometimes done after the neck of the bottle and the deposits have been frozen. After *dégorgement,* a small amount of syrup melted in old champagne is added to the bottle and the wine is recorked. Champagne to which little or none of this sugar is added is labeled brut, or extra dry; somewhat sweeter is sec, and wine with larger quantities is demi-sec. All of these are sweeter than the words indicate.

Champagne bottles are made in many sizes: the split (equal to ¼ bottle), the half-bottle, the bottle (0.75 litres), the magnum (equal to two bottles), the jeroboam (equal to four bottles), the methuselah (equal to eight bottles), the salmanazar (equal to 12 bottles), the balthazar (equal to 16 bottles), the nebuchadnezzar (equal to 20 bottles), and the most recent creation, the sovereign (equal to more than 33 bottles). The larger bottles (from the balthazar on up), originally hand-blown, proved to be so dangerous that they were discontinued until 1986, when a safer method of production was introduced.

substantially, and the number of holdings have been greatly reduced since 1955, numerous small farms disappearing. By the late 1990s there were fewer than 700,000 holdings, compared with more than 2,000,000 in the mid-1950s and more than 1,000,000 in the late 1980s. The average size of farms has risen considerably, to close to 100 acres (40 hectares). Large holdings are located primarily in the cereal-producing regions of the Paris Basin, while small holdings are most common in Mediterranean regions, the lower Rhône valley, Alsace, and Brittany. Important technical changes have also occurred, ranging from the increased use of intermediate products such as fertilizers and pesticides to the widespread use of irrigation (nearly one-tenth of agricultural land is now irrigated) and the growth of crops within controlled environments, such as under glass or plastic canopies. Marketing systems have also been modified, as an increasing

ROQUEFORT

Roquefort is one of the oldest known cheeses. The classic blue cheese is made from ewe's milk, and it is often considered one of the greatest cheeses of France. It was reportedly the favourite cheese of the emperor Charlemagne, and in France it is called *le fromage des rois et des papes* ("the cheese of kings and popes"). Roquefort cheese is widely imitated throughout the world, and its name is used rather indiscriminately on processed cheeses and salad dressings. True Roquefort is noted for its sharp, tangy, salty flavour and its rich, creamy texture. Today some authentic Roqueforts are made in Corsica, but all still undergo final aging in the limestone caves of Roquefort near Toulouse in southern France,

Roquefort cheese. Steve Moss/Food Features

where the cool and humid atmosphere promotes growth of the mold *Penicillium roqueforti*. By French law, only cheese that is processed at Roquefort, France, may be labeled "Roquefort cheese"; other French blue-veined cheeses are called "bleu" cheese.

Roquefort is generally formed in 5-pound (2.3-kg) cylinders of about 7-inch (18-cm) diameter and 4-inch (10-cm) thickness. The white paste of the interior is marbled with blue mold; the cheese is wrapped in foil bearing a traditional insignia of red sheep. Dry red wine is considered an ideal accompaniment.

proportion of output is grown under contract. Together such changes have led to a remarkable increase in output of major agricultural products, but they have also resulted in a large reduction in the number of agricultural workers and the increased indebtedness of many farmers, and the related negative effects on the environment have given rise to the organic farming movement.

FORESTRY

With more than 57,000 square miles (148,000 square km) of woodland, France possesses one of the largest afforested areas in western Europe, offering direct employment to more than 80,000 people. Forested areas are unevenly distributed, with the majority lying to the east of a line from Bordeaux to the Luxembourg border. Aquitaine and Franche-Comté have a particularly dense forest cover. This vast resource is, however, generally underexploited, partly because of the multitude of private owners, many of whom are uninterested in the commercial management of their estates. Less than one-fourth of the afforested area is controlled by the National Office of Forests.

FISHING

Despite the extent of France's coastlines and its numerous ports, the French fishing industry remains relatively small. Annual catches have averaged about 700,000 tons since the mid-1970s, and by the 21st century there were fewer than 16,500 fishermen. The industry's problems are related to its fragmented character and to inadequate modernization of boats and port facilities, as well as to overfishing and pollution. Activity is now concentrated in the port of Boulogne in Nord–Pas-de-Calais and to a lesser degree in ports in Brittany such as Concarneau, Lorient, and Le Guilvinic. France is also known for its aquaculture, with activity increasing over recent years along the coastal waters of western France. Oyster beds are found particularly in the southwest, centred on Marennes-Oléron.

RESOURCES AND POWER

Compared with its agricultural resources, the country is far less well-endowed with energy resources. Coal reserves are estimated at about 140 million tons, but French coal suffered from being difficult and expensive to mine and from its mediocre quality. In 1958 annual production amounted to some 60 million tons; 40 years later this total had dropped to less than 6 million tons; and in 2004 the last coal mine was shuttered. Imported coal had long supplemented indigenous production. Imports originate mainly from Australia, the United States, South Africa, and Germany.

Other energy resources are in short supply. Natural gas was first exploited in southwestern France (near Lacq) in 1957. Production then increased substantially, only to decline after 1978 as reserves became exhausted. By the late 1990s, production was negligible, requiring a high level of imports, principally from the North Sea (Norway and the Netherlands), Algeria, and Russia. France has few oil reserves, and production from wells in Aquitaine and the Paris Basin is extremely limited. Uranium is mined in the Massif Central, and, although recoverable reserves are estimated at approximately 50,000 tons, more than half of the annual consumption has to be imported. France, however, does possess fast-moving rivers flowing out of highland areas that provide it with an ample hydroelectric resource.

MINERALS

The metal industry is poorly supplied by indigenous raw materials, although traditionally France was an important producer of iron ore and bauxite. Iron ore output exceeded 60 million tons in the early 1960s, originating principally in Lorraine; but production has now ceased, despite the continued existence of reserves. Low in metal content and difficult to agglomerate, Lorraine ores were thus long supplemented and have now been replaced by richer overseas supplies from such countries as Brazil, Sweden, and Australia. Bauxite production is negligible, though other mineralized ores, such as those containing lead, zinc, and silver, are mined in very small quantities. Greater amounts of potash (mined in Alsace), sodium chloride (from mines

in Lorraine and Franche-Comté and from salt marshes in western and southern France), and sulfur (derived from natural gas in Aquitaine) are produced, but again the trend is toward declining output as reserves are depleted. The supply of stone, sand, and gravel is relatively ubiquitous.

ENERGY

Through the post-World War II years, the increase in the demand for energy has closely followed the rate of economic growth. Thus, for much of the period until 1973, consumption increased rapidly. Then, in the wake of the two oil price rises of 1973 and 1979, demand stabilized, followed by a fall in the early 1980s until growth rates recovered after the mid-1980s.

The demand for different types of energy has changed considerably over time. In the early postwar years, coal provided the larger part of energy needs. By the 1960s, however, oil, as its price fell in real terms, was being used in ever-greater quantities, so that by 1973 about two-thirds of energy consumption was accounted for by crude oil. Since then a more diversified pattern of use has emerged. Coal now plays only a minor role, while the use of oil has also fallen, replaced partly by natural gas and notably by nuclear energy, which now accounts for more than one-third of primary energy consumption. One of the main consequences of these changes has been a reduction in the country's previously high dependence on external sources of supply.

Oil has long been France's principal energy import, which has led to the growth of a major refining industry, with plants concentrated in two areas of the lower Seine valley (Le Havre and Rouen) and in the region around Fos-sur-Mer and the Étang de Berre. Many markets are supplied with oil products by pipeline, which is also the distribution method for natural gas. Algerian imports arrive in the form of liquefied natural gas (primarily methane) and are unloaded at French ports where regasification plants operate.

Since the early 1980s one of the most significant changes in energy supply has been the greatly increased role of nuclear power, at the expense of fuel oil and coal; even the production of hydroelectric power has stabilized, as most suitable sites have already been exploited, particularly those of the Rhine and Rhône valleys, the Massif Central, and the Alps. In contrast, nuclear production, benefiting from major government investment from the early 1970s, expanded enormously in the 1980s, notably with the construction of sites in the Rhône and Loire valleys, a reflection of the need for large quantities of cooling water. By the 21st century more than three-fourths of electricity in France was produced in nuclear plants, the highest proportion in the world, which enabled the country to become a large exporter of such energy. More recently development has slowed substantially, as demand has eased and environmental groups have campaigned against further investment. France's nuclear industry also includes a large uranium-enrichment factory at Pierrelatte in the lower Rhône valley and a waste-reprocessing plant at La Hague, near Cherbourg.

In the early 21st century renewable energy sources, such as solar and wind power, gained new prominence. Although wind power generated less than 3 percent of the electricity consumed in France in 2010, the country's "wind potential" was the second largest in Europe, and new facilities were planned in accordance with EU renewable energy directives. In addition, France's installed solar capacity increased by almost 700 percent between 2009 and 2011, and its 2.5 gigawatts of production represented almost 4 percent of the world's total.

MANUFACTURING AND INDUSTRIAL TRENDS

French industry was long the powerhouse of the country's postwar economic recovery. Yet, after a period of substantial restructuring and adjustment, particularly during successive periods of recession since the late 1970s, this sector (including construction and civil engineering) now employs only about one-fourth of the country's workforce and contributes the same proportion of GDP.

Both production and employment grew rapidly during the 1950s and '60s as industrial development was stimulated by the opening of new markets and by rising incomes. Industrial production went into decline in the mid-1970s, however, and a period of major deindustrialization followed as manufacturers responded to reduced domestic demand and to more intense foreign competition. Investment fell, delaying modernization and further compromising French competitiveness. In recent years investment and output have again increased, although at a lower rate and in a more erratic fashion than in the earlier postwar period. Nevertheless, industrial employment is still declining. There is an ever-increasing concentration of ownership as a result of the expansion of large multinational groups, which also allows foreign markets to have a greater impact on French industry.

Changes in industrial location have also occurred. Industrial expansion in the 1960s and '70s was accompanied by large-scale decentralization, favouring many areas of the Paris Basin (where there was an abundant and relatively cheap supply of labour) at the expense of the capital. Few company headquarters followed the dispersion of manufacturing plants, however, so that the centre of industrial operations remained rooted in the Paris region. The decline of industrial employment since the mid-1970s has had the greatest impact in traditional manufacturing regions, such as Nord–Pas-de-Calais and Lorraine. Nevertheless, the broad arc of *régions* stretching through northern and eastern France,

from Haute-Normandie to Rhône-Alpes, remains the most heavily industrialized part of the country.

On the basis of employment and turnover, seven branches of manufacturing stand out as particularly important: vehicles, chemicals, metallurgy, mechanical engineering, electronics, food, and textiles. The vehicle industry is dominated by the activities of the two automobile manufacturers, Peugeot SA (including Citroën) and Renault, which together produce nearly four million cars annually. Automobile production generates a substantial number of direct jobs as well as employment in subsidiary industries, such as the major tire manufacturer Michelin. France also possesses an important industry for the manufacture of railway locomotives and rolling stock, for which the expanding high-speed train (*train à grande vitesse*; TGV) network represents a major market.

Within the chemical industry, manufacturing ranges from basic organic and inorganic products to fine chemicals, pharmaceuticals, and other parachemical items, including perfumes. Because of the capital-intensive nature of these activities, a dominant role is played by large manufacturers such as Rhône-Poulenc. Extensive research is carried out in this field. Basic chemical production is concentrated in areas offering access to raw materials, such as Nord–Pas-de-Calais, Étang-de-Berre, and Rhône-Alpes, whereas pharmaceutical production is more closely related to

MICHELIN

Headquartered at Clermont-Ferrand, Michelin (in full Compagnie Générale Des Établissements Michelin) is a leading French manufacturer of tires and other rubber products. Founded in 1888 by the Michelin brothers, André (1853–1931) and Édouard (1859–1940), the company manufactured tires for bicycles and horse-drawn carriages before introducing pneumatic tires for automobiles in the 1890s. To show that demountable pneumatic tires could be used successfully on motor vehicles, the Michelins equipped a car with such tires held onto the rims by bolts and entered and drove it in the 1895 Paris–Bordeaux road race. Although they did not win the race, they created popular interest in pneumatic tires. Their company became a major producer of tires in Europe. In 1948 Michelin was the first to introduce steel-belted radial tires.

The company established its first foreign plant at Turin, Italy, in 1906 and today operates facilities in a number of countries. Michelin was reorganized as a holding company in 1951, with interests in tires, other rubber products, and synthetic rubber.

The company also publishes an international series of travel guides known as Michelin guides (French: Guide Michelin) and a series of road maps. The guides were initiated by André Michelin, whose aim was to promote tourism by car and thus to support his tire industry. The first Red Guide (1900), an aid to travel in France, was a pocket-size, alphabetical listing of French towns of interest that were large enough to contain hotels and garages. It included the prototypical rating symbols for which Michelin has become famous; this now-extensive list of symbols indicates such features of lodgings as comfort level (from luxurious to modest comfort) and the presence of such amenities as swimming pools, gardens, tennis courts, and air conditioning. The Red Guide also includes restaurant ratings, noting those that provide serviceable but inexpensive meals as well as a select few (indicated by the presence of three stars) that provide "cooking worth a special journey." In 1957 the company began publishing Red Guides to other western European countries, including guides to Spain and Portugal, Italy, Great Britain and Ireland, the Benelux countries (Belgium, Netherlands, and Luxembourg), and West Germany.

In addition to the Red Guides, the most popular of the Michelin guides, Michelin offers supplementary Green Guides, which can be of aid to the traveler in search of more information on the museums, natural wonders, and other points of interest in a region. Michelin also publishes a great number of highly detailed and informative maps.

major market areas and research centres, notably Île-de-France.

The metallurgical industry, dominated by the production of steel, experienced major restructuring in the late 1970s and the '80s as demand fell and competition from other international producers increased. Originally concentrated in Lorraine because of the presence of iron ore, steel production shifted to the coastal sites of Dunkirk and Fos-sur-Mer, which relied on imported ore and coal. France is also an important producer of aluminum, notably through the Pechiney group. Such basic metal industries support a diverse range of engineering activities, spread widely throughout France but with important concentrations in the highly urbanized and industrialized régions of Île-de-France and Rhône-Alpes. Similar features characterize the electrical engineering and electronics industries. France is a major manufacturer of professional electronics, such as radar equipment, but is weakly represented in the field of consumer electronics, which has led to a high level of imports. The country also has a number of high-tech aerospace industries, which manufacture aircraft, missiles, satellites, and related launch systems. These industries are concentrated in the Paris region and in the southwest around Toulouse and Bordeaux.

Food and beverage industries represent a large branch of French manufacturing, reflecting the considerable volume and diversity of agricultural production. Although present in most regions, food manufacturers are particularly concentrated in major urban market areas and in western agricultural regions such as Brittany, Pays de la Loire, and Basse-Normandie. The beverage sector is dominant in the main wine-growing areas of northern and northeastern France; it represents an important source of exports.

Textile and clothing industries have experienced a long period of decline in the face of strong foreign competition, with substantial job losses and plant closures affecting the major production areas of northern France and Rhône-Alpes (textiles), as well as Île-de-France (clothing). Unlike other major industrial branches, these activities remain characterized by small firms.

A varied group of construction and civil engineering industries employs about one-fourth of the labour in the industrial sector. Activity and employment have fluctuated considerably in relation to changing government and private investment programs and the varying demand for new homes. This sector is characterized by the coexistence of a large number of small firms with a limited number of large companies, many of which work on civil engineering contracts outside France.

FINANCE

Although the French financial sector employs less than 13 percent of the labour force, it accounts for roughly one-third of the country's total gross domestic product. Home to some of Europe's largest banks and its second largest stock exchange, France is a key player in the continent's financial markets.

BANKING AND INSURANCE

France possesses one of the largest banking sectors in western Europe, and its three major institutions, Crédit Agricole, BNP-Paribas, and Société Générale, rank among the top banks on the continent. Traditionally, banking activities were tightly controlled by the government through the Banque de France. However, deregulation beginning in the 1960s led to a substantial increase in branch banking and bank account holders, and legislation in 1984 further reduced controls over banks' activities, which thereby enabled them to offer a wider range of services and led to greater competition. Since then, encouraged by the lifting of restrictions on the free movement of capital within the EU in 1990, banks have broadly internationalized their activities. In 1993 the Banque de France was granted independent status, which freed it from state control. In general, employment in the banking sector has declined, largely because of the widespread computerization of transactions and this restructuring. At the turn of the 21st century, the franc gave way to the euro as the legal currency in France.

France has a large insurance industry dominated by major companies such as Axa, CNP, and AGF but also including a number of important mutual benefit societies, which administer pension plans. The deregulation of this sector has led to vast reorganization, with activity still concentrated in Paris though a number of provincial towns have developed as specialist centres through the location of various mutual societies.

THE STOCK EXCHANGE

Share transactions in France were historically centred on the Bourse de Paris (Paris Stock Exchange), a national system that in the late 20th century incorporated much smaller exchanges at Lyon, Bordeaux, Lille, Marseille, Nancy, and Nantes. Share dealings and stock market activity increased greatly beginning in the early 1980s, corresponding with a period of deregulation and modernization: official brokers lost their monopoly on conducting share transactions; a second market opened in 1983 to encourage the quotation of medium-size firms; and in 1996 the "new market" was launched to help finance young, dynamic companies in search of venture capital. Also in 1996 the Bourse was restructured, reinforcing the powers of its controlling body, Commission des Opérations de Bourse. In 2000 the Bourse merged with the Amsterdam and Brussels stock exchanges to form the Euronext equities market, which in 2006 merged with the New York Stock Exchange.

FOREIGN INVESTMENT

Financial deregulation, the movement toward a single European market, and the general freeing of world trade are among the influences that have encouraged investment by French firms outside France and increased the reverse flow of foreign investment funds into the country. In the industrial field French companies have shown a growing interest in investing in other advanced economies, especially the United States. Over recent years investments have also multiplied in the developing economies of Asia and eastern Europe. Foreign firms investing in France have been principally from the EU (notably the United Kingdom, the Netherlands, and Germany) and the United States. Most investment is related to the fields of engineering, electronics, and chemicals and generally is directed at the more highly urbanized centres of the country. The sources and nature of foreign investment in France are becoming more diverse, however. Japanese interests have increased substantially, for instance, and investment in property and the service industry has been growing, particularly in and around Paris.

TRADE

France, a leading trading nation, has grown into one of the world's foremost exporting countries, with the value of exports representing more than one-fifth of GDP. France is also a major importer, especially of machinery, chemicals and chemical products, tropical agricultural products, and traditional industrial goods such as clothes and textiles. The high level of imports led to a trade deficit for much of the period between the early 1970s and early 1990s. However, from 1992 France experienced a trade surplus, combined with a positive balance from invisible (nonmerchandise) transactions, especially tourism.

Most foreign trade is based on the exchange of goods. In the case of agricultural commodities, France has become an increasingly important net exporter of raw agricultural products (such as grains) as well as agro-industrial products, such as foods and beverages, including wines, tinned fruits and vegetables, and dairy products. The need to import large quantities of oil (and to a lesser extent gas and coal), however, has resulted in a sizable deficit for those exchanges. Although France imports a great deal of industrial goods, the country has long been a major exporter of vehicles and transport equipment, as well as armaments and professional electronics. More recently exports of pharmaceuticals and parachemical products have risen.

The greater part of foreign trade is carried out with other developed countries, and some four-fifths of transactions take place with Organisation for Economic Co-operation and Development (OECD) countries. Among these the EU plays a major role, reflecting the growing exchange of goods and services between its member countries. More than three-fifths of French exports and imports are destined for or originate in EU countries, of which Germany is easily the most important. Outside the EU the United States is France's other major trading partner, although Russia and China claimed a growing percentage of trade in the 21st century. EU countries are an important source of industrial imports, whereas fuel products and raw materials tend to originate from more distant sources. Conversely, agricultural and food exports are oriented predominantly toward European markets, whereas industrial goods are exported to a more global marketplace.

SERVICES

The various service, or tertiary, industries in France account for about two-thirds of the country's employment and of GDP. These levels were reached following an extended period of sustained growth, notably since the 1960s. This sector covers a highly diverse range of activities, including social and administrative services, such as local government, health, and education; wholesaling, distribution, and transport and communication services; consumer services, such as retailing and the hotel and catering trades; and producer or business services, including banking, financial, legal, advertising, computing, and data-handling services.

Not all tertiary activities have developed in the same way. For example, rationalization in the banking and financial services sector has limited the creation of jobs. Conversely, the continuously strong growth, since the early 1970s, of hypermarkets and other large freestanding retail outlets that allow for purchasing in bulk and in greater variety has led to a significant rise in related employment. In particular the large group of producer services has expanded rapidly. In part this trend is the inevitable

consequence of the increasingly complex and highly competitive nature of the modern economy. It also results from companies' strategies of externalizing (outsourcing) such service requirements for reasons of efficiency and cost savings.

Tertiary activities are located predominantly in urban areas, especially the larger cities. Such concentration is most evident in relation to the capital. The Île-de-France région (Paris region) alone accounts for nearly one-fourth of all tertiary employment while containing less than one-fifth of the population. In Paris the sector's importance is qualitative as well as quantitative. Paris houses more than two-thirds of the headquarters of the country's major companies and a disproportionately large share of senior management and research staff. This attraction to the capital is influenced by a number of factors, including the size and diversity of the labour market, the high level of accessibility to other French and international business centres, prestige, and the presence of numerous specialized services.

CIVIL SERVICE

The largest groups of employees are those in national education and the postal system. As in the judicial system, French administration has been strongly marked by a strict hierarchy since the time of Napoleon. Civil servants are grouped into different corps and different ranks and are classified according to their recruitment level into four different categories. Entry is by a competitive examination. At the highest level, category A civil servants are recruited through a national school of administration, created in 1945, which gives access to the grands corps de l'État, including the Court of Accounts, the Inspection of Finance, the prefectural corps, the diplomatic service, and the civil administrators' corps. The duties and rights of civil servants are defined by a general statute of 1946, which was partly modified in 1959. The career guarantees and disciplinary code are extensive and are protected by the Conseil d'État (Council of State). In return, civil servants are duty-bound to be discreet in expressing any personal opinions, and the right to strike, which is recognized by the constitution for all French citizens, is severely limited for them, although this varies according to the corps. Most civil servants belong to labour unions.

TOURISM

With France's variety of landscapes and climatic conditions, its cultural diversity, and its renowned cuisine, it is of little surprise that tourism should have become a major industry. Directly and indirectly this activity employs about 10 percent of the workforce and contributes approximately 9 percent of GDP, earning French businesses a substantial income from foreign visitors and more than compensating for the amount spent by French tourists abroad. France is one of the world's leading tourist destinations, visited by up to 70 million foreign tourists each year at the end of the 20th century.

The tourist industry has grown rapidly since the 1960s, with an increasingly large number of French families taking a holiday each year, encouraged by greater affluence, more leisure time, and, since 1982, five weeks' statutory paid holiday. In response to this increase in demand, the industry itself has changed. An activity traditionally distinguished by small businesses has been transformed by the growth of increasingly large hotel and holiday firms; new resorts have been built, notably along the Languedoc and Aquitaine coasts and in the French Alps, and new tourist products have been developed, including spectacular theme parks. The Disneyland complex on the eastern fringe of Paris, which opened in 1992, epitomized this trend.

Comparatively few French people take their holidays abroad. Conversely, France receives a large influx of foreign visitors, mainly from European countries, especially Germany. On average such tourists remain for only a short period, and their stays are more evenly spread over the course of the year and between the various regions of the country than those of their French counterparts. Nevertheless, Paris and the Mediterranean areas remain preferred destinations.

The unequal impact of tourism on different regions is a key feature of this

Skiing at Chamonix in the *département* of Haute-Savoie, France. © Peter Miller/Photo Researchers

activity. In summer a restricted number of coastal areas, notably in the Midi and in Brittany, receive the heaviest influx of holidaymakers; in winter mountainous regions become the preferred destination, particularly the northern Alps, with such major ski resorts as Chamonix, Tignes, La Plagne, and Les Arcs. Paris itself is an enormous tourist attraction, especially for foreign visitors and for events such as exhibitions and conferences; indeed, the capital is perhaps the world's leading centre for international conferences. The uneven geographic pattern of tourism is matched by an unbalanced seasonal pattern. Despite attempts to spread holidays more evenly throughout the year, the months of July and August overwhelmingly dominate as the period chosen for travel by a large majority of the French. Another problem is the environmental stress caused by mass tourism, which has led to official efforts to promote more sustainable forms of tourism in mountainous and coastal regions.

TRANSPORTATION AND TELECOMMUNICATIONS

The transportation sector includes such dynamic companies as the National Society of French Railways (Société Nationale des Chemins de Fer Français), the state-owned railways operator, and Air France, the national airline. Closely allied are manufacturers of transport equipment and the civil engineering concerns responsible for constructing new infrastructure. Generally, France benefits from a dense and diversified transport network, limited only by its still excessive focus upon the capital city. For land-based movements the road network has become increasingly important. For example, a vast majority of all freight traffic, in terms of the volume and distance of goods moved, goes by road. This dominance has been achieved at the expense of railways and inland waterways.

ROADS

Traffic on the highways has more than doubled since 1970, and about one-fifth of vehicles are commercial. An extensive road system totaling about 600,000 miles (965,000 km) has been developed to deal with increasingly heavy traffic conditions. However, only a small proportion of this network consists of main trunk roads (the *routes nationales*) and motorways. Construction on the latter began much later than in neighbouring countries, and it was not until the mid-1960s that a major development program was under way. To speed progress, building concessions were granted to private and semiprivate companies, which, in return for their investment, were authorized to levy tolls. Since that period the major radial routes from the capital have been completed, as well as embryonic regional networks focusing on large urban centres, such as Paris, Lyon, Marseille, and Lille. Traffic is heavily concentrated on the main north-south axis between these cities. In extending the system, emphasis has been placed on improving international links and developing national routes that avoid Paris, as between Calais and Dijon, as well as Bordeaux and Clermont-Ferrand. Numerous rural roads and lanes supplement the main system, as do new bridges, such as the Millau Bridge in the Tarn valley, which opened in 2004 as the world's highest road bridge (343 metres [1,125 feet]).

RAILROADS

By the end of the 19th century, the present rail network was largely in place, dominated by the main lines radiating from Paris. Since World War II many little-used rural sections have been closed. In contrast, since the early 1980s certain new lines have been opened in conjunction with the introduction of high-speed passenger trains (*trains à grande vitesse*; TGV) between Paris and a number of provincial cities. Southeastern France was the first area to be provided with such services, reflecting the already high density of traffic between Paris, Lyon, and the Mediterranean coast. New lines are also in operation to western and northern France, with longer-term plans to serve eastern regions. International service also exists to Geneva, Lausanne, and Brussels, as well as to London, by means of the Channel Tunnel, which opened in 1994 after six years of construction. It is used for passenger and freight trains as well as for transporting cars and commercial vehicles. By the end of the 20th century, the Eurostar passenger trains linked Paris to London in three hours and carried more than nine million travelers annually. In France the TGV network alone accounts for more than one-half of passenger miles and has attracted many new customers to the railways. Generally, however, fewer than one-fifth of passenger movements in France were accounted for by rail

A high-speed TGV (train à grande vitesse) *traversing the Burgundy région between Tournous and Mâcon, France.* © Riviere—Rapho/Photo Researchers

services, with traffic heavily concentrated along the main, electrified radial routes from the capital, particularly in the direction of southeastern France. Freight traffic has declined, partly because of fallen demand for products such as coal, iron, and oil, traditionally carried by rail, and partly because of intense competition from road haulers. Like passenger traffic, freight movements are concentrated along the main radial routes, as well as along the lines linking the industrial centres of northern and northeastern France.

Within an increasing number of urban areas, investment has been made in new underground rail and tram systems in an effort to reduce congestion on the roads and related problems of pollution. Provincial cities such as Lyon, Marseille, Lille, and Toulouse now boast metro networks, while a growing number of other cities (such as Lille, Nantes, Strasbourg, and Grenoble) are served by tramways, a solution increasingly favoured because of its comparatively lower cost. However, this has not stopped further substantial investment in the Paris Métro or the high-speed regional system (Réseau Express Régional; RER). Lines have been extended farther into the suburbs, and major new capacity has been added in central Paris.

WATERWAYS

Despite the presence of major rivers such as the Seine, Rhine, and Rhône, inland waterways carry little freight. Although they are still used to transport goods such as construction materials and agricultural and oil products, their role has progressively declined in the face of cheaper and faster alternatives. Traffic has also been lost because of the reduced inland movement of heavy raw materials and fuel products and an inefficiently organized industry with too many small-barge operators. The uneven and disjointed pattern of the waterways further restricts use. Less than a third of the commercial waterway system is of European standard gauge; moreover, the principal river and canal systems remain unconnected for the passage of large barges, so that no truly national or international network exists.

France is served by a large number of maritime ports, which reflects not only its extensive coastline but also its importance as a trading nation. As in other Western countries, however, France's merchant fleet has steadily shrunk, largely because of the difficulty of competing with lower-cost carriers. Freight traffic, consisting mostly of imports, is concentrated in a limited number of ports, principally Marseille and Le Havre, followed by Dunkerque, Calais, Nantes-Saint-Nazaire, and Rouen. This imbalance is partly explained by the still-sizable quantities of crude oil that are unloaded. Passenger traffic is less important but is dominated by cross-channel movements from the port of Calais and the nearby Channel Tunnel.

AIR TRANSPORT

Air freight and passenger traffic have expanded rapidly and, like other forms of transport, are centred around Paris. The capital's two major airports (Roissy [Charles de Gaulle] and Orly) represent the second largest airport complex in western Europe (after London), handling roughly two-thirds of all French passenger traffic. Other French airports are far less important, though the country has a comprehensive network of local and regional airports. The majority of routes, however, are between provincial towns and cities and the capital rather than between regional centres, which reemphasizes the persistent centralization of economic activity and decision making in France. Nice and Marseille are the busiest regional air centres and, along with Lyon, Bordeaux, Toulouse, and Strasbourg, are the only provincial airports to have significant international traffic.

TELECOMMUNICATIONS

At the beginning of the 21st century, France had some 35 million main telephone lines, almost all with digital capacity. Over 62 million cellular telephones were in use in 2010, creating a ratio of almost one phone per person. The country had over 40 million personal computers, and roughly 70 percent of French people were Internet users. The comparatively low Internet use statistics were due in part to restrictive government controls on e-commerce and the presence of an existing network called Minitel (founded 1983 and owned by France Telecom)—obstacles that began to fall away in the first years of the 21st century. Indeed, although Minitel had achieved widespread usage among groups that were otherwise averse to new technology, it was shuttered in 2012 due to rising costs.

CHAPTER 4

GOVERNMENT AND SOCIETY

Over recent decades France has experienced extensive change. Rapid urbanization and suburbanization have transformed many former rural areas. At the same time, many of the large cities have been faced with a growing need for renovation and rehabilitation, often in the face of rising levels of crime. The once dominant industrial regions of northern France have seen their traditional manufacturing base decline and their economies restructured. Conversely, areas of western and southern France that were once sparsely industrialized have become the focus for the growth of new manufacturing and service activities, particularly in advanced technology. These have also proved to be increasingly attractive areas in which to live, work, and vacation.

These demographic trends have been facilitated by substantial improvements to the transport infrastructure, in the form of new motorways and the development of TGV, the high-speed train network. Despite spontaneous movements and policies of decentralization, as well as challenges from new forms of local governance, Paris retains its dominant role in the nation.

GOVERNMENT

When France fell into political turmoil after the May 1958 insurrection in Algeria (then still a French colony), General Charles de Gaulle, an outspoken critic of the postwar constitution who had served as the provisional head of government in the mid-1940s, returned to political life as prime minister.

He formed a government and, through the constitutional law of June 1958, was granted responsibility for drafting a new constitution. With the assistance of Michel Debré, de Gaulle crafted the constitution of the Fifth Republic.

THE 1958 CONSTITUTION

The drafting of the constitution of the Fifth Republic and its promulgation on October 4, 1958, differed in three main ways from the former constitutions of 1875 (Third Republic) and 1946 (Fourth Republic): first, the parliament did not participate in its drafting, which was done by a government working party aided by a constitutional advisory committee and the Council of State; second, French overseas territories participated in the referendum that ratified it on September 28, 1958; and, third, initial acceptance was widespread, unlike the 1946 constitution, which on first draft was rejected by popular referendum and then in a revised form was only narrowly approved. In contrast,

French prime minister Jean-Marc Ayrault addresses members of parliament. Patrick Kovarik/ AFP/Getty Images

the 1958 constitution was contested by 85 percent of the electorate, of which 79 percent were in favour; among the overseas territories only Guinea rejected the new constitution and consequently withdrew from the French Community.

THE DUAL EXECUTIVE SYSTEM

In order to achieve the political stability that was lacking in the Third and the Fourth Republic, the constitution of 1958 adopted a mixed (semipresidential) form of government, combining elements of both parliamentary and presidential systems. As a result, the parliament is a bicameral legislature composed of elected members of the National Assembly (lower house) and the Senate (upper house). The president is elected separately by direct universal suffrage and operates as head of state. The constitution gives the president the power to appoint the prime minister (often known as the premier), who oversees the execution of legislation. The president also appoints the Council of Ministers, or cabinet, which together with the prime minister is referred to as the government.

THE ROLE OF THE PRESIDENT

The French system is characterized by the strong role of the president of the republic. The office of the president is unique in that it has the authority to bypass the parliament by submitting referenda directly to the people and even to dissolve the parliament altogether. The president presides over the Council of Ministers and other high councils, signs the more important decrees, appoints high civil servants and judges, negotiates and ratifies treaties, and is commander in chief of the armed forces. Under exceptional circumstances, Article 16 allows for the concentration of all the powers of the state in the presidency. This article, enforced from April to September 1961 during the Algerian crisis, has received sharp criticism, having proved to be of limited practical value because of the stringent conditions attached to its operation.

De Gaulle's great influence and the pressures of unstable political conditions tended to reinforce the authority of the presidency at the expense of the rest of the government. Whereas the constitution (Article 20) charges the government to "determine and direct" the policy of the nation, de Gaulle arrogated to himself the right to take the more important decisions, particularly concerning foreign, military, and institutional policies, and his successors adopted a similar pattern of behaviour. The constitution of 1958 called for a presidential term of seven years, but, in a referendum in 2000, the term was shortened to five years, beginning with the 2002 elections.

The role of the prime minister, however, has gradually gained in stature. Constitutionally, the office is responsible for the determination of governmental policy and exercises control over

French prime minister Jean-Marc Ayrault answers journalists upon his arrival at the Economic, Social, and Environmental Council of France. Martin Bureau/AFP/Getty Images

the civil service and the armed forces. Moreover, while all major decisions tended to be taken at the Élysée Palace (the residence of the president) under de Gaulle, responsibility for policy, at least in internal matters, has slowly passed to the head of the government. Especially since the mid-1970s, a working partnership between the president and the prime minister has tended to be established. Finally, the power of the president is tied to the parliamentary strength of the parties that support him and that form a majority in the National Assembly. It is possible, however, for the president's parties to become a minority in the assembly, in which case the president must appoint a prime minister from the majority faction. Beginning in 1986, France experienced several periods of divided government, known as "cohabitation," in which the president and the prime minister belonged to different parties.

PARLIAMENTARY COMPOSITION AND FUNCTIONS

The National Assembly is composed of 577 deputies who are directly elected for a term of five years in single-member constituencies on the basis of a majority two-ballot system, which requires that a runoff take place if no candidate has obtained the absolute majority on the first ballot. The system was abandoned for proportional representation for the 1986 general election, but it was reintroduced for the 1988 election and has remained in place ever since. In 2012 the Senate was composed of 348 senators indirectly elected for six years by a *collège électoral* consisting mainly of municipal councillors in each *département*, one of the administrative units into which France is divided. The parliament retains its dual function of legislation and control over the executive but to a lesser extent than in the past. The domain of law (Article 34) is limited to determining the basic rules and fundamental principles concerning such matters as civil law, fiscal law, penal law, electoral law, civil liberties, labour laws, amnesty, and the budget. In these matters the parliament is sovereign, but the government can draw up the details for the application of laws.

The government is responsible for all other matters, according to Article 37 of the constitution, and the assemblies can in no way interfere; the Constitutional Council is responsible for ensuring that these provisions are respected. The parliament can temporarily delegate part of its legislative power to the government, which then legislates by ordinances. This procedure has been used on matters concerning Algeria, social security, natural disasters, European integration, and unemployment. Finally, government and the parliament are advised by an Economic and Social Council, composed of 230 representatives of various groups (e.g., trade unions and employers' and farmers' organizations) that must be consulted on long-term programs and on developments and that may be consulted on any bill concerning economic and social matters.

The right to initiate legislation is shared by the government and the parliament. Bills are studied by parliamentary committees, although the government does control the agenda. The government can also, at any point during the debate over a bill, call for a single vote on the whole of the bill's text. Parliamentary control over the government can be exercised, but it is less intense than in the British system. There are questions to ministers challenging various aspects of performance, but these take place infrequently and are primarily occasions for lesser debates and do not lead to effective scrutiny of the government's practices. Committee inquiries are also relatively rare. The National Assembly, however, has the right to censure the government, but, in order to avoid the excesses that occurred before 1958 (as a result of which governments often fell once or twice a year), the motion of censure is subject to considerable restrictions. Only once in the first 50 years of the Fifth Republic, in 1962, did the National Assembly pass a motion of censure, when it stalled de Gaulle's referendum for direct election of the president by universal suffrage, which ultimately met with approval. The government is also strengthened by its constitutional power to ask for a vote of confidence on its general policy or on a bill. In the latter case a bill is considered adopted unless a motion of censure has obtained an absolute majority.

THE ROLE OF REFERENDA

The people may be asked to ratify, by a constituent referendum (Article 89), an amendment already passed by the two houses of the parliament. The constitution made provision for legislative referenda, by which the president of the republic has the authority to submit a proposed bill to the people relating to the general organization of the state (Article 11).

This procedure was used twice in settling the Algerian question of independence, first in January 1961, to approve self-determination in Algeria (when 75 percent voted in favour), and again in April 1962, approving the Évian Agreement, which gave Algeria its independence from France (when 91 percent voted in favour). The use of this latter procedure to amend the constitution without going through the preliminary phase of obtaining parliamentary approval is constitutionally questionable, but it led to a significant result when, in October 1962,

the election of the president by universal suffrage was approved by 62 percent of those voting. In April 1969, however, in a referendum concerning the transformation of the Senate into an economic and social council and the reform of the regional structure of France, fewer than half voted in favour, and this brought about President de Gaulle's resignation.

Through the end of the 20th century, national referenda were met with low voter turnout. The procedure was used in 1972 for the enlargement of the European Economic Community (EEC) by the proposed addition of Denmark, Ireland, Norway, and the United Kingdom; in 1988 for the proposed future status of the overseas territory of New Caledonia; and in 1992 for approval of the Maastricht Treaty, which established the European Union. In 1995, when minor modifications were made to the constitution, the use of the referendum was enlarged to include proposed legislation relating to the country's economic and social life. In 2000 a referendum shortened the presidential term from seven to five years. A 2005 referendum on a proposed constitution for the European Union was soundly defeated, and the setback forced EU officials to consider alternative means to further European integration.

THE ROLE OF THE CONSTITUTIONAL COUNCIL

The Constitutional Council is appointed for nine years and is composed of nine members, three each appointed by the president, the National Assembly, and the Senate. It supervises the conduct of parliamentary and presidential elections, and it examines the constitutionality of organic laws (those fundamentally affecting the government) and rules of parliamentary procedure. The council is also consulted on international agreements, on disputes between the government and the parliament, and, above all, on the constitutionality of legislation. This power has increased over the years, and the council has been given a position comparable to that of the U.S. Supreme Court.

REGIONAL AND LOCAL GOVERNMENT

The main units of local government, defined by the constitution as *collectivités territoriales* ("territorial collectivities"), are the *régions*, the *départements*, the *communes*, and the overseas territories. A small number of local governments, known as *collectivités territoriales à statut particulier* ("territorial collectivities with special status"), have slightly different administrative frameworks; among these are the island of Corsica and the large cities of Paris, Lyon, and Marseille.

THE *RÉGIONS*

One of the main features of decentralization in French government has evolved through the creation of the *régions*. These include the 21 metropolitan *régions* of mainland France as well as the 5 overseas *régions* of Guadeloupe, Martinique, French Guiana, Mayotte, and Réunion. (The overseas régions are simultaneously administered as overseas départements.) Although Corsica is still commonly described as one of 22 *régions* of metropolitan France, its official status was changed in 1991 from *région* to *collectivité territoriale à statut particulier*; its classification, unique among France's local governments, provides Corsica greater autonomy than the *régions*.

After a number of limited changes lasting two decades, a 1982 law set up directly elected regional councils with the power to elect their executive. The law also devolved to the regional authorities many functions hitherto belonging to the central government, in particular economic and social development, regional planning, education, and cultural matters. The *régions* have gradually come to play a larger part in the administrative and political life of the country.

THE *DÉPARTEMENTS*

The *région* to an extent competes with the *département*, which was set up in 1790 and is still regarded by some as the main intermediate level of government. With the creation in 1964 of new *départements* in the Paris region and the dividing in two of Corsica in 1976, the number of *départements* reached 100: 96 in metropolitan France and 4 overseas (Guadeloupe, Martinique, French Guiana, and Réunion, which are simultaneously administered as *régions*). In 2009 voters in Mayotte voted overwhelmingly in favour of *département* status, and two years later it became France's fifth overseas (and its 101st total) *département*. Each *département* is run by the General Council, which is elected for six years with one councillor per canton. There are between 13 and 70 cantons per *département*. The General Council is responsible for all the main departmental services: welfare, health, administration, and departmental employment. It also has responsibility for local regulations, manages public and private property, and votes on the local budget.

A law passed in 1982 enhanced decentralization by increasing the powers and authority of the *départements*. Formerly, the chief executive of the *département* was the government-appointed prefect (*préfet*), who also had strong powers over other local authorities. Since the law went into effect, however, the president of the General Council is the chief executive and the prefect is responsible only for preventing the actions of local authorities from going against national legislation.

THE *COMMUNES*

The *commune*, the smallest unit of democracy in France, dates to the parishes of the ancien régime in the years before the Revolution. Its modern structure dates from a law of 1884, which stipulates that *communes* have municipal councils that are to be elected for six years, include at least nine members, and be responsible for "the affairs of the commune." The council administers public land, sets up public undertakings, votes on its own budget, and over recent years has played an increasing role in promoting local economic development. It elects a mayor and the mayor's assistants. Supervision by the central government, once very tight, has been markedly reduced, especially since 1982.

The mayor is both the chief executive of the municipal council and the representative of the central government in the *commune*. The mayor is in charge of the municipal police and through them ensures public order, security, and health and guarantees the supervision of public places to prevent such things as fires, floods, and epidemics. The mayor also directs municipal employees, implements the budget, and is responsible for the registry office. French mayors are usually strong and often dominate the life of the *commune*. They are indeed important figures in the political life of the country.

French *communes* are typically quite small; there are more than 36,500 of them. Efforts have been made to group *communes* or to bring them closer to one another, but these have been only partly successful. In certain cities, such as Lyon and Lille, cooperative urban communities have been created to enable the joint management and planning of a range of municipal services, among them waste disposal, street cleaning, road building, and fire fighting. A similar approach has been adopted elsewhere, including rural areas, with the establishment of *syndicats intercommunaux* that allows services to be administered jointly by several *communes*. Moreover, since the 1999 law on Regional Planning and Sustainable Development, the *communes* within urban areas of more than 50,000 inhabitants have been encouraged to pool resources and responsibilities to promote joint development projects by means of a new form of administrative unit known as the *communauté d'agglomération*.

THE OVERSEAS TERRITORIES

The status of many of France's overseas territories—vestiges of the French Empire—changed in the 1970s. Independence was proclaimed in 1975 by the Indian Ocean archipelago of the Comoros, with the exception of Mayotte (Mahoré) island, which chose to remain within French rule; in 1977 by Djibouti, on the Horn of Africa; and in 1980 by the Anglo-French Pacific Ocean condominium of the New Hebrides, under the

French Polynesian capital Papeete. Paul Chesley/Stone/Getty Images

name of Vanuatu. Mayotte was elevated to the status of territorial collectivity in 1976, and in North America the island territory of Saint-Pierre and Miquelon was elevated to the same status in 1985. France granted Mayotte, known as a departmental collectivity from 2001, the status of overseas *département* in 2011.

The only places retaining overseas territory status are French Polynesia (with its capital at Papeete on the island of Tahiti), New Caledonia, the Wallis and Futuna islands in the Pacific, and the Adélie Land claim in Antarctica. These territories have substantial autonomy except in matters reserved for metropolitan France, such as diplomacy and defense. They are governed through various but similar administrative structures, usually involving an elected council and a chief executive, but they are subject to the tutelage of a representative of the French Republic. A 1998 decision regarding New Caledonia envisaged the progressive transfer of political responsibilities to the island over a period of 15 to 20 years.

JUSTICE

In France there are two types of jurisdictions: the judiciary that judges trials between private persons and punishes infringements of the penal law and an administrative judicial system that is responsible for settling lawsuits between public bodies, such as the state, local bodies, and public establishments, as well as private individuals.

THE JUDICIARY

For civil cases the judiciary consists of higher courts (*grande instance*) and lower courts (*tribunaux d'instance*), which replaced justices of the peace in 1958. For criminal cases there are *tribunaux correctionnels* ("courts of correction") and *tribunaux de police*, or "police courts," which try minor offenses. The decisions of these courts can be referred to one of the 35 courts of appeal. Felonies are brought before the assize courts established in each *département*, consisting of three judges and nine jurors.

All these courts are subject to the control of the Court of Cassation, as are the specialized professional courts, such as courts for industrial conciliation, courts-martial, and, from 1963 to 1981, the Court of State Security, which tried felonies and misdemeanours against national security. Very exceptionally, in cases of high treason, a High Court of Justice (Cour de Justice de la République), composed of members of the National Assembly and of senators, is empowered to try the president of the republic and the ministers. They can also be tried by this court if they have committed felonies or misdemeanours during their term of office. These are the only situations in which the Court of Cassation is not competent to review the case. Otherwise, the court examines judgments in order to assess whether the law has been correctly interpreted; if it finds that this is not the case, it refers the case back to a lower court.

The more than 5,000 judges are recruited by means of competitive examinations held by the National School of the Magistracy, which was founded in 1958 and in 1970 replaced the National Centre for Judicial Studies. A traditional distinction is made between the *magistrats du siège*, who try cases, and the *magistrats de parquet* (public prosecutors), who prosecute. Only the former enjoy the constitutional guarantee of irremovability. The High Council of the Judiciary is made up of 20 members originally appointed by the head of state from among the judiciary. Since 1993, however, its members have been elected, following reforms designed to free the judiciary from political control. The Council makes proposals and gives its opinion on the nomination of the *magistrats du siège*. It also acts as a disciplinary council. Public prosecutors act on behalf of the state. They are hierarchically subject to the authority of the minister of justice. Judges can serve successively as members of the bench (*siège*) and the public prosecutor's department. They act in collaboration with, but are hierarchically independent of, the police.

ADMINISTRATIVE COURTS

One of the special characteristics of the French judicial system is the existence of a hierarchy of administrative courts whose origins date to Napoleon. The duality of the judicial system has been sometimes regarded unfavourably, but the system has come to be gradually admired and indeed widely adopted in continental European countries and in the former French colonies. The administrative courts are under the control of the Council of State, which examines cases on appeal. The Council of State thus plays a crucial part in exercising control over the government and the administration from a jurisdictional point of view and ensures that they conform with the law. It is, moreover, empowered by the constitution to give its opinion on proposed bills and on certain decrees.

POLITICAL PROCESS

Universal suffrage at the age of 21 has existed in France since 1848 for men and since 1944 for women; the age of eligibility was lowered to 18 in 1974. Legislation enacted in the late 1990s penalizes political parties for failing to maintain sufficient parity between male and female candidates. Candidates for the National Assembly must receive a majority, not a plurality, of votes, and, if no candidate receives an absolute majority, then a second ballot is held the following week and the post is awarded to the plurality winner. Elections follow the model of single-member districts rather than proportional representation within a district. Two-phase voting is also used for the presidency, with the exception that, if an absolute majority is not reached after the first ballot, then only the two highest vote getters are considered for the second ballot, which is contested two weeks later.

French president Charles de Gaulle salutes the Eternal Flame at the Arc de Triomphe, Paris, on November 12, 1965. Reg Lancaster/Hulton Archive/Getty Images

Historically, French political parties have been both numerous and weak, which is generally accepted as the reason governments fell frequently before the advent of the Fifth Republic in 1958. Since then there has been a degree of streamlining, although, especially among centrist groups, parties are still poorly organized and highly personalized. Indeed, there have been many vicissitudes in the fortunes of the main parties since the late 1950s. In the 1960s and early '70s, Charles de Gaulle's centre-right party—first named Union for the New Republic (UNR) and later Rally for the Republic (RPR)—dominated the elections. After the election of the centrist Valéry Giscard d'Estaing to the presidency in 1974, the Gaullist party declined, while the centrists (from 1978 as the Union for French Democracy; UDF) and Socialists gained in strength. From 1981 and with the election of the Socialist president François Mitterrand, the Socialist Party became dominant, its gains being made primarily at the expense of the Communists. It was the first time since 1958 that the left had taken the leadership in French politics. While the Gaullists achieved a comeback with the appointment of Édouard Balladur as prime minister in 1993 and the election of Jacques Chirac as president in 1995, the Socialists regained control of the government during 1997–2002, when Lionel Jospin served as prime minister. In 2002 Chirac was reelected to the presidency under the coalition banner of the Union for Presidential Majority (UMP), decisively putting down Jean-Marie Le Pen of the far-right National Front, who had surprised many with his strong showing in the first round of balloting. The UMP retained control of the presidency and the government following the 2007 election of Nicolas Sarkozy, but it was swept from office by the Socialists in 2012. François Hollande defeated the incumbent Sarkozy in the presidential race, and the Socialist bloc captured a clear majority in the National Assembly.

The French party system has continued to display volatility, though less so than in the past. Because the dominance of the Gaullist party was relatively short-lived, with other groups from the centre eroding its strength, the parliamentary base of the governments of the centre-right shrank; this was especially so since the centrists remained a loose confederation of several groupings, each of which tended to adopt different tactics. The precarious nature of political balance was underscored by recent periods of cohabitation between presidents and prime ministers of opposing parties.

SECURITY

The overall responsibility for national defense rests with the president, who is the constitutional chief of the armed services and presides over the higher councils and committees on national defense. Since a decree in 1964, the president can give the order to bring the air and strategic forces into action. The prime minister, assisted by the secretary-general for national defense, oversees the armed forces according to the terms of the constitution, but it is the minister of defense who actually directs the land, air, and naval forces and who, moreover, has authority over the armament policy and the arsenal.

ARMED FORCES

Since 1958 the military administration has been divided by various functions; it includes strategic nuclear forces, territorial-defense forces, mobile forces, and task forces. France has had the atomic bomb since 1960 and the hydrogen bomb since 1968. The nation withdrew from the integrated military command of the North Atlantic Treaty Organization (NATO) in 1966, but in 1995 it took a seat on the NATO Military Committee, and in 2009 it announced its plan to return to the organization's command structure. An all-volunteer army was in place by 2002, though previously every French male 18 years of age had been subject to one year of compulsory military service.

POLICE SERVICES

The police are responsible primarily for maintaining public law and order. Under the authority of the minister of interior, they are responsible to the prefects in the *départements* and to the prefect of police in Paris and adjacent suburban *communes*. The police force is divided into public security forces and specialized police forces, such as the vice squad. The security police include the State Security

French police ride down the Champs-Elysees during the 2011 Bastille Day parade in Paris. Miguel Medina/AFP/Getty Images

FRENCH FOREIGN LEGION

The French Foreign Legion (*Légion étrangère*) is a military corps that consisted originally of foreign volunteers in the pay of France but now includes many Frenchmen. It was founded in 1831 as a highly disciplined professional army to help control French colonies in Africa. Since its founding, it has been in almost continuous combat; its forces have fought or been stationed in such places as Europe, Mexico, Syria, and Southeast Asia. The new volunteer swears to serve not France but the legion; after three years of service with good conduct, foreign-born soldiers are eligible for French citizenship. Since the legion keeps a volunteer's past secret, it has been romanticized as a haven for those seeking new identities, including criminals, but legionnaires typically are professional soldiers. Originally headquartered in Algeria, the legion moved its headquarters to France after Algerian independence.

Police (Compagnies Républicaines de Sécurité; CRS), responsible for public order; the judicial police, who carry out criminal investigations and hunt down suspects; and the complex internal intelligence and antiespionage units. The municipal forces are responsible to the mayor. There is also the national gendarmerie, a kind of state police, which is responsible to the minister of defense, combats terrorism, and is of particular importance in the rural areas.

SOCIAL SECURITY AND HEALTH

Almost everyone is covered by the social security system, notably after the reform of 1998 that extended coverage to those previously excluded owing to lack of income. Social insurance was introduced in 1930 and family allowances in 1932, but the comprehensive rules for social security were established in 1946. A network of elected social security and family allowance *caisses primaires* ("primary boards"), headed by national *caisses*, manages a considerable budget. This budget relies on employers' and employees' social security contributions, as well as the proceeds from a special tax, introduced in 1991 (*contribution sociale généralisée*), on all forms of income. Deficits are made up by the state. The majority of expenditure is devoted to retirement benefits (pensions) and the partial reimbursement of most medical expenses. Other payments include family benefits for dependent children, unemployment indemnities, and housing subsidies. Since 1988, in response to a long-term problem of unemployment in France, people with little or no income have been able to benefit from a special government subsidy known as the social minimum (*revenu minimum d'insertion*).

France complies with the principles of liberal medicine, with patients free to choose doctors and treatment. Since

1960, however, agreements have been signed at a regional level between the *caisses* and the professional medical associations that regulate fees. Although doctors need not necessarily adhere to them, reimbursements from social security are based on these scales.

The hospital reform of 1960 joined hospitals and medical schools through the creation of teaching hospitals. Private hospitals and clinics operate alongside public hospitals, and the cost of treatment in private facilities may also be partially reimbursed from social security funds. Since the enactment of legislation in 1991, the government has sought to rationalize the distribution of hospitals to take advantage of shifting population densities, changing health care needs, and new technology.

HOUSING

In the first years after World War II, France experienced a continuous housing crisis. Although the Fourth Republic successfully carried out reconstruction following the war, this did not substantially reduce housing requirements, which were intensified by urbanization, population growth, the repatriation of one million French nationals from Algeria, immigration, and the deterioration of buildings (by the turn of the 21st century, 35 percent of the nation's housing predated 1948). The government encourages construction through premiums, loans (particularly for low-rent housing), and tax incentives. Municipal and other public bodies also have engaged in a vast program of subsidized public housing (*habitation à loyer modéré*; HLM), which was especially prominent in the 1960s and '70s. In 1970 the procedure for receiving building permits for private construction was greatly simplified, and since 1982 mayors have been responsible for granting construction permits and devising local housing policies for both the public and private sectors. The government has also sought to encourage home ownership through low-interest loans. As a result of continuing suburbanization, far greater emphasis is now placed on building houses rather than apartments. From the late 1960s city planning in France became more organized through such programs as *zone d'aménagement concerté* (ZAC), which often link both private and public developers. Reforms in 2000 updated long-term development plans (*schéma de cohérence territoriale*; SCOT) and detailed land-use plans (*plan local d'urbanisme*; PLU). The current emphasis of urban policy is on rehabilitation, particularly of the many peripheral housing estates built in the 1960s and '70s but also of older central districts.

WAGES AND THE COST OF LIVING

Despite a history of high inflation, over recent years levels have been similar to those of other industrialized countries. Indeed, since the mid-1980s inflation has been particularly low in France. A minimum wage law has been in effect since 1950, and since 1970 it has been supplemented by a provision known as the *salaire minimum interprofessionel de croissance* (SMIC; general and growth-indexed minimum wage), which has increased the lowest salaries faster than the inflation rate. Its level is set annually, and all employers must abide by it. Women are, in general, paid less well than men. A worker earns nearly twice as much in Paris as in the less-developed *départements* of central France. The differentials between the earnings of manual workers and those of managers, while still large, have diminished progressively. In general, the majority of French society has benefited from a very substantial increase in purchasing power over the last half century.

EDUCATION

The organization of national education is highly centralized. Since 1968, however, following rioting among university students seeking a greater voice in their administration, a movement toward decentralization has been in progress in higher education. Reforms have sought to modify the character and structure of education, not only at the university level but also in primary and secondary schools; in the latter case one of the principal government aims has been to enable 80 percent of secondary-school students to obtain their *baccalauréat*.

France has both public and private education. All public education is free and is administered by the Ministry of National Education, which draws up the curricula, employs the staff, and exercises its authority through rectors placed at the heads of academies. However, while the state retains control of the educational programs and faculty, responsibility for the provision and maintenance of schools has been decentralized since the early 1980s; the *communes* look after primary schools, while in secondary education the *départements* are responsible for the *collèges* and the *régions* maintain the *lycées*.

PRIMARY AND SECONDARY EDUCATION

Education is free and compulsory between the ages of 6 and 16. Children under the age of 6 can attend *écoles maternelles* (nursery schools). Primary schools provide elementary education for those between the ages of 6 and 11. Secondary education begins in the *collèges* from the ages of 11 to 15 with further secondary education offered in general or technical *lycées*, leading to the national *baccalauréat* examination. Courses of study lasting for two or three years can lead to professional certificates or diplomas. School councils allow teachers and representatives of parents (and pupils at the secondary level) to gather to discuss the operation of schools.

The first day of nursery school (écoles maternelles) *in Nancy, France.* Francis Demange/ Gamma-Rapho/Getty Images

HIGHER EDUCATION

Following the student riots of May 1968, higher education was profoundly changed with the enactment of reforms on November 12, 1968, though many centralizing features from the past remain. Previously, universities had been divided into faculties or colleges according to the subjects taught. After 1968 the faculties were replaced by teaching and research units regrouped into autonomous multidisciplinary universities comanaged by representatives elected from among the teaching staff, students, and administration. These institutions substantially determine their own research programs, teaching methods, and means of assessment. Much of the curriculum is still validated at the national level, however.

The state grants funds to the universities, which they divide among their departments. The degrees awarded are the *licence* (roughly comparable to the British-American bachelor's degree), *maîtrise* (master's degree), and doctorate. There are also special teaching qualifications, one of which is the *agrégation*, a rigorous competitive examination. Traditional university courses were considerably diversified by the creation of specialized technological sections (Instituts Universitaires de Technologies; IUT) in 1966 and by the establishment in 1991 of vocational units (Instituts Universitaires Professionnalisés; IUP), which work closely with businesses. Students may also apply to a number of prestigious *grandes écoles*, which are even more highly regarded than the universities, especially in the engineering and technical fields. The best-known among these is the École Polytechnique ("Polytechnic School"); founded in 1794 to recruit and train technicians for the army, it has become the most important technical school in both the public and private sectors.

OTHER FEATURES

Private education is mostly Roman Catholic. Although the French constitution proclaims that the state is secular, a 1959 law allows private establishments to sign government contracts that procure financial support in exchange for some control. Despite attempts made by the Socialist government of the early 1980s to bring private schools closer to the public sector, the system has remained basically unchanged.

Teachers are highly unionized and belong largely to the Federation for National Education and the National Syndicate of Instructors, as well as other left-wing unions. The main student unions are the National Union of French Students (Union National des Étudiants de France; UNEF), the quasi-communist UNEF Renouveau, the Union of Communist Students of France, and the National Confederation of French Students.

CHAPTER 5

CULTURAL LIFE

For much of its history, France has played a central role in European culture. With the advent of colonialism and global trade, France reached a worldwide market, and French artistic, culinary, and sartorial styles influenced the high and popular cultures of nations around the globe. Today French customs, styles, and theories remain an influential export, as well as a point of great national pride, even as French intellectuals worry that the rise of globalism has prompted, in the words of the historian Pierre Nora, "the rapid disappearance of our national memory."

CULTURAL MILIEU

French culture is derived from an ancient civilization composed of a complex mix of Celtic, Greco-Roman, and Germanic elements. Monuments, especially from the period of Roman occupation, are numerous and include the amphitheatre at Arles, the *arènes* ("arenas") in Paris, and the aqueduct at Pont du Gard.

During the Middle Ages a rich culture developed, fostered in particular by monks and scholars in monasteries and universities and encouraged well into the 18th century by a system of royal and aristocratic patronage. Important trade fairs in growing cities such as Paris, Nancy, Strasbourg, and Lyon enabled the spread of artistic ideas and cultural trends to and from other regions, placing France at the centre of a nascent European high culture that would reach its greatest expression in the Renaissance. From the early 1700s and with the development of a middle class, the bourgeoisie, culture became more generally accessible. This was the age of the Enlightenment, of inquiry and question. Cultural activity remained largely centred in Paris, but smaller cities such as Aix-les-Bains, Grenoble, and Lyon were vital in their own right. The culture of the Enlightenment was built on reason and analytic argumentation, mirrored, as political scientist Alexis de Tocqueville remarked, in the French Revolution's

> attraction for general theories, for general systems of legislation, the exact symmetry of laws...the same desire to remake the entire constitution at once following the rules of logic and in accordance with a single plan, instead of seeking ways to amend its parts.

Among its tenets was the idea of meritocracy, or an aristocracy of ability and intelligence, which accorded a central place to intellectuals unknown in most other societies and opened France's schools to students from the provinces without regard for social class.

With free primary education compulsory by the late 19th century, basic literacy ensured that the general cultural level was raised. This was further aided by the increase in the number of newspapers and, later, by the development of radio, cinema, television, and the Internet. After World War II the intellectual and social development of lower-income groups benefited from the decision to make free secondary education compulsory up to age 16. Cultural literacy expanded as newspaper circulations rose, lending libraries proliferated, and in 1954 a revolution began in paperback books (*livre de poche*). This last development met with enormous success, providing people of all ages and classes with much greater access to literature and other forms of specialized knowledge.

The Ministry of Culture and Communications oversees the major cultural institutions of the nation. The department, first led by novelist André Malraux, seeks to redouble arts awareness among ordinary people, support the creation of new art, and protect existing French forms and properties as wide-ranging as monuments and language. The cultural map of France remains firmly centred on Paris, despite increased expenditure by local authorities on cultural activities following the decentralization legislation of the early 1980s. Yet, while serving, often self-consciously, the interests of the whole nation, the capital is aware of its own internal differences. Most of the city's *arrondissements* (municipal districts) have groups actively researching their history and traditions, and local art exhibitions and concerts are encouraged. In the rest of the country, provincial culture is strong and often fiercely defended—for example, in Brittany, parts of the south, and Alsace.

French culture has felt the impact made by immigrants, especially those from North Africa beginning in the 1960s. The Muslim communities that have formed, notably in Paris and Marseille, have not escaped discrimination, but there is a widespread acknowledgment of their contributions to cuisine, music, dance, painting, and literature. Verlan, a slang of standard French that reverses and reshuffles French syllables and spellings, traces its roots to the 19th century but was revived by postwar immigrant communities and in recent decades has made inroads into mainstream society. Beginning in the 1980s, second- and third-generation North Africans were often referred to as *les beurs*, and *beur* cinema, *beur* comics, and *beur* radio, among other forms of expression, have found a large audience. The label *beur* is itself a Verlan term for *arabe*, the French word for Arab. In addition, Asian and sub-Saharan African immigrants have attained prominence as artists, writers, and musicians in France's increasingly multicultural society.

DAILY LIFE AND SOCIAL CUSTOMS

In comparison with the immediate postwar era, the French now devote far more time to leisure and cultural pursuits, largely as a result of a shorter workweek, more years spent in education, and greater affluence. The increasing emphasis on home entertainment provided by television, stereo, and personal computers has not reduced cinema or theatre attendance. On the contrary, the number of moviegoers grew significantly in the 1990s, and though it varied

somewhat during the first decade of the 21st century, it reached its highest level in 45 years in 2011, with more than 215 million tickets sold.

The popularity of cultural activities is also evident, with increasing visits to historic monuments, art galleries, and museums. Especially attractive are interactive exhibitions at museums, such as the Cité de Sciences et de l'Industrie (City of Science and of Industry) at Le Parc de la Villette in Paris or the Futuroscope theme park near Poitiers. Interest also has been revived in local and regional cultures, often as part of new initiatives to develop tourism, and annual national festivals, such as the Fête de la Musique, are extremely successful.

Although French cuisine has a reputation as a grand national feature, regional differences are marked. Some local dishes have achieved international fame, even if they are often poorly imitated. Among these are the seafood soup, *bouillabaisse*, from Marseille; *andouillette*, a form of sausage from Lyon; *choucroute*, pickled cabbage from Alsace; and *magret de canard*, slices of breast of duck from Bordeaux. France is also renowned for the range and quality of its cheeses. More than 300 varieties are recognized. The majority are produced from cow's milk, including Camembert (Normandy), Brie (Île-de-France), Comté (Franche-Comté), Saint-Nectaire (Auvergne), and Reblochon (Savoy). Cheese is also made from ewe's milk, as in the case of Roquefort (Aveyron), as well as from goat's milk. Perhaps the best-known

Christian Dior. Popperfoto/Getty Images

exports of France are the wines from some of the world's great vineyards in Burgundy, Bordeaux, and the Rhône valley. However, the reputation of French cuisine has not prevented the proliferation of fast-food outlets in France, especially over the past few decades. French consumption of wine and tobacco has dropped steadily since the mid-20th century, a mark of the nation's increased attention to health.

Paris is internationally known for its haute couture, exemplified by such houses of high fashion as Coco Chanel, Christian Dior, Hubert de Givenchy, Yves Saint Laurent, Jean-Paul Gaultier, and Christian Lacroix. Traditional dress is occasionally seen in many regions, although it is largely reserved for official ceremonies and festivals. Regional differences often reflect local customs of dressmaking and embroidery, the availability of fabrics, and adaptations to local climatic conditions. Headdresses vary greatly, ranging from elaborate lace wimples found in Normandy and Brittany to the more sober beret of southwestern France or the straw hat, worn typically in and around the area of Nice.

In addition to the Roman Catholic holy days, the French celebrate Bastille Day on June 14, commemorating the rise of the French Republic via the fall of the prison fortress of the Bastille in Paris in 1789 at the start of the French Revolution. "La Marseillaise," the French national anthem and one of the world's most recognizable national anthems, also memorializes the Revolution.

THE ARTS

The French people as a whole highly value artistic creativity. As the arts have flourished, they have spread the influence of French culture throughout the world. The French have made invaluable contributions to literature, painting, music, ballet, sculpture, motion pictures, and photography, among other arts.

LITERATURE

French literature has a long and rich history. Traditionally it is held to have begun in 842 with the Oath of Strasbourg, a political pact between Louis the German and Charles the Bald, the text of which survives in Old French. The Middle Ages are noted in particular for epic poems such as *La Chanson de Roland* (c. 1100; *The Song of Roland*), the Arthurian romances of Chrétien de Troyes, and lyric poetry expressing romantic love. In the 16th century the

Renaissance flourished, and figures such as the poet Pierre de Ronsard, the satirist and humorist François Rabelais, and the quintessential essayist Michel de Montaigne, were to become internationally acknowledged. French Neoclassical drama reached its apotheosis during the next hundred years in the tragedies of Pierre Corneille and Jean Racine. During the same period, Molière displayed his vast and varied talents in the theatre, particularly as a writer of comedies; Jean de La Fontaine produced moralistic verse in his *Fables*; and Madame de La Fayette created the classic *La Princesse de Clèves* (1678), generally considered the first French psychological novel.

Voltaire, Denis Diderot, and Jean-Jacques Rousseau dominated the 18th century, especially with their philosophical writings, though they made major contributions to all genres, and Voltaire's novel *Candide* (1759) is notable for its literary quality and distillation of Enlightenment ideals. Other authors of the period include playwright Pierre-Augustin Caron de Beaumarchais, best known for works such as *Le Mariage de Figaro* (1784; *The Marriage of Figaro*), and Pierre Choderlos de Laclos, remembered for his epistolary novel *Les Liaisons dangereuses* (1782; *Dangerous Acquaintances*). The 19th century witnessed the emergence of a series of writers who substantially influenced the development of literature worldwide, including the novelists Honoré de Balzac, Stendhal, Gustave Flaubert, and Émile Zola along with the poets Charles

Portrait of Voltaire, circa 1740. Stock Montage/Archive Photos/Getty Images

Baudelaire, Stéphane Mallarmé, and Arthur Rimbaud. Added to these was the Romantic writer Victor Hugo, whose creative energy expressed itself in all literary forms, as well as in painting.

French literature in the 20th century both carried on the earlier traditions and transformed them, and French authors have won a number of Nobel Prizes for Literature. While the complexity of French poetry continued in the work of Paul Valéry, Guillaume Apollinaire, Paul Claudel (also a major dramatist), Saint-John Perse, Paul Éluard, Louis Aragon, René Char, and Yves Bonnefoy, the art of the novel was given new direction by Marcel Proust, in *À la recherche du temps perdu* (1913–27; *Remembrance of Things Past*). The first half of the century also produced such notable writers as André Gide, François Mauriac, André Malraux, Albert Camus, and Jean-Paul Sartre, the last arguably the chief exponent of existentialist philosophy. Their work was followed in the 1950s by the *nouveau roman* ("new novel") and by the emergence of writers such as Alain Robbe-Grillet, Nathalie Sarraute, Michel Butor, Claude Mauriac, Marguerite Duras, and Claude Simon, whose works have entered the canon of literature. Since the 1970s Michel Tournier, Patrick Modiano, Erik Orsenna, and Georges Perec have become leading novelists; feminist writers, including Hélène Cixous, Annie Leclerc, Jeanne Champion, and Marie Cardinal, have also made significant contributions. The closing years of the century were a time of adjustment to political, economic, and social changes. The slow recognition that France no longer played the tremendous role in global politics that it once had was accompanied by a reassessment of the leading part the country still had on the cultural stage—not least in Europe, where cultural politics became increasingly important in France's bid for power within the new European Union.

As the century closed, on the far side of the distress caused by the gradual demise of the old regime, it was possible to see new and vital trends emerging. Pierre Nora, writing in 1992 the closing essay to his great project of national cultural commemoration, *Les Lieux de mémoire* (*Realms of Memory*), begun in 1984, was struck by the elegiac tone of the finished work and commented that a different tone might have emerged if he had invited his contributors to focus on more marginal groups. Indeed, the literature of the 20th century was notable for its openness to nonnative writers: the Irish writer Samuel Beckett, for instance, the Czech expatriate Milan Kundera, the Russian emigrant Andreï Makine, and Chinese exile Gao Xingjian have all produced major works in French. Georges Simenon and Marguerite Yourcenar, both born in Belgium in 1903, were considered French writers, though they often lived outside France. The postcolonial literature of the late 20th and early 21st centuries offered insights into the tensions of cross-cultural identity by Francophone writers from North Africa, sub-Saharan Africa, and the Caribbean.

The works of French playwrights have enjoyed international acclaim for centuries, from the 17th-century comic theatre of Molière to the 19th-century cabaret productions known as Grand Guignol. In theatre in the 20th and 21st centuries three important currents can be discerned. Traditional playwriting was carried on largely by Jean Anouilh, Claudel, Jean Giraudoux, Henry de Montherlant, and Camus, but experimentation with both form and content also developed. Before World War II, Jean Cocteau in particular made his mark (as did to a lesser degree Claudel), but innovation came with Fernando Arrabal, Arthur Adamov, Beckett, Jean Genet, and the Romanian exile Eugène Ionesco. Since the 1950s producers have also made an important contribution to theatre; Roger Planchon, Jean-Louis Barrault, Peter Brook, Marcel Maréchal, and Ariane Mnouchkine in particular have shared in both creating new works and revitalizing traditional ones.

Philosophy and criticism have always played a central part in French intellectual and cultural life. The Surrealist movement, led by André Breton, among others, flourished in the 1920s and '30s. Existentialism in both Christian and atheist forms was a powerful force in the mid-20th century and was championed by Sartre, Étienne Gilson, Gabriel Marcel, and Camus (though he rejected the label). More broadly, Roman Catholicism and Marxism in orthodox or revised forms have influenced a large number of creative writers, including the Roman Catholic Georges Bernanos and Sartre, who was a Marxist of a sort. Since the 1950s, new criticism, which began with structuralism—itself largely inspired by the anthropological work of Claude Lévi-Strauss in *Mythologiques*, 4 vol. (1964–71), and *Tristes Tropiques* (1955)—has challenged the monopoly of the historical approach to works of art and especially literature. Not limited to literary criticism, structuralism was an important component of philosophy among proponents such as Louis Althusser. The most popular expression of this approach was perhaps the work of Roland Barthes, including *Mythologies* (1957), but his work fragmented into various branches—linguistic, genetic, psychobiographical, sociocultural—each with its exponents and disciples increasingly embroiled in academic, and often abstruse, debate. Following on the heels of structuralism, poststructuralism was associated with such figures as Jacques Derrida, Michel Foucault, Jacques Lacan, Julia Kristeva, Giles Deleuze, Hélène Cixous, Luce Irigaray, and Jean-François Lyotard. Other philosophers of recent note include André Glucksmann, Bernard Henri-Lévy, and Michel Serres.

THE FINE ARTS

French traditions in the fine arts are deep and rich, and painting, sculpture, music, dance, architecture, photography, and film all flourish under state support.

PAINTING AND SCULPTURE

In painting there was a long tradition from the Middle Ages and Renaissance that, while perhaps not matching those of Italy or the Low Countries, produced a number of religious subjects and court portraits. By the 17th century, paintings of peasants by Louis Le Nain, of allegories and Classical myths by Nicolas Poussin, and of formally pastoral scenes by Claude Lorrain began to give French art its own characteristics.

Within the next hundred years, styles became even more wide-ranging: mildly erotic works by François Boucher and Jean-Honoré Fragonard; enigmatic scenes such as *Pierrot*, or *Gilles* (c. 1718–19), by Antoine Watteau; interiors by Jean-Siméon Chardin that were often tinged with violence, as in *La Raie* (c. 1725–26; "The Ray"); emotive portraits by Jean-Baptiste Greuze; and rigorous Neoclassical works by Jacques-Louis David.

Much as the Académie Francaise regulated literature, painting up to this time was subject to rules and conventions established by the Academy of Fine Arts. In the 19th century some artists, notably J.-A.-D. Ingres, followed these rules. Others reacted against academic conventions, making Paris, as the century progressed, a centre of the Western avant-garde. Beginning in the 1820s, the bold eroticism and "Orientalism" of the works of Romantic painter Eugène Delacroix angered the academy, while at midcentury the gritty Realism of the art of Gustave Courbet and Honoré Daumier was viewed as scandalous.

Perhaps the greatest break from academic conventions came about through the Impressionists, who, inspired in part by the daring work of Édouard Manet, brought on a revolution in painting beginning in the late 1860s. Some artists from this movement whose work became internationally celebrated include Claude Monet, Camille Pissarro, Alfred Sisley, and Edgar Degas. Important Post-Impressionists include Paul Cézanne, Henri de Toulouse-Lautrec, Paul Gauguin, Pierre-Auguste Renoir, and Georges Seurat.

French sculpture progressed from the straight-lined Romanesque style through various periods to reach its height in the work of Auguste Rodin, who was a contemporary of the Impressionists and whose sculpture reflected Impressionist principles. Another from this time, Aristide Maillol, produced figures in a more Classical style.

Pablo Picasso, one of the most influential forces in 20th-century art, was born in Spain but spent most of his artistic life in France. His oeuvre encompasses several genres, including sculpture, but he is best known for the Cubist paintings he created together with French artist Georges Braque at the beginning of the century. One of Picasso's greatest rivals was French painter Henri Matisse, whose lyrical work, like Picasso's, spanned the first half of the century. In the period between the World Wars, Paris remained a major centre of avant-garde activity, and

Decorative Figure on an Ornamental Background, *oil painting by Henri Matisse, 1925-26; in the National Museum for Modern Art, Paris.* S.P.A.D.E.M., Paris/V.A.G.A., New York City, 1985; photograph, Musée National d'Art Moderne, Centre Georges Pompidou, Paris

branches of prominent international movements such as Dada and Surrealism were active there.

By midcentury, however, Paris's dominance waned, and the focus of contemporary art shifted to New York City. Prominent artists working in France have included Jean Dubuffet, Yves Klein, Swiss-born Jean Tinguely, Hungarian-born Victor Vasarely, Niki de Saint-Phalle, Bulgarian-born Christo, Daniel Buren, and César.

Major art exhibits are held regularly, mainly in Paris, and training for aspiring artists is provided not only at the prestigious École des Beaux-Arts ("School of Fine Arts") in Paris but also at a number of provincial colleges. Courses for art historians and restorators are available at the School of the Louvre. Building on their country's rich history as a leader in furniture design and cabinetry, French craftsmen of all sorts today study at the National Advanced School of Decorative Arts and other institutions.

MUSIC

The growth of classical music parallels that of painting. Despite work from earlier periods by Louis Couperin, Jean-Philippe Rameau, and Jean-Baptiste Lully, for example, French music gained a broad international following only in the 19th and early 20th centuries. Such composers as Hector Berlioz, Camille Saint-Saëns, Maurice Ravel, Claude Debussy, and the Polish-born Frédéric Chopin created a distinctively French style, further developed in the 20th century by composers such as Pierre Boulez, Darius Milhaud, and Erik Satie. In the late 20th century much experimentation occurred with electronic music and acoustics. The Institute for Experimentation and Research in Music and Acoustics (Institut de Recherche et Coordination Acoustique/Musique), in Paris, remains devoted to musical innovation. A new generation of French musicians includes the pianists Hélène Mercier and Brigitte Engerer.

Training for the musical profession remains traditional. Local conservatoires throughout the country provide basic grounding; some provincial schools—at Lyon and Strasbourg, for example—offer more advanced work, but young people with talent aim for the National Conservatory of Music in Paris, where Nadia Boulanger taught. Since World War II, Paris has hosted internationally famous conductors, such as Herbert von Karajan and Daniel Barenboim, who have made contributions in revitalizing an interest in classical music. Major visiting orchestras perform at the Châtelet Theatre or the Pleyel Concert Hall, and concerts are given by smaller groups in many of the churches. There is a network of provincial orchestras.

Although interest in classical music has grown at the amateur level, it is practiced by a relatively small number. The young tend to be preoccupied with popular music, especially that imported from the United States and the United Kingdom. The tradition of the French chanson, the romantic French ballad, has continued, however, following such legendary stylists as Juliette Gréco, Edith Piaf, Belgian-born Jacques Brel, Charles Aznavour, and Georges Brassens. Moreover, France has produced rock performers such as Johnny Hallyday and the group Téléphone, as well as chanteuses of the 1960s such as Francoise Hardy, known for pop music called *yé-yé* ("yeah-yeah"). Other well-known artists of the late 20th century include Julien Clerc, Jean-Jacques Goldman, and Renaud. However, all were considerably more popular nationally than internationally.

Singer-songwriter Serge Gainsbourg achieved global popularity for his sensual music as well as his romantic links to actresses Brigitte Bardot and Jane Birkin. Later, Gainsbourg's daughter Charlotte emerged as a force in her own right, garnering acclaim for her acting skills as well as her finely crafted pop songs. Perhaps France's biggest international music act of the 21st century was the electronic duo Daft Punk, who brought dance-club beats to stadium-sized crowds around the world.

The Paris Opéra, established in 1669, prospered under the efforts of Lully, Rameau, Christoph Gluck, Berlioz, Georges Bizet, and Francis Poulenc. France was known for the traditions of opéra comique and grand opera, among others.

DANCE

France is famous for developing ballet. In 1581 the *Ballet comique de la reine* was performed at the French court of Catherine de Médicis. Because it fused the elements of music, dance, plot, and design into a dramatic whole, it is considered the first ballet. The *ballet comique* influenced the development of the 17th-century *ballet de cour* (court ballet), an extravagant form of court entertainment.

In 1661 Louis XIV established the Académie Royale de Danse (now the Paris Opéra Ballet); the company dominated European theatrical dance of the 18th and early 19th centuries. Pierre Beauchamp, the company's first director, codified the five basic ballet positions. Extending the range of dance steps were virtuosos such as Gaétan Vestris and his son Auguste Vestris and also Marie Camargo, whose rival Marie Sallé was known for her expressive style.

In his revolutionary treatise, *Lettres sur la danse et sur les ballets* (1760), Jean-Georges Noverre brought about major reforms in ballet production, stressing the importance of dramatic motivation, which he called *ballet d'action*, and decrying overemphasis on technical

virtuosity. In 1832 the Paris Opéra Ballet initiated the era of Romantic ballet by presenting Italian Filippo Taglioni's *La Sylphide*. Jean Coralli was the Opéra's ballet master at the time, and the company's dancers of this period included Jules Perrot and Arthur Saint-Léon.

In the 20th century ballet was rejuvenated under the leadership of Russian impresario Sergey Diaghilev, who founded the avant-garde Ballets Russes in Paris in 1909. For the next two decades it was the leading ballet company in the

Philippe Starck presenting his design of the "Bordeaux Bike," a hybrid of a bicycle and a scooter.
Pierre Andrieu/AFP/Getty Images

West. The original company was choreographed by Michel Fokine. Elsewhere in Paris, Serge Lifar, the Russian-born ballet master of the Paris Opéra, reestablished its reputation as a premier ballet troupe.

Dance entertainments of a lighter kind also were developed in France. In 19th-century Paris the all-female cancan became the rage. After 1844 it became a feature of music halls, revues, and operetta.

ARCHITECTURE

With a rich and varied architectural heritage (which helped to spawn, among other styles, Gothic, Beaux Arts, and Art Deco) and an organized and competitive program of study, France has shown itself to be open to a variety of styles and innovations. For example, Le Corbusier, much of whose work can be found in France, was Swiss. The development of architecture has also been sustained by the central government's penchant for *grands projets*, or great projects. The country, however, has not produced as many designers of international repute in recent years as have other Western nations. Major achievements such as the Pompidou Centre, the pyramid entrance to the Louvre, and the Grand Arch have resulted from plans submitted in open competition by foreign architects. Recent architects of acclaim, of French origin or working in France, have included Jean Nouvel, Dominique Perrault, Adrien Fainsilber, Paul Andreu, Swiss-born Bernard Tschumi, and Catalonian

Ricardo Boffil of Spain. Among important contemporary designers are Andrée Putman and Philippe Starck.

PHOTOGRAPHY

Jacques Daguerre, one of the recognized founders of modern photography in the early 19th century, began the evolution of an art form that has flourished in France. In the 20th century the work of such photographers as Eugène Atget, Henri Cartier-Bresson, and Robert Doisneau ensured that the art had a dimension beyond journalistic and commercial purposes, which was apparent in the installation art of later figures such as Christian Boltanski. In 1969 an annual festival was established at Arles, and in 1976 a national museum was created. The French popularization of photography through posters and postcards was one of the most remarkable cultural events of the late 20th century.

THE CINEMA

French cinema has occupied an important place in national culture for more than a hundred years. August and Louis Lumière invented a motion-picture technology in the late 19th century, and Alice Guy-Blaché and others were industry pioneers. In the 1920s French film became famous for its poetic realist mode, exemplified by the grand historical epics of Abel Gance and the work in the 1930s and '40s of Marcel Pagnol and others. A generation later the *nouvelle*

Anna Karina and Eddie Constantine in Alphaville *(1965), directed by Jean-Luc Godard.* Pathé Contemporary Films; photograph from a private collection

vague, or New Wave, produced directors such as Jean-Luc Godard and François Truffaut, who "wrote" with the camera as if, in critic André Bazin's words, it were a *caméra-stylo* ("camera-pen"). This shift was accompanied by an "intellectualization" of the cinema reflected in the influential review *Cahiers du cinéma*, in the establishment of several schools in Paris and the provinces where film could be studied, and in the founding of film museums such as the Cinémathèque ("Film Library") in Paris.

Other directors of international stature include Jean Renoir, Jacques Tati, Jean-Pierre Melville, Alain Resnais, Eric Rohmer, Robert Bresson, and Louis Malle. They exemplified the auteur theory that a director could so control a film that his or her direction approximated authorship. Filmmakers such as Agnès Varda, Claude Chabrol, Jacques Demy, Bertrand Tavernier, and Claude Bérri, as well as Polish-born Krzystof Kieslowski, extended these traditions to the end of the century, while directors such as Luc

NEW WAVE

New Wave (*nouvelle vague*) was the name given to the style developed by a number of highly individualistic French film directors of the late 1950s. Preeminent among New Wave directors were Louis Malle, Claude Chabrol, François Truffaut, Alain Resnais, and Jean-Luc Godard, most of whom were associated with the film magazine *Cahiers du cinéma*, the publication that popularized the auteur theory in the 1950s. The theory held that certain directors so dominated their films that they were virtually the authors of the film.

Films by New Wave directors were often characterized by a fresh brilliance of technique that was thought to have overshadowed their subject matter. An example occurs in Godard's *Breathless* (1960), in which scenes change in rapid sequence ("jump cuts") to create a jerky and disconnected effect. Although it was never clearly defined as a movement, the New Wave stimulated discussion about the cinema and helped demonstrate that films could achieve both commercial and artistic success.

Beeson, Patrice Leconte, Laurent Cantet, and Clare Denis carried on with them in the 21st century.

The leading film stars of the 20th century ranged from Fernandel, Maurice Chevalier, and Arletty to Brigitte Bardot, Gérard Depardieu, and Catherine Deneuve. Among those French actors winning accolades in the 21st century were Audrey Tautou, Juliette Binoche, and Vincent Cassel. One of the world's premier film festivals is held annually at Cannes, where the Palme d'Or is awarded to the best motion picture—most, in recent years, have come from outside France, a source of consternation to French film devotees. As in television, the French film industry faces competition from the United States and the United Kingdom. This led the government in the early 1990s to elicit the support of the European Commission to protect its native film industry.

CULTURAL INSTITUTIONS

Despite increasing support from the private sector, various ministries, such as those of National Education and of Culture and Communications, are ultimately responsible for the promotion of cultural activities. Local authorities, particularly those representing the major towns and cities, as well as a variety of associations also fund cultural activities. The importance attached to culture is reflected in the substantial increase in expenditure and personnel working in this field and the growth of related industries (music, publishing, broadcasting technologies). About one-third of the populace belong to some form of cultural association. Abroad, French culture is promoted through the work of counselors and attachés at embassies, visiting speakers, the Alliance Française, and the French lycées in major cities. French institutes provide lectures, language courses, and access to books and newspapers. There are also associations ensuring international links, such as the United Nations Educational, Scientific and Cultural Organization and the International Association of French Teachers, both headquartered in Paris.

MUSEUMS AND MONUMENTS

Support and encouragement for cultural activities of all kinds are provided by a large number of museums, centres, and galleries, many of which are ultimately the responsibility of government ministries. In the provinces many museums traditionally reflecting their region's activities have been expanded and renovated and, like those at Saint-Étienne and Strasbourg, have achieved national importance. It is in Paris, however, that the nation's principal museums are to be found. The Louvre Museum, containing one of the world's great art collections, was extensively remodeled at the end of the 20th century, with a notable addition of a dramatic steel-and-glass pyramid entrance. The Musée d'Orsay, created out of a former railway station, houses a fine, large collection of 19th- and early 20th-century art and artifacts, while the Georges Pompidou National Centre of Art and Culture, with its industrially

inspired architecture, concentrates on the 20th century. The centre has an important library and media collection, and the square in front of it provides an open-air stage for jugglers, musicians, fire-eaters, and other street performers. Smaller museums, often containing substantial private collections, are numerous; three of particular interest are the Marmottan, Cognacq-Jay, and Orangerie. In addition to the larger museums, the Grand Palais and the Petit Palais regularly provide the setting for important exhibitions, and many of the national institutes offer French people the opportunity to appreciate works from different cultures. Particularly important in this respect are the Museum of the Arab World and the Museum of African and Oceanic Arts.

Since the 1950s there has been a national program for the conservation and renovation of important historic areas. The medieval *vieux quartiers* of Lyon have been tastefully restored, as has the 18th-century Place du Parlement in Bordeaux, for example. Many significant buildings have been saved by private funding, and government financial assistance is also available, usually on the condition that the property is opened to the public. In Paris the houses in the Marais district and on the Île Saint-Louis have had their original splendour restored, while around Montparnasse, for example, poor areas of 19th-century building have been bulldozed to make room for fashionable modern apartment blocks. Four structures in particular mark the later years of the 20th century:

the entrance to the Louvre; the Bastille Opera; the Grand Arch in La Défense, a futuristic business district west of Paris; and the national library, Bibliothèque François Mitterrand, all of which received the strong support of Mitterrand as monuments to his presidency.

SPORTS AND RECREATION

Although the French have recently developed a taste for a new range of sporting activities, such as mountain biking, cross-country skiing, and rock climbing, the most common forms of recreation in France seem to be nonphysical or relatively sedentary—talking, reading, eating, going to the cinema, and so on. This no doubt has something to do with the relative absence of programmed physical education at school. Certainly organized sport has a place in French society, however, with cycling, swimming, football (soccer), skiing, tennis, boules (pétanque), and, increasingly, golf, basketball, and martial arts being the most popular activities. Walking and jogging, too, are important, and a national network of paths (grandes randonnées) is well maintained. Popular seaside vacation resorts include Saint-Tropez, Cannes, and Cap d'Agde on the Mediterranean, the Île de Ré and La Baule-Escoublac on the Atlantic coast, and Le Touquet on the English Channel. Inland the French Alps, the Massif Central, and the national and regional parks, such as the Morvan regional nature park in Burgundy, attract campers and hikers. Newer, artificially created attractions include a growing number of theme parks, ranging from Disneyland at Paris to more specialized sites such as the Nausicaä seaworld museum at Boulogne-sur-Mer.

The nation's showcase sporting event is the Tour de France, an international cycling road race that attracts hundreds of thousands of spectators each year. Established more than a century ago, the annual summer race covers some 3,600 km (2,235 miles) over the course of three weeks, finishing in Paris. Football, especially in the larger towns, is extremely popular. The 1998 World Cup was both hosted by France and won by a French

TOUR DE FRANCE

The Tour de France is the world's most prestigious and most difficult bicycle race. Staged for three weeks each July—usually in some 20 daylong stages—the Tour typically comprises 20 professional teams of 9 riders each and covers some 3,600 km (2,235 miles), mainly in France, with occasional and brief visits to such countries as Belgium, Italy, Germany, and Spain. Although the race may start outside France—as was the case in 2007, when England hosted the opening stage for the first time—it always heads there quickly; the Tour is France's premier annual sporting event and has deep cultural roots. It is watched by huge crowds from

Miguel Indurain (Spain) riding in the penultimate stage of the 1993 Tour de France; Indurain won the race for the third successive year. AP

the roadside and is televised around the world as one of the supreme tests of athletic endurance. Part of the difficulty cyclists face in the Tour is that it is divided among time-trial racing and racing stages covering both flat land and great stretches of mountainous inclines. It is a rare cyclist who can perform well at both time trials and climbing, and those who can usually wear the yellow jersey (maillot jaune) of victory at the end of the race in Paris.

Established in 1903 by Henri Desgrange (1865–1940), a French cyclist and journalist, the race has been run every year except during the World Wars. Desgrange's newspaper, *L'Auto* (now *L'Equipe*), sponsored the Tour to boost circulation. Two events sparked spectator interest in the race: in 1910 the riders were sent, for the first time, over the treacherous "circle of death" in mountain passes in the Pyrenees; and 1919 marked the introduction of the yellow jersey—yellow being the colour of paper on which *L'Auto* was printed. The yellow jersey is an honour accorded to the cyclist who has the lowest cumulative time for the race at the end of each day. (A racer might well win a stage of a race on any given day but will not necessarily be given a yellow jersey, as that depends on the lowest overall time.) Three other types of jerseys are awarded during the Tour. Bonus sprints, awarding both points and a deduction of overall elapsed time, are held at several sites along the route each day during the race, and points are also awarded and time deducted for the first three finishers of each stage; the winner of the most points receives a green jersey. A polka-dotted jersey is given to the "king of the mountains," the rider who has the most points in the climbing stages, racing over small hills as well as steep mountains. The white jersey is awarded to the rider age 25 and under who has the lowest cumulative time.

In 2005 Lance Armstrong of the United States became the first rider to win the Tour seven times (1999–2005; he was stripped of his titles in 2012 for using performance-enhancing drugs). Four riders have won five times each: Jacques Anquetil of France (1957 and 1961–64), Eddy Merckx of Belgium (1969–72 and 1974), Bernard Hinault of France (1978–79, 1981–82, and 1985), and Miguel Indurain of Spain (1991–95).

team led by Zinedine Zidane. More than five million French people ski, and many children have the opportunity to go on school skiing trips in February; the principal resorts are in the northern Alps, notably in Savoy (Savoie). French bowls, or *boules*, is played by thousands and is highly organized at both national and local levels. Handball has an avid following, and rugby is mostly played in the southwest. Educator Pierre, baron de Coubertin, revived the Olympic Games in modern form in 1896 and founded the International Olympic Committee. Games in Paris soon followed in 1900 and 1924. Chamonix was the site of the inaugural Winter Olympic Games in 1924, followed by Grenoble in 1960 and Albertville in 1992. Olympic highlights include the successes of skier Jean-Claude Killy in 1968, the national football team in 1984, and runner Marie-José Pérec in the 1990s.

BROADCAST MEDIA

In 1989 the Socialist government formed the Supreme Audiovisual Council (Conseil Supérieur de l'Audiovisuel; CSA) to supervise radio and television broadcasting. There are both public and private stations. Programs also have been broadcast and received via satellite since 1984, and cable broadcasting began in 1987.

Television has made a significant contribution to cultural life. There are three state-controlled television channels and more than 100 private ones. More than three-fourths of the population watch television an average of 22 hours per week. Programs are varied, with a number of quality discussions, interviews, and documentary reports, as well as a broad combination of quiz and variety shows and dramas. In the 1980s the literature program *Apostrophes* enjoyed immense success and had a direct effect on book sales, as did its successor *Bouillon de culture*. As elsewhere in Europe, however, there has been a tendency to show an increasing number of American films and programs, which is hedged by official efforts to promote French programming; as critics point out, it is less expensive to buy 10 episodes of an American television show than to produce an hour-long documentary. By the 1980s the arrival of the videocassette recorder had created new opportunities for home film viewing, which expanded at the turn of the century with the introduction of digital videodisc (DVD) players.

Although it has been largely eclipsed by television and video, radio still has cultural impact. Two agencies managed by Radio France—France Culture and France Musique—provide the bulk of the cultural programs, but they are often indifferently presented. Major stations such as France-Inter (public) or Europe No. 1 (private) have resorted increasingly to a mix of popular music, news items, quizzes, and talk shows. Smaller private stations cater to specialized interests—for example, Radio Notre Dame (religion) and Radio Classique (classical music). Popular music stations such as Fun Radio and Skyrock have grown rapidly. Since 1994, however, with the aim of protecting French culture, such stations have been obliged to dedicate 40 percent of their playlists to songs in French.

THE PRESS

The newspaper has a long history and a strong tradition in France. The French press, in the form of reviews and news sheets, has its origins in the early 17th century with Théophraste Renaudot's *La Gazette*, which began in 1631. It was not for another 250 years, however, with the passage of an act in 1881 allowing greater freedoms, that the press began to expand significantly. At the beginning of World War II, Paris offered some 30 daily papers, many with national followings and most with a clear political affiliation. The number of newspapers (and periodicals as well) declined sharply after the war, in some cases for political reasons but in others as a result of takeovers, collaborative ventures, and competition from television. In 1944 the Paris-based *Le Monde* was founded, and it became the most informed and influential of modern French newspapers. Other influential and widely circulating Paris dailies include *Le Figaro*, *Libération*, and *France-Soir*. Among the smaller dailies are the Roman Catholic *La Croix l'Événement* and the communist *L'Humanité*. In the 1950s illustrated magazines began to proliferate (echoing a trend of the 1930s); some of these were popular magazines of general interest and some were directed at specific markets, such as *Elle*, *Marie-Claire*, and *Vogue Paris* for women and *L'Express*, *Le Point*, and *Le Nouvel Observateur*, which are political. Few, however, have enjoyed the popular success and wide distribution of the news-oriented *Paris-Match*. By the late 20th century, three specific factors characterized the French press: first, the expansion of the regional daily paper, with *Ouest-France* enjoying the largest circulation in the country; second, the growth of specialized magazine journalism; and third, the appearance since the early 1960s of free newspapers essentially for advertising purposes, which are distributed weekly in the millions.

CHAPTER 6

EARLY HISTORY

From its creation as a Roman province in the first century BCE to its role as a founding member of the European Union, France has played an important part in global affairs for two millennia. The Napoleonic Code formed the basis for civil law codes throughout Europe and Latin America, and French political thought has run the gamut from absolutism to radicalism. Although France no longer commands a colonial empire, its influence remains strong throughout the world.

GAUL

Gaul, in this context, signifies only what the Romans, from their perspective, termed Transalpine Gaul (Gallia Transalpina, or "Gaul Across the Alps"). Broadly, it comprised all lands from the Pyrenees and the Mediterranean coast of modern France to the English Channel and from the Atlantic Ocean to the Rhine River and the western Alps. The Romans knew a second Gaul, Cisalpine Gaul (Gallia Cisalpina, or "Gaul This Side of the Alps"), in northern Italy—which, however, does not belong to the history of France. Transalpine Gaul came into existence as a distinct historical entity in the middle of the 1st century BCE, through the campaigns of Julius Caesar (c. 100–44 BCE), and disappeared late in the 5th century CE. Caesar's heir, the emperor Augustus (reigned 27 BCE–14 CE), divided the country into 4 administrative provinces: Narbonensis, Lugdunensis, Aquitania (Aquitaine), and Belgica. Realizing the impossibility of large-scale expansion beyond the Rhine, rulers of the Flavian dynasty (69–96) annexed the region between the middle Rhine and upper Danube rivers, roughly the Black Forest region, to secure communications between Roman garrisons, by then permanently established on both rivers. This area was called the Agri Decumates, which may have referred to a previous settlement made up of 10 cantons. Its eastern border, conventionally referred to as the limes, assumed its final shape, as a defended palisade and ditch, under Antoninus Pius (138–161). The Agri Decumates were attached to Upper Germany (Germania Superior), 1 of 2 new frontier provinces (the other being Lower Germany [Germania Inferior]) created by the last Flavian emperor, Domitian (reigned 81–96). For greater administrative efficiency, the emperor Diocletian (reigned 284–305) subdivided all 6 Gallic provinces, forming a total of 13.

THE PEOPLE

Gaul was predominantly a Celtic land, but it also contained pre-Celtic Ligurians and Iberians in the south and southwest and more recent Germanic immigrants in the northeast. Neighbouring Celtic communities on the Danube and in northern Italy, however, were not included. The south, in addition, had been heavily influenced by the Greek colony of Massilia (modern Marseille, founded c. 600 BCE) and its daughter cities. In brief, the Gaul that was the foundation of medieval France was not a "natural" unit but a Roman construct, the result of a decision to defend Italy from across the Alps.

THE ROMAN CONQUEST

In the 2nd century BCE Rome intervened on the side of Massilia in its struggle against the tribes of the hinterland, its main aim being the protection of the route from Italy to its new possessions in Spain. The result was the formation, in 121 BCE, of "the Province" (Provincia, whence Provence), an area spanning from the Mediterranean to Lake Geneva, with its capital at Narbo (Narbonne). From 58 to 50 BCE Caesar seized the remainder of Gaul. Although motivated by personal ambition, Caesar could justify his conquest by appealing to deep-seated Roman fear of Celtic war bands and further Germanic incursions (late in the 2nd century BCE the Cimbri and Teutoni had invaded the Province and threatened Italy). Because of chronic internal rivalries, Gallic resistance was easily broken, though Vercingetorix's Great Rebellion of 52 BCE had notable successes before it expired in the cruel siege of Alesia (Alise-Sainte-Reine).

GAUL UNDER THE HIGH EMPIRE (c. 50 BCE–c. 250 CE)

The first centuries of Roman rule were remarkable for the speedy assimilation of Gaul into the Greco-Roman world. This was a consequence of both the light hand of the Roman imperial administration and the highly receptive nature of Gallic-Celtic society. Celtic culture had originated on the upper Danube about 1200 BCE. Its expansion westward and southward, through diffusion and migration, was stimulated by a shift from bronze- to ironworking. Archaeologically, the type of developing Celtic Iron Age culture conventionally classified as Hallstatt appeared in Gaul from about 700 BCE; in its La Tène form it made itself felt in Gaul after about 500 BCE. Initially the Romans, who had not forgotten the capture of their city by Brennus, the leader of Celtic war bands, about 390 BCE, despised and feared the Celts as barbarian savages. Until the end of the 1st century BCE, they disparaged Gaul beyond the Province as Gallia Comata ("Long-Haired Gaul"), mocked and exploited the Gauls' craving for wine, and generally mismanaged the Province itself.

Gaul by then, however, was not far behind Rome in its evolution. In the south, Ligurian communities had long emulated the Hellenic culture of Massilia, as may be seen in the settlement of Entremont (near Aquae Sextiae [Aix-en-Provence]). In the Celtic core, Caesar found large nations (his *civitates*) coalescing out of smaller tribes (*pagi*) and establishing urban centres (*oppida*—e.g., Bibracte [Mont Beuvray], near Augustodunum [Autun]), which, though quite unlike the Classical city-states, were assuming significant economic and administrative functions. After the corrupt Roman Republic was replaced by the empire and its more prudent rule, these advances in Transalpine Gaul could be exploited for the imperial good. The Province, now Narbonensis, was planted with settlements of retired Roman soldiers (*coloniae*, "colonies"—e.g.,

Arelate [Arles]); it soon became a land of city-states and was comparable to Italy in its way of life. In the remaining "three Gauls"—Lugdunensis, Aquitania, and Belgica—such colonies were few; there the *civitates* were retained, as was the habit of fierce rivalry between their leaders. Competition, however, was diverted from war: status was now measured in terms of the level of Romanization attained by both the individual and his community.

Northern Gaul therefore became a Romanized land too. This is dramatically reflected in the dominance of Latin as the language of education and government; French was to be a Romance tongue. Archaeologically, however, Romanization in Gaul is most evident in the emergence of the Greco-Roman city. Although the *civitates* were too large to act as true city-states, they contained towns, either already in existence (e.g., Lutetia Parisiorum [Paris]) or newly founded (e.g., Augustodunum ["Augustusville"]), that could be designated as their administrative centres and developed, by local magnates at their own expense, in accordance with Classical criteria. Thus, these civitas-capitals, as scholars term them, were characterized by checkerboard street grids and imposing administrative and recreational buildings such as forums, baths, and amphitheatres. Although they display vernacular architectural traits, they essentially follow the best Mediterranean fashion. Most were unwalled—an indicator of the Pax Romana, a tranquil period of about 150 years.

VERCINGETORIX

Julius Caesar had almost completed the subjugation of Gaul when Vercingetorix (died 46 BCE) led a general uprising of the Gauls against him in 52 BCE. Vercingetorix was named the king of the Arverni and general of the confederates. After an initial defeat at Noviodunum Biturigum, Vercingetorix used guerrilla warfare to harass Caesar's supply lines and cleverly offered to engage Caesar's forces on terrain unfavourable to the Romans. He successfully held the Arvernian hill-fort of Gergovia against an assault by Caesar. Vercingetorix followed up this victory by an attack on the Roman army, the failure of which compelled him to retreat with 80,000 troops to the prepared fortress of Alesia (in east-central France). Caesar, with a force of 60,000 men, laid siege to the fortress and was able to force its surrender after he had defeated the Gauls' reserve army in the field. Vercingetorix was taken to Rome in chains, exhibited in Caesar's triumph (52 BCE), and executed six years later.

The mark of Rome is also discernible in the countryside, in the shape of villas. Villas of this period were, however, working farms as much as Romanized country residences—manor houses, not palaces. The survivors of the great Gallic aristocracy of the pre-Roman period, who first adopted Roman ways and who might eventually have constructed rural palaces, persisted into the 1st century CE but then seem to have been eclipsed by lesser landowners.

Scholars dispute the extent to which the mass of the Gallic population (about 10 million, or 15 persons per square kilometre [39 persons per square mile], large for a preindustrial economy), free or slave, benefited from the new conditions, but there is no doubt that the landowners prospered. One of the great engines of their wealth was the Rhine army, which stimulated trade by purchasing its supplies from the interior. Commerce was greatly facilitated by a road network and system of river transport that had been expanded and improved under Roman administration. It is no accident that the capital of high imperial Gaul was Lugdunum (Lyon), the main Gallic road junction and a great inland port on the river route that led north to Colonia Agrippinensis (Cologne), the chief city of the two German provinces.

It is not surprising, therefore, that there was relatively little resistance to Roman rule and that Vercingetorix's rebellion was ultimately unsuccessful. There were localized revolts in 21 CE and 69–70, but these were easily suppressed. They may have accelerated the demise of the old Gallic aristocracy; few Gauls subsequently pursued imperial Roman careers (for example, as senators). This diffidence, perhaps initially due to lingering Roman prejudice against Celts but reinforced by Gallic contentment with local responsibilities, may have served to keep Gallic wealth in Gaul.

GAUL UNDER THE LATE ROMAN EMPIRE (c. 250–c. 400)

High Roman Gaul came to an end in an empirewide crisis characterized by foreign invasions and a rapid succession of rulers, as increased pressure on the empire's frontiers exacerbated its internal economic and political weaknesses. Priority was given to holding the Danube and the East; despite sporadic visits by emperors, the West was neglected. In 260 and 276 Gaul suffered depredation by two recent confederations of Germanic peoples, the Alemanni and the Franks (facing Upper and Lower Germany, respectively). The ensuing civil war left Gaul, Britain, and (for a while) Spain governed by a line of "Gallic" emperors (beginning with Postumus [reigned 260–268]). These lands were reconquered by the Roman emperor Aurelian in 274, though there was further revolt about 279–80. Although unity was reestablished and order of a sort restored by Aurelian (reigned 270–275), Probus (276–282), and Carinus (283–285), the country was much altered. For example, about 260 the Agri Decumates were abandoned, and, from about the reign of Probus, there began an extensive program of city fortification, though on very restricted circuits that cut through, and even used as building material, the proud structures of the previous age. The countryside was prey to marauding peasants. There was, however,

no move to exploit the crisis to gain independence: the "Gallic Empire," though closely involving leading Gallic civilians, depended on the loyalty of the Rhine army; it thus championed Gallo-Roman, not Gallic, interests (essentially, the maintenance of a strong Rhine frontier).

After Diocletian and his successors radically reformed the empire in the late 3rd and early 4th centuries, Gaul enjoyed a new stability and even an enhanced role in imperial life. The reason for this was the empire's renewed commitment to defend Italy from the Rhine. To ensure the loyalty of the Rhine garrison and the civil population that depended on it for protection, imperial representation in the frontier region became permanent. An official of the highest rank, a praetorian prefect, was based there, and a series of emperors and usurpers (in particular, Constantine I [reigned 306–337], Julian [355–363], Valentinian I [364–375], Gratian [375–383], and Magnus Maximus [383–388]) resided there for at least part of their reigns. Their seat of government was usually Augusta Treverorum (now Trier, Germany), the former civitas-capital of the Treveri and capital of Belgica, now "the Rome of the West." (An interesting exception to the rule was Julian, who, with Trier rendered inhospitable by war, wintered in Paris, giving that city its first taste of future greatness.) Throughout the 4th century and especially in its latter half, the ever-present German menace as well as internecine strife occasionally caused the Rhine frontier to be broken, but it was always vigorously restored.

Some recovery of economic prosperity occurred, though it was fragile and uneven. The levying of taxes in kind rather than in cash may have weakened commerce, and the settlement of captive barbarians on the land indicates a rural labour shortage. Trier was endowed with magnificent buildings, but most Gallic cities failed to recover their Classical grandeur. The well-to-do, who were for the most part probably not descended from the aristocracy of high Roman Gaul (destroyed in the 3rd-century crisis), had loftier ambitions than their predecessors. Looking beyond the civitates, they eagerly sought posts in the imperial administration, now conveniently close at hand, basing their claim to advancement on their learning. (Gallo-Roman education, drawing vitality from the Gallo-Celtic love of eloquence, had long been renowned, but it blossomed fully in the 4th century in famous universities such as the one at Burdigala [Bordeaux].) As the century progressed, some educated Gauls grew extremely powerful; the best-known, Ausonius (c. 310–c. 393), a poet and professor at Burdigala, was appointed tutor of the future emperor Gratian and became his counselor. These worldly aristocrats, when not at court, favoured the country life; the latter 4th century saw the rise of the palatial villa, especially in the southeast. Other Gauls looked to serve an even higher power; Christianity, thought to have been introduced in the region about 250 by St. Denis of Paris, took root deeply in the land in the century following. An episcopal hierarchy (based on the Roman provinces and civitates) was developed, and monasticism was introduced by Martin of Tours (c. 316–397).

THE END OF ROMAN GAUL (c. 400–c. 500)

From 395 the division of the Roman Empire into an eastern and a western half reinforced acute internal political stresses that encouraged barbarian penetration of the Danube region and even Italy. The Rhine frontier was again neglected, and the seat of the Gallic prefecture was moved to Arelate. The result was Germanic invasion, most dramatically the mass crossing of the Rhine in 405–406, and civil war. By 418, Franks and Burgundians were established west of the Rhine, and the Visigoths settled in Aquitania (Aquitaine). These Germans, however, were nominally allies of the empire, and, mainly because of the energy of the Roman general Flavius Aetius, they were kept in check. The death of Aetius in 454 and the growing debility of a western imperial government hamstrung by the loss of Africa to the Vandals created a power vacuum in Gaul. It was filled by the Visigoths, at first indirectly through the nomination of the emperor Avitus (reigned 455–456) and then directly by their own kings, the most important being King Euric (466–484). Between 460 and 480 there was steady Visigothic encroachment on Roman territory to the east; the Burgundians followed suit, expanding westward from Sapaudia (now Savoy). In 476 the last imperial possessions in Provence were formally ceded to the Visigoths.

Gaul suffered badly from these developments. Communities near the Rhine were destroyed by war. Refugees fled south, to Roman territory, only to find themselves burdened by crippling taxation and administrative corruption. As is evident from the works of the writer Sidonius Apollinaris (c. 430–c. 490), however, the economic power and with it the lifestyle of the Gallo-Roman aristocracy remained remarkably resilient, whether under Roman emperors or barbarian kings. Many aristocrats, such as, for example, Sidonius himself, also confirmed their standing in their communities by becoming bishops. Until the middle of the 5th century, the leaders of Gallic society, lay and clerical, while learning to live with the barbarian newcomers, still looked to Rome for high office and protection. Thereafter they increasingly cooperated with the German rulers as generals and counselors. Thus, at least in the centre and south of the country, the Gallo-Roman cultural legacy was bequeathed intact to the successor-kingdoms.

MEROVINGIAN AND CAROLINGIAN AGE

The period of the Merovingian and Carolingian Frankish dynasties (450–987) encompasses the early Middle Ages. After the 4th and 5th centuries, when Germanic peoples entered the Roman Empire in substantial numbers and brought the existence of that Mediterranean state to an end, the Franks played a key role in Gaul, unifying it under their rule. Merovingian and, later, Carolingian monarchs created a polity centred in an area between the Loire and Rhine rivers but extending beyond the Rhine into large areas of Germany.

EARLY FRANKISH PERIOD

In the second quarter of the 5th century, various groups of Franks moved southward. The Ripuarian Franks, as they would be known, settled in the middle Rhine area (near Cologne) and along the lower branches of the Moselle and Meuse rivers, and the Salian Franks, as they came to be known, found homes in the Atlantic coastal region. In the latter area, separate groups took possession of Tournai and Cambrai and reached the Somme River. These Franks along the coast were divided into many small kingdoms. One of the better-known groups established itself in and around the city (*urbs*) of Tournai; its kinglet (*regulus*) was Childeric (died c. 481/482), who traditionally is regarded as a close relative in the male line of Merovech, eponymous ancestor of the Merovingian dynasty and descendant of a sea god. Childeric placed himself in the service of the Roman Empire.

GAUL AND GERMANY AT THE END OF THE 5TH CENTURY

Preceding the arrival of the Franks, other Germans had already entered Gaul. The area south of the Loire was divided between two groups. One, the Visigoths, occupied Aquitaine, Provence, and most of Spain. Their king, Euric (reigned 466–484), was the most powerful monarch in the West. The other group, the Burgundians, ruled much of the Rhône valley. In northern Gaul the Alemanni occupied Alsace and moved westward into the area between the Franks and Burgundians, while the first British immigrants established themselves on the Armorican peninsula (now Brittany). Substantial parts of Gaul were ruled by Syagrius, a Roman king (*rex*) with his capital at Soissons.

In spite of the influx of Germans, whose numbers have been exaggerated, Gaul, which had been part of the Roman Empire for about 500 years, remained thoroughly Romanized. Because many of its administrative institutions withstood the crisis of the 5th century, Gaul's traditional Roman civilization survived, at least in attenuated form, especially among the aristocratic classes. The core of political, social, economic, and religious life remained in the *civitas* with the *urbs* at its heart. In addition, the Germans themselves were, to varying degrees, Romanized. This influence was stronger among the Burgundians and the Visigoths, who had lived within the empire for a longer time and had intermingled with other Germanic peoples to a great extent, than it was among the Franks and Alemanni, who had only recently entered the empire even though they had fought alongside or against Rome since the 3rd century. On the other hand, the Burgundians and Visigoths were often seen in an unfavourable light by the Romans because they adopted a heretical form of Christianity—Arianism. The Franks and Alemanni, who preserved limited contacts with Germans living outside the boundaries of the Roman Empire, remained pagan, which the Romans viewed less harshly than heresy.

In effect, the Germanic peoples who penetrated into Roman Gaul were but a small segment of the Germanic world. The northern Germans (Angles, Jutes, Saxons, and Frisians) still occupied the coastal regions of the North Sea east of the Rhine, and the Thuringians and Bavarians divided the territory between the Elbe and Danube. The Slavic world began on the opposite bank of the Elbe.

THE MEROVINGIANS

As the Roman Empire declined in the 5th century, Germanic peoples settled in Gaul and other parts of the Roman world. The most successful of these peoples were the Franks, who settled in northern Gaul. The greatest of the early Frankish leaders was Clovis, who ruled from 481 to 511. He expanded Frankish power throughout much of Gaul and founded the Merovingian dynasty.

CLOVIS AND THE UNIFICATION OF GAUL

Clovis (reigned 481/482–511), the son of Childeric, unified Gaul with the exception of areas in the southeast. According to the traditional and highly stylized account by Gregory of Tours that is now generally questioned by scholars in its particulars, Clovis consolidated the position of the Franks in northern Gaul during the years following his accession. In 486 he defeated Syagrius, the last Roman ruler in Gaul, and in a series of subsequent campaigns with strong Gallo-Roman support he occupied an area situated between the Frankish kingdom of Tournai, the Visigothic and Burgundian kingdoms, and the lands occupied by the Ripuarian Franks and the Alemanni, removing it from imperial control once more. It was probably during this same period that he eliminated the other Salian kings. In a second phase he attacked the other Germanic peoples living in Gaul, with varying degrees of success. An Alemannian westward push was blocked, probably as a result of two campaigns—one conducted by the Franks of the kingdom of Cologne about 495–496 at the Battle of Tolbiacum (Zülpich), the second by Clovis about 506, after his annexation of Cologne. Clovis thus extended his authority over most of the territory of the Alemanni. Some of the former inhabitants sought refuge in the Ostrogothic kingdom of Theodoric the Great, the most powerful ruler in the West at that time.

In the late 490s, according to the traditional chronology, Clovis absorbed the region between the Seine and the Loire (including Nantes, Rennes, and Vannes) and then moved against the Visigothic kingdom. He defeated Alaric II at Vouillé (507). He annexed Aquitaine, between the Loire, Rhône, and Garonne, as well as Novempopulana, between the Garonne and the Pyrenees. Opposed to a Frankish hegemony in the West, Theodoric intervened on behalf of the Visigothic king. He prevented Clovis from annexing Septimania, on the Mediterranean between the Rhône and the Pyrenees, which the Visigoths retained, and occupied Provence. In addition, Clovis eliminated various Frankish kinglets in the east and united the Frankish people under his own leadership.

Clovis established Paris as the capital of his new kingdom, and in 508 he received some sort of recognition from Emperor Anastasius, possibly an honorary consulship, and the right to use the imperial insignia. These privileges gave the new king legitimacy of sorts and were useful in gaining the support of his Gallo-Roman subjects.

THE CONVERSION OF CLOVIS

According to Gregory of Tours, Clovis came to believe that his victory at Tolbiacum in 496 was due to the help of the Christian God, whom his wife Clotilda had been encouraging him to accept. With the support of Bishop Remigius of Reims, a leader of the Gallo-Roman aristocracy, Clovis converted to Catholic Christianity with some 3,000 of his army in 498. This traditional account of the conversion, however, has been questioned by scholars, especially because of the echoes of the conversion of Constantine that Gregory so clearly incorporated in his history. Scholars now believe that Clovis did not convert until as late as 508 and did not convert directly from paganism to Catholic Christianity but accepted Arian Christianity first. Clovis did, however, convert to the Catholic faith, and this conversion assured the Frankish king of the support not only of the ecclesiastical hierarchy but also of Roman Catholic Christians in general—the majority of the population. It also ensured the triumph in Gaul of Roman Christianity over paganism and Arianism and spared Gaul the lengthy conflicts that occurred in other Germanic kingdoms.

THE SONS OF CLOVIS

Following the death of Clovis in 511, the kingdom was divided among his four sons. This partition was not made according to ethnic, geographic, or administrative divisions. The only factor taken into account was that the portions be of equal value. This was defined in terms of the royal fisc (treasury), which had previously been the imperial fisc, and tax revenues from land and trade, which were based upon imperial practices. Boundaries for the division were poorly defined.

Clovis's lands included two general areas: one was the territory north of the Loire River (the part of Gaul that was conquered earliest); the other, to the south, in Aquitaine, was a region not yet assimilated. Theodoric I, Clovis's eldest son by one of the wives he married in Germanic style before Clovis married Clotilda and converted to Christianity, received lands around the Rhine, Moselle, and upper Meuse rivers, as well as the Massif Central. Clodomir was given the Loire country to the other side of the Rhine, which was the only kingdom not composed of separated territories. Childebert I inherited the country of the English Channel and the lower Seine and, probably, the region of Bordeaux and Saintes. Chlotar I was granted the old Frankish country north of the Somme and an ill-defined area in Aquitaine. Their capitals were centred in the Paris Basin, which was divided among the four brothers: Theodoric used Reims; Clodomir, Orléans; Childebert, Paris; Chlotar, Soissons. As each brother died, the survivors partitioned the newly available lands among themselves. This system resulted in bloody competition until 558, when Chlotar, after his brothers' deaths, succeeded in reuniting the kingdom under his own rule.

THE CONQUEST OF BURGUNDY

In spite of these partitions, the Frankish kings continued their conquests. One of their primary concerns was to extend their dominion over the whole of Gaul. It took two campaigns to overcome the Burgundian kingdom. In 523 Clodomir, Childebert I, and Chlotar I, as allies of Theodoric the Great, king of the Ostrogoths, moved into Burgundy, whose king, Sigismund, Theodoric's son-in-law, had assassinated his own son. Sigismund was captured and killed. Godomer, the new Burgundian king, defeated the Franks at Vézeronce and forced them to retreat; Clodomir was killed in the battle. Childebert I, Chlotar I, and Theodebert I, the son of Theodoric I, regained the offensive in 532–534. The Burgundian kingdom was annexed and divided between the Frankish kings. Following Theodoric the Great's death in 526, the Franks were able to gain a foothold in Provence by taking advantage of the weakened Ostrogothic kingdom. The Franks were thus masters of all of southeastern Gaul and had reached the Mediterranean. But, in spite of two expeditions (531 and 542), they were unable to gain possession of Visigothic Septimania. Also, at least a portion of Armorica in the northwest remained outside the Frankish sphere of influence. During this period, British colonization of the western half of the Armorican peninsula was at its height.

THE CONQUEST OF SOUTHERN GERMANY

To the east, the Franks extended their domain in southern Germany, subjugating Thuringia (about 531 Chlotar I carried off Radegunda, a niece of the Thuringian king), the part of Alemannia between the Neckar River and the upper Danube (after 536), and Bavaria. The latter was created as a dependent duchy about 555. The Franks were less successful in northern Germany; in 536 they imposed a tribute on the Saxons (who occupied the area between the Elbe, the North Sea, and the Ems), but the latter revolted successfully in 555.

Theodebert I and his son, Theodebald, sent expeditions into Italy during a struggle between the Ostrogoths and Byzantines (535–554), but they achieved no lasting results.

THE GRANDSONS OF CLOVIS

At the death of Chlotar I (561), the Frankish kingdom, which had become the most powerful state in the West, was once again divided, this time between his four sons. The partition agreement was based on that of 511 but dealt with more extensive territories. Guntram received the eastern part of the former kingdom of Orléans, enlarged by the addition of Burgundy. Charibert I's share was fashioned from the old kingdom of Paris (Seine and English Channel districts), augmented in the south by the western section of the old kingdom of Orléans (lower Loire valley) and the Aquitaine Basin. Sigebert I received the kingdom of Reims, extended to include the new German conquests; a portion of the Massif Central (Auvergne) and the Provençal territory (Marseille) were added to his share. Chilperic I's portion was reduced to the kingdom of Soissons.

The death of Charibert (567) resulted in further partition. Chilperic, the principal beneficiary, received the lower Seine district, including a large tract of the English Channel coast. The remainder, most notably Aquitaine and the area around Bayeux, was divided in a complex manner; and Paris was subject to joint possession. The partitions of 561 and 567, which reaffirmed the division of Francia, were the sources of innumerable intrigues and family struggles, especially between, on the one hand, Chilperic I, his wife the former slave Fredegund, and their children, who controlled northwestern Francia, and, on the other hand, Sigebert I, his wife the Visigothic princess Brunhild, and their descendants, the masters of northeastern Francia.

THE SHRINKING OF THE FRONTIERS AND PERIPHERAL AREAS

These events undermined the Frankish hegemony. In Brittany the Franks maintained control of the eastern region but had to cope with raids by the Bretons, who had established heavily populated settlements in the western part of the peninsula. To the southwest the Gascons, a highland people from the Pyrenees, had been driven northward by the Visigoths in 578 and settled in Novempopulana; in spite of several Frankish expeditions, this area was not subdued. In the south the Franks were unable to gain control of Septimania; they tried to accomplish this by means of diplomatic agreements, which were buttressed by dynastic intermarriage, and by military campaigns occasioned by religious differences (the Visigothic kings were Arians). In the southeast the Lombards, who had recently arrived in Italy, made several raids on Gaul (569, 571, 574); Frankish expeditions into Italy (584, 585, 588, 590), led by Childebert II, were without result. Meanwhile the Avars, a people of undetermined origin who settled along the Danube in the second half of the 6th century, threatened the eastern frontier; in 568 they took Sigebert prisoner, and in 596 they attacked Thuringia, forcing Brunhild to purchase their departure.

THE PARCELING OF THE KINGDOM

Internal struggles resulted in the emergence of new political configurations. At the time of the partitions of 561 and 567, new political-geographic units began to appear within Gaul. Austrasia was created from the Rhine, Moselle, and Meuse districts, which had formerly been the kingdom of Reims, and from the areas east of the Rhône conquered by Theodoric I and his son Theodebert; Sigebert I (died 575) transferred the capital to Metz to take advantage of the income provided by trade on the Rhine. Neustria was born out of the partition of the kingdom of Soissons; a portion of the kingdom of Paris was added to it, thus endowing the area with a broad coastal section and making the lower Seine valley its centre. Its first capital, Soissons, was returned to Austrasia following the death of Chilperic I; its capital was later moved to Paris, which had been controlled by Chilperic. The kingdom of Orléans, without its western territory but with part of the old Burgundian lands added to it, eventually became Burgundy; Guntram fixed its capital at Chalon-sur-Saône. Aquitaine submitted to the Frankish kingdoms centred farther north in Gaul; its civitates were the object of numerous partitions made by sovereigns who regarded it as an area for exploitation. Aquitaine did not enjoy political autonomy during this period.

THE FAILURE OF REUNIFICATION (613–714)

Territorial crisis was partially and provisionally averted during the first third of the 7th century. Chlotar II, son of Chilperic I and Fredegund and king of Neustria since 584, took control of Burgundy and Austrasia in 613 upon the brutal execution of Brunhild, and thus a united kingdom once again was created. He fixed his capital at Paris and, in 614, convoked a council there, at which he recognized the traditional prerogatives of the aristocracy (Gallo-Roman and Germanic) in order to gain their support in the governing of the kingdom. His son Dagobert I (reigned 629–639) was able to preserve this unity. He journeyed to Burgundy, where the highest political office, mayor of the palace, was maintained; to Austrasia; and then to Aquitaine, which was given the status of a duchy. He thus recognized

structures of imperial origin.

Dagobert had only limited success along the frontier. In 638 he placed the Bretons and the Gascons under nominal subjection, but ties with these peripheral peoples were tenuous. He intervened in dynastic quarrels of Spain, entering the country and going as far as Zaragoza before receiving tribute and quitting. Septimania remained Visigothic. On the eastern frontier there were incidents involving Frankish merchants and Moravian and Czech Slavs; after the failure of a campaign conducted by Dagobert, with the assistance of the Lombards and Bavarians (633), the Slavs attacked Thuringia. The king reached an agreement with the Saxons, who would protect the eastern frontier in return for remission of a tribute they had paid since 536. Thus, Dagobert used traditional imperial techniques to protect the frontiers with more or less Romanized barbarians.

THE HEGEMONY OF NEUSTRIA

The territorial struggles began anew after 639. In Neustria, Austrasia, and Burgundy, power was gradually absorbed by aristocratic leaders, particularly the mayors of the palace. Ebroïn, mayor of the palace in Neustria, attempted to unify the kingdom under his leadership but met with violent opposition. Resistance in Burgundy was led by Bishop Leodegar, who was assassinated about 679 (he was later canonized). Austrasia was governed by the Pippinid mayors of the palace, who were given the office as a reward for their founder's support of Chlotar in the over-throw of Brunhild; Pippin I of Landen was succeeded by his son Grimoald, who tried unsuccessfully to have his son, Childebert the Adopted, crowned king, and by Pippin II of Herstal (or Héristal), whom Ebroïn was briefly able to keep from power (c. 680).

Frankish hegemony was once more threatened in the peripheral areas, especially to the east where Austrasia was endangered. The Thuringians (640–641) and Alemanni regained their independence. The Frisians reached the mouth of the Schelde River and controlled the towns of Utrecht and Dorestat; the attempted conversion of Frisia by Wilfrid of Northumbria had to be abandoned (c. 680). In southern Gaul the duke Lupus changed the status of Aquitaine from a duchy to an independent principality.

AUSTRASIAN HEGEMONY AND THE RISE OF THE PIPPINIDS

The murder of Ebroïn (680 or 683) reversed the situation in favour of Austrasia and the Pippinids. Pippin II defeated the Neustrians at Tertry in 687 and reunified northern Francia under his own control during the next decade. Austrasia and Neustria were reunited under a series of Merovingian kings, who retained much traditional power and authority while Pippin II consolidated his position as mayor of the palace. At the same time, Pippin II partially restabilized the frontiers of northern Francia by driving the Frisians north of the Rhine and by restoring Frankish suzerainty over the Alemanni. But control of southern Gaul continued to elude Pippin II and his supporters. In the early 8th century, Provence became an autonomous duchy, while power in Burgundy was divided.

THE CAROLINGIANS

Representatives of the Merovingian dynasty continued to hold the royal title until 751. Chroniclers in the service of their successors, the Carolingians—as the Pippinids would come to be known—stigmatized the Merovingians as "do-nothing kings." Although some of the later Merovingian kings inherited the title as children and died young, they retained at least some power into the 8th century, and only in the 720s did they become mere puppets. At the same time, however, effective power was increasingly concentrated in the hands of the Pippinids, who, thanks to their valuable landholdings and loyal retainers, maintained a monopoly on the office of mayor of the palace. Because of their familial predisposition for the name Charles and because of the significance of Charlemagne in the family's history, modern historians have called them the Carolingian dynasty.

CHARLES MARTEL AND PIPPIN III

Pippin II's death in 714 jeopardized Carolingian hegemony. His heir was a grandchild entrusted to the regency of his widow, Plectrude. There was a revolt in Neustria, and Eudes, duc d'Aquitaine, used the occasion to increase his holdings and make an alliance with the Neustrians. The Saxons crossed the Rhine, and the Arabs crossed the Pyrenees.

CHARLES MARTEL

The situation was rectified by Pippin's illegitimate son, Charles Martel. Defeating the Neustrians at Amblève (716), Vincy (717), and Soissons (719), he made himself master of northern Francia. He then reestablished Frankish authority in southern Gaul, where the local authorities could not cope with the Islamic threat; he stopped the Muslims near Poitiers (Battle of Tours; 732) and used this opportunity to subdue Aquitaine (735–736).

The Muslims then turned toward Provence, and Charles Martel sent several expeditions against them. At the same time, he succeeded in reestablishing authority over the dissident provinces in the southeast (737–738) with the exception of Septimania. Finally, he reestablished his influence in Germany. In his numerous military campaigns he succeeded in driving the Saxons across the Rhine, returned the Bavarians to Frankish suzerainty, and annexed southern Frisia and Alemannia. He also encouraged missionary activity, seeing it as a means to consolidate his power. Most notably, Charles supported the Anglo-Saxon missionaries, especially Winfrith (the future St. Boniface), who spread the faith east of the Rhine. The work of the Anglo-Saxons was sanctioned by the papacy, which was beginning to seek support in the West at the same time that St. Peter's prominence was growing among the Franks. Moreover, long-lasting ties with England brought Boniface to Rome for papal blessing of missionary work, and his activities strengthened ties between the pope and the Franks.

Charles Martel had supported a figurehead Merovingian king, Theodoric IV (reigned 721–737), but upon the latter's death he felt his own position secure enough to leave the throne vacant. His chief source of power was a strong circle of followers who furnished the main body of his troops and became the most important element in the army because local

BATTLE OF TOURS

The Battle of Tours (also called the Battle of Poitiers) resulted in a victory for Charles Martel, the de facto ruler of the Frankish kingdoms, over Muslim invaders from Spain in October 732. The battlefield cannot be exactly located, but it was fought somewhere between Tours and Poitiers, in what is now west-central France.

'Abd-ar-Raḥmān, the Muslim governor of Córdoba, had invaded Aquitaine (present southwestern France) and defeated its duke, Eudes. Eudes appealed for help to Charles, who stationed his forces to defend the city of Tours from the northward progress of the Muslims. According to

Battle of Poitiers, *in October 732, oil on canvas by Charles de Steuben, 1834–37; in the Versailles Museum, France.* Photos.com/Thinkstock

tradition, the Muslim cavalry attacks broke upon Charles's massed infantry, ʿAbd-ar-Raḥmān was killed in the fighting, and the Arabs then retired southward. There were no further Muslim invasions of Frankish territory, and Charles's victory has often been regarded as decisive for world history, since it preserved western Europe from Muslim conquest and Islamization. The victory also served to consolidate Charles's leadership of the Franks, and he was able to assert his authority in Aquitaine, where Eudes swore allegiance to him.

dislocation of government had weakened the recruitment of the traditional levies of freemen. He attached them to himself by concessions of land, which he obtained by drawing on the considerable holdings of the church. This gave him large tracts of land at his disposal, which he granted for life (*precaria*). He was thus able to recruit a larger and more powerful circle of followers than that surrounding any of the other influential magnates.

PIPPIN III

At the death of Charles Martel (741), the lands and powers in his hands were divided between his two sons, Carloman and Pippin III (the Short), as was the custom. This partition was followed by unsuccessful insurrections in the peripheral duchies—Aquitaine, Alemannia, and Bavaria. The seriousness of these revolts, however, encouraged Pippin and Carloman to place the Merovingian Childeric III, whom they conveniently discovered in a monastery, on the throne in 743.

Carloman's entrance into a monastery in 747 reunited Carolingian holdings. Pippin the Short, who as mayor of the palace had held de facto power over Francia, or the regnum Francorum ("kingdom of the Franks"), now desired to be king. He was crowned with the support of the papacy, which, threatened by the Lombards and having problems with Byzantium, sought a protector in the West. To accomplish this goal, he sent a letter to Pope Zacharias in 750 asking whether he who had the power or the title should be king, and he received the answer he desired. In 751 Pippin deposed Childeric III; he then had himself elected king by an assembly of magnates and consecrated by the bishops, thus ending the nominal authority of the last Merovingian king. The new pope, Stephen II (or III), sought aid

from Francia; in 754 at Ponthion he gave Pippin the title Patrician of the Romans, renewed the king's consecration, and consecrated Pippin's sons, Charles and Carloman, thus providing generational legitimacy for the line.

As king, Pippin limited himself to consolidating royal control in Gaul, thus establishing the base for later Carolingian expansion. Despite Pippin's efforts, the situation at the German frontier was unstable. The duchy of Bavaria, which had been given to Tassilo III as a benefice, gained its independence in 763; several expeditions were unable to subdue the Saxons. On the other hand, Pippin achieved a decisive victory in southern Gaul by capturing Septimania from the Muslims (752–759). He broke down Aquitaine's resistance, and it was reincorporated into the kingdom (760–768). Pippin campaigned in Italy against the Lombards twice (754–755; 756) on the appeal of the pope and laid the foundations for the Papal States with the so-called Donation of Pippin. He exchanged ambassadors with the great powers of the eastern Mediterranean— the Byzantine Empire and the Caliphate of Baghdad. He also continued a program of reform of the church and religious life that he had begun with Carloman.

CHARLEMAGNE

Pippin III was faithful to ancient customs, and upon his death in 768 his kingdom was divided between his two sons, Charles (Charlemagne) and Carloman.

The succession did not proceed smoothly, however, as Charlemagne faced a serious revolt in Aquitaine as well as the enmity of his brother, who refused to help suppress the revolt. Carloman's death in 771 saved the kingdom from civil war. Charlemagne dispossessed his nephews from their inheritance and reunited the kingdom under his own authority.

THE CONQUESTS

Charlemagne consolidated his authority up to the geographic limits of Gaul. Though he put down a new insurrection in Aquitaine (769), he was unable to bring the Gascons and the Bretons fully under submission. However, Charlemagne extended considerably the territory he controlled and unified a large part of the Christian West. He followed no grand strategy of expansion, instead taking advantage of situations as they arose.

He pursued an active policy toward the Mediterranean world. In Spain he attempted to take advantage of the emir of Córdoba's difficulties; he was unsuccessful in western Spain, but in the east he was able to establish a march, or border territory, south of the Pyrenees to the important city Barcelona. Pursuing Pippin's Italian policy, he intervened in Italy. At the request of Pope Adrian I, whose territories had been threatened by the Lombards, he took possession of their capital city, Pavia, and had himself crowned king of the Lombards. In 774 he fulfilled Pippin's promise and created a papal state; the situation on the peninsula remained unsettled, however, and many expeditions were necessary. This enlargement of his Mediterranean holdings led Charlemagne to establish a protectorate over the Balearic Islands in the western Mediterranean (798–799).

Charlemagne conquered more German territory and secured the eastern frontier. By means of military campaigns and missionary activities he brought Saxony and northern Frisia under control; the Saxons, led by Widukind, offered a protracted resistance (772–804), and Charlemagne either destroyed or forcibly deported a large part of the population. To the south, Bavaria was brought under Frankish authority and annexed. Conquests in the east brought the Carolingians into contact with new peoples—Charlemagne was able to defeat the Avars in three campaigns (791, 795, 796), from which he obtained considerable booty; he was also able to establish a march on the middle Danube, and the Carolingians undertook the conversion and colonization of that area. Charlemagne established the Elbe as a frontier against the northern Slavs. The Danes constructed a great fortification, the Danewirk, across the peninsula to stop Carolingian expansion. Charlemagne also founded Hamburg on the banks of the Elbe. These actions gave the Franks a broad face on the North Sea.

The Frankish state was now the principal power in the West. Charlemagne claimed to be defender of Roman Christianity and intervened in the religious affairs of Spain. Problems arose over doctrinal matters that, along with questions concerning the Italian border and the use of the imperial title, brought him into conflict with the Byzantine Empire; a peace treaty was signed in 810–812. Charlemagne continued his peace policy toward the Muslim East: ambassadors were exchanged with the caliph of Baghdad, and Charlemagne received a kind of eminent right in Jerusalem.

THE RESTORATION OF THE EMPIRE

When by the end of the 8th century Charlemagne was master of a great part of the West, he reestablished the empire in his own name. He was crowned emperor in Rome on Christmas Day, 800, by Pope Leo III, who had been savagely attacked by rivals in Rome in 799 and who hoped that the restoration of an imperial authority in western Europe would protect the papacy. Charlemagne's powers in Rome and in relation to the Papal States, which were incorporated, with some degree of autonomy, into the Frankish empire, were clarified. Although his new title did not replace his royal titles, it was well suited to his preponderant position in the old Roman West. The imperial title, later known as Holy Roman emperor, indicates a will to unify the West; nevertheless, in his succession plan of 806, Charlemagne preserved the kingdom of Italy, giving the crown to one of his sons, Pippin, and made Aquitaine a kingdom for his other son, Louis. The continuing dispute with the Byzantines over the imperial title may have led to his reluctance to pass it on, or,

more likely, he saw it as a personal honour in recognition of his great achievements.

LOUIS I

Only chance ensured that the empire remained united under Louis I (the Pious), the last surviving son of Charlemagne. Louis was crowned emperor in 813 by his father, who died the following year. The era of great conquests had ended, and, on the face of it, Louis's principal preoccupation was his relationship with the peoples to the north. In the hope of averting the threat posed by the Vikings, who had begun to raid the coasts of the North Sea and the Atlantic Ocean, Louis proposed to evangelize the Scandinavian world. This mission was given to St. Ansgar but was a failure.

During Louis's reign, the imperial bureaucracy was given greater uniformity. Louis the Pious saw the empire, above all, as a religious ideal, and in 816 in a separate ceremony the pope anointed him and crowned him emperor. At the same time, Louis took steps to regulate the succession so as to maintain the unity of the empire (Ordinatio Imperii, 817). His eldest son, Lothar I, was to be sole heir to the empire, but within it three dependent kingdoms were maintained: Louis's younger sons, Pippin and Louis, received Aquitaine and Bavaria, respectively; his nephew Bernard was given Italy. He also replaced the dynasty's customary relationship with the pope with the Pactum Hludowicianum in 817, which clearly defined relations between the two in a way that favoured the emperor.

The remarriage of Louis the Pious to Judith of Bavaria and the birth of a fourth son, who would rule as Charles II (the Bald), upset this project. In spite of opposition from Lothar, who had the support of a unity faction drawn from the ranks of the clergy, the emperor sought to create a kingdom for Charles the Bald. These divergent interests would undermine Louis's authority and cause much civil strife.

THE PARTITIONING OF THE CAROLINGIAN EMPIRE

In 830 Louis faced a revolt by his three older sons, and in 833–834 he confronted a second, more serious revolt. In 833 he was abandoned by his followers on the Field of Lies at Colmar and then deposed and forced by Lothar to do public penance. Judith and Charles were placed in monasteries. Lothar, however, overplayed his hand and alienated his brothers, who restored their father to the throne. Lothar lived in disgrace until a final reconciliation with his father near the end of Louis's life.

THE TREATY OF VERDUN

After the death of Louis the Pious (840), his surviving sons continued their plotting to alter the succession. Louis II (the German) and Charles II (the Bald) affirmed their alliance against Lothar I with the Oath of Strasbourg (842). After several battles, including the bloody one at Fontenoy, the three brothers came to an agreement in the Treaty of Verdun (843).

The empire was divided into three kingdoms arranged along a north-south axis: Francia Orientalis was given to Louis the German, Francia Media to Lothar, and Francia Occidentalis to Charles the Bald. The three kings were equal among themselves. Lothar kept the imperial title, which had lost much of its universal character, and the imperial capital at Aix-la-Chapelle (now Aachen, Germany).

THE KINGDOMS CREATED AT VERDUN

Until 861 the clerical faction tried to impose a government of fraternity on the descendants of Charlemagne, manifested in the numerous conferences they held, but the competition of the brothers and their supporters undermined clerical efforts.

Francia Media proved to be the least stable of the kingdoms, and the imperial institutions bound to it suffered as a result. In 855 the death of Lothar I was followed by a partition of his kingdom among his three sons: the territory to the north and west of the Alps went to Lothar II (Lotharingia) and to Charles (kingdom of Provence); Louis II received Italy and the imperial title. At the death of Charles of Provence (863), his kingdom was divided between his brothers Lothar II (Rhône region) and Louis II (Provence). After the death of Lothar II in 869, Lotharingia was divided between his two uncles, Louis the German and Charles the Bald. Louis, however, did not gain control of his share until 870. Charles was made master of the Rhône regions of the ancient kingdom of

Provence, while Louis turned most of his attention to fighting the Muslims who threatened the peninsula and the papal territories.

In Francia Occidentalis Charles the Bald was occupied with the struggle against the Vikings, who ravaged the countryside along the Scheldt, Seine, and Loire rivers. More often than not, the king was forced to pay for their departure with silver and gold. Aquitaine remained a centre of dissension. For some time (until 864) Pippin II continued to have supporters there, and Charles the Bald attempted to pacify them by installing his sons—first Charles the Child (reigned 855–866) and then Louis II (the Stammerer; 867–877)—on the throne of Aquitaine. The problems in Aquitaine were closely connected to general unrest among the magnates, who wished to keep the regional king under their control. By accumulating countships and creating dynasties, the magnates succeeded in carving out large principalities at the still unstable borders: Robert the Strong and Hugh the Abbot in the west; Eudes, son of Robert the Strong, in this same region and in the area around Paris; Hunfred, Vulgrin, Bernard of Gothia, and Bernard Plantevelue (Hairyfoot), count of Auvergne, in Aquitaine and the border regions; Boso in the southeast; and Baldwin I in Flanders. Nevertheless, Charles the Bald appeared to be the most powerful sovereign in the West, and in 875 Pope John VIII arranged for him to accept the imperial crown. An expedition he organized in Italy on the appeal of the pope failed, and the magnates of Francia Occidentalis rose up. Charles the Bald died on the return trip (877). Charles's son Louis the Stammerer ruled for only two years. At his death in 879 the kingdom was divided between his sons Louis III and Carloman. In the southeast, however, Boso, the count of Vienne, appropriated the royal title to the kingdom of Provence. The imperial throne remained vacant. The death of Louis III (882) permitted the reunification of Francia Occidentalis (except for the kingdom of Provence) under Carloman.

In Francia Orientalis royal control over the aristocracy was maintained. But decentralizing forces, closely bound to regional interests, made themselves felt in the form of revolts led by the sons of Louis the German. He had made arrangements to partition his kingdom in 864, with Bavaria and the East Mark to go to Carloman, Saxony and Franconia to Louis the Younger, and Alemannia (Swabia) to Charles III (the Fat). Although Louis the German managed to gain a portion of Lotharingia in 870, he was unable to prevent Charles the Bald's coronation as emperor (875). When Louis the German died in 876, the partition of his kingdom was confirmed. At the death of Charles the Bald, Louis's son Carloman seized Italy and intended to take the imperial title, but ill health forced him to abandon his plans. Carloman's youngest brother, Charles the Fat, benefited from the circumstances and restored the territorial unity of the empire. The deaths of Carloman (880) and Louis the Younger (882) without heirs allowed Charles the

Fat to acquire successively the crown of Italy (880) and the imperial title (881) and to unite Francia Orientalis (882) under his own rule. Finally, at the death of Louis the Stammerer's son Carloman, Charles the Fat was elected king of Francia Occidentalis (885); the magnates had bypassed the last heir of Louis the Stammerer, Charles III (the Simple), in his favour. Charles the Fat avoided involving himself in Italy, in spite of appeals from the pope, and concentrated his attention on coordinating resistance to the Vikings, who had resumed the offensive in the valleys of the Scheldt, Meuse, Rhine, and Seine. He was unsuccessful, however, and in 886 had to purchase the Vikings' departure: they had besieged Paris, which was defended by Count Eudes. The magnates of Francia Orientalis rose up and deposed Charles the Fat in 887.

THE FRANKISH WORLD

The settlement of Germanic peoples in Roman Gaul brought people from two entirely different backgrounds into contact. Linguistic barriers were quickly overcome, for the Germans adopted Latin. At the same time, German names were preponderant. Although there were religious difficulties in those regions settled by peoples converted to Arianism (Visigoths, Burgundians), Clovis's eventual conversion to Catholic Christianity simplified matters. The Germans who settled in Gaul were able to preserve some of their own judicial institutions, but these were heavily influenced by

Roman law. The first sovereigns, under Roman influence, committed the customs of the people to writing, in Latin (Code of Euric, c. 470–480; Salic Law of Clovis, c. 507–511; Law of Gundobad, c. 501–515), and occasionally had summaries of Roman rights drawn up for the Gallo-Roman population (Papian Code of Gundobad; Breviary of Alaric). By the 9th century this principle of legal personality, under which each person was judged according to the law applying to his status group, was replaced by a territorially based legal system. Multiple contacts in daily life produced an original civilization composed of a variety of elements, some of which were inherited from antiquity, some brought by the Germans, and many strongly influenced by Christianity.

SOCIAL CLASSES

The collapse of Roman imperial power and the influx of Germans did not destroy the old Roman senatorial and landed aristocracy; the 6th-century kings called on its members to serve in the administration. A sort of military aristocracy had existed among the Germans: at the time of their settlement within the empire, its members were given tax revenues and lands confiscated from the Gallo-Roman aristocracy or awarded from the fisc (royal treasury). The two groups fused rapidly. They shared a common life, discharging public and religious duties and frequenting the court. By the beginning of the 7th century, there arose an aristocracy of office, whose signs of prestige were the possession of land and service to the king and church. This aristocracy increased in importance during the conflicts between the Merovingian sovereigns. The ascendance of the Pippinids, Carolingian rule, and the power struggles in the 9th century furnished these magnates, on whom those in power were dependent, with a means of enriching themselves and augmenting their political and social influence.

Parallel to this class of lay magnates and largely drawn from the same families was an ecclesiastical aristocracy, which was one both of office and of land. The church found itself in possession of a vast landed fortune. At the beginning of the 7th century, at least, the church frequently benefited from immunity, and governmental rights were conferred on abbots or bishops.

A class of small and middle-size landholders apparently existed, about which little is known. It appears that both the power of the magnates and the practices born of the ancient patronage system, combined with extensive military service, had the effect of diminishing the size of this class.

During the Merovingian epoch, slavery, inherited from antiquity, was still a viable institution. Slaves continued to be obtained in war and through trade. But the number of slaves decreased under the influence of the church, which encouraged manumission and sought to prohibit the enslavement of Christians. Under the Carolingians, the slaves in Gaul formed only a residual class, although the slave trade was still active. Taken increasingly from the Slavic territories (the term *slavus* replaced the traditional *servus*), slaves were a commodity for trade with the Muslim lands of the Mediterranean.

DIFFUSION OF POLITICAL POWER

During the period of insecurity and turbulence that marked the end of the Merovingian epoch, bonds of personal dependence, present in both Roman and Germanic institutions, competed with weakened governmental institutions. In the 7th century these bonds took one of two forms: commendation (a freeman placed himself under the protection of a more powerful lord for the duration of his life) and precarious contract (a powerful lord received certain services in return for the use of his land for a limited time under advantageous conditions). In the 8th century the Pippinids increased their personal circle of followers. Charlemagne sought to establish a personal bond with the entire free population through oaths of loyalty. He encouraged an increase in the number of royal vassals and gave them administrative functions. During the 9th-century power struggles, however, some administrative offices became hereditary, though this represented a distortion of the vassalic relationship. In addition, before the end of the century, a man could place himself in vassalage to several lords. Finally, the usurpation of governmental powers led to the formation of territorial principalities, resulting in a great weakening of royal authority.

INSTITUTIONS

The institutions of government underwent great changes under the Frankish monarchs. Ties between the throne and Rome were emphasized, to the extent that the chief duty of the king (and, later, emperor) was to defend the pope.

KINGSHIP

Kingship was the basic institution in the Merovingian realm. Since Clovis's reign, the power of the king had extended not only over a tribe or tribes but also over a territory inhabited by Germans of divergent backgrounds and by Gallo-Romans as well. The king exercised power within legal limitations, which, when violated, led to efforts to reestablish political equilibrium by means of civil war, assassination, and an appeal to God and the saints. Royal power was dynastic and patrimonial. The Frankish kings successfully eliminated the Germanic practice of the magnates electing the king (the Frankish king was content to present himself to the magnates who acclaimed him) and accepted the hereditary principle as a personal right. The kings partitioned the kingdom at each succession. Royal power also had a sacred aspect; under the Merovingians the external sign of this was long hair.

The nature of the Frankish monarchy was profoundly changed during the Carolingian epoch. When Pippin III usurped the office of king, he had himself consecrated first by the bishops of his realm (possibly including Boniface) in 751 and then by the pope in 754. This rite, originated by the biblical kings of Israel, had already been adopted by the Visigoths; it gave Christian legitimacy to royal authority because it reinforced the religious character of the monarchy and signified the king's receipt of special grace from God. The king was permitted to reign and was given a stature above that of the common level because of this grace. Acclamation by the magnates became a pledge of obeisance to a king whom God had invested with power.

To this new royal status Charlemagne, who had been called *rex et sacerdos* (Latin: "king and priest") in the 790s, added the title of emperor, which had not been held by a ruler in the West since 476. Although, according to his biographer, Charlemagne was surprised by the ceremony on Christmas Day in 800, he must surely have known of the coronation. Indeed, during the previous decade his advisers, especially Alcuin, had developed the idea that Charlemagne was a worthy successor to Constantine, the first Christian emperor. Among the clerical ranks that formed the entourage of the new emperor, the revival of the empire was regarded as a magistracy conferred by God in the interests of Western Christianity and the church; imperial authority was considered a kind of priesthood, and its bearer was obligated to lead and protect the faithful. This idea reached fruition under Louis the Pious, who understood his role as that of a Christian emperor and dispensed with the royal designations that his father included in his official title. He also redefined Carolingian relations with the pope, who crowned Louis in 816 and whose role became central in the act of coronation. Later Carolingians were deemed emperors only after coronation by the pope, and, as a result of the divisions of the empire, the emperor's most important duty was defense of the pope.

THE CENTRAL GOVERNMENT

By the time of Clovis, the ancient Germanic assembly of freemen participated only in the conduct of local affairs and was consigned largely to a military role. Within each kingdom, the king's court, of Roman imperial origin but adapted and modified by the Frankish sovereigns, encompassed domestic services (treasury, provisioning, stables, clergy), a bureau of accounts, and a military force. The court was presided over by three men—the seneschal, the count of the palace, and, foremost, the mayor of the palace, who also presided over the king's estates. They traveled with the king, who, while having various privileged places of residence, did not live at a fixed capital. Only under Charlemagne did this pattern begin to change; while not abandoning the itinerant life, Charlemagne nonetheless wished to make Aachen the centre of his state. It was there that he constructed a vast palace, which was based upon a late imperial Roman model and of which only the Palatine Chapel remains.

LOCAL INSTITUTIONS

Except in the north, which was divided into districts called *pagi* (singular *pagus*), the Merovingians continued to use the city (the Roman *civitas*) as the principal administrative division. A count, installed in each *pagus* and city (*urbs*), delegated financial, military, and judicial authority. Groups of counts were occasionally placed under the authority of a duke, whose responsibilities were primarily military.

THE DEVELOPMENT OF INSTITUTIONS IN THE CAROLINGIAN AGE

The Carolingians contented themselves with refining their administrative system to strengthen royal control and to solve the problems posed by a large empire. The kingdom's cohesion was augmented by an oath of fidelity, which Charlemagne exacted from every freeman (789, 793, 802), and by the publication of legislation—the capitularies—that regulated the administration and exploitation of the kingdom. In the marches, local governments were established.

To improve government further, the episcopate (the body of bishops) was given a central role in the administration, and a new class of judges (*scabini*) was created. Charlemagne extended the use of the *missi dominici*—i.e., envoys who also served as liaisons between the central government and local agents and who were responsible for keeping the latter in line. To strengthen his control over the population, Charlemagne attempted to develop intermediary bodies; he tried to use both vassalage and immunity as means of government—in the first instance by creating royal vassals and giving them public offices and in the second by controlling protected institutions such as monasteries and the Jewish community.

ECONOMIC LIFE

Agriculture was the principal economic activity, and during the entire Frankish age the great estate, inherited from antiquity, was one of the components of rural life. These estates were, according to contemporary documents known as *polyptyques*, an important source of income for the aristocracy. The estates appear to have long been placed under cultivation by servile labour, which was abundant at the time. The heavy work was done with the assistance of day labourers. A portion of the land, however, was given to the tenants—the *coloni*—who were compelled to pay annual charges. With the decline in slavery at the end of the Merovingian era, the number of tenancies increased, and tenants were compelled to render significant amounts of labour to cultivate land held directly by the lord. This bipartite system, in which the lord's "reserve" coexisted with tenant holdings, was not adopted throughout the Frankish

empire but became characteristic of the future French heartland between the Loire and the Rhine. Farming techniques were rudimentary and crop yields were low, putting a damper on population growth and economic expansion; during the Merovingian and Carolingian periods, the total population remained below the peak it had reached in Roman times. The Carolingian period, however, especially after 800, witnessed the beginning of climatic and technological change that would lay the foundation for later economic and demographic expansion.

TRADE

Despite the Islamic conquests, Mediterranean commerce did not decline abruptly. In Gaul, goods such as papyrus, oil, and spices were imported from the East, and there were numerous colonies of Syrians. Currency continued to be based on the gold standard, and imperial units were still used. All signs, moreover, point to the existence of manufacturing for trade (marble from Aquitaine, Rhenish glass, ceramics). However, in the Carolingian age, Mediterranean trade no longer occupied a primary place in the economy. The adoption of a new monetary system based on silver, along with a reduction in the number of Oriental goods and merchants, are signs of the change. After the 7th century, trade among the countries bordering the English Channel and the North Sea and in the Meuse valley increased steadily. The Scandinavians, with their great commercial centres at Birka in Sweden and Hedeby in Denmark, were both pirates and traders; they established new contacts between East and West.

In addition to this large-scale commerce, there was agriculturally based local trade. The number of markets increased, and market towns began to appear alongside the former Gallo-Roman cities, which survived as fortresses and population centres and served as the basis for religious organization and political administration.

FRANKISH FISCAL LAW

The Frankish fiscal system reflected the evolution of the economy. Frankish kings were unable to continue the Roman system of direct taxation of land as the basis for their income. Their principal sources of income were the exploitation of the domains of the fisc (royal treasury), war (booty, tribute), the exercise of power (monetary and judicial rights), and the imposition of a growing number of *telonea* (taxes collected on the circulation and sale of goods).

THE CHURCH

The episcopate and the diocese were practically the only institutions to survive the collapse of Roman imperial power largely unchanged. Many bishops played important roles in defending the population during the German conquest. During the Frankish era, bishops and abbots occupied a socially prominent position because of both their great prestige among the people and their landed wealth.

INSTITUTIONS

The organization of the secular church took its final form under the Merovingian and Carolingian kings. The administrative bodies and the hierarchy of the early Christian church were derived from institutions existing during the late Roman Empire. In principle, a bishop was responsible for the clergy and faithful in each district (*civitas*). The bishop whose seat was in the metropolitan city had pre-eminence and was archbishop over the other bishops in his archdiocese. The monarchy dominated the church. Kings most often appointed bishops from among their followers without regard for religious qualifications; the metropolitan see was often fragmented in the course of territorial partitions and tended to lose its importance, and the church in Francia increasingly withdrew from papal control despite papal attempts to reestablish ties. The first Carolingians reestablished the ecclesiastical hierarchy. They restored the authority of the archbishops and established cathedral chapters so that the clergy living around a bishop were drawn into a communal life. They also maintained the right to nominate bishops, whom they considered agents of the monarchy.

During the 4th and 5th centuries success at converting the countryside made it necessary for the bishops to divide the dioceses into parish churches. Initially there was a limit of between 15 and 40 of these per diocese. In the Carolingian era they were replaced by small parish churches better suited to the conditions of rural life.

MONASTICISM

Monasticism originated in the East. It was introduced in the West during the 4th century and was developed in Gaul, mainly in the west (St. Martin of Tours) and southeast (St. Honoratus and St. John Cassian). In the 6th century the number of monasteries throughout Gaul increased, as did the number of rules regulating them. Introduced by St. Columban (c. 543–615), Irish monasticism was influential in the 7th century, but it was later superseded by the Benedictine rule, which originated in Italy. The monasteries suffered from the upheavals affecting the church in the 8th century, and the Carolingians attempted to reform them. Louis the Pious, acting on the advice of St. Benedict of Aniane, imposed the Benedictine rule, which became a characteristic feature of Western monasticism. The Carolingians, however, continued the practice of having lay abbots.

EDUCATION

In the 6th century, especially in southern Gaul, the aristocracy and, consequently, the bishops drawn from it preserved an interest in traditional Classical culture. Beginning in the 7th century, the Columbanian monasteries insisted on the study of the Bible and the celebration of the liturgy. In the Carolingian era these innovations shared the focus of education with works of Classical antiquity.

RELIGIOUS DISCIPLINE AND PIETY

Characteristic of the church in the 6th century were frequent councils to settle questions of doctrine and discipline. In time, however, the conciliar institution declined, leading to liturgical anarchy and a moral and intellectual crisis among the clergy. Charlemagne and Louis the Pious attempted to impose a uniform liturgy, inspired by the one used at Rome. They also took measures to raise the standard of education of both clerics and the faithful.

The cults of saints and relics were an important part of religion during late antiquity and the Middle Ages. Relics, the remains of the holy dead, were thought to have miraculous powers that could convert pagans and cure the sick. Consequently, the great desire to obtain relics led to the commercial exchange and even theft of them. Rome, with its numerous catacombs filled with the remains of the earliest Christians, was one of the key centres of the relic trade. It also became the most prominent Western pilgrimage site at a time when pilgrimage, at first to local shrines and then to international ones, became increasingly important. The desire on the part of the faithful to be buried near relics changed funeral practices. Ancient cemeteries were abandoned, and burials in or near churches (burials *ad sanctos*) increased.

THE INFLUENCE OF THE CHURCH ON SOCIETY AND LEGISLATION

The progressive Christianization of society influenced Frankish institutions significantly. The introduction of royal consecration and the creation of the empire afforded the clergy an opportunity to elaborate a new conception of power based on religious principles. The church was involved in trying to discourage slavery and in ameliorating the legal condition of those enslaved. It was during the Carolingian period that, in reaction to the polygyny practiced in German society, Christian doctrines of marriage were more strictly formulated.

MEROVINGIAN LITERATURE AND ARTS

During the entire 6th century many writers, inspired by Classical tradition, produced works patterned on antique models; such writers included Sidonius Apollinaris (died *c.* 488) and Venantius Fortunatus (died *c.* 600). In the late 6th century, Gregory of Tours produced influential works in history and hagiography—the writing of saints' lives, which became the most widespread literary genre of the period. Nevertheless, the standard of literature continued to decline, becoming more and more conventional and artificial. The use of popular Latin became more common among writers.

Religious architecture remained faithful to the early Christian model (churches of basilican type, baptisteries, and vaulted mausoleums with central plans). Because of the development of the cult of saints and the practice of burying *ad sanctos*, mausoleums became common in churches. As had been the case in antiquity, marble was the principal sculptural material. In the Pyrenees, sculptors produced antique-style capitals and sarcophagi, which they exported throughout Gaul; these workshops reached their zenith in the 7th century. The development of the art of metalwork (fibulae, buckles) was another characteristic of the Merovingian age. Germanic craftsmen adapted Roman techniques (e.g., cloisonné and damascene work). A new aesthetic standard, characterized by the play of colour and the use of stylized motifs, eventually predominated.

CAROLINGIAN LITERATURE AND ARTS

Although its roots can be traced to the 7th century, a cultural revival, or renaissance, blossomed under the Carolingians. Indeed, the Carolingian kings actively promoted the revival as part of their overall reform of church and society. Inspired by his sense of duty as a Christian king and his desire to improve religious life, Charlemagne promoted learning and literacy in his legislation. He also encouraged bishops and abbots to establish schools to educate the young boys of the kingdom. His reforms attracted some of the greatest scholars of his day, including the Anglo-Saxon Alcuin and the Visigoth Theodulf of Orléans. The renaissance continued into the 9th century and gained renewed support from Charles the Bald, who sought to revive the glory of his grandfather's court.

After raising the standard of the clergy, Charlemagne assembled a group of scholars at his court. Although, contrary to legend, there was no formal school established in the imperial palace, numerous schools opened in the vicinity of churches and monasteries. An attempt was also made to reform handwriting. Research was carried on simultaneously under the auspices of several monastic centres (most notably Tours) for the purpose of standardizing writing; this effort resulted in the adoption of a regular, easily readable script (Carolingian minuscule). Improved teaching and a desire to imitate Classical antiquity helped to revivify the Latin used by writers and scribes.

The imperial court and monasteries throughout the realm were centres of literary production. Carolingian authors produced a number of works of history, such as Einhard's *Vita Karoli Magni* (*Life of Charlemagne*), the Astronomer's *Vita Hludowici imperatoris* (*Life of Louis the Pious*), Nithard's *Historiarum libri IV* (*History of the Sons of Louis the Pious*), and Hincmar's *De ordine palatii* ("On the Government of the Palace"). They also wrote original works of theology on such matters

as predestination and the Eucharist. These authors also copied numerous works of Christian and Classical antiquity, which otherwise would have been lost, and Alcuin prepared a new edition of St. Jerome's Vulgate. Many of the more important books were beautifully illustrated with miniatures, sometimes decorated in gold, that revealed the Roman, Germanic, and Christian influences of these artists and their patrons.

Beginning in the mid-9th century, however, the kingdoms formed from the partitions of the empire saw a renaissance of regional cultures. The fact that the Oath of Strasbourg was drawn up in Romance and German is an early indication of this development. There is a striking contrast between the *Annales Bertiniani* (*The Annals of St. Bertin*), written at the court of Charles the Bald, and the *Annales Fuldenses* (*The Annals of Fulda*), written at the principal intellectual centre in Francia Orientalis. They are, respectively, the western and eastern narratives of the same events.

Some of the great imperial monuments erected during the Carolingian age (palace of Ingelheim, palace of Aachen) reveal the permanence of ancient tradition in their regular plans and conception. The churches were the subjects of numerous architectural experiments; while some were constructed on a central plan (Germigny-des-Prés, Aachen with its internal octagon shape), most remained faithful to the traditional T-shape basilican type. Liturgical considerations and the demands of the faith, however, made certain modifications necessary, such as crypts on the east or a westwork, or second apse on the west. These church buildings afforded architects an opportunity to make experiments in balancing the arches. The extension of the vaults over the entire church and the more rational integration of the annexes and church proper gave rise to Romanesque architecture.

The buildings of the period were richly decorated with paintings, frescoes, painted stucco, and mosaics in which figural representation increasingly replaced strictly ornamental decoration. North Italian ateliers were popularizing the use of interlace (i.e., ornaments of intricately intertwined bands) in chancel decoration. Sumptuary arts became more common, especially illumination, ivory work, and metalwork for liturgical use (reliquaries).

CHAPTER 7

THE EMERGENCE OF FRANCE

From the 9th to the 11th century the peoples and lands dominated by western Frankish kings were transformed. The Carolingian protectorate of local order collapsed under the pressures of external invasions and internal usurpations of power. Growing populations and quickening economies were reorganized in principalities whose leaders struggled to carry on the old programs of kings, bishops, and monks; one of these lands, centred on the Paris-Orléans axis and later known as the Île-de-France, was the nucleus of a new dynastic kingdom of France. This kingdom may be spoken of as Capetian France (the first king of the new dynasty having been Hugh Capet), but it was not until the 13th century that this France came to approximate the modern nation in territorial extent. The emergence of a greater France as a social and cultural entity preceded the political expansion of Capetian France; already in the 12th century Crusaders, when speaking of "Franks" from Romance-speaking lands, meant something like "Frenchmen," while the persistence of old boundaries between populations of Romance and Germanic speech perpetuated the idea of a greater West Frankland.

FRENCH SOCIETY IN THE EARLY MIDDLE AGES

A foremost circumstance of the later 9th and the 10th century was the inability of the western Frankish Carolingian kings to keep order. The royal estates that had theretofore supported them, mostly in the north and east, were depleted through grants to retainers uncompensated by new acquisitions.

Hindered by poor communications, the kings lost touch with lesser counts and bishops, while the greater counts and dukes strove to forge regional clienteles in fidelity to themselves. These princes (as they were called) were not rebels. More often allied with the king than not, they exercised regalian powers of justice, command, and constraint; it was typically they who undertook to defend local settlements and churches from the ravages of Magyars invading from the east, of Muslims on Mediterranean coasts, and of Vikings from northern waters.

Of these invaders, the Northmen, as contemporaries called the Vikings, were the most destructive. They raided landed estates and monasteries, seizing provisions and movable wealth. Striking as far inland as Paris by 845, they attacked Bordeaux, Toulouse, Orléans, and Angers between 863 and 875. From a base in the Somme estuary, they pillaged Amiens, Cambrai, Reims, and Soissons. But they were drawn especially to the Seine valley. Between 856 and 860 they laid waste the country around its lower reaches and repeatedly attacked Paris thereafter. Sometimes they were turned back by defenses but more often by payments of tribute. After 896 the invaders began to settle permanently in the lower Seine valley, whence they spread west to form the duchy of Normandy. Maritime raiding continued into the 10th century, then subsided.

Lords such as the counts of Flanders, Paris, Angers, and Provence were well situated to prosper in the crisis. They were often descended from or related to Carolingian kings. Adding protectorates over churches to their inherited offices, domains, and fiefs while acquiring other lordships and counties through marriage, they built up principalities that were as precarious as they were powerful. The lords tried to avoid dismemberment of the patrimony by limiting their children's right of succession and marriage, but it was only in the 12th century that these dynastic principles came to prevail in the French aristocracy. The princes, moreover, found it almost as hard as the kings to secure their power administratively. They exploited their lands through servants valued less for competence than for fidelity; these servants, however, were men who tended to think of themselves as lords rather than agents. This tendency was especially marked among the masters of castles (castellans), who by the year 1000 were claiming the power to command and punish as well as the right to retain the revenues generated from the exercise of such power. In this way was completed a devolution of power from the undivided empire of the 9th century to a checkerboard of lordships in the 11th—lordships in which the control of castles was the chief determinant of success.

The devolution of power led to a fragmented polity; at every level lords depended on the services of sworn retainers who were usually rewarded with the tenures of lordship called fiefs (*feuda*). In the 9th century fiefs were not yet numerous enough to undermine the public order protected by kings and their delegates. Indeed, fiefs were at first rewards for public service made from fiscal (royal) lands; this practice persisted in the south into the 11th century. By then, however, castles, knights, and knights' fiefs were multiplying beyond all control, resulting in a fracturing of power that few princes succeeded in reversing before 1100. Counts were unwilling to admit that their counties were fiefs or that they owed the same sort of allegiance to kings or dukes as their vassals did to them. Tainted with servility as well as with the brutality of needy knights on the make, vassalage was slow to gain respectability. The multiplication of fiefs was a violent process of subjugating free peasants and abusing churches.

THE POLITICAL HISTORY OF FRANCE (*c.* 850–1180)

The fragmentation of political power resulting from the decline of the Carolingians meant that the kings of France were forced into rivalries, alliances, and conflicts with the princes, who were for many generations the real rulers of their territories. Even after a new dynasty, the Capetians, took over the crown in 987, it took several centuries before they were able to impose their authority on most of present-day France.

PRINCIPALITIES NORTH OF THE LOIRE

Outside the dynastic royal domain (centred around Paris) the foremost northern powers were Flanders, Normandy, Anjou, Brittany, Blois-Champagne, and Burgundy.

The northernmost of these was Flanders, whose founder, Baldwin I (Iron-Arm; reigned 862–879), managed not only to abduct the Carolingian king's daughter and marry her but also to win that king's approval as count of Ghent. His authority was consolidated under his son Baldwin II (879–918) and grandson Arnulf I (918–965), the latter a violent and ambitious prince who undertook to restore the Flemish church as if he were an emperor. Fertile and precocious in trading activity, Flanders became home to a dense network of prosperous cities and monasteries; monks at Saint-Bertin and Ghent celebrated the dynastic feats of the counts.

In the time of Robert I (the Frisian; 1071–93), efforts were made to systematize the count's lordship over castles as well as his fiscal rights, but the results fell short of giving the count effective sovereign power. When the foreign-born Charles the Good (1119–27) tried to pacify the county at the expense of lesser knightly families, he was murdered. Stability together with a new and centralized mode of fiscal accountancy was achieved by Thierry of Alsace (1128–68) and his son Philip (1163–91). Toward 1180 Flanders was a major power in northern France.

The duchy of Normandy was created in 911, when the Viking chieftain Rollo (Hrolf) accepted lands around Rouen and Evreux from King Charles III (the Simple). With its pastures, fisheries, and forests, this territory was a rich prize, and Rollo's successors extended their domination of it aggressively. Early Norman history, however, is more obscure than Flemish, lacking the records that only Christian clerics could write. The acquisitions of the second duke of Normandy, William I (Longsword; 927–942), were threatened when he was murdered by Arnulf I of Flanders in 942. It was only in the reign of his son Richard I (942–996) that something like administrative continuity based on succession to fiscal domains and control of the church was achieved. The dukes (as they then came to be styled) allied with the ascendant duke Hugh Capet had little to lose from the latter's accession to the kingship in 987; it was at this time that a new Norman aristocracy in ducal control took shape. Under Robert I (the Devil; 1027–35) agrarian and commercial prosperity favoured the multiplication of castellanies and knights, and Duke William II (1035–87; William the Conqueror) had to put down a dangerous rising of Norman barons and castellans in 1047 before proceeding, surely in deliberate consequence, to establish a firmly central control of castles that was without precedent in France. His conquest of England in 1066 made William the most powerful ruler in France. At the same time, knights from lesser elite families in Normandy were establishing territorial lordships in southern Italy.

Norman ducal lordship was crude but effective. Under Henry I (1106–35) a unified exploitation of patronage, castles, and revenues was developed for the kingdom of England and the duchy of Normandy alike. Normandy passed to Henry's son-in-law Count Geoffrey of Anjou in 1135 and to his grandson Henry II (1150–89), in whose time it became the heartland of an Angevin dynastic empire.

Anjou, in the lower Loire valley, was among the lands delegated to Robert the Strong in 866. In the 10th century a series of vigorous counts established a dynastic patrimony that expanded under the great Fulk III Nerra (987–1040) and his son Geoffrey Martel (1040–60) to include Maine and Touraine. Strategically situated, this principality prospered in its early times of external danger, but it was surrounded by aggressive dynasts; the control of castles and vassalic fidelities were the count's somewhat precarious means of power.

Brittany, to the west of Anjou and Normandy, was set apart by its strongly Celtic tradition. It achieved identity in the 9th century under the native leader Nomenoë, who seized Nantes and Rennes in defiance of Charles the Bald. His successors, badly battered by the Vikings, were recognized as dukes in the 10th century but were unable to consolidate their power over lesser counts and castellans. With little more than an unenvied independence, the duchy persisted into the 12th century, when a series of succession crises enabled King Henry II of England to subject it to the Plantagenet domains. Only after 1166 were the Bretons to feel the impact of systematic territorial administration.

The area around Blois, to the east of Touraine, had also been entrusted to Robert the Strong and remained in his family's hands until about 940, when Theobald I (the Old) seized control of it and founded a line of counts of Blois. His successors, notably the fearsome Eudes II (996–1037), annexed the counties of Sancerre (1015) and Champagne (1019–23), thereby creating a principality comparable in strength to Flanders and more threatening to the king, whose patrimonial domains it encircled. A dynastic aggregate lacking natural cohesion, Blois-Champagne achieved its greatest strength under Theobald IV (the Great; Theobald II of Champagne, 1125–52), who was a formidable rival of Kings Louis VI and Louis VII. The main lands were divided under his sons Theobald V (1152–91) and Henry (1152–81), themselves prestigious lords; and the Champagne of Henry the Liberal was among the richest, best organized, and most cultured French lands of its day.

Finally, there was Burgundy, to the south of Champagne (not to be confused with the old kingdom and the later imperial county of Burgundy), which first achieved princely identity under Richard the Justiciar (880–921). Defeating Magyars and Vikings as well as exploiting the rivalries of his neighbours, Richard was regarded (like his near contemporary Arnulf I of Flanders) as virtually a king. Ducal power was contested and diminished thereafter, but it survived as the patrimony of a Capetian family until 1361.

Thus, by the later 12th century, France north of the Loire consisted of several large principalities (some of them associated with the English crown) coexisting with each other and with the king, who struggled to impose his lordship on them.

THE PRINCIPALITIES OF THE SOUTH

South of the Loire emerged another set of lands: Provence, Auvergne, Toulouse, Barcelona, and Aquitaine.

Provence, lying in what is now the southeastern corner of France, was not part of the western Frankish domains. Included in the middle kingdom (Francia Media) from 843, it passed to the kings of Burgundy after 879 and to the emperors in the 11th century. But it was local counts once again who won prestige as defenders against pillagers, in this case the Muslims, and who profited from urban growth to establish a dynastic authority of their own. This authority was fractured in the early 12th century, when the houses of Barcelona and Toulouse secured portions by marriage; a cadet dynasty of Barcelona continued to rule the county until 1245.

The county of Barcelona, formed from a delegation of Frankish royal power in 878, came to dominate all other eastern Pyrenean counties in the 11th century. Prospering at the expense of the Muslims, Count Ramon Berenguer I (reigned 1035–76) reduced his castellans to submission (as did his contemporary William in Normandy). His great-grandson Ramon Berenguer

IV (1131–62) organized the strongest principality in the south. He and his successors acted as fully independent sovereigns, although the king of France retained a theoretical lordship over Barcelona until 1258.

Auvergne is the best example of a region whose masters failed to subordinate rival counts and castellans. A tradition of superior comital unity had survived in the claims of two related counts before their patrimonies were absorbed by the crown in the 13th century.

Toulouse had been a centre of delegated Frankish power from the 8th century, but its pretension to princely status dated from 924, when Raymond III Pons (924–after 944) added control of coastal Gothia to that of Toulouse and its hinterland. Dynastic continuity, here as elsewhere, however, was badly interrupted, and none of the succeeding counts were able to organize a coherent lordship. Raymond IV of Saint-Gilles (1093–1105) acquired the Crusader land of Tripoli (Syria), but he and his successors were weakened at home by conflicts with Barcelona and Aquitaine.

The duchy of Aquitaine might at first have seemed the most promising of all these principalities. A kingdom in the 9th century, it was reconstituted under William the Pious (died 926) and again, more imposingly, under William V (994/5–1029), who was acclaimed as one of the greatest rulers of his day and even offered the imperial crown in 1024. An advocate of religious reform, William sought to strengthen his control over Aquitaine by promoting alliances with the monasteries and imposing his will on lesser nobles. His efforts were not always successful, and he and his successors suffered reverses at the hands of the Angevin counts. In the 12th century the vast duchy was conveyed by the marriages of its heiress Eleanor successively to the kings of France and England.

Of these principalities, only Barcelona had achieved territorial cohesion and cultural unity by the later 12th century; it was then becoming known as Catalonia. The others, less toughened by external invasion and less resistant to the Cathari (or Albigensian) religious heresy from within, were vulnerable to an expanding Capetian monarchy.

THE MONARCHY

The kingdom of France was descended directly from the western Frankish realm ceded to Charles the Bald in 843. Not until 987 was the Carolingian dynastic line set aside, but there had been portentous interruptions. The reunited empire of Charles the Fat (reigned 884–888) proved unworkable: the Viking onslaught was then at its worst, and the king proved incapable of managing defenses, which fell naturally to the regional magnates. Among these was Eudes, son of that Robert the Strong to whom counties in the lower Loire valley had been delegated in 866. Eudes's resourceful defense of Paris against the Vikings in 885 contrasted starkly with Charles the Fat's failures, and in 887 the western Frankish magnates deposed

Charles and later elected Eudes king. In so doing, they bypassed an underage grandson of Charles the Bald, also named Charles, who was crowned at Reims in 893 with the support of the archbishop there. Although gaining undisputed title to the crown upon Eudes's death in 898 and imposing a crushing defeat on Rollo and forcing his conversion to Christianity before granting Normandy to the Viking leader, Charles the Simple was unable to recover the undivided loyalty of the nobility. He then sought to reward the service of lesser men but lost the crown in 922 to Eudes's brother Robert I, who was killed in battle against Charles in 923. Thereupon Robert's son-in-law Rudolf (Raoul of Burgundy) was elected king, and Charles the Simple was imprisoned, to die in captivity in 929. Yet, when Rudolf died in 936, the Robertian candidate for the crown, Robert's son Hugh the Great, stood aside for another Carolingian restoration in the person of Louis IV, son of Charles the Simple and called Louis d'Outremer ("Louis from Overseas") because he had been nurtured in England since his father's deposition. Louis IV acted energetically to revive the prestige of his dynasty, leaving the crown undisputed at his death in 954 to his son Lothar (954–986). But Lothar's dynastic resources were too seriously impaired to command the full allegiance of the magnates. When his son Louis V (986–987) died young, the magnates reasserted themselves to elect Hugh Capet king. This time, despite the survival of a Carolingian claimant,

Charles of Lorraine, the dynastic breach was permanent.

The election of 987 coincided with a more general crisis of power. The pillaging of Vikings gave way to that of castellans and knights; the inability of kings (of whatever family) to secure professions of fidelity and service from the mass of people in lands extending beyond a few counties shows how notions of personal loyalty and lordship were replacing that of public order. Just as castellans were freeing themselves from subordination to counts, so the monks claimed exemption from the supervision of bishops: in a famous case the bishop of Orléans was opposed by the learned Abbo of Fleury (died 1004). There was a new insistence on the virtue of fidelity—and on the sin of betrayal.

Hugh Capet (reigned 987–996) and his son Robert II (the Pious; 996–1031) struggled vainly to maintain the Carolingian solidarity of associated counts, bishops, and abbots; after about 1025 Robert and his successors were hardly more than crowned lords, and their protectorate was valued by few but the lesser barons and churches of the Île-de-France. Neither Henry I (1031–60) nor Philip I (1060–1108) could match the success (such as it was) of their rivals in Normandy and Flanders in subordinating castles and vassals to their purposes.

Yet even these relatively weak kings clung to their pretensions. They claimed rights in bishops' churches and monasteries far outside their immediate domain, which was concentrated around

Paris, Orléans, Compiègne, Soissons, and Beauvais. Henry I married a Russian princess, whose son was given the exotic name of Philip; and the choice of Louis, a Carolingian name, for Philip's son was even more obviously programmatic. Louis VI (1108–37) spent his reign reducing the robber barons of the Île-de-France to submission, thereby restoring respect for the king's justice; he worked cautiously to promote the royal suzerainty over princely domains. It was a sign of newly achieved prestige that he secured the heiress Eleanor of Aquitaine as a bride for his son Louis VII (1137–80). But Louis VI was less successful in border wars with Henry I of Normandy; these conflicts became more dangerous when, upon the failure of her first marriage, Eleanor married Henry II of Anjou, who came thereby to control lands in western France of much greater extent than the Capetian domains. Louis VII proved nonetheless a steady defender of his realm. He never relinquished his claim to lordship over the Angevin lands, and he allowed lesser men of his entourage the freedom to develop a more efficient control of his patrimonial estate. Not least, he fathered—belatedly, by Queen Adele of Champagne, his third wife, amid transports of relieved joy—the son who was to carry on the dynasty's work.

The early Capetian kings thus achieved the power of a great principality, such as Normandy or Barcelona, while harbouring the potential to reestablish a fully royal authority over the greater realm once ruled by Charles the Bald. The princes were their allies or their rivals; they sometimes did homage and swore fealty to the king, but they were reluctant to admit that their hard-won patrimonies were fiefs held of the crown. Royal lordship over peasants, townspeople, and church lands was for many generations a more important component of the king's power in France. It was exercised personally, not bureaucratically. The king's entourage, like those of the princes, replicated the old Frankish structure of domestic service. The seneschal saw to general management and provisioning, a function (like that of the mayors of the palace) with the potential to expand. The butler, constable, and chamberlain were also laymen, the chancellor normally a cleric. The lay officers were not agents in the modern sense; their functions (and incomes) were endowed rewards or fiefs, for which they seldom accounted and which they tended to claim as by hereditary right. In a notorious case, Stephen of Garland tried to claim the seneschalsy as his property and for a time even held three offices at once; but this abuse was soon remedied and taught caution to Louis VI and his successors. The chancellor drafted the king's decrees and privileges with increasing care and regularity. He or the chamberlain kept lists of fiscal tenants and their obligations on the lord-king's estates and in towns for use in verifying the service of provosts who collected the rents and profits of justice. But this service was hardly less exploitative than that of the household officers; the royal domain lagged behind the princely ones of Flanders and Normandy in the imposition of accountability on its servants. The abbot Suger of Saint-Denis (died 1151), once a provost on his monastery's domains, was instrumental in furthering administrative conceptions of power in the court of Louis VII.

ECONOMY, SOCIETY, AND CULTURE IN THE MIDDLE AGES (c. 900–1300)

The breakdown of royal authority in the 10th century coincided with the beginning of a long era of population growth and economic expansion. Population had fallen sharply after the end of the Roman Empire, not only because of the period's political disruptions but because of a series of epidemics and other disasters. Farming methods in the Merovingian and Carolingian periods were primitive and crop yields too low to permit any recovery.

ECONOMIC EXPANSION

As early as 800 and more dramatically after 950, improved climatic conditions, the disappearance of deadly diseases, and the development of improved agricultural techniques set the stage for the development of a new, more prosperous civilization. All indicators suggest growth—e.g., expansion of old towns, founding of new villages, the rising price of land—but no exact measurements are possible. A register of hearths, tallied for tax purposes, dating from 1328 has been estimated variously to point to a total

population of 15 million to 22 million; the total, not much below the figure for the end of Louis XIV's reign in 1715, was probably slightly reduced after a crest toward the end of the 13th century. By the 1280s large portions of France had enjoyed many years of relative security and prosperity, even though private warfare had not disappeared, despite royal prohibitions. Brigandage seems actually to have worsened in the south about 1200. The ravages and massacres of the Albigensian Crusade, the 13th-century war against the "Good Men," or Cathar heretics, made Languedoc an insecure southern frontier for still another generation. Though it eventually stamped out this heresy, the harsh response of the Inquisition, beginning in the 1230s, apparently did not seriously disrupt urban or rural prosperity.

The broad tendencies of social change were in keeping with political and institutional progress. The conjugal family gained in importance: Roman and especially canon law favoured its authority over the wider solidarities of clan or kin (extended family); rulers made the hearth a basis of fiscal responsibility. The growing population remained overwhelmingly agrarian, but changes in farming practices made their efforts more efficient. The clearing of new lands and more flexible schemes of crop rotation and improved technology, such as better yokes and horse collars that allowed draft animals to pull plows that could effectively till the heavy soils of northern France, led to better harvests.

The spread of water-powered mills to grind grain allowed an improvement in diet, as bread replaced gruel. The diet was further improved by the greater cultivation of private gardens, which produced protein-rich legumes and green leafy vegetables. The social condition of the peasantry also changed. Outright slavery, common in earlier periods, tended to disappear. Some peasants retained their independence, as in the Massif Central and the Pyrenees, although they were not necessarily better off than serfs in more prosperous regions. Most peasants were organized in subjection to lords—bishops, abbots, counts, barons, or knights—whose estates assumed diverse forms. In northern France lords typically reserved the proceeds of a domain worked by tenants, who had their own parcels of land to live on. Lords were not simply landowners, however. They were also able to extract a variety of dues and labour services from their tenants, to compel them to use the lord's mill, oven, and winepress, and to bring their legal disputes to the lord's court. The income from these dues and services was often more important to local lords than the rents they collected.

URBAN PROSPERITY

Increasing productivity stimulated trade, the improvement of roads and bridges, and the growth of towns, as well as competition for the profits of agrarian lordship. After about 1050, townspeople, especially merchants, sought to free themselves from the arbitrary lordship of counts and bishops, usually peaceably, as at Saint-Omer, but occasionally in violent uprisings, as at Le Mans and Laon. Town life continued to flourish. A few places, favoured by political, ecclesiastical, and economic circumstances, grew far larger than the rest. Paris could probably count close to 200,000 inhabitants by the late 13th century, and some great provincial centres—e.g., Toulouse, Bordeaux, Arras, Rouen—may have surpassed 25,000, but most of the older cities grew more modestly. Jewish communities, which existed almost everywhere, were especially important in the towns of Champagne and Languedoc. Emigration from the countryside probably increased as peasants sought better opportunities and independence, yet the towns remained somewhat indistinct in appearance and activity from their rural surroundings. Many urban properties had agrarian attachments, often within the walls; Paris itself was, to a surprising extent, an aggregation of expanded villages. Nevertheless, the progress of commerce, together with an important ancillary development of industry, chiefly accounts for medieval urban prosperity.

The trades not only grew in volume but also became more diversified and specialized. New markets, often regional in nature, arose to supplement the older centres that had developed on the basis of the long-distance exchange of relatively high-priced imperishables. Regional markets featured agrarian staples such as grains and wines as well as animals, cloth, weapons, and tools, and they facilitated the introduction of foreign goods, such as glassware and spices. An increasing reliance on coinage or on monetary values may be connected with these provincial trades; sensitivity to the intrinsic values of the many French coinages was increasing everywhere toward 1200, even in the hinterlands away from main trading routes. In the late 13th century the need for money in denominations larger than the age-old penny (denarius)—primarily for use in the great commercial centres—caused Louis IX (reigned 1226–70) to issue the *gros tournois* (worth 12 pennies) and the gold coin (which, however, had little importance before the 14th century). A gradual long-term inflation tended to favour commercial activity.

The towns of northern France, notably in Artois, Burgundy, the Île-de-France, and especially Champagne, prospered not only from regional exchange but also from the great overland trade flows connecting Normandy, England, the Baltic, and the Low Countries with the cities of Italy. The fairs of Champagne, becoming the leading entrepôt of European merchants, reached their apogee in the 13th century. Favoured by the count's privilege, the traders operated at Lagny, Bar-sur-Aube, or—in greater numbers—Provins and at the "warm fair" of Troyes in June; the "cold fair" of Troyes ended the yearly cycle in October. The fairs were designated as occasions for payment and repayment, contributing significantly to the progress of banking and business accounting.

Enlarged and more diversified demand encouraged urban growth and prosperity. Townsmen were eating better: in the north, at least, the per capita consumption of meat, butter, and cheese, as well as of spices, seems to have increased by the 13th century. As for wine, not only was more being drunk but the taste for *vins de qualité* became more acute, and the great regional vintages, notably that of Gascony, were established. Townspeople furnished their houses more amply than in the past (lamps, wooden chests, and draperies came into common use), and they produced more articles themselves.

The progress of industry, in fact, was a remarkable feature of the period. Crafts in metal, wood, leather, and glass expanded in such large towns as Paris. Cloth work—weaving, dyeing, fulling—prospered in regional centres such as Toulouse, with specialities in fine cloths concentrated in Artois and Flanders. In most places, however, the crafts remained in the shadow of commercial enterprise, in which greater fortunes continued to be made. Artisanal associations proliferated everywhere; often termed brotherhoods (*confratria, confraternitas*), they fostered new urban and suburban solidarities for charitable and ceremonial purposes as well as for the promotion of economic interests.

Urban society became more competitive and more stratified. At Lyon, Bordeaux, and elsewhere, some fortunes were established enough, usually from commerce, to enable their possessors to live as landlords, build stone houses, buy rural property, and aspire to titles of nobility. This patriciate—despite occasional setbacks at the hands of "new men," a rising class of administrators chosen over men of high birth for their expertise in politics—dominated municipal governments, acting as mayors and magistrates (*échevins*) in the north or as consuls in the south. While not altogether self-serving—they supported civic projects such as the building or decorating of churches—they were disinclined to share power. Below them, often as their tenants or debtors, were small entrepreneurs, middlemen in trade (or between local industry and regional trade), master craftsmen, and bankers; and below all— and increasingly restive—was a swelling class of impoverished artisans, servants, vagabonds, and beggars.

RURAL SOCIETY

Rural life changed more gradually. The expanding markets favoured well-endowed or efficient lords or peasants who could produce a surplus of goods for sale. Such conditions were less common in the south than in the north, although they could be found in most wine-producing areas. But, while rising prices benefited producers, they contributed to certain difficulties in the countryside. Fixed revenues in coin proved an unsatisfactory alternative to payments in kind, which landlords specified when new land was put under cultivation. Moreover, needs and tastes became more expensive and tended to exceed aristocratic resources; lavish generosity continued to be an admired and practiced virtue, and costly Crusades—occasionally lapsing into speculative adventures—regularly attracted noblemen after the end of the 11th century. Larger lordships began to employ salaried estate managers, while in the south the division of landed fortunes among numerous heirs resulted in a multiplied and impoverished petty nobility. Many rural landlords fell into debt in the 13th century. And, as wealth and nobility became less correlated, some nobles, especially those who were financially hard-pressed, sought to close ranks against the intrusion of new men or creditors. They insisted on noble birth as a condition for knighthood, reserving the designation of "squire" (or *donzel*, in the south) for those of noble birth awaiting or postponing the expensive dubbing (*adoubement*). At the upper extreme, a noble elite, the barons, achieved recognition in administration and law.

Peasant societies also became stratified. Men unable to set aside a surplus against times of famine and those who had to borrow or rent their tools or teams found it difficult to avoid dependence on other men. In some areas serfdom was renewed, or confirmed, as jurists interpreted the more stringent types of peasant obligation in the light of the revived Roman law of slavery. But here again economic and legal status did not necessarily coincide. Rich peasants who employed other men to drive their teams could be found in any village; such people as the mayor, the lord's provost, and the peasant creditor established themselves as a rural elite, whose resources insured them against calamity and opened up diverse opportunities in prospering regional economies. Where enfranchisement occurred, the lord usually received a good payment; even when servility persisted, there was a tendency to commute the arbitrary tallage into fixed common sums. New villages continued to be established, especially in the south, where many previously existent communities of peasants also received charters of elementary liberties in the 13th and early 14th centuries.

These conditions notwithstanding, the manor, or *seigneurie*, resisted fragmentation. The favourable market for grain and the psychological attachment of lords to their fathers' possessions preserved demesne land (for use by leasehold, not freehold, tenants) as the chief source of seigneurial income through the 13th century. The lords also continued to require the services of labourers, although the shortfall increased between work owed and work needed. Accordingly, lords resorted to paid seasonal labour, so that the margin between profit and loss became a more critical calculation than in the past. A new alternative was to lease the demesne to paid managers or sharecroppers, but this practice spread more slowly in France than in neighbouring countries. Whether lords had demesnes and servile tenants or not, the association

between landlordship and power remained close. Tenancies or properties smaller than the grand old residences known as manses appeared everywhere but especially in the north, where horsepower and three-field crop rotations were making possible more productive agriculture. The burgeoning viticultures of Burgundy and Gascony proved incompatible with traditional demesne lordship and encouraged sharecropping and peasant initiative. Innovation was less common in the uplands of the centre and south, where the manse tended to retain its identity and fiscal utility.

RELIGIOUS AND CULTURAL LIFE

The Christian church was badly disrupted by the invasions of the 800s and early 900s as well as by the rise of the local strongmen that accompanied the invasions. In Normandy five successive bishops of Coutances resided at Rouen, far from their war-torn district, which had converted to paganism under the Vikings. Elsewhere standards of clerical deportment declined, threatening the moral leadership with which Carolingian prelates had supported public order. Renewal came in two influential forms.

First, monks in Burgundy and Lorraine were independently inspired to return to a strict observance of the Benedictine rule and thereby to win the adherence of laypeople anxious to be saved. The monastery of Cluny, one centre of reform, was founded in 910 by William I (the Pious), a duke of

Aquitaine with a bad conscience; dedicated to Saints Peter and Paul, it thus came under the protection of the pope. The Cluniac reform, whose influence gradually radiated beyond Cluny and encouraged reforms in other monastic houses, stressed independence from lay control, opposed simony and clerical marriage, and practiced an elaborate routine of liturgical prayer. In the 11th century Cluny came to direct an order of affiliated monasteries that extended throughout France and beyond. Cluny's religious hegemony was challenged only in the 12th century with the rise of a yet more ascetic Benedictine observance, of which St. Bernard of Clairvaux (1090–1153) was the great proponent. Centred at Cîteaux (Latin Cistercium, whence the appellation Cistercian) in Burgundy, this movement combined ascetic severity with introspective spirituality and economic self-sufficiency. A newly personal devotionalism was diffused from monastic cloisters into lay society.

Second, the bishops, in the absence of royal leadership, renewed Carolingian sanctions against violence. The Peace of God was instituted in synods of southern France in the late 10th and early 11th centuries. Solemnized in relic processions and oaths and supported by large crowds of the laity, it was an effort to restrain the increasing number of knights from violating the traditional rights of peasants and churches. It was supplemented from the 1020s by the Truce of God, which forbade fighting on certain days or during particular seasons of the year and which helped to mold a new conception of the knight as a Christian warrior prohibited from shedding the blood of other Christians. These movements were warmly embraced by the Cluniac pope Urban II when he preached the First Crusade at the Council of Clermont in 1095, which resembled the Peace councils earlier in the century. The ideals and reforms of the Peace and Truce of God contributed to a new understanding of knighthood as an honourable estate of Christian leadership. When young princes were dubbed to knighthood in the 12th century, they assumed a mode of respectability fashioned by the church; this eased the way for lesser knights to be recognized as nobles as well.

Scholars such as Gerbert of Aurillac, the future pope Sylvester II, were forced to wander from city to city in the pursuit of learning (Gerbert had to travel to Spain to study advanced mathematics); nevertheless, the growing wealth and stability of regional societies, such as those in Burgundy, Flanders, and Normandy, encouraged new impulses in the arts and letters. Cathedral schools revived the traditional curriculum of learning, stressing reading, writing, speaking, and computation. Fulbert of Chartres (c. 960–1028) was fondly remembered as a humane teacher by students who often became teachers themselves. A century later, famous masters could be found at Laon and Paris as well as (probably) at Chartres, attracting young clerics to their lectures in swelling numbers. The Breton Peter Abelard (1079–1142) taught and wrote so brilliantly on logic, faith, and ethics that he established Paris's reputation for academic excellence. His famous correspondence with his beloved Héloïse reveals the emerging humanism in 12th-century letters, demonstrating a knowledge of Classical authors and depth of emotion characteristic of the age. Traditional pursuits of contemplative theology and history gave way to new interests in logic and law. Men trained in canon and Roman law found their way increasingly into the service of kings, princes, and bishops.

Everywhere churches were built in Romanesque style, and they continued to be built in the south long after some architects, such as Suger at Saint-Denis in the 1140s, introduced the new aesthetic of Gothic style, a distinctive French innovation. Lay culture found expression in vernacular epics, such as *La Chanson de Roland* (*The Song of Roland*) in Old French, and in the Provençal lyrics of southern France. These poems are witness to diverse zones of linguistic evolution from spoken Latin; by the 12th century the *langue d'oïl* (Old French) north of the Loire was broadly differentiated from the *langue d'oc* (Occitan, or Provençal, language) to the south. The cultural cleavage so marked ran deeper than language and was not entirely overcome by the spread of modern French, descended from the *langue d'oïl*, into the south.

At the same time that society and the church underwent reform and expansion, they also faced the first expressions of popular heresy since late antiquity. In the early 11th century, episodes of heresy occurred in Aquitaine, Arras, Orléans, and Vertus. The heretics, possibly influenced by foreign missionaries and certainly reacting against the abuses of the church and failures of reform, rejected the church and its sacraments, abstained from sexual intercourse and eating meat, and lived pious lives. By the mid-11th century the church had successfully repressed the heretics, burning a dozen or so at Orléans under order of the king. Heresy disappeared until the early 12th century, when a number of heretical leaders, such as Peter of Bruys and Henry of Lausanne, developed large followings in various cities. These leaders, again reacting to the flaws of the church and inadequacies of reform, rejected the church, its ministers, and its sacraments and advocated lives of simple piety in imitation of the Apostles.

THE AGE OF CATHEDRALS AND SCHOLASTICISM

Religious faith began to assume a new coloration after 1000 and evolved along those lines in the 11th and 12th centuries. Whether in the countryside or in town, a new, more evangelical Christianity emerged that emphasized the human Jesus over the transcendent Lord. The Crusading impulse was kept alive in France by the desire to vindicate the true faith against Muslim infidels and Byzantine schismatics. More intense Christian faith was also reflected in hostility toward France's Jewish communities. As early as 1010 Jews had

THE ALBIGENSIAN CRUSADE

The Albigensian Crusade was called by Pope Innocent III against the heretical Cathari of southern France. The war, which lasted from 1209 to 1229, pitted the nobility of northern France against that of southern France, and it eventually involved the king of France who established his authority over the south. The Crusade ended with the Treaty of Paris (1229), which took away the independence of the southern princes and largely destroyed the culture of Provence. The Crusade caused much devastation and injustice, which Innocent came to regret, but did not bring about the extirpation of the Albigensian heresy (named for its center in the town of Albi, France). The heresy lingered on into the 13th–14th centuries and became the object of the Inquisition.

suffered persecution and were forced to choose between conversion or exile. Anti-Jewish sentiment grew during the next two centuries and led to further offenses. Expelled from royal territories by Philip II Augustus in 1182, Jews were readmitted in 1198 but suffered further persecutions, including a formal condemnation of the Talmud under Louis IX. Philip IV (the Fair) renewed the policy of expulsion in 1306.

The church was not always in a position to satisfy the religious demands of the population, however. The regular clergy could no longer be relied upon to set standards of piety and penitence; their observance was either too relaxed or too severe to suit the new conditions brought on by a rising population and the growth of towns. The canonical movement of the later 12th century produced a secular clergy that could respond to the needs of the laity in ways that the traditional monastic orders could not. The Cistercian order, even though it continued to

expand, was incapable of sustaining its ascetic impulse completely; its houses, as well as those of the older Benedictines, were often remote from the new population centres. Nor was the higher secular clergy much better situated to fulfill pastoral obligations. The bishop was by now remote from his flock, acting usually as diocesan supervisor, judge, or lord; his subordinates—the archdeacon and cathedral canons—likewise functioned primarily as administrators. Archbishops were required by the fourth Lateran Council (1215) to hold annual synods of provincial clergy, a ruling that—although imperfectly observed—probably contributed to some strengthening of discipline.

Failure to improve the standards of parish ministry or respond fully to changing social conditions left the door open for the spread of heretical sects. The critical reform was that of the parish ministry. When emphatic measures to improve the education and supervision of priests were adopted in the fourth Lateran Council, it was already too late in France. For most of the 12th century, the same evangelical impulses that led to the reforms of the orders of canons and monks also contributed to anticlericalism and doctrinal heresy, especially in the towns and villages of the east and south. There was a suspicion that sinning priests could not be trusted to mediate God's grace effectively, and the virtue of poverty as an antidote to the worldly cupidity of a prospering society was attractive to many.

The merchant Valdes (Peter Waldo), who gave up his property and family in the 1170s, took it upon himself to preach in the vernacular to his fellow townsfolk of Lyon. Although he gained the pope's approval for his lifestyle, Valdes did not receive the right to preach. Nonetheless, he and his followers—"the Poor" or "Poor Men"—continued to do so and were condemned by the church, which drove them to more extreme positions on doctrine and practice. Despite strong opposition from the church, the Waldensian movement spread to southern towns, and small groups of adherents were found in Europe through modern times.

Another heretical movement, that of the "Good Men," or Cathars (Albigenses), posed an even stronger threat to religious orthodoxy. Flourishing in the hill towns and villages between Toulouse and Béziers, the Cathars were dualists. They taught, among other things, that the material world was created by the Devil, that Christ did not assume the flesh but only appeared to, and that the church and its sacraments were the Devil's work. In stark contrast to the often ignorant and worldly Catholic clergy, the Cathar elite, the *perfecti*, lived rigorously ascetic lives.

For this challenge, the secular clergy of Languedoc were no match. To establish an effective counterministry of learned and respectable men, the pope deputed Cistercians to Languedoc; they were soon succeeded by St. Dominic, who spent a decade as mendicant preacher in Languedoc. In 1217, with his order of preachers recognized by the bishop of Toulouse and confirmed by the pope, Dominic set out with his fellow friars to work in the wider world "by word and example."

Meanwhile, the murder of the legate Peter of Castelnau (1208) had stirred Innocent III to promote a Crusade against the heretics of Languedoc. Led by Simon de Montfort, northern barons attacked towns in the viscounty of Béziers and later in the county of Toulouse with singular fury. The Albigensian Crusade brought the south under northern subjection, as massacres and the establishment of a papal Inquisition (1233) eventually drove the Cathars into exile in Italy or back to Catholicism. The Inquisition, which spread to many parts of France, was usually entrusted to Dominicans; it relied on the active pursuit of suspects, secret testimony, and—in case of conviction and obstinacy—delivery of the heretic to the "secular arm" for capital punishment.

Like the Dominicans, the Franciscans had spectacular success in a variety of endeavours. Highly organized, with provincial and international administrative institutions, both orders had houses in Paris by 1220, and their members were soon working everywhere in France. Becoming preachers and confessors, they also secured chaplaincies, inspectorships, and professorships as their initiatives in piety, probity, and learning were recognized. Conflict with the secular priesthood naturally resulted; the seculars attempted unsuccessfully to exclude the mendicants from the ministry of sacraments and inveighed against conventual endowments that seemed to contradict the friars' professions of poverty. Despite this conflict, the friars, women's orders such as the Poor Clares, and similar groups such as the Beguines stimulated a more active piety among laypeople, encouraging charitable works and foundations, private devotions, and penitential reading.

CULTURE AND LEARNING

Literacy and elementary learning became more widespread after 1000. Indeed, the growth in literacy was heralded by the heresy of Vilgard of Ravenna, who, according to Radulfus Glaber, was betrayed by demons in the guise of Virgil and other ancient writers in the late 10th century. By the later 11th and the 12th century, cathedral schools had emerged as centres of learning, and literacy had become an increasingly important tool of government. A form of Christian humanism took shape in the 12th century that was expressed in the letters of John of Salisbury and others. The courtly tastes of the 12th century, while not obliterated, were overtaken by a more flexible and ironic sensibility evident in vernacular ballads, fables, satires, and moralizing literature, most popular in the northern towns. The burgher or knight began to take a keen interest in the tangible world about him. The taste for clarity, proportion, and articulation reached mature expression in the great Gothic cathedrals of northern France, such as those in Amiens, Paris (Notre-Dame), and Reims. Architectural innovations—the pointed arch and the flying buttress—allowed the construction of soaring naves and walls pierced by large windows filled with the exquisite stained glass that was a great technological achievement of the period. And the taste for order is illustrated by the reorganization of masters, students, and studies as *studia generalia* (or universities). Montpellier became a leading centre of medical learning, and Toulouse (founded in 1229 to prepare clerics to combat heresy) and Orléans were noted for law. Paris remained preeminent among the early universities; its famous schools became associated as the faculties of arts, canon law, medicine, and theology, gaining jurisdictional independence under papal protection by 1231.

During the same years, philosophical doctrines in conflict with Christian orthodoxy began to trouble the theologians as translations of the metaphysical and scientific works of Aristotle and his commentators reached Paris. For a time the teaching of Aristotle was prohibited there, but by midcentury, when some of the "artists" who had been most attracted to the new philosophy were advancing to theological degrees, efforts were made to incorporate Aristotelian learning in enlarged summaries of Christian knowledge. The *Summa theologiae* (1266–72) by the Italian Thomas Aquinas was the greatest synthesis of this type. Its serene power breathes no hint of the controversies in which its author was involved. St. Thomas had taken his theological degree, together with St. Bonaventure, in 1257, when the secular masters were bitterly disputing the friars' privileges within the university. In the end the Dominicans and Franciscans each retained a chair on condition of submitting to university regulations. Thomas's work, however, came under suspicion. A reaction set in against the arts faculty's increasing disposition to take a naturalistic view of all reality. When Étienne Tempier, the bishop of Paris, condemned some philosophical principles as "error" in 1270 and 1277, the repercussions were so sweeping as to render even Thomas suspect.

Thomas's synthesis was to have no immediate imitators. Nevertheless, the social consequences of the emergence of academic learning in the 12th and 13th centuries were profound; it created new estates of professional men—lawyers, notaries, trained clerks, and physicians, many of them laymen—whose rational and legalist outlook became firmly rooted in French culture.

The dogmatic condemnations of the 1270s were symptomatic. Prosperity and confidence were shaken in many ways in the late 13th century. The papacy, hitherto a support for progressive causes, found itself discredited after its fiasco in a Crusade against Aragon. While the removal of the papal court to Avignon in the time of Clement V created a new centre of patronage for arts and letters, it did little to arrest the waning prestige of the church. The burdens of renewed warfare increased social tensions in the towns and depressed civic enterprise; the Jews had their assets confiscated before being expelled in 1306, and the Lombard bankers suffered like treatment in 1311. Economic indicators—while few and difficult to interpret—are generally held to suggest growing difficulties in many parts of France. The business of the fairs of Champagne was falling off by 1300, if not before, while records of Normandy reveal declining agrarian revenues in the half-century after 1260. Some regions were "saturated" with people: their existent economic technology could no longer sustain growth. Probably the population was already leveling off, if not yet decreasing, when, from 1315 to 1317, crop failures and famine caused serious disruption.

THE CAPETIAN AND VALOIS DYNASTIES

In 987 the Carolingian dynasty was replaced by a new ruling family, the Capetian dynasty. This line of kings would rule France until 1328 and would restore royal authority throughout the kingdom. In the 11th century Capetian kings gradually built up power and extended their authority outside of Paris. In the 12th and 13th centuries they strengthened the monarchy through war and marriage alliances. Through such actions, the Capetian kings laid the foundation of the French nation-state.

THE KINGS AND THE ROYAL GOVERNMENT

The age of Gothic cathedrals and Scholastic theology was also an age of splendour for the French monarchy. Royal authority was greatly strengthened by Louis VII's successor, Philip II (Augustus; reigned 1180–1223), who could claim descent from Charlemagne through his mother. Philip proved to be the ablest Capetian yet to reign. He was practical and clear-sighted in his political objectives; the extension of territorial power and the improvement of mechanisms with which to govern an expanded realm were his consistent policies. Perhaps it was not accidental that royal documents began to refer to the "king of France" (*rex Franciae*) instead of using the customary formula "king of the Franks" (*rex Francorum*) within a year or two of Philip's accession.

PHILIP AUGUSTUS

Philip's outstanding achievement was to wrest control from the Plantagenets of most of the domains they held in France. Intervening in struggles between Henry II of England and his sons, Philip won preliminary concessions in 1187 and 1189. He acquired strategic lands on the Norman borders following wars with Henry's sons, King Richard and King John (1196 and 1200). And, when in 1202 John failed to answer a summons to the vassalic court of his lord, Philip Augustus confiscated his fiefs. Normandy fell to the Capetian in 1204. Maine, Anjou, and Touraine fell rapidly (1204–06), leaving only Aquitaine and a few peripheral domains in the contested possession of England. By the Truce of Chinon (September 18, 1214), John recognized the conquests of Philip Augustus and renounced the suzerainty of Brittany, although the complete submission of Poitou and Saintonge was to take another generation.

Philip's other acquisitions of territory, if less spectacular, were no less important for consolidating the realm. In the north he pressed the royal authority to the border of Flanders. Artois, which came under his control as a dowry with his first wife, was fully secured in 1212. Vermandois and Valois (1213) and the counties of Beaumont-sur-Oise and Clermont-en-Beauvais were annexed during his last years. On the southern limits of the Île-de-France Philip rounded out prior possessions in Gâtinais and Berry. Much of Auvergne, whose suzerainty had been ceded by Henry II in 1189, passed to royal control in 1214, while in the more distant south Philip extended his influence by gaining lordship over Tournon, Cahors, Gourdon, and Montlaur in Vivarais. As the reign ended, only Brittany, Flanders,

Champagne, Burgundy, and Toulouse, among principalities later annexed, lay outside the royal domain. At the end of Philip's reign, rising concern about the heretical stance of the Albigenses set the stage for the Albigensian Crusade and later conquest of southern lands.

Because the territorial expansion was accomplished through traditional means—dynastic, feudal, and military— the curial administration was, outwardly, little changed. Household officers such as the butler and the constable continued to function as in the past. But Philip Augustus was even more suspicious of the seneschalship and chancellorship than his father had been; he allowed both offices to fall vacant early in his reign, entrusting their operations to lesser nobles or to clerics of the entourage. Although their activity is obscure, some of these men were beginning to specialize in justice or finance. The curia as such, however, remained undifferentiated; characteristically, the committee of regents, appointed in 1190 to hold three courts yearly while the king was absent on Crusade, was expected to concern itself with both justice and the administration of the kingdom on those occasions. Prelates and nobles of the curia also served as counselors; enlarged councils convened, at the king's summons, on festivals or when major political or military issues were contemplated.

Philip Augustus acted vigorously to improve the efficiency of his lordship. He was, indeed, practically the founder of royal administration in France. His chancery began to keep better records of royal activities. Documents were copied into registers before being sent out, and lists of churches, vassals, and towns were drawn up to inform the king of his military and fiscal rights. These lists replaced others lost on the battlefield of Fréteval (1194), a disaster that may have hastened the adoption of a new form of fiscal accountancy. One may draw this conclusion because it is unlikely that the Capetians had previously troubled to record the balances of revenues and expenses in the form first revealed by a record of the year 1202. Its central audit was connected with other efforts to improve control of the domains dominated directly by the king. From early in his reign Philip appointed members of his court to hold periodic local sessions, to collect extraordinary revenues, to lead military contingents, and to supervise the provosts. The new officers, called bailiffs (*baillis*), at first had no determined districts in which to serve (they resembled the circuit commissioners of Angevin government, whose office may have been the model for the Capetian institution). From the outset the bailiffs were paid salaries; they were more reliable than the provosts, who by the later 12th century generally farmed the revenues. In the newly acquired lands of the west and south, Philip and his successors instituted seneschals—functionaries similar to the bailiffs but with recognized territorial jurisdiction from the start.

Philip Augustus's policy toward his conquered domains was shrewd.

He retained the deep-rooted customs and administrative institutions of such flourishing provinces as Anjou and Normandy; indeed, the superior fiscal procedures of Normandy soon exercised perceptible influence on Capetian accounting elsewhere. On the other hand, to secure the loyal operation of provincial institutions, Philip appointed men of his own court, typically natives of the Île-de-France. It was a compromise that was to work well for generations to come.

The character of Philip's rule may likewise be deduced from his relations with the main classes of the population. A devoted son of the church, if not unswervingly faithful, he favoured the higher clergy in many of their interests. He opposed the infidels, heretics, and blasphemers; he supported the bishops of Laon, Beauvais, Sens, and Le Puy (among others) in their disputes with townspeople; and he granted and confirmed charters to monasteries and churches. Yet he was more insistent on his rights over the clergy than his predecessors had been. He required professions of fidelity and military service from bishops and abbots, summoned prelates to his court, and sought to limit the jurisdiction of ecclesiastical courts. He supported papal policies or submitted to papal directives only to the extent that these were consistent with his temporal interests. Cases in point were his reserved support of Crusades and his notorious rejection of Queen Ingeborg, whom he married, abandoned, and then, in response to the pope's censure, feigned to reconcile.

Toward the lay aristocracy, Philip Augustus acted energetically as suzerain and protector. Indeed, no Capetian was more fully the "feudal monarch." His war with John resulted from John's refusal to appear at court as a vassal of the French king to answer for his mistreatment of the count of La Marche. He regarded Flanders and Toulouse as well as Normandy as fiefs held by the crown. As with ecclesiastical vassals, Philip insisted upon the service due from fiefs, and he required his vassals to reserve their fealty for him alone. He extended his influence by entering into treaties (*pariages*) with minor lords, often distant ones; and, by confirming the acts of nobles in unprecedented numbers, he recovered the force of the royal guarantee.

The policy toward the lesser rural and urban populations was to increase their loyalty and contribution to the crown without significantly reducing their dependence on the king and other lords. Philip offered his protection to exploited villages, and, especially during his early years, he confirmed existing "new towns," extended their privileges to other villages, and otherwise favoured peasant communities. Townsmen, notably those in semiautonomous communes, gained confirmation of their charters; and the king created some new communes. Most of the latter were located in strategic proximity to the northern frontiers of the expanded royal domain; this fact, together with the obligations of service and payment specified in the charters, suggests that military motives were paramount in these foundations. More generally evident in these charters, as in others, was the desire to gain the political fidelity of a prospering class. At Paris Philip Augustus acted as did no other local lord to promote the civic interest, improving sanitation, paving streets, and building a new wall. Parisian burghers financed and administered these projects; they were associated in the fiscal supervision of the realm when the king went on Crusade, but they were not favoured with a communal charter.

LOUIS VIII

The reign of Louis VIII (1223–26) had an importance out of proportion to its brevity. It was he (this frail husband of the formidable Blanche of Castile and father of famous sons) who first brought Languedoc under the crown of France and who inaugurated the appanages— grants of patrimonial land to members of the royal family or royal favourites that reverted to the crown if their holders died without heirs—thereby creating a familial condominium through which the expanded France of later generations was to be governed. The conquest of Languedoc, following the Albigensian Crusade (against heretics in southern France) that was only tepidly supported by Philip Augustus, was not complete until the 1240s, but the royal seneschalsies of

Beaucaire and Carcassonne were already functioning when Louis VIII died. And it was in keeping with that ruler's will of 1225 that the great appanages passed to his younger sons as they came of age—Artois to Robert in 1237; Poitou, Saintonge, and Auvergne to Alphonse in 1241; and Anjou and Maine to Charles in 1246.

LOUIS IX

The real successor to Philip Augustus, however, was his grandson, Louis IX (reigned 1226–70), in whose reign were fulfilled some of the grand tendencies of prior Capetian history.

Louis IX, who was canonized in 1297, is the best-known Capetian ruler. He impressed all who came in touch with him, and the records of his reign—anecdotal and historical as well as official—leave no doubt that he commanded affection and respect in a combination and to an extent that were unique. He regarded himself as a Christian ruler, duty-bound to lead his people to salvation. He led by example, precept, and correction. He earned a reputation for fairness and wisdom that enabled him to rule as absolutely as he wished; only with the Crusade, perhaps, did his judgment falter. His reign was marked by consolidation, maturation, and reform rather than by innovation.

In his early years baronial revolts, supported by Henry III of England, were put down by the regency, headed by the queen mother, with singular firmness and skill. Poitou and Saintonge remained restive largely because of the stubborn machinations of Isabella of Angoulême (King John's widow); it was only in 1243, after a revolt planned to coincide with an uprising in Languedoc, that the adjudication of 1202 was fulfilled in Aquitaine. The revolt of Raymond Trencavel, dispossessed heir to the viscounty of Béziers, halfheartedly supported by Raymond VII of Toulouse, was no more successful; its failure resulted in the vindictive destruction of the petty nobility of Languedoc, and many fiefs thereupon passed to the crown. In 1239 a childless count of Mâcon sold his domains to the king.

Such were the principal territorial acquisitions of Louis IX; the balance of his work, however, was to be affected further by three characteristic events. First, despite his victory of 1243, Louis remained disposed to compromise with Henry III; in the Treaty of Paris (December 1259) Henry regained title to lands and reversionary rights in Guyenne in exchange for renouncing all claims to Normandy, Anjou, Maine, Touraine, and Poitou. Similarly, by the Treaty of Corbeil (May 1258) Louis himself had abandoned ancient claims to Catalonia and Roussillon in exchange for the renunciation of Barcelona's rights in Gévaudan and Rouergue. Meanwhile, upon the death of Raymond VII in 1249, the county of Toulouse had passed to Raymond's son-in-law, Alphonse of Poitiers, who proceeded to govern it as effectively as his appanage lands; and when he and his wife died without issue in 1271, their enormous inheritance reverted to the royal domain.

The ancient household administration died out in the 13th century. Offices such as the chancery and treasury became more specialized and bureaucratic, while the greater advisory personnel formed a fluctuating corps of reliable favourites: bishops, abbots, and minor nobles of the old Capetian homelands. The counselors, meeting in diverse political and ceremonial capacities, continued to assemble with other prelates and barons during festivals or ad hoc. But the fiscal and judicial activities of the court were growing in volume and technicality. Ordinary revenues expanded apace with the royal domains; taxes ceased to be exceptional. Toward 1250, judgments of the curia began to be recorded centrally; and the judicial sessions, now often called *parlements*, derived an ever-expanding jurisdiction from the king's repute.

Meanwhile, a real local administration evolved as the bailiffs and seneschals became well established in territorial circumscriptions. Complaints arose when these men, and more particularly their subordinate officers, abused their powers for personal profit or the king's. Commissions of investigation, first appointed in 1247, provided means for redress; and these investigators continued to function after Louis returned from his first Crusade in 1254.

Although previous rulers had legislated on occasion, Louis IX was the first to express his will regularly in statutory form. A great ordinance for administrative reform in 1254 resulted from the remedial inquiries. In other enactments, characteristically moral and authoritarian, Louis sought to curb private warfare (about 1258) and to promote the use of royal money while limiting that of baronial (1263–65).

Toward the clergy Louis IX manifested a sympathy born of conservatism and exceptional piety, but he was nonetheless a firm master. He opposed efforts to expand clerical jurisdictions. During his later years he supported papal taxes on the clergy for the Crusade, although in the 1240s he had joined his clergy in opposing papal preferments and impositions for a war against the emperor Frederick II. The lay nobles found Louis IX a frustrating ruler. Sharing few of their values, he consistently tried to limit their ability to cause disorder. He allowed royal officials to encroach on baronial jurisdiction in many cases, and he welcomed appeals from baronial judgments. On the other hand, he respected such rights as were sanctioned by provincial custom and was less forceful in exploiting feudal relationships than his grandfather had been.

The royal interest in order and justice was especially beneficial to townspeople and peasants, who had suffered most from exploitative agents and private war. Louis IX confirmed municipal charters, but he also taxed the towns heavily. When oligarchical urban governors mismanaged finance to the disadvantage of the lower classes as well as the king, he moved energetically (1259–62) to place the fiscal administration of 35 communes directly under the crown. A Crusade of peasants known as the Pastoureaux (1251) was inspired by loyalty to the king, then in trouble in the Holy Land; when its impulse was dissipated in agitation against the propertied classes, the regent, Blanche of Castile, had it suppressed.

LATER CAPETIANS

Louis IX was succeeded by his son, Philip III (reigned 1270–85); his grandson, Philip IV (the Fair; 1285–1314); and three great-grandsons, Louis X (1314–16), Philip V (1316–22), and Charles IV (1322–28). The most significant of these last Capetian reigns was that of Philip the Fair. Worldly and ambitious yet pious and intelligent, he was less accommodating than his forebears and more devoted to his power than to his reputation. He brought the monarchy to a degree of coordinated strength it was not again to have in the Middle Ages. But, in so doing, he strained the resources and patience of his subjects. His sons had to give in to the demands of a country beginning to suffer from the natural disasters, such as the great famine and the Black Death, that would mark the 14th century. They did so, however, without abandoning their father's objectives. When Charles IV died without a male heir in 1328, as his brothers had done before him, the royal succession was claimed by a collateral Capetian family.

The reigns of the later Capetian kings were marked by further territorial consolidation. Marrying his son to the heiress of Champagne and Navarra in 1284, Philip III prepared the way for a reversion no less important than that of Toulouse (1271). Philip the Fair secured the heiress to the county of Burgundy for his son Philip in 1295 and annexed southern Flanders and Lyon in 1312. Smaller acquisitions, cumulatively of great importance, resulted from purchase: the counties of Guînes (1281), Chartres (1286), and La Marche and Saintonge (1308); the viscounties of Lomagne and Auvillars (1302) and La Soule (1306); and a number of untitled lordships.

Through treaties, Philip the Fair extended his jurisdiction into the ecclesiastical principalities of Viviers, Cahors, Mende, and Le Puy. With his greatly expanded domain, the king could assert unprecedented authority everywhere in France. Yet it does not appear that territorial policy as such had changed. Appanages were still to be granted and to be recovered by the later Capetians. The monarchs continued to do without Brittany, Burgundy, and many lesser lordships, which did not prevent them from legislating for these lands along with the rest.

Government became more engrossing, specialized, and efficient. Although the royal curia continued to exist as an aggregate of favourites, magnates, prelates, and advisers, its ministerial element—comprising salaried officers serving at the king's pleasure—functioned increasingly in departments. The small council acquired definition from an oath first mentioned in 1269. With its sessions lengthening under a growing burden of cases, Parlement was divided into chambers of pleas,

requests, and investigations (1278), and its composition and jurisdiction were regulated. Older provincial tribunals, such as the Norman Exchequer and the Jours of Troyes, became commissions of Parlement. While the direction of finance was left with the council, the Chambre des Comptes (Chamber of Accounts), apart from the treasury, was organized to audit accounts. Council and chamber as well as Parlement developed appropriate jurisdiction, and all three bodies kept archives. The chancery, serving all departments, remained in the hands of lesser functionaries until 1315, when Louis X revived the title of honour.

Local administration was marked by the proliferation of officers subordinate to the bailiffs and seneschals. The chief judge (*juge-mage*) assumed the seneschal's judicial functions in the south; receivers of revenues, first appearing in Languedoc, were instituted in the bailiwicks at the end of the 13th century. Commissions of investigation continued to traverse the provinces under the later Capetians, but all too often they now functioned as fiscal agents rather than as reformers.

Many of the officers who served Philip the Fair were laymen, and many were lawyers. Impressed with the power they wielded, they promoted loyalty to the crown and a conception of the royal authority approaching that of sovereignty. Without claiming absolute power for the king, they thought in terms of his "superiority" over all men within national boundaries now (for the first time) strictly determined; and they did not hesitate to argue from Roman law that, when the "state of the kingdom" was endangered, the monarch had an overriding right to the aid of all his subjects in its defense. While this doctrine, in a notorious case, was made a justification for imposing on the clergy, the later Capetians did not lose the religious mystique they had inherited from their predecessors' efforts in Christian causes. Even as political loyalties were being engrossed by the lay state, the "religion of monarchy" derived impetus from the fervent utterance of those who saw in Philip the Fair a type of Christ or the ruler of a chosen and favoured people.

It was in the requirements of war and finance that the claims of the monarchy found most concrete expression. In the 1270s, for his campaigns in the south, Philip III requested military aid from men theretofore exempt from such service. Philip the Fair, renewing these demands for his wars in Gascony and Flanders, went so far as to claim the military obligation of all freemen as the basis for taxing personal property. The most persistent and lucrative taxation after 1285 was that imposed on the clergy, generally in the form of tithes (taxes on income) and annates (taxes on property); sales taxes, customs, tallages on Jews and foreign businessmen, and forced loans likewise supplemented older revenues of the domain to support increased administrative expenses as well as costs of war. The most unpopular fiscal expedients were the revaluations of coinage after 1295, by which the king several times increased the profits of his mints to the confusion of merchants and bankers. The imbalance between ordinary resources and the needs of an expanding government became chronic at the end of the 13th century. Yet, in spite of the statist arguments of their lawyers, none of the later Capetians were moved to regard taxation as an established and justified requirement of a national government.

Such restraint is one reason why, with momentary lapses, the strongest of the later Capetians was not regarded as an arbitrary ruler. Philip the Fair revered St. Louis (Louis IX) as much as did his people; like Louis, he took counsel from a relatively few unrepresentative persons. But, when Philip's own policies broke with the past, he resorted to great councils and assemblies, not so much to commit the nation as to justify his course. Whether a tax was sanctioned by custom or not, even if approved by assembled magnates or townsmen, he had it negotiated—re-explained and collected—in the provinces and localities. Large central assemblies in 1302, 1303, 1308, and 1312 met to enable the king and his ministers to arouse political support for his measures against the pope or the Knights Templars.

Among these gatherings were the earliest national assemblies to include representatives of towns and villages, which has caused historians to see them as early versions of what became the Estates-General, meetings of deputies representing the clergy, the nobility, and the commoners of the entire kingdom that were convoked beginning in the 14th century. Under Philip the Fair and his sons, however, these convocations were not yet understood to be representative of the estates of society; only when Philip V began to summon northern and southern men separately to deliberate on fiscal matters were the estates (which made up the Estates-General) in any way anticipated. Almost simultaneously the provincial Estates were foreshadowed in the petitions of magnates and towns in several regions for relief from administrative violations of traditional privilege; but the resulting charters of 1314–15 were poorly coordinated. They did little to limit royal power, although the fiscal rights later claimed by the Estates of Normandy could be traced to the Norman Charter of 1315.

If the policies of Philip the Fair evoked the complaint of all classes of people, it was because he had favoured none in particular; in fact, except in war and finance, the later Capetians may be said to have maintained a traditional politics toward both the nobles and the towns. With the church, however, it was otherwise. Philip the Fair's insistence on taxing the clergy for defense led immediately to his conflict with Pope Boniface VIII. The latter, in the bull *Clericis laicos* (1296), forbade the payment of taxes by clergymen to lay rulers without papal consent. Boniface had some support in the south, but Philip outmaneuvered the pope by prohibiting the export of bullion from France. The following year the

pope abandoned his position and conceded to kings the right to tax the clergy without papal approval in time of need.

The quarrel was renewed in 1301, when the king and the magnates accused the bishop of Pamiers of treason and heresy. Boniface not only revoked the concessions of 1297 but rebuked Philip for seizing clerical property and debasing the coinage, among other things, and he summoned French prelates to Rome to proceed with a reform of the kingdom. Once again the clergy were split; many bishops and abbots attended an assembly at Paris in 1302 where they joined men of the other estates in addressing a remonstrance to the pope. A year later the king adopted rougher tactics: in June 1303 many prelates acquiesced in a scheme to try the pope before a general council, and in September the king's envoy Guillaume de Nogaret and his accomplices seized Boniface at Anagni. Rescued by the Romans, the aged pope died a month later. Upon his death the papal monarchy that had been erected over the preceding two centuries collapsed entirely. The Gascon pope Clement V (reigned 1305–14) moved the Holy See to Avignon, and a mass of his compatriots were appointed cardinals.

With this pliant pontiff, the way was cleared for the strangest act of violence of the reign of Philip the Fair—the destruction of the Knights Templars. Founded in the 12th century, the Templars were an important Crusading order whose privileges seemed poorly justified after the fall of the last Crusader outpost in the Holy Land. The Templars remained an influential order, however, whose great wealth and power attracted Philip's attention. In 1307 Philip ordered the arrest of every Templar in France and the seizure of their goods and property because of alleged heresy and immorality. Under torture, the Templars confessed to homosexual practices, spitting on the cross, idol worship, and other things. In 1310 many of the Templars recanted their confessions, but Philip proceeded in his quest against them and in 1312 persuaded the pope to formally suppress the order. Their last leaders were imprisoned for life, and the two highest-ranking authorities were burned at the stake.

FOREIGN RELATIONS

France assumed a more active role in the politics of Christian Europe from the end of the 12th century. The most heavily populated region of Europe, the kingdom of France provided its rulers with greater resources than any of their rivals. Philip Augustus led French contingents on the most fully international of the great Crusades (1190–91), although, having once demonstrated his energy in that work of piety, he could not afterward be persuaded to renew his vow. He preferred, through dynastic schemes and opportunism, to pursue his rivalry with the Plantagenets. His ambition seems to have embraced England as early as 1193, when he married Ingeborg, whose brother, the king of Denmark, had an old claim to the throne of England. When Philip, for private reasons, repudiated Ingeborg the day after the wedding and sought to have the marriage annulled, she and her brother appealed to the pope; her case, punctuated by reconciliations with Philip dictated more by policy than by sentiment, dragged on through the pontificate of Innocent III.

Meanwhile, in 1200, Philip's son Louis married Blanche of Castile, granddaughter of Henry II, through whom another claim to England was heralded. Louis's career as prince was marked by aggressive designs against King John. Innocent III was prepared to recognize Louis as king of England in 1213; and the policy was dropped only after Louis's abortive invasion of 1216–17.

It was in the play of rival coalitions that Philip Augustus had his greatest diplomatic anxiety and success. Philip countered John's alliance with Otto IV of Brunswick, his nephew and claimant to the empire, by supporting a second claimant, Philip of Swabia. When Otto became Holy Roman emperor in 1209 and the counts of Flanders and Boulogne were alienated from their Capetian suzerain, Philip found himself seriously threatened in his northern heartlands. John's desire to avenge the loss of his French fiefs finally prompted him to act in 1214; he led a force from the west, and his major allies marched on Paris from the north. Philip Augustus met the allied forces at Bouvines in July 1214 and won a decisive victory. As John retreated and his coalition collapsed, there could be no doubt that Capetian France had achieved hegemony in Christian Europe.

Louis IX acted astutely, though in ways unlike his grandfather's, to preserve the prestige of France. His treaties with Aragon and England, designed to extend and secure his domains, resulted from a cordiality better appreciated abroad than by the royal counselors. From Navarra and Lorraine as well as from within the realm were brought disputes for his judgment; and in the Mise of Amiens (1264) Louis responded to the appeal of Henry III and the English barons to pronounce on the validity of the Provisions of Oxford (a written agreement between the king and magnates in England to reform the state of the realm). But the more absorbing issues of Louis's diplomacy lay in the east. He resisted papal urgings to take sides against Otto's successor, Frederick II, believing in the equal legitimacy of empire and papacy. On the other hand, he allowed his brother Charles I of Anjou to accept the crown of Sicily from the pope; for this enterprise, as well as for his own Crusades, he allowed the papacy to tax the French clergy. His paramount foreign interest was to recover the holy places of Christ, a traditional ambition characteristically associated in his mind with the hope of converting the infidel: the Mongols or the emir of Tunis.

Louis IX first took the cross in 1244, upon learning that a Turkish-Egyptian coalition had driven the Christians of the Levant back to precarious coastal positions. His expedition, which was well planned and well financed, set out in 1248, only to founder in the plague-ridden floodwaters of Egypt a year and a half later. Louis himself was captured; upon his release he spent four years in Syria in support of the Christian cause. He renewed his Crusader's vow in 1267, in circumstances clouded by Angevin-Sicilian politics. Charles, whose inordinate Mediterranean ambitions had little in common with the traditional Crusade, secretly persuaded the new expedition to divert to Tunis. It broke up there with the king's death in 1270.

The prestige of France in Christendom lost little from these failures of Louis IX. Nor was it generally foreseen that Aquitaine and Sicily would become battlegrounds in the future. The apparent strength of his father's diplomacy deterred Philip III from changing it, even though circumstances had changed. When in 1282 the misrule of Charles of Anjou caused the Sicilians to revolt in favour of Peter III of Aragon, leading to the War of the Sicilian Vespers, a test of the Angevin policy could no longer be deferred. Charles's friend Pope Martin IV (reigned 1281–85) excommunicated the king of Aragon and offered the vacant throne to Philip for one of his sons. Because at this juncture the crown of Navarra was destined for Philip's son and successor, Philip the Fair, the whole Spanish March seemed ripe for recovery by the French. Yet the Crusade against Aragon, blatantly political and impractical, came to a catastrophic end: the king himself died as his battered forces staggered out of Catalonia (October 1285).

Charles of Anjou and Martin IV also died in 1285. Understandably, Philip the Fair, who had foreseen the folly of the ill-conceived attack on Aragon, no longer permitted Mediterranean concerns to dominate foreign policy. The issue over Sicily dragged on, but minor Capetian interests in the Pyrenees and in Castile were allowed to lapse.

The extension of French influence and domain toward the north and east was the result of resourceful diplomacy at the expense of the empire. Philip's interest in that direction was emphasized when his sister married the son of Albert I of Germany and when he proposed first his brother and later his son as candidates for the imperial title. But it was against the English holdings in France that Philip exercised his most aggressive and portentous diplomacy.

Questions over spheres of administrative rights in Aquitaine had been creating tensions for many years. By the Treaty of Amiens (1279) the Agenais, whose status had been left in doubt when Alphonse of Poitiers died, passed to Edward I of England, who also had unsettled claims in Quercy. Serious conflict was precipitated in 1293, when clashes between French and English seamen caused Philip the Fair to summon his vassal to Parlement. When Gascon castles occupied by the French as part of the settlement were not returned to the English on schedule, Edward renounced his homage and prepared to fight for Aquitaine. The war that ensued (1294–1303) went in favour of Philip the Fair, whose armies thrust deep into Gascony. Edward retaliated by allying with Flanders and other northern princes. His dangerous campaign, concerted with the count of Flanders in 1297, met defeat from a French force led by Robert of Artois, and during a truce from 1297 to 1303 the rival monarchs reestablished the status quo ante. Edward married Philip's sister, and a marriage was projected between Prince Edward and Philip's daughter.

A consequence of this first war was to be the chronic insubordination of Flanders. After the count's surrender and imprisonment, it was left to the Flemish burghers to revolt against the French garrisons, and the French knights suffered a terrible defeat at Courtrai in July 1302. Thereafter the tide turned. But it was only in 1305 that a settlement satisfactory to the king could be reached; even then it proved impossible to win full ratification from the Flemish townsmen, whose resistance remained an invariable factor in the latent hostility between France and England.

In 1320 Philip the Fair's son, Philip V, obtained Edward II's personal homage, but friction was increasing in Gascony again. When Edward refused to do homage to Philip V's brother and successor, Charles IV, an old issue relating to French rights in Saint-Sardos (in Agenais) flamed into a war that once again went in favour of the French. By the Treaty of Paris (March 1327) France recovered Agenais and Bazadais and imposed a heavy indemnity on England, but a number of issues were left unresolved. Meanwhile, having married the emperor Henry VII's daughter, Charles was tempted to negotiate for the vacant imperial title in 1324; but nothing came of this. The last Capetians, although troubled at home, retained their international standing among neighbouring states, which were no less troubled.

THE PERIOD OF THE HUNDRED YEARS' WAR

At the accession of the house of Valois in 1328, France was the most powerful kingdom in Europe. Its ruler could muster larger armies than his rivals elsewhere; he could tap enormous fiscal resources, including taxes authorized by sympathetic popes of French extraction; there remained only four great fiefs—the duchies of Aquitaine, Brittany, and Burgundy and the county of Flanders—outside the direct royal domain; and the king's courts continued to press a jurisdictional supremacy that was felt everywhere in the realm. It did not follow, however, that France's superior armies would fight better than its foes or that its resources would not sometimes be dissipated or withheld. France remained a collection of traditional provinces whose peoples believed that a king should "live off his own," while military success continued to depend on the personal leadership of dynastic rulers whose qualifications as strategists had been less refined by experience and institutional progress than their judicial or administrative competence. The history of France in the 14th century is dominated by efforts of its kings to maintain their suzerainty over the Plantagenets in Aquitaine—efforts that, despite French advantages, were long frustrated. The sufferings inflicted on the kingdom by a century of intermittent warfare were exacerbated by other hardships, especially the devastating Black Death of 1347–50. After more than three centuries generally characterized by peace, prosperity, and a growing population, France entered a period of troubles that would last in some respects until the early 1700s. The ongoing warfare between England and France would be known later as the Hundred Years' War.

PHILIP VI

Philip VI of Valois (reigned 1328–50), grandson of Philip III, was of mature age when he became regent of France in 1328. Upon the birth of a daughter to the widow of his cousin Charles IV, the familiar issue of the succession was posed anew. It was the regent's experience, together with the circumstance that Edward III of England, grandson of Philip the Fair, was under the influence of his disreputable mother, Isabella of France, that probably disposed the council at Vincennes to recognize Philip as king (April 1328).

Philip's reign began well. Within months he crushed a revolt of the Flemish cloth towns that concluded at the Battle of Cassel in August 1328, thereby recovering the effective suzerainty over

Flanders that had eluded his predecessors for a generation. And in 1329 he obtained Edward III's personal homage for the duchy of Aquitaine, an act that not only secured Philip's leadership but also nullified Edward's claim to the crown of France.

This initial success was soon undone. Jurisdictional questions in Gascony remained unsettled. In 1336 Philip VI appeared to be preparing massive support for David II, the Scottish king at war with Edward; and in 1337, alleging defaults in feudal service, Philip ordered the confiscation of Aquitaine. Edward III renounced his homage and again laid claim to the crown of France, starting the period of conflict that would come to be known as the Hundred Years' War. Despite the new Plantagenet pretensions, the basic causes of conflict were feudal and jurisdictional, not dynastic.

Edward proceeded deliberately and ominously. He fomented discontent among the Flemish cloth workers and then treated with the towns; in so doing he negated the count's fidelity to France; he also purchased the fidelity and service of many princes in the Rhineland and Low Countries. But, to succeed, the English needed a prompt and massive victory on French soil, something Philip VI was able to prevent. Despite Edward's naval triumph off Sluys (1340), which confirmed English control of the seas, his initial advantage was lost as his resources and allies melted away. A truce in September 1340 was extended for several years, during which time Edward intervened in a disputed succession to the duchy of Brittany, while Philip's officials increased their pressure on Gascony. In 1345 English armies counterattacked French posts on the duchy's borders; their success emboldened Edward. Landing in Normandy (July 1346) with a well-disciplined army, he captured Caen, only to be overtaken in Picardy by a much larger French army as he moved to join his Flemish allies. At Crécy (August 26, 1346), despite serious disadvantages, the English forces won the first major battle of the war. Their victory, however, proved difficult to exploit; Edward moved on to capture Calais after a long siege, but he could then only return to England with more glory than accomplishment to his credit.

Nevertheless, Philip's failures were proving costly in money and political support. In 1340–41 he had been able to raise "extraordinary" revenue through taxes on sales, salt, and hearths, despite regional protests. The continuance of sales and salt taxes in 1343 could be extracted from the Estates of Paris only in return for the restoration of a stable coinage; in the following years regional assemblies in the north proved even more obstinate. In the Estates of Paris in November 1347 the king heard ringing denunciations of his mismanagement and defeats and was fortunate to obtain new subsidies to support an invasion of England. But that prospect, like the war itself, evaporated when the Black Death struck Europe late in 1347, destroying life, fiscal resources, and resolve for several years thereafter.

Philip VI cannot be judged by his military failures alone. The royal domain was significantly enlarged by his acquisition of Dauphiné (technically an endowment for his grandson; 1343–49) and the city of Montpellier, the last (and wealthiest) Aragonese fief in Languedoc. As administrative expertise continued to progress, the services, such as Parlement and the treasury, were regulated. Within the departments of the court and notably in the Chambre des Comptes (Chamber of Accounts), power came increasingly into the hands of royal favourites, whose rivalries were stimulated by the courtly predilections of the king. Their influence and embezzlement together with the familiar injustices of local government came under attack in the Estates of 1343 and 1347, which, in their conditional grants of subsidy, asserted a more nearly constitutional authority than French assemblies had yet enjoyed; the fiscal powers of the provincial Estates likewise originated during this reign.

JOHN THE GOOD

John II (the Good; reigned 1350–64) succeeded to a weakened authority and kingdom; he was a mediocrity whose suspicions and impetuosity were ill suited to the changed circumstances. John hoped to rally baronial loyalties to himself. But he failed to reconcile Charles II (the Bad), king of Navarra, whose strong dynastic claim to the throne (he was the grandson of Louis X) was matched by his ambition; Charles's conspiracy—at first appeased, then too violently put down—seriously weakened John during 1355–56, when the English war broke out anew. When Charles sought alliance with Edward III, French diplomats abandoned full sovereignty over Aquitaine, a reversal of policy too gratuitous to hold for long; its prompt revocation, with papal support, encouraged Edward's son, Edward the Black Prince, to undertake destructive raids through Languedoc in 1355. That November the Estates of Languedoïl, meeting at Paris, insisted on controlling the military appropriations they voted; when the Black Prince advanced from Bordeaux to Touraine in the summer of 1356, John hastened to prevent his union with rebellious Norman barons. The armies met near Poitiers in September. Once again the French had the advantage of numbers and position, only to suffer a disastrous defeat. King John allowed himself to be taken prisoner.

France was to experience no worse years than those of the regency, during John's captivity, of the dauphin Charles (1356–61). Unpaid or poorly disciplined armies ravaged the countryside. The dynasts, nobles, and townspeople had new reasons to resist the monarchy. The dauphin (crown prince) showed no sign of adjusting to meet the crisis. The Estates-General, convoked in 1356 to provide for the king's ransom, demanded sweeping administrative reforms, even imposing upon the regent a council representing the Estates. Their program proved unworkable, and Charles tried to resume power on terms already rejected by the Estates. This move radicalized Étienne Marcel, provost of the Parisian merchants and leader of the urban estate. Marcel arranged the brutal murders of two of the dauphin's noble associates, which created an irreconcilable breach with the dauphin, who fled Paris and convoked his own assembly at Compiègne. Marcel's enthusiasm mounted as his position became more precarious; he drew strength from alliance with Charles the Bad but failed to win the Flemish towns to his cause. The climactic complication was a terrible uprising of the peasants (the Jacquerie), which broke out in Picardy in May 1358 and which antagonized Marcel's noble supporters, notably Charles the Bad, who helped to quell the disturbances. Marcel was increasingly isolated when loyalist sentiment mounted and administrative failures became evident. His assassination on July 31, 1358, not only secured the dauphin's authority but ended the burgher influence that had originated in the Estates of 1355.

Intense efforts were then made to end the English war. Negotiations dragged past the term of truce set in 1356; when an initial and too humiliating treaty was rejected by the dauphin, Edward made yet another demonstration in France (1359). At Brétigny (May 8, 1360) King John's ransom was set at three million gold crowns, while England was assigned full sovereignty over Aquitaine (including Poitou). Two months later John arrived in Calais, where a first payment of ransom was made. In the definitive Treaty of Calais (October 24, 1360), for reasons not clear, the monarchs' renunciations—Edward's claim to the crown of France, John's claim to sovereignty over the ceded territories—were postponed. The Black Prince, however, proceeded to take control of Aquitaine, while the regent tried with little success to extract additional money for the ransom from an exhausted country. When the Estates at Amiens (October 1363) refused to ratify an irresponsible agreement between the king's replacement hostages and Edward III, John returned to captivity in London, where he died a few months later.

CHARLES V

Under the former dauphin, now Charles V (reigned 1364–80), the fortunes of war were dramatically reversed. Charles had a high conception of royalty and a good political sense. While he shared the house of Valois's taste for luxury and festivity, he reverted to the Capetian tradition of prudent diplomacy. He observed the Treaty of Calais, which helps to explain why Edward III did not press to conclude the renunciations; but he reserved his authority in Aquitaine by inserting in his coronation oath a clause prohibiting the alienation of rights attached to the crown.

The early years of his reign were filled with baronial politics. Charles the Bad once again revolted unsuccessfully, his dynastic claim to Burgundy running afoul of the king's; the succession to Brittany was settled by arms in favour of the Anglophile Jean de Montfort (who became John IV [the Valiant]). Most significant for the future, Charles V obtained the heiress to Flanders for his brother Philip II (the Bold), to whom Burgundy had been granted in appanage. Meanwhile, companies of mercenary soldiers, many based in strongholds of central France, were paralyzing the countryside. Charles V commissioned the Breton captain Bertrand du Guesclin to neutralize them. Between 1365 and 1369 Bertrand employed the companies in adventurous conflicts in Spain; many of the mercenaries were killed or dispersed. The Black Prince had also intervened in Spain, and his taxes and administration in Aquitaine aroused protest. In 1369 the lords of Albret and Armagnac, having refused to permit levies of subsidy in their lands, appealed to Charles V for the judgment of his court. Although Charles hesitated, his eventual decision to accept the appeals was in keeping with the letter of the Treaty of Calais and his coronation oath.

The war with England soon broke out again. Two new factors worked in favour of France. First, Charles's alliance with Henry II of Trastámara, king of Castile, cost the English their naval supremacy; a Castilian fleet destroyed English reinforcements off La Rochelle in 1372, which effectively secured the success of French operations in the west. Second, Charles abandoned the defective policy of massive engagement with the enemy. Unable to command in person, he appointed Bertrand du Guesclin constable in 1370; the latter proceeded to harry the enemy and to prey on supplies with great effectiveness. Through skirmishes and sieges, the French forces soon reconquered Guyenne and Poitou, leaving only some port towns (Calais, Cherbourg, Saint-Malo, Bordeaux) in English hands. To finance these operations, Charles continued to levy the taxes on merchandise, salt (gabelles), and hearths that had been intended to raise John's ransom; despite serious inequities and defaults, these taxes persisted to the end of the reign. In Languedoc they were voted, assessed, and expended by the Estates; elsewhere, by transforming into royal officers the deputies first chosen by the Estates in the time of John, Charles created a fiscal administration independent of popular control. His military success owed much to the improved regulation of armed forces and defenses. Ordinances provided for the inspection and repair of fortifications, the encouragement of archery, a more dependable discipline, pay for fighting men, and even the establishment of a navy.

The last years of the reign brought disappointments. Truces were arranged; but, as there could be no more talk of ceding French sovereignty over Aquitaine, there could be no assurance of peace. More serious, the papal-French alliance collapsed. Charles V, unable to prevent Pope Gregory XI from returning to Rome in 1376, chose to support the candidacy of Robert of Geneva against the Italian Urban VI in 1378, but only Scotland and Naples followed the French lead. A schismatic pope could no longer help France much; rival popes could hardly promote peace between their political supporters. Although he had reestablished the political unity of France, Charles V left an uncertain future.

CHARLES VI

Charles VI (reigned 1380–1422) was a minor when he succeeded his father. His uncles, each possessed of the ambition and resources to pursue independent policies, assumed control of the government. Louis II, duc d'Anjou, soon removed himself from influence by seeking the throne of Naples; Jean, duc de Berry, received the lieutenancy of Languedoc, by then virtually an appanage; and it was left to Duke Philip II (the Bold) of Burgundy to set the young king's policy. He imposed his own cause upon the king in his policy toward Flanders (whose ruler, Count Louis II, was Philip's father-in-law). An uprising by the workers of Ghent, spreading to other towns, was met by royal force that won a crushing victory at Roosebeke in 1382. The young king returned in triumph to deal forcefully with restive populations at Paris and Rouen and in Languedoc. The provostship of the merchants was suppressed at Paris, bringing that municipality under direct royal control.

In 1388 Charles VI assumed full authority himself. He recalled his father's exiled advisers, the Marmousets, who undertook to reform the royal administration in keeping with the practice of Charles V. But the country was again wearying of taxation. The annual levies of Charles V had been discontinued in 1380 but then were reestablished—helping to cause the urban unrest already mentioned—and were being dissipated blatantly in royal and princely extravagance. In 1392 the king lost his sanity, a shocking event that aroused popular solicitude for the crown. His recurrent lapses into insanity, however, played into the hands of his uncles. Philip the Bold again dominated the council. Fortunately for France, England was incapable of renewing the war. The duke of Burgundy planned an invasion of England in 1386, but, after major preparations in Flanders, it came to nothing. A series of truces, beginning in 1388, was followed by a reconciliation between Richard II of England and Charles VI in 1396, when the truce was extended for 28 years. Meanwhile, French nobles were reviving the Crusade, imagining a reunited West following their lead; John the Fearless's defeat at Nicopolis in 1396 was the most famous of several enterprises. To restore unity in the church, the masters of the University of Paris began to speak out vigorously; the conciliar theory (according to which the church was to be governed by an ecumenical council), which finally prevailed to end the schism, owed much to them.

When conflict with England was renewed in the 15th century, circumstances had changed. Henry IV of England was committed to the recovery of English rights in France; moreover, in a civil war between Louis I, duc d'Orléans, and John the Fearless (duke of Burgundy since 1404) over control of the king, both parties

SAINT JOAN OF ARC

Joan of Arc (born c. 1412, Domrémy, Bar, France—died May 30, 1431, Rouen; canonized May 16, 1920; feast day May 30) was a peasant girl who from an early age believed she heard the voices of Saints Michael, Catherine, and Margaret. When she was about 16, her voices began urging her to aid France's dauphin and save France from the English attempt at conquest in the Hundred Years' War. Dressed in men's clothes, she visited the dauphin and convinced him, his advisers, and the church authorities to support her. With her inspiring conviction, she rallied the French troops and raised the English siege of Orléans in 1429. She soon defeated the English again at Patay. The dauphin was crowned king at Reims as Charles VII, with Joan beside him. Her siege of Paris was unsuccessful, and in 1430 she was captured by the Burgundians and sold to the English. Abandoned by Charles, she was turned over to the ecclesiastical court at Rouen, which was controlled by French clerics who supported the English, and tried for witchcraft and heresy (1431). She fiercely defended herself but finally recanted and was sentenced to life imprisonment. When she again asserted that she had been divinely inspired, she was burned at the stake.

sought English support. And, when John arranged Orléans's assassination in Paris (November 23, 1407), the popular horror magnified the conflict. John exploited the situation by pressing for reforms; his rival's cause was taken up by Bernard VII of Armagnac, whose daughter married Orléans's son. But John's alliance with the turbulent Parisians was no more secure than the temper of the angriest burghers; a major ordinance for administrative reform (1413) collapsed in a riot of the butchers, and in the ensuing reaction the Armagnac faction regained control of Paris. John's dangerous response was to encourage the new king of England, Henry V, to claim the French throne for himself. Henry's invasion of 1415, reminiscent of the campaign ending at Crécy, had the same result—at Agincourt the

French suffered yet another major defeat, after which, characteristically, the English withdrew—but the civil war in France enabled Henry V to exploit his strength, as Edward III had not been able to do. In 1418 the Burgundian party recovered control of Paris, and the dauphin Charles embarked on a long exile in Armagnac company.

John's limitless duplicity led him to meet with the dauphin in 1419 and offer to betray the English, but he was assassinated by the dauphin's followers. His successor, Philip III (the Good), renewed the alliance with Henry V. By the Treaty of Troyes (1420) the deranged Charles VI was induced to set aside the dauphin's right of succession in favour of Henry V, who married Charles VI's daughter. The ancient dream of a dynastic union between France and England seemed to be realized; and, when Henry and Charles died within weeks of each other in 1422, the infant Henry VI became king in both lands.

CHARLES VII

Charles VI's son, Charles VII (reigned 1422–61), for his part, did not fail to claim his inheritance, though he had no proper coronation. Residing at Bourges, which his adversaries pretended was the extent of his realm, he in fact retained the fidelity of the greater part of France, including Berry, Poitou, Lyonnais, Auvergne, and Languedoc. For a time the Valois cause suffered from the ineptness of its leader and from his advisers and retainers, who prospered from the unresolved conflict. Incapable himself of military leadership, Charles put his hope in reconciliation with Philip of Burgundy, a diplomacy that thoroughly discomfited King Henry's regent, the duke of Bedford. Nevertheless, French prestige collapsed with the abasement of the monarchy; Charles VII appears to have doubted his own legitimacy, and disorder spread again.

Then Joan of Arc appeared. Stirred by the popular memory of traditional French kingship, she found her way from her peasant home at Domrémy (on the border of Champagne and Bar) to Chinon, where she confronted Charles with her astonishing inspiration: her "voices" proclaimed a divine commission to aid the king. In April 1429 she entered Orléans, long besieged, rallying the garrison to effective sorties that soon caused the English to lift the siege. Other victories followed, in which Joan's influence was manifest, although probably exaggerated in tradition. On her insistence that only consecration at Reims could make a true king, chosen by God (a view doubtless supported by the chancellor Regnault, archbishop of Reims), it was decided to advance boldly across the Île-de-France to Reims. Charles was anointed there on July 17, 1429.

RECOVERY AND REUNIFICATION, 1429–83

The coronation of Charles VII was the last pivotal event of the Hundred Years' War. From Reims the king's army moved on triumphantly, winning capitulations from Laon, Soissons, and many lesser places and even threatening Paris before disbanding. The popular devotion to monarchy that had produced Joan was undermining English positions almost everywhere in France; the urgent necessity to discredit her explains the callous efficiency of the inquisition to which she was subjected, upon being captured by the Burgundians and turned over to the English in 1430. Under duress, she confessed to heresy, then boldly retracted her confession. She was burned at the stake in Rouen on May 30, 1431.

Charles and his party made no move through ecclesiastical channels to save

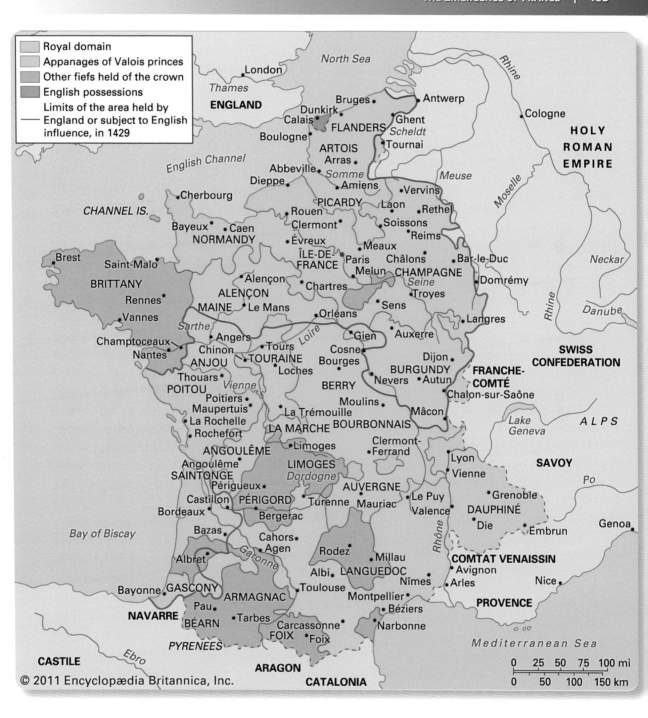

France in 1453. Encyclopædia Britannica, Inc.

Joan. They then proceeded deliberately to make peace with Burgundy. In the Treaty of Arras (September 21, 1435), Philip the Good bargained strongly; confirmed in the possession of domains ceded by the English, he also obtained Charles's humiliating disavowal of the murder of the duke's father, John the Fearless. The act, however damaging to the royal vanity, set Charles free from political obligation to the Armagnacs; the factional king now became the supreme king of France. Within a year, English support collapsed in the Île-de-France, and royal soldiers entered Paris. The Truce of Tours (1444) provided for a marriage between Henry VI and the niece of Queen Mary of France; extensions of the truce gave Charles time to strengthen his military resources. War flared again in 1449, when England intervened against a duke of Brittany who had done homage to Charles VII. In 1449–50 a vigorous campaign resulted in the French conquest of Normandy, and in 1451 most of Guyenne fell to the French.

When the English lost the minor Battle of Castillon in 1453, the Hundred Years' War was over. That fact was not altogether clear to contemporaries, for no treaty was concluded and skirmishes were to recur for many years to come. But only Calais, enclosed in the Burgundian domains, remained of English possessions in France. Charles VII issued medals to commemorate his soldiers, and he ordered a review of Joan of Arc's trial, which resulted in a verdict of rehabilitation in 1456.

GOVERNMENTAL REFORMS

As hostilities were waning (1435–49), Charles VII presided over a major reorganization of government. Tested by adversity and strengthened by fortune, he had grown in political competence. The principal administrative services—chancery, Parlement, accounts—were reestablished at Paris. The replacement of Burgundian sympathizers, notably in Parlement, seems to have been accomplished with moderation and tact; in local offices no purges were necessary. But it quickly became evident that the reunited country was now too large and its officials too numerous to get along very well with a government as centralized as Parisian bureaucrats preferred.

Remedial legislation was consistent with tendencies long apparent. Revenues from the domain were collected in the treasury, the work of which Charles VII reorganized in four regional offices. Extraordinary revenues had been administered since the 1350s in districts (*élections*), whose numbers had vastly increased since the time of Charles V. The *élections* were now subordinated to four regional *généralités*, corresponding to the offices of treasury. The old Chambre des Comptes had lost parts of its jurisdiction to more specialized courts in 1390, of which the Cour des Aides (board of excise) had provincial divisions set up at Toulouse in 1439 and at Rouen in 1450. A provincial *parlement* was definitively established at Toulouse in 1443, and there were to be others at Grenoble and Bordeaux. With all these changes, the conciliar structure of government survived; policy continued to be made by the king in concert with favourites, whose numbers had not been limited by reforms. The proliferation of lesser offices, many filled by lawyers, created a new stratum of gentlemen who enjoyed the king's privilege.

While the reform of offices did nothing to obliterate the older distinction between ordinary and extraordinary revenue, the work of Charles VII effectively belied the notion that the monarchy should subsist on its domain alone. That the king as lord could no longer pay his officers and soldiers was apparent to almost everyone. Early in his career Charles had resorted to the Estates to raise *aides* and tailles (as the old levies on sales and hearths were now called), but after convocations in the 1430s he continued these taxes through annual ordinances no longer sanctioned by the Estates. Moreover, the preparation of annual budgets for ordinary and extraordinary revenues gave way in 1450 to a single "general statement" of finance, which, being related to demonstrable necessities, effectively institutionalized taxation in France. As the Middle Ages ended, France comprised a central core of *élections*, where local Estates, when they met at all, had little to do with fiscal matters, and a surrounding belt of "lands of Estates" (e.g., Languedoc, Brittany, Normandy, and Burgundy), where custom continued to allow for the administration of taxes. Having originated in times of fiscal demands thought uncustomary and excessive, representative institutions could not generally survive once the royal impositions, from very repetition, had ceased to seem arbitrary; even where Estates persisted, their votes were more like approval than sovereign consent.

MILITARY REFORMS

The fiscal reorganization facilitated equally significant military reforms. The Peace of Arras, rather than pacifying France, had only thrown the people once again to the mercies of disbanded mercenaries and brigands. In 1439 an ordinance made the recruitment of military companies the king's monopoly and provided for uniform strength in contingents, supervision, and pay. Following the Truce of Tours in 1444, no general demobilization occurred; instead, the best of the larger units were reconstituted as "companies of the king's ordinance," which were standing units of cavalry well selected and well equipped; they served as local guardians of peace at local expense. With the creation of the "free archers" (1448), a militia of foot soldiers, the new standing army was complete. Making use of a newly effective artillery, its companies firmly in the king's control, supported by the people in money and spirit, France rid itself of brigands and Englishmen alike.

REGROWTH OF THE FRENCH MONARCHY

Thus, the monarchy recovered much of the authority it had lost during the early stages of the Hundred Years' War. Although its influence in Burgundy and Flanders (now united in a formidable dynastic association) had declined, its definitive recovery of Aquitaine consolidated a direct domain, again extensive enough to free the Valois royalty from anxiety about landed resources. It had exploited not only a widespread distaste for the destructive self-interest of barons and warlords but also an incipient nationalism, which, besides reviving the "religion of monarchy," put new stresses on the foreignness of Englishmen. How renewed power and Gallicanism went together was demonstrated in the Pragmatic Sanction of Bourges (1438), by which papal benefices and revenues from France were severely curtailed and the royal influence in the French church strengthened. Nevertheless, the survival of powerful dynasts and provincial interests, as a legacy of the war and the fertility of the royal house, represented a counterpoise to the crown that Philip the Fair had never known. And, with the son of Charles VII, the monarchy was to be tested yet again.

Louis XI (reigned 1461–83) was shamelessly impatient for his father's death. It must be said of this strange man that he had worthy policies to pursue: the securing of the royal domain against Burgundy, Orléans, and Brittany, among others, and the promotion of commerce and industry within national boundaries. His foreign policy was less consistent, ranging from the cautious in Italy to the chimerical in Spain; yet it was at the expense of Aragon that he regained title to Roussillon and Cerdagne. His methods rather than his ends were what made the reign of this ambitious, nervous, and capricious ruler so turbulent. No French king had ever imposed himself so totally and so tyrannically as did Louis XI. Forgetful of past loyalties, he was betrayed as often as he himself betrayed others. Toward the clergy as toward his officials, he could be brutal and vindictive. He antagonized the nobles by revoking the Valois pensions and some ceremonial trappings and by promoting the independence of seigneurial towns. As for the royal towns, Louis respected their constitutions only so far as was consistent with royal supervision and the payment of heavy taxes; he tolerated the resurgence of urban oligarchies. Fiscal pressures in support of the army, government, and diplomacy mounted fearfully.

Louis XI's determined efforts to strengthen royal authority provoked the princes to establish the formidable League of the Public Weal, which in 1465 appealed to the people against misgovernment and proposed a regency of the princes supported by the three estates. Louis, in turn, as on later occasions, used assemblies and proclamations to divide the princes. But the settlement of October 1465 was a grave setback for the king, whose brother Charles gained title to Normandy while Charles the Bold, soon to inherit Burgundy, acquired strategic counties and towns in Artois. To the undoing of this treaty Louis devoted great energy. Fomenting strife between Brittany and Normandy, he soon recovered the latter and isolated the former. Deaths among his rivals in Gascony enabled him to secure successions that were more divided and less hostile—such as in Armagnac. Increasingly, Louis's tortuous diplomacy fastened on Burgundy. The king succeeded in reconciling the Swiss cantons with Austria to form a coalition with France and the Rhenish cities; this coalition invaded Burgundy and defeated and killed Charles the Bold at Nancy (January 5, 1477). While the legal reversion of Burgundy to the crown could not be given practical effect, Louis prevented the emergence of a powerful state on France's northern and eastern borders and did recover Artois. Moreover, even as he enjoyed this decisive triumph over his most dangerous rival, the entire Angevin inheritance (Anjou, Provence, and Mediterranean claims) devolved to the crown upon the death of René I of Anjou in 1480. Through accident and design and the inability of the princes to collaborate effectively, Louis had succeeded in countering the threat of a princely constitution and had considerably extended the royal domain.

ECONOMY, SOCIETY, AND CULTURE IN THE 14TH AND 15TH CENTURIES

The long war against the English, fought almost entirely in France, benefited few but the captains and peculators; it injured almost everyone. Even the best-disciplined companies lived off the land, so that French peasants and defeated townsfolk in effect paid the expenses of both sides; and undisciplined mercenary bands were a wearisome scourge in times of truce after the middle of the 14th century.

ECONOMIC DISTRESS

But the war alone did not cause economic distress. Even before it broke out, bad weather and commercial dislocations, together with overpopulation in some areas, resulted in worse and more frequent famines than in the past. However, what most terribly damaged life and security was sickness.

The Black Death, a pandemic of both bubonic and pneumonic plague that was carried on shipboard from the Levant, reached Provence in 1347, ravaged most of France in 1348, and faded out only in 1350. Nothing worked to check the disease in populations without immunity—neither bonfires to disinfect the air, nor collective demonstrations of penitence in northern towns, nor persecutions of Jews or friars. The mortality was staggering—the French chronicler Jean Froissart's estimate that the first wave carried off one-third of the population was perhaps not far wrong; evidence shows that rural areas were no less afflicted than towns. And there were recurrent outbreaks of plague in later years. These afflictions and related factors were responsible for a general decline of population. Toulouse seems to have lost half of its population, which fell from 40,000 to 20,000; the population of Normandy is estimated to have declined by two-thirds between 1300 and 1450. The trend was not reversed until the middle of the 15th century.

The hard times affected classes and regions in different ways, degrees, and rhythms. Some places almost escaped the ravages that afflicted others repeatedly. In the countryside, especially—save for the greatest personages—those who had most to lose suffered most. Whether for landlords or rich peasants, surpluses became harder to obtain or preserve; to many lesser lords the dangerous fortunes of war probably seemed an attractive alternative to declining yields in money or produce. Standards of living, as measured in diets or furnishings, declined. Onerous obligations and services tended to disappear as shortages of rural labour made themselves felt; the transition from servile to rental tenures was largely completed in the 15th century. Peasant uprisings, such as the Jacquerie in the relatively prosperous Île-de-France and the Tuchins in Languedoc, both betrayed desperation born of recurrent taxation and were associated with the expression of egalitarian ideas; the Jacquerie coincided with a weakened grain market and may have been hastened by efforts of lords to enforce labour services and payments after the Black Death. The manor survived, but little remained of its human identity in the 15th century. Even minor lords lived away from their peasant tenants, protected them poorly if at all, and relied on salaried managers to collect payments that, in some cases, had lost all social justification; lordship had degenerated into an unsentimental economic practice.

THE CITIES

Urban society was also troubled. During the centuries of relative peace after 1000, towns had been able to neglect fortifications and surround themselves with growing suburbs; the threat of warfare required them to make heavy investments in new walls that broadened the separation between city and countryside. Royal taxation, often inequitably administered, exacerbated old tensions in the towns; fiscal policy or the regulation of wages or supplies was largely at issue in the uprisings of Flemish towns (1323–28), in Paris

(1357–58, 1380–82), and in Rouen (1382). Communes continued to be revoked in the 14th century, although the kings as a rule were less interested in governing the towns than in securing their resources and fidelity. The concentration of trades and crafts in guilds became more complete and more exclusive.

Some leading commercial centres of the 13th century suffered as new trade routes developed in the empire and by sea and as textile manufactures and money markets—the latter suffering from unstable coinages—became more dispersed. The fairs of Champagne declined rapidly after 1310. Only a few capitals, such as Avignon, Bordeaux, and Paris, prospered; and even they were hard-hit by plague. Nor did the French merchant or manufacturer keep up with the new business techniques being developed in Italy and the Low Countries. His work often unspecialized, his bookkeeping old-fashioned, his tastes simple, he typically looked forward to securing his future by the purchase of land.

THE CHURCH

The organized church, despite losses from war and plague, continued to be better endowed economically than morally. The popes of Avignon were less distant and—save perhaps to their French relatives, merchants, and artists—less admirable than the reformer popes of the past; their authority was disputed by their rivals in Rome, and the French higher clergy were confirmed in their incipient Gallicanism (a movement advocating administrative independence from papal control). While organized heresy had almost disappeared, reforms intended to strengthen the parish priesthood languished. Jurisdictional disputes continued to rage between mendicants and seculars and between bishops and canons or archdeacons. Even more than in the past, Christian piety sought encouragement in mystical or individual devotions or readings and in collective observances of the Holy Spirit or the Virgin or the patron saints of the trades that promoted elementary solidarity and charity in the towns; such confraternities were not always welcome to ecclesiastical authorities, whose deportment or jurisdiction they sometimes challenged, whether directly or merely by example. The popular religion of saints—more particularly of the Virgin and the Pietà—and fear of demons worked more deeply into the collective imagination, becoming very evident in the 15th century. Associated with intensified anxieties about sin and damnation, these experiences thrived in times of recurrent and inscrutable disaster, such as the Black Death.

CULTURE AND ART

Cultural circles remained strongly oriented to aristocratic values and the past. With the accession of the house of Valois came a high nobility, distinguished by lavish and exclusive conceits. When John II formed the Order of the Star (1351), an institution imitated by the great lords for their clientages, chivalry stood incorporated as the most distinguished of religious confraternities. The dream of the Crusade remained strong, notably among princes of the fleur-de-lis, who dominated the public life of Valois France to the point of eclipsing the monarch; beneath them many noble families disappeared, while new ones emerged among the captains, lawyers, and patricians. Jean Froissart spun out chronicles of the war at once detailed and grand, full of the frivolous courtly protocol that marked the aristocratic life of his day. Tapestries created for courtly patrons idealized a life of enticing gardens, tournaments, and the hunt. Paintings as well as tapestries decorated the walls of chambers that were smaller and more elegant than the cavernous halls of earlier centuries. The delicate Gothic Rayonnant style of the Île-de-France remained in favour through the 14th century, inspiring the chapel built by Charles V at Vincennes, while the decorative arts of furnishings and manuscripts exploited the Gothic tendencies to articulation and grace. The evocation of the Classical past became less fantastic and more heroic in the humanist circles of Pierre Bersuire and Petrarch; their interests helped to attract copyists and artists to the papal court of Avignon. Books of hours (the most popular private devotional works of the later Middle Ages) could become "very rich," as in the case of a sumptuous manuscript undertaken for Jean, duc de Berry (c. 1410); more typically they were pocket books for general use by the literate, whose numbers continued to increase.

Stimulated by the commissions of Charles V, the chasm between learned and vernacular cultures narrowed: Raoul de Presles translated St. Augustine; Nicolas Oresme translated Aristotle. Christine de Pisan (1364–c. 1430) challenged traditional assertions of women's inferiority, incorporated in texts such as the *Roman de la Rose* (*The Romance of the Rose*), the most popular literary work of the 13th century. Music resounded in old forms (ballad, virelay) even while becoming more articulate or flamboyant; Guillaume de Machaut (died 1377), the great musician-poet of the mid-14th century, composed the first polyphonic mass as well as many motets and secular lyrics. Time and space came to be better represented and measured, as evidenced by the first attempts to render perspective in art and by the erection of public clocks at Paris and Caen.

By 1400 Paris regained cultural leadership as a result of a new synthetic (or international) style in painting and of the initiatives of the university masters in ecclesiastical politics and theology. The efflorescence, however, was soon destroyed in the civil wars. Provincial universities (like *parlements*) proliferated at the expense of Paris, which became the preserve of an antiquated and pedantic theology. Painters, architects, and writers regrouped under princely patrons or even under bourgeois ones, flourishing in postwar trade (Jacques Coeur's palace at Bourges exemplifies the flamboyantly decorated solidity of late medieval taste in France). A new style in painting, as in architecture, characterized by vigour and an enlarged scale, contrasted with the more traditional style in Burgundy, where the dukes were building on a grand and continuous past. Italianate humanism, together with the new philology, stirred in France only in the latter third of the 15th century.

CHAPTER 8

THE SUN KING AND THE NAPOLEONIC ERA

French kings of the 16th and 17th centuries strengthened the monarchy and gave it grandeur. Under their patronage, the arts flourished and exploration in the Americas brought France an empire in the New World. Rivalries in Europe, however, continued to be a drain on the treasury, and unsuccessful wars did little to expand French power.

FRANCE IN THE 16TH CENTURY

When Charles VIII (reigned 1483–98) led the French invasion of Italy in 1494, he initiated a series of wars that were to last until the Peace of Cateau-Cambrésis in 1559. These wars were not especially successful for the French, but they corresponded to the contemporary view of the obligations of kingship. They also had their effects upon the development of the French state; in particular, they threatened to alter not only the military and administrative structure of the monarchy but even its traditional role.

MILITARY AND FINANCIAL ORGANIZATION

The French kings of the early 16th century could look back with satisfaction at the virtual expulsion of the English from French soil in the course of the preceding century. This success offered a shining precedent for further military sallies, this time against the growing power of the Habsburgs. In 1445 the first steps had been taken to fashion a royal French

army out of the ill-disciplined mercenary bands upon which French kings
had traditionally relied. It was a small
force—no more than 8,000 men—but it
was a beginning. The role of the nobility
in the army was strong, for the art of war
was still considered a noble pursuit par
excellence. The core of Charles's army
that marched into Italy, the *compagnies d'ordonnance*, known collectively
as the gendarmerie, consisted of noble
volunteers. The infantry, however, was
made up of non-nobles, and by the
middle of the 16th century there were
more than 30,000 infantrymen to a mere
5,000 noble horsemen. As this infantry
force grew in number, its organization
changed. After a brief experiment in the
1530s with a system of legions organized
on a provincial basis (the Breton Legion,
the Norman Legion, etc.), a regimental
system, based on large units under a
single command, was adopted. This latter organization appeared during the
Wars of Religion of the 16th century and
survived until the time of Louis XIV. Of
great significance, too, was the involvement of the provincial governors as
commanders of the gendarmerie at the
heart of the royal army. Yet such reorganization did not immediately reduce the
army to a pliant tool of the crown. Not
until late in the 17th century could the
royal army be considered fairly under the
king's control. Until then, notably during
the Wars of Religion and the outbreaks
of the Fronde (1648–53), the loyalty of
the commanders and the devotion of

the troops were conspicuously inadequate. In the later part of the 17th
century, the reforms of the army by
Michel Le Tellier and his son the marquis de Louvois provided Louis XIV
with a formidable weapon.

The growth of a large royal army,
however, was only one effect of the
increased level of military activity. The
financial administration of the country
also underwent a drastic reorganization, which had far-reaching economic
and social consequences. The king,
despite his ambitions, possessed neither
the resources nor the administrative
machinery to maintain a large army. The
medieval idea that the king should live
off the revenue of his own domain persisted into the 18th century and helps to
explain the formal distinction made until
the reign of Francis I (1515–47) between
ordinary and extraordinary finance—
i.e., between revenue emanating from
the king's patrimonial rights and taxes
raised throughout the kingdom. By the
reign of Francis I, the king, even in times
of peace, was unable to make do with
his ordinary revenue from rents and
seigneurial dues. In 1523 Francis established a new central treasury, the Trésor
de l'Épargne, into which all his revenues,
ordinary and extraordinary, were to be
deposited. In 1542 he set up 16 financial and administrative divisions, the
généralités, appointing in each a collector general responsible for the collection
of all royal revenues within his area. In
1551 Henry II added a treasurer general;

from 1577 the *bureaux des finances,* new supervisory bodies composed of a collector general and a number of treasurers, made their appearance in each *généralité.*

The actual collecting of taxes, moreover, was increasingly handed over to tax farmers. The more efficient methods of collection by tax farmers enabled the crown to gather a larger proportion of its revenue than previously but did not solve the problem of royal finance. Even the extraordinary taxes, now added to the crown's ordinary revenue, notably the taille (a direct tax levied on all but the nobility and the clergy), customs duties, and the purchase tax on wine, fish, meat, and especially salt (the gabelle), were not adequate resources for Renaissance princes whose chief glory lay in the expensive art of war. The taille, the only direct tax, which weighed most heavily upon the underprivileged classes, went up from about 4.5 million livres under Louis XI (1461–83) to 55 million under Jules Cardinal Mazarin in the mid-17th century.

Successive monarchs were forced, therefore, to seek additional revenue. This was no simple matter, because French kings traditionally could not tax their subjects without their consent. Indeed, there were many areas of the country where the taille itself could not be collected and where the king was dependent upon local agreements. The early Valois kings had negotiated with the Estates-General or with the provincial Estates for their extra money; but in the middle of the 15th century, when the Hundred Years' War with England was reaching a successful conclusion, Charles VII was able to strike a bargain with the Estates. In return for a reduction in overall taxation, he began to raise money to support the army without having to seek the Estates' approval. In some areas of central France, the *pays d'élection,* the provincial assemblies, ceded their right to approve taxation and disappeared altogether. But, in those provinces where the provincial Estates survived (the *pays d'état*), the right to vote the amount of royal taxation also survived. During the Italian wars, meetings of the Estates became more frequent as the king's financial demands became more strident, and, though the Estates never felt themselves able to refuse to provide money, they retained the right to provide less than the monarch requested. The king continued to rely upon the support of the provincial assemblies to provide extra revenue long after 1614, when the cumbersome Estates-General ceased to play a role in opposing financial resources for the crown.

THE GROWTH OF A PROFESSIONAL BUREAUCRACY

But the king also found another means of filling his exchequer that had nothing to do with traditional methods: he began to sell offices on a large scale. Venality, or the sale of offices, was not novel in early 16th-century France; traces of the practice can be found in the 13th century. But it was Francis I who opened the floodgates.

The number of judges proliferated. In the Parlement of Paris alone, the king created two new chambers, each containing 20 members, and a further score of judges. In 1552 Henry II established a new kind of court, the *présidial*, whose jurisdiction lay between the *parlement* and the bailiwick. Each of the 65 new courts had a complement of nine judges; this brought in a sizable revenue but appears to have made little difference to the efficiency of the judicial system. Nor were judicial offices the only ones put up for sale; it was also possible to purchase financial offices, such as those of treasurer general, treasurer, or the immediately inferior *élu*. It has been estimated that during the 16th century some 50,000 offices were sold by the crown.

The partial rationalization of the financial system produced an increasing number of professional advisers, who formed the embryo of a bureaucratic elite. In the course of the 16th century, as specialization grew apace, the king's council became a much more complex institution. The Conseil d'État (Council of State), with its various subdivisions, formed the hub of royal government. Its members were drawn from a variety of backgrounds. The king's immediate family expected to be consulted, as did great officers of the crown, such as the chancellor, the constable, and the admiral. Also included in the council were the great territorial magnates, members of powerful aristocratic families, and the country's leading prelates. There were also masters of requests (*maîtres de requêtes*), lawyers whose expertise was invaluable when the council sat in a judicial capacity. But in the council the professional element that assumed the greatest significance in the course of the 16th and 17th centuries was the holders of the office of secretary of state. In the early years of the 14th century, royal secretaries had already acquired the right to sign documents on the king's authority. From this stage, granted the stability of the crown, the development of the office from a position of subordinate but considerable importance to one of complete indispensability was predictable. Henry II gave four of his secretaries the official title of *secrétaire d'état*, and in 1561 they became full members of the royal council. Closely associated with them and destined to overshadow them in importance in the first half of the 17th century were the superintendents of finance, formally established in 1564, though exercising an already well-established function. Their responsibility was to control and safeguard royal finances and especially to prepare annual budgets containing estimates of revenue and expenditure for the following year. They also played a leading part in assessing the amount to be levied each year from the taille and in deciding upon the imposition of new taxes. Below the superintendents but also in the royal council in the 16th century were the intendants of finance. Originally masters of requests, they became a separate group specializing in the increasingly complex task of advising the sovereign in financial matters. In time, their role outstripped in prestige that of the other masters of requests who counseled the king.

There thus grew up close to the crown a more specialized class of administrators, whose expertise rather than birth was the key to their influence; the sale of office allowed wealthy families to establish a firm base for later political and social advancement. In addition, the needy crown was perfectly prepared to sell titles of nobility as well as offices and, in return for a cash payment, to allow both nobility and office to become hereditary. Although this advancement of new men within the government might suggest a social readjustment of considerable proportions, in fact the element of continuity was more important than it might at first appear. Even though it is true that some of the ancient noble families and the king's own relatives found it increasingly difficult to fulfill their old advisory roles, the new men were not rejecting the established order but rather were being absorbed into it. The king's counselors, whatever their background, became leading noblemen by virtue of their high office: service to the crown was what mattered, and elevation to the office depended on the king's choice. It was not the first time that a new wave of royal servants had begun to overtake established advisers; in the 13th century the new *magistri*, or "masters," had ousted the great barons and prelates from the Curia Regis without effecting a social revolution. What took place in the 16th and 17th centuries was another turn of the social wheel by which new men seized the opportunity to pursue those dignities and honours held by men who were themselves descendants of new men.

THE AGE OF THE REFORMATION

The professional class that grew up in the 16th century was different in one respect from those that had gone before: it represented a predominantly secular culture—the product of Renaissance humanism. The Italian wars had brought French elites into contact with the new art, literature, and learning; Charles VIII, Louis XII, and especially Francis I imported numerous Italian painters, sculptors, and architects. French scholars such as Jacques Lefèvre d'Étaples and Guillaume Budé devoted themselves to the study of Classical Greek and Latin and attempted to reform the French language. The establishment in 1530 of the Collège de France institutionalized humanist studies, in opposition to the University, where the legacy of medieval Scholasticism, satirized in François Rabelais's bawdy prose works, *Gargantua and Pantagruel*, still dominated. Later in the century, the group of poets known as La Pléiade, of whom Pierre de Ronsard and Joachim du Bellay are the best-known, created a new style of French verse inspired by Classical models.

Many of the French humanists were initially receptive to ideas about returning to the original sources of the Christian religion that began to spread in France soon after Martin Luther publicized his famous Ninety-five Theses in 1517. Lutheran works first appeared in Paris in 1519; in 1521 Francis I, who was on the point of war with Emperor Charles V and King Henry VIII of England and who wanted to demonstrate his orthodoxy, forbade their publication. Yet interest in the new faith continued to grow, especially in the humanist circle of Lefèvre. Having published in 1512 an edition of the letters of St. Paul with a commentary that anticipated Martin Luther in its assertion of the doctrine of justification by faith, Lefèvre became the leader of a small group of moderate but orthodox Reformers in the tradition of the great Dutch humanist Desiderius Erasmus. This group included Guillaume Briçonnet, the bishop of Meaux; the mystic Gérard Roussel; and Margaret of Angoulême, the king's own sister. Although this circle was dispersed in 1525, Lutheranism had already established itself, especially in such trading centres as Lyon, where it found support among the poorer classes. The progress of the Reformation in France depended on the crown's attitude; although Francis for political reasons had initially shown hostility, his feelings were far from clear. He was favourably disposed toward Lefèvre and toward orthodox reform in general, though he naturally feared those extreme movements that threatened social upheaval. In addition, Francis I saw political advantages in establishing good relations with the Lutheran German princes. On the other hand, unlike them, he had no great incentive to assert his independence from Rome, because the Gallican church already enjoyed a large measure of autonomy. In 1516 the Concordat of Bologna had given the king effective control over the church in France.

In 1534, however, royal policy changed radically. The posting of anti-Catholic placards that began to appear in Paris and even at the royal court alarmed Francis I, who feared losing control of the religious movement. He responded with the first of a series of persecuting edicts. French Protestantism itself had changed, reinforced from the mid-1530s by the spread among the poorer classes of Languedoc and the seaboard towns of Normandy and Brittany of the ideas of John Calvin, a French exile in Geneva. Henry II (1547–59) pursued his father's harsh policies, setting up a special court (the *chambre ardente*) to deal with heresy and issuing further repressive edicts, such as that of Écouen in 1559. His sudden death from a jousting accident in 1559 and the demise the following year of his eldest son, Francis II, left royal policy uncertain. Meanwhile, the infusion of Calvinism, or Huguenotism, into the French Reformation had stiffened the Protestant opposition. Protestant pastors, trained in Geneva, infiltrated the country; by 1562 there were some 2,000 highly organized Calvinist churches in France. Calvinism provided both a rallying point for a wide cross section of opposition and the organization necessary to make that opposition effective. Each Huguenot community created its own administrative structure to provide a tight disciplinary framework through which the community could ensure its spiritual and material independence. The new creed attracted several elements in French society: small artisans, shopkeepers, and the urban unemployed, who were suffering in particular from steeply rising prices; many rich townspeople and professional men who thought that material advancement would be easier to procure as Calvinists; and, after the Treaty of Cateau-Cambrésis in 1559, many nobles, especially the poorer ones who had lost with the peace their best hope of wealth and status.

The adherence of large numbers of the nobility had two important effects upon the movement in France: it caused many peasants to join the new creed in imitation of their noble seigneurs, thus swelling the overall number and widening its social composition, and it brought a new military element into the Calvinist communities. Under the leadership of the nobility, secret religious meetings were transformed into mass public demonstrations against which the king's forces were impotent. Such demonstrations sometimes involved upward of 20,000 people. Similarly, the administrative structure that was so important in aiding the survival of the proscribed faith was transformed into a military organization. This organization was ultimately headed by Louis I de Bourbon, prince de Condé, who assumed the title of protector general of the churches of France, thus putting all the prestige of the house of Bourbon behind the Huguenot cause. By doing so, he added a new dimension to the age-old opposition of the mighty feudal subject to the crown: that opposition was now backed by a tightly knit military organization based on the Huguenot communities, by the financial contributions of wealthy bankers and businessmen, and by the dedicated religious zeal of the faithful, inspired by the example of Geneva.

At a time when the threat to the crown had never been greater, the monarchy itself presented a sorry spectacle. The struggle between the families of Guise, Bourbon, and Montmorency for political power at the centre of government after Henry II's death; the vacillating policy of Catherine de Médicis, widow of Henry II, who strongly influenced the three sons who successively became king; and, most important, the ineptitude of those rulers—Francis II (1559–60), Charles IX (1560–74), and Henry III (1574–89)— meant that local government officials were never confident of their authority in seeking to curb the growing threat of Huguenotism. After the death of Francis II, Catherine de Médicis, who was ruling in the name of her second son, Charles IX, abandoned the repressive religious policy of Francis I and Henry II and attempted to achieve religious reconciliation. Guided by the moderate chancellor Michel de L'Hospital, Catherine summoned the French clergy to the Colloquy of Poissy (1561), at which an unsuccessful attempt was made to effect a religious compromise with the Huguenots; in the following year she issued the Edict of January, which allowed the Calvinists a degree of toleration. These signs of favour to the Protestants brought a violent reaction from devout Catholics, who found leadership in the noble house of Guise, the champions of Roman Catholicism in France. The first civil war began with the massacre of a Huguenot congregation at Vassy (March 1562) by the partisans of François, 2e duc de Guise.

THE WARS OF RELIGION

Guise's forces occupied Paris and took control of the royal family while the Huguenots rose in the provinces, and their two commanders—Louis I de Bourbon, prince de Condé, and Admiral Gaspard II de Coligny—established headquarters at Orléans. The deaths of the opposing leaders—the Protestant Anthony of Bourbon, king consort of Navarra, and the Catholic marshal Jacques d'Albon, seigneur de Saint-André—and the capture of Condé caused both sides to seek peace. After the Battle of Dreux (December 1562) the war drew to a close, despite the assassination of the duc de Guise by a Protestant fanatic. A compromise was reached at the Peace of Amboise in March 1563: liberty of conscience was granted to the Huguenots, but the celebration of religious services was confined to the households of the nobility and to a limited number of towns.

The second war was precipitated by Huguenot fears of an international Catholic plot. Condé and Coligny were persuaded to attempt a coup to capture Catherine and Charles IX at Meaux in September 1567 and to seek military aid from the Protestant Palatinate. In the following brief war, the Catholic constable Anne, duc de Montmorency, was killed at the Battle of Saint-Denis (November 1567). The Peace of Longjumeau (March 1568) signaled another effort at compromise. This peace, however, proved little more than a truce; a third war soon broke out in September 1568. In an attempt to restore their authority, Catherine and King Charles dismissed L'Hospital in September and restored the Guise faction to favour. The edicts of pacification were rescinded; Calvinist preachers faced expulsion from France, and plans were made to seize Condé and Coligny. The former was killed at the Battle of Jarnac (1569), and the Huguenots were again defeated in that year at Moncontour. But the Catholic side failed to consolidate its successes, and yet another compromise was arranged at the Peace of Saint-Germain in August 1570.

Coligny subsequently regained the king's favour but not the queen mother's, and he remained an object of hatred with the Guises. In 1572 he was murdered. At the same time, some 3,000 Huguenots who gathered in Paris to celebrate the marriage of Margaret of Valois (later Margaret of France) to Condé's nephew, Henry IV of Navarre, were massacred on the eve of the feast day of St. Bartholomew, and several thousand more perished in massacres in provincial cities. This notorious episode was the signal for the fifth civil war, which ended in 1576 with the Peace of Monsieur, allowing the

Huguenots freedom of worship outside Paris. Opposition to these concessions inspired the creation of the Holy League, or Catholic League. Local Catholic unions or leagues had begun to appear in the 1560s, headed by nobles and prelates. In 1576, after the Peace of Monsieur with its concessions to the Huguenots, these local leagues were fused into a national organization. The league was headed by the Guise family and looked to Philip II of Spain for material aid. It sought, like the Protestants, to attract mass support; its clandestine organization was built around the house of Guise rather than the monarchy, from which it was increasingly alienated. In 1577 King Henry III (reigned 1574–89) tried to nullify the league's influence, first by putting himself at its head and then by dissolving it altogether. This maneuver met with some success.

Renewed fighting broke out in 1577 between Catholic and Protestant noblemen, who defied Henry III in his attempt to assert royal authority. The Huguenots were defeated and forced by the Peace of Bergerac (1577) to accept further limitations upon their freedom. An uneasy peace followed until 1584, when, upon the death of François, duc d'Anjou, the Huguenot leader Henry of Navarra became the heir to the throne. This new situation produced the War of the Three Henrys (1585–89), during which the Guise faction—led by Henri I de Lorraine, 3e duc de Guise—sought to have Navarra excluded from the succession. The threat of a Protestant king led to the revival of the Catholic League, which now took on a more radical form. This movement was centred in Paris among middle-class professional men and members of the clergy and soon spread among the Parisian artisans, guilds, and public officials. Henry III, who was considered far too tolerant toward the Huguenots, was an object of attack. In town after town, royalist officials were replaced by members of the league. In Paris the mob was systematically aroused; in 1588, on the famous Day of the Barricades (May 12), Henry III was driven from his own capital. In a welter of intrigue and murder, first the duc de Guise (December 1588) and his brother Louis II de Lorraine, 2e cardinal de Guise (December 1588), and then Henry III himself (August 1589) were assassinated, allowing the Protestant Henry of Navarra (Henry IV) to ascend to the throne. After the murder of the Guises, the league came out in open revolt against the crown. Towns renounced their royal allegiances and set up revolutionary governments. In Paris, however, where the league was most highly organized, a central committee called the Sixteen set up a Committee of Public Safety and conducted a reign of terror in a manner similar to the much more famous one that occurred during the revolution 200 years later. Paradoxically, this genuinely populist and revolutionary element in the Holy League paved the way for the triumph of Henry IV (1589–1610), the first king of France from the house of Bourbon (a branch of the house of Capet). The aristocratic members of the league took fright at the direction in which the extreme elements in the movement were proceeding. Their fears reached a climax in 1591, when the Sixteen arrested and executed three magistrates of the Parlement of Paris. The growing split in the ranks of the members of the league, combined with Henry's well-timed conversion to Roman Catholicism, enabled Henry to seize the initiative and enter Paris, almost unopposed, in 1594. In its final stages, the war became a struggle against Spanish forces intervening on behalf of Isabella Clara Eugenia, the daughter of Philip II of Spain and Elizabeth of Valois, who also laid claim to the French throne. The Peace of Vervins (1598), by which Spain recognized Henry IV's title as king, and the Edict of Nantes of the same year, which granted substantial religious toleration to the Huguenots, ended the Wars of Religion.

POLITICAL IDEOLOGY

The religious wars had posed a new and fundamental threat to the monarchy and therefore to the whole French state, which makes the strong position that Henry IV achieved by the time of his death that much more remarkable. Part of his success lay in the unwillingness of his great (noble) subjects to contemplate a social and political upheaval that would displace them as well as the king from their positions of power and prestige. The religious wars also engendered a luxuriant growth of political ideas that in the end provided a strong theoretical basis for the reassertion of royal authority.

A strong element in Calvin's teaching was the importance of passive obedience to secular authority—an idea that became impossible for the Huguenots to support after the Massacre of St. Bartholomew's Day. They began instead to advocate the right to attack the king if he would not guarantee them toleration. The most important Huguenot contribution in this change was the anonymous pamphlet *Vindiciae contra tyrannos* (1579; "A Defense of Liberty Against Tyrants"), which raised fundamental questions about the prince's power and the rights of his subjects. The pamphlet advanced the idea of a twofold contract: the first contract, between God and ruler on the one hand and the ruler and his subjects on the other, recognized the belief that the king ruled under the aegis of Divine Providence; the second contract, between the king and the people, obliged the king to govern justly and the people to obey him so long as he did so. It followed from the argument in the *Vindiciae* that subjects had the right to rebel if the prince disobeyed the laws of God or refused to govern his people justly. This twofold contract was not intended to be a license for private and personal rebellion but was interpreted as justifying the corporate opposition of whole towns and provinces.

A second element in the realm of political ideas, deeply opposed to the contractual theory of the Huguenots, was that of the Jesuit supporters of Ultramontanism. The Ultramontanists feared that a strong national monarchy would mean the subordination of the church to its authority and the diminution of papal authority. They feared the triumph of both Huguenotism and Gallicanism in France. Their most effective controversialist was the Italian prelate Robert Bellarmine, whose *Disputationes*, 3 vol. (1586–93), and *De potestate summi pontificis in rebus temporalibus* (1610; "Concerning the Power of the Supreme Pontiff in Temporal Matters") gave definite form to the theory of papal supremacy. By no means were all members of the league supporters of Bellarmine, though their extreme Catholicism made many of them sympathetic to his ideas. The definitive Gallican reply came in 1594 with Pierre Pithou's *Les Libertés de l'église gallicane* ("Liberties of the Gallican Church"), which reiterated the basic tenets of Gallican doctrine: that the pope had no temporal authority in France and no more spiritual power than that bestowed on him by such conciliar decisions as the monarchy chose to recognize.

The growing support for Gallican opinion was a reflection of the emergence of the Politique Party after the Massacre of St. Bartholomew's Day. In the opinion of this moderate Catholic group, toleration should be granted to the Huguenots for the sake of peace and national unity. The Politiques were the spiritual heirs of the chancellor L'Hospital and represented an attitude of mind rather than an organized movement. Under the pressure of political events, this group became convinced of the need to support a strong monarchy that could resist both Ultramontane and Huguenot excesses and the divisive influence of noble factions. They therefore increasingly identified themselves with the Gallican position. The Huguenots, too, were not slow to see the advantages for themselves of this new attitude, and the ideas of the *Vindiciae* gave way to the theory of passive obedience. The wheel had turned full circle.

With this emphasis upon passive obedience emerged the theory of the divine right of kings. The first written statement of the theory in France is contained in the works of Pierre de Belloy, especially his *De l'autorité du roi* (1588; "Of the Authority of the King"). He asserted that the monarchy was created by God and that the king was responsible to God alone. Any rebellion against the ruler, therefore, was a rebellion against the Almighty. The essential premise of the divine-right idea is that the right to command obedience cannot be bestowed by man; only God can grant such authority. God therefore chooses the king, and there can be no contractual relationship between the king and his people; to rebel even against an unjust ruler is to challenge God's choice. If the king breaks his contract with God, then he is answerable to God alone. On the wave of such ideas, Henry of Navarra became king of a united France, supported by Huguenots and moderate Politique Catholics alike. The universalist doctrine of Bellarmine gave way to the national one of Pithou as the country closed ranks against Spain, the common enemy.

One other concept emerged about this time that helped to set the seal on Henry's authority: the idea of sovereignty, as expounded by Jean Bodin. In his *Six Livres de la république* (1576; *The Six Bookes of a Commonweale*, 1606) Bodin argued that the political bond that made every man subject to one sovereign power overrode religious differences. Bodin provided the link divine right did not allow between the king and his people; divine right was concerned with the source of the ruler's power, sovereignty with its exercise. The needs of the political situation forced Bodin to give his sovereign virtually unlimited authority, though he insisted—as was traditionally the case in France—that the ruler should respect the sanctity of the natural law, of the fundamental laws of the kingdom, of property, and of the family. In 1614, on the occasion of the last meeting of the Estates-General before the Revolution, the Third Estate sought to have it made a fundamental law of the realm that under no pretext whatever was it permissible to disobey the king. This effort gives some indication of the extent to which the ideas of divine right and sovereignty had provided a firm theoretical base for the reestablishment of monarchical power after the dangerous years of civil war.

FRANCE IN THE EARLY 17TH CENTURY

The 17th century is known as France's great century. Colonies expanded and trade increased. Art and literature reached new heights. And able ministers, such as the duke de Sully, Cardinal Mazarin, and Jean-Baptiste Colbert, helped make France the foremost power in Europe.

HENRY IV

The restoration of royal authority was not, of course, simply a matter of adjusting theories of kingship; there was a clear practical reason for Henry's success. The country had tottered on the brink of disintegration for three decades. By the time of Henry's succession, it was generally recognized that only a strong personality, independent of faction, could guarantee the unity of the state, even though unity meant religious toleration for the Protestant minority. In the Edict of Nantes (April 13, 1598) Henry guaranteed the Huguenots freedom of conscience and the right to practice their religion publicly in certain prescribed areas of the country. As a surety against attack, the Huguenots were granted a number of fortresses, some of them, such as La Rochelle and Montpellier, extremely formidable. Huguenots were made eligible to hold the same offices as Roman

Catholics and to attend the same schools and universities. Finally, to ensure impartial justice for them, the Edict established in the Parlement of Paris—the supreme judicial court under the king—a new chamber, the Chambre de l'Édit, containing a number of Protestant magistrates who would judge all cases involving Huguenots. Although the problem of religion was not finally settled by the Edict of Nantes, Henry did succeed in effecting an extended truce during which he could apply himself to the task of restoring the royal position.

The chief need of the monarchy was to improve the financial situation, parlous since the days of Henry II's wars and aggravated by the subsequent internecine conflict. Henry was fortunate in this connection to have the services of Maximilien de Béthune, duc de Sully, who was admitted to the king's financial council in 1596. Sully at once embarked upon a series of provincial tours, enforcing the repayment of royal debts, thereby increasing the king's revenues. He also provided the first real statements of government finances in many years; by 1598 he had become the effective head of the royal financial machine as well as a trusted member of the king's inner cabinet. He held a variety of offices: superintendent of finances, grand master of artillery, superintendent of buildings, governor of the Bastille, and others. But it was in the field of finance that he made his greatest contribution to the welfare of the state. Sully was not an original financial thinker. He undertook no sweeping

changes, contenting himself with making the existing system work, for example, by shifting the emphasis from direct to indirect taxation. He succeeded in building both an annual surplus and substantial reserves.

The only measure Sully championed that might be described as novel and far-reaching was the introduction in 1604 of a new tax, the *paulette*, named after the financier Charles Paulet, which enabled *officiers* (officeholders) to assure the heritability of their offices by paying one-sixtieth of the purchase price each year. The *paulette* was intended to increase royal revenues, though it had considerable political implications too, in effect making government offices practically hereditary. Politically, the *paulette* was to increase the independence of a wide range of royal officials; it did, however, give these officiers a stake in the strengthening of the royal government. In addition, Sully did much to reorganize fortifications and to rebuild roads and bridges after the devastation of the religious wars. In transportation his greatest work was the Briare Canal project to join the Seine and Loire rivers—the first such scheme in France—completed under Louis XIII.

Sully, however, favoured a much more cautious domestic policy overall than did his sovereign; because Sully disliked merchants and manufacturers, he opposed many of the king's economic ventures. Henry IV believed in direct state intervention, and he took steps to fix wages and to prohibit strikes and illegal combinations of workmen. Henry's policies bore fruit especially in the textile industries, where the production of luxury silk goods and woolen and linen cloth greatly increased. Henry also took the initiative in making commercial treaties with Spain and England, thereby increasing the volume of French trade and stimulating the export of grain, cattle, and wine. Yet his efforts were not entirely successful, not least because merchants remained more concerned with buying land and office (and thereby status) than with plowing back their profits into further industrial development. Though the country did assume a more prosperous air under Henry IV, that change was chiefly because of the domestic and foreign calm that followed the Peace of Vervins.

Even after Spain's agreement in 1598 to the restoration of the territorial position as it had existed in 1559, Henry was not free of international complications. But he was able to prevent them from once more dividing his kingdom. He did have to counter a conspiracy led by one of his own marshals, Charles de Gontaut, baron et duc de Biron, who plotted with the king of Spain and almost succeeded in raising southwestern France in revolt. Henry, however, had Biron arrested and executed in 1602; this strong action against an old friend and powerful enemy had the effect of subduing the political rising and strengthening Henry's own authority. In central government Henry gave increasing power to Sully at the expense of the rest of his council, while in the provinces the responsibilities of

the intendant, an official first regularly employed during the reign of Henry III, were widened to include the supervision of potentially dissident groups. The intendants also represented the crown at meetings of provincial estates, enforced royal laws, and advised the king on a variety of local problems—fiscal, administrative, and military. When Henry IV was assassinated by François Ravaillac, a Catholic fanatic, in May 1610, he had gone a long way toward restoring the monarchy to a position of authority similar to that held by Francis I and Henry II and had reunified a state greatly threatened at his accession from both within and without.

LOUIS XIII

From 1610 to 1617, Henry's widow, Marie de Médicis, ruled on behalf of their young son Louis XIII (reigned 1610–43). Once more the security of the country was threatened as factions disputed around the throne. The work of Henry IV seemed likely to be undone. Crown and country, however, were rescued by probably the greatest minister of the whole Bourbon dynasty—Armand-Jean du Plessis, cardinal et duc de Richelieu. Richelieu first came to the attention of the government in 1614, when he was chosen to present the final address of the clergy at the meeting of the Estates-General. His eloquence and political expertise on this occasion won him the notice of Marie de Médicis, who later appointed him her secretary. By 1616

Richelieu was secretary of state for war and foreign affairs. His career, however, received a check in the following year when a palace revolution overthrew the regency of the queen mother, exiling her to Blois. Richelieu was banished first to Luçon and subsequently to Avignon (1618). He began the climb back to power by negotiating the Treaty of Angoulême (1619), which reconciled Louis XIII to his mother. After the death in 1621 of Louis's favourite, Charles d'Albert, duc de Luynes, Richelieu regained effective power; he became a cardinal in 1622 and in April 1624 gained access to Louis XIII's council. On the disgrace in 1624 of the superintendent of finance, Charles de La Vieuville, Richelieu became Louis's principal minister—a position that he maintained until his death some 18 years later.

Richelieu proved an indefatigable servant of the French crown, intent on securing absolute obedience to the monarchy and on raising its international prestige. The first objective required him to crush a number of revolts of the nobles, the first of which, in 1626, involved the king's younger brother and heir, Gaston, duc d'Orléans. Louis acted ruthlessly, and one of the conspirators, Henri de Talleyrand, comte de Chalais, was executed. Then, in 1630, came the notorious Day of Dupes (November 10), when the queen mother, now allied with Gaston and the keeper of the seals, Michel de Marillac, prepared to move against Richelieu. After initially agreeing to the cardinal's dismissal, the king recovered and chose to support Richelieu against the wishes of his mother, his wife, and his confessor. Finally, at the very end of his life, the cardinal had to overcome another conspiracy headed by the young royal favourite, Henri Coiffier de Ruzé, marquis de Cinq-Mars, in which Gaston was once more implicated. Through all these crises, Richelieu retained the king's support, for it was in Louis's interests, too, that such intrigues be firmly dealt with.

In the course of strengthening royal absolutism, Richelieu also came into conflict with the Huguenots. He believed that their right under the Edict of Nantes to maintain armed fortresses weakened the king's position at home and abroad. Protestant rebellions in 1625 and 1627 persuaded the cardinal of the need for a direct confrontation. The major Huguenot citadel of La Rochelle was attacked by royal troops in 1627 and, despite attempts by the English to assist the Protestants, fell in the following year. Another royal army marched into Languedoc, where the Huguenot forces were concentrated, and quickly overcame them. The Peace of Alais (1629) left the Huguenots free to enjoy religious and civil liberties, but they lost the military power that had made them a threat to the government. They were never to pose that sort of threat again, and little more would be heard of them until Louis XIV decided to repeal Henry IV's Edict of Nantes.

Richelieu also took a great interest in economic matters. To promote economic self-sufficiency, he encouraged the manufacture of tapestry, glass, silk, linen, and woolen cloth. He gave privileges to companies that established colonies in the Americas, Africa, and the West Indies. To protect trading and colonial interests, he created a navy, which by 1642 had 63 oceangoing vessels.

On the basis of these policies, Richelieu was able to pursue an increasingly ambitious foreign policy. His first aim was the security of France, which he hoped to achieve through the occupation of key points on the country's frontiers lying along imperial and Spanish territories. He thus involved France in the War of the Mantuan Succession (1628–31) in northern Italy. Through diplomatic means he worked for the dismissal of Albrecht Wenzel von Wallenstein, the brilliant general fighting on the side of Emperor Ferdinand II, whose forces were threatening to destroy the Protestant princes of Germany in the Thirty Years' War. To undermine the power of the Habsburgs, he prolonged this conflict, negotiating with the United Provinces; with Gustav II Adolf of Sweden, with whom he concluded the subsidy Treaty of Bärwalde in 1631, agreeing to pay the Swedish king one million livres per year to continue the war; with Gustav's successor, Greve (count) Axel Oxenstierna; and with Bernhard, duke of Saxe-Weimar. Eventually, in 1635, Richelieu committed France to direct conflict with the Habsburgs; and before his death he had savoured the triumph of having French arms in the Spanish Netherlands, Lorraine, Alsace, and Roussillon.

Richelieu's foreign policy was not only ambitious but extremely expensive. Annual government expenditure tripled from 1620 to 1640, two-thirds of the money going to the military. The drastic increase in taxes needed to pay for the war sparked a series of provincial rebellions in the 1630s. The population's resentment of the monarchy's rising demands was exacerbated by the fact that these years marked the end of a long cycle of prosperity, encompassing most of the 16th century and the beginning of a period of economic difficulties that would extend through the reign of Louis XIV. Crop failures, great fluctuations in prices, and outbreaks of famine further accentuated the misery. Although most participants in the revolts of the 1630s came from the lower classes, municipal authorities such as those of Lyon in 1632, provincial nobles in Périgord in 1636, and even princes of the blood such as Louis de Bourbon, comte de Soissons, in 1641, took advantage of the discontent to incite protests against the increasing centralization of royal power and Richelieu's efforts to abrogate local privileges. Indeed, peasants often turned to local nobles to lead their movements.

Although these revolts were unwelcome distractions from the minister's efforts to project French power abroad, they did not pose a revolutionary threat. Dispersed and uncoordinated, they were put down by a combination of temporary concessions, such as the suspension of efforts to collect unpopular taxes, and the exemplary execution of a few ringleaders. There was little sign of the revolutionary attitude that had characterized aspects of the 16th-century Wars of Religion and that would surface again in 1789. On the contrary, there were positive signs of continuing loyalty to the crown, with such rebel slogans as "Vive le roi sans la gabelle" ("Long live the king, but not the salt tax") or "Vive le roi sans la taille" ("Long live the king, but not the direct tax") indicating that the resistance was focused on the taxes themselves. Nor was the other great bastion of the establishment, the church, attacked. The substantial tax of the *dîme* (the tithe, or tenth) continued to be paid to the church without complaint. The first half of the 17th century was a period of revival for French Catholicism, as the church reforms called for by the Council of Trent began to show their effects. Improved seminary training produced more educated and devout priests, who worked to inspire stricter observance among their flocks. New religious orders, inspired by such figures as Francis of Sales, Vincent de Paul, Jane Frances of Chantal, and Louise de Marillac (all later canonized), emphasized practical activities such as teaching and the provision of medical care. These orders—such as the Oratorians and the Vincentians (Lazarists), for men, and the Ursulines and Sisters of Charity, for women—rooted the church more strongly in French society.

The career of Richelieu bears something of a contradictory aspect. He undoubtedly added to the earlier success of Henry IV and Sully in overcoming the threat of anarchy and disorder that was the legacy of the late 16th century. Indeed, his contemporary reputation was one of supreme ruthlessness and arbitrariness in the application of power. Yet he was never more than the king's creature, incapable of pursuing a course of action of which Louis disapproved, always vulnerable to the loss of royal favour and support. He was ambitious, but he recognized that his desire for power could be satisfied best within the confines of dutiful royal service. Richelieu was no innovator: he devised neither new administrative procedures nor novel methods of taxation to secure the king's authority. Indeed, the power of the great financiers grew with the government's need for additional war revenue, posing a different threat to royal absolutism. Richelieu's unique contribution lay in the single-minded devotion he gave to the task of increasing royal authority at home and abroad. He also succeeded in accumulating a vast personal fortune as a result of his years in power. Richelieu died in 1642, and Louis XIII died the following year. France was once again ruled by a regent, the queen mother, Anne of Austria. But the task of governing the country fell increasingly into the hands of another cardinal, Jules Mazarin.

THE FRONDE

The years of Louis XIV's minority were dominated by the Fronde, a series of civil disturbances that lasted from 1648 to 1653. The government's financial difficulties were once more at the root of the trouble. In the first few years of the regency a variety of expedients were tried to raise additional revenue for the war with Spain. There was about these expedients an air of arbitrariness and compulsion that antagonized a wide cross section of Parisian society, notably the Parlement of Paris, and the animosity was heightened by Mazarin's use of intendants in the localities to cut across traditional legal hierarchies. Although most of the disputes were superficially concerned with financial exactions, below the surface an older constitutional argument was developing, as Mazarin followed Richelieu in attempting to dictate from the centre in the interests of the state. The climax came when the government failed to renew the paulette for the members of the provincial parlements and for some of the chief legal officers in the capital, in the Cour des Aides, the Chambre des Comptes, and the Great Council. This decision was not a gratuitous rebuff to these magistrates but yet another attempt to gain additional revenue, this time by offering a renewal of the paulette in lieu of four years' salary.

At this point, the first phase of the disturbances (the Fronde of the Parlement) began with the outraged magistrates of the three courts concerned joining with the Parlement of Paris to demand redress. Their demands included the abolition of the office of intendant, a reduction in the level of the taille, and the restoration of normal judicial procedure in registering financial edicts in the Parlement. The regent and Mazarin at first took a conciliatory attitude, but each side gradually moved to more committed and extreme positions, and civil disturbances in Paris exacerbated an already delicate situation. The magistrates increasingly aimed their fire at Mazarin, for he, like Richelieu before him, seemed to be taking over the king's authority and using it in uncharted and illegal areas. The magistrates, however, were not revolutionaries, and the state of disorder in the capital frightened them. That fact, allied with fears of a Spanish invasion (for the war was continuing with Spain despite the Peace of Westphalia in 1648), persuaded them in 1649 to make the Peace of Rueil with the government, the terms of which were for the most part favourable to the magistrates' original demands. At this stage the second civil war broke out, the Fronde of the Princes, headed by the Great Condé. The second phase was a pale reflection of the aristocratic resistance during the Wars of Religion; and, although Condé succeeded in gaining control of Paris, he did not acquire the support of the Parlement except briefly and under duress. In October 1652 Condé fled to Spain, and Louis XIV reentered his capital in triumph.

Neither phase of the Fronde posed the grievous threat to the very basis of the state that had existed in the previous century. Mazarin was the chief object of enmity, and that fact itself helps to explain the less serious nature of the threat. What was at issue was not the king's authority per se but the manner in which it had been exercised since Richelieu's time.

After the Fronde, Mazarin continued to play a key role in government as chief adviser to the young king, whose respect and affection he had long possessed. His career ended on a high note with a successful conclusion of the war with Spain negotiated by the Peace of the Pyrenees (1659). According to its terms, France gained Roussillon and Cerdagne in the south and Artois and a number of border towns in the north; and the Rhine became France's frontier in the east. By the treaty, too, Louis XIV was betrothed to the infanta Marie-Thérèse, the elder daughter of Philip IV of Spain. It was by any reckoning a triumphant peace, though it sowed the seeds of future European conflict over the issue of the Spanish succession. When Mazarin died in 1661, Louis was confident enough to take up the reins of government without recourse to another first minister.

THE AGE OF LOUIS XIV

Throughout his long reign Louis XIV (1643–1715) never lost the hold over his people he had assumed at the beginning. He worked hard to project his authority in the splendid setting of Versailles and to depict it in his arrogant motto "Nec pluribus impar" ("None his equal") and in his sun emblem. He buttressed his authority with the divine-right doctrines elaborated by Bishop Jacques-Bénigne Bossuet and proclaimed it across Europe by force of arms. Yet he made surprisingly few institutional or administrative changes in the structure of government. Like Richelieu, Louis used the system that he had inherited and adapted it to suit his own personality and outlook. This practice may be seen first in his attitude to the machinery of central government.

THE DEVELOPMENT OF CENTRAL GOVERNMENT

Louis's inner council was based on the model of the royal council in Richelieu's days, a High Council (Conseil d'en Haut) consisting of only three or four members and excluding the king's own relatives. Members of this council were known as ministers, but they held no formal right to the title and ceased to be a minister if the king chose not to summon them. The first of these great men were Michel Le Tellier, Hugues de Lionne, and Nicolas Fouquet; but the last was disgraced within a year, and by 1665 his place had been taken by Mazarin's former secretary, Jean-Baptiste Colbert. These three men dominated the government in the early years of Louis's personal reign, but always, as with Richelieu and Louis XIII, under the watchful and jealous eye of the king. Le Tellier had been secretary of state for military affairs under Mazarin's regime, and his greatest contribution under Louis was to reorganize the army along lines that were hardly changed until after 1789. He created a royal army that wore the king's uniform; it was commanded by his officers and was ultimately responsible to the sovereign. It was a standing army of hitherto undreamed-of size, reaching 400,000 men in times of war and requiring close regulation in matters of discipline, training, recruitment, supply, and overall organization. The success of Le Tellier and of his son Louvois, who succeeded him, goes far to explain the dominance of French arms in Europe during Louis's reign.

Lionne, the expert in foreign affairs, had been the chief French negotiator at the Peace of the Pyrenees. His effective influence on Louis is difficult to gauge; he certainly was not the sole source of advice in foreign affairs. Lionne remains a more elusive personality than his colleagues, though there can be no doubt of his importance. It should be remembered that all important matters of state were reviewed at the High Council; and the king's ministers were expected to give advice and opinions on all that was discussed, not simply on matters in the area of their particular expertise.

Colbert, however, remains the best-known of these intimate counselors. Of the 17 ministers summoned by Louis XIV to the High Council during his reign, 5 were members of the Colbert family. In 1664, Colbert was appointed superintendent of the king's buildings; in 1665, controller general of finances; in 1669, secretary of state for the navy. His capacity for work and his grasp of detail were remarkable; but he was not an original, much less a revolutionary, thinker. His chief contribution to the king's finances, like Sully's, was to make the machinery more efficient,

not to substitute any new mechanisms. Colbert's first achievement was to present the king with a monthly statement of the financial situation, though his annual estimates for the following year never persuaded Louis of the need for economies if his mind was set in other directions. Yet, within 10 years of taking office, Colbert, mainly by tightening up on the tax-collecting administration and by rationalizing the gathering of indirect taxes, did succeed in producing a surplus. He turned a large part of central and northern France into a free-trade area and gave the responsibility for collecting all indirect taxes there to a new syndicate of tax farmers called the Farmers-General. Under Colbert, the total sum levied from indirect taxation rose from 36 million livres to 62 million.

In his industrial policy Colbert believed that France needed to produce for itself those manufactured goods that it was importing. To achieve this mercantilist goal, derived from, among other sources, the ideas of Richelieu, Colbert was willing to invoke a variety of improvisations: direct subsidies, exemptions from the taille, monopoly grants, and controls exercised through town guilds. Skilled foreign workmen were persuaded to settle in France and to pass on their skills to native artisans; protective tariffs were imposed. The famous tapestry works of the Gobelin family was made a state enterprise, and France became largely self-sufficient in the production of woolen cloth. Colbert also had some success in other industries, such as sugar refining, plate-glass making, and the production of silk, naval stores, and armaments. The overall results of his hard work, however, were disappointing. French economic growth lagged behind that of England and the Netherlands, where governments permitted greater entrepreneurial initiative.

Much more successful were Colbert's efforts at fostering the growth of the navy. He reorganized the recruitment system on a rotating basis, whereby seamen served in the royal navy for six months every three years. He refurbished the hospitals in each of the major ports; rebuilt the arsenals at Toulon and Rochefort; and increased the size of the navy from about 25 ships in 1661 to 144 in 1677. He also established schools of marine engineering, hydrography, and cartography. His interest in reestablishing French sea power was, in part, to challenge the commercial supremacy of the Dutch. He encouraged the building of the French mercantile marine and established a number of overseas trading companies, in particular the East India and Levant companies, neither of which had much success. He also attempted to protect French colonial interests in the West Indies and Canada. The Code Noir of 1685, imposed after Colbert's death, legalized slavery in the French colonies, even though it was banned in France itself.

Besides the High Council, the king's council also met for somewhat less vital matters under a variety of different guises. The Council for Dispatches (Conseil des Dépêches), or, more loosely,

the Council for the Interior, had particular responsibility for home affairs, including the activities of the intendants; the Royal Council for Finances (Conseil Royal des Finances) supervised important matters affecting financial aspects of the king's domain lands. These two councils, like the High Council, were presided over by the king in person. But the royal council also met without the king under three further titles to deal with judicial and administrative matters. The Privy Council (Conseil Privé) judged disputes between individuals or bodies and dispensed the king's supreme and final judgments. The State Council for Finances (Conseil d'État et Finances) expedited financial matters of secondary importance, while the Financial Arbitration Court (Grande Direction des Finances) was an administrative tribunal that settled disputes between the state and individuals or corporations. Each of these subdivisions of the king's council contained more members than the exclusive High Council, made up of the secretaries of state and of financial and judicial experts.

The initial group composing the High Council contributed a great deal to the basic pattern of Louis's reign, particularly in military, fiscal, naval, and commercial attitudes, partly because many of those who followed as ministers came from the same tightly knit group of royal servants. In addition to the five members of the Colbert family, there were also three Le Telliers; and, while only one member of the Phélypeaux family, Louis II, comte de Pontchartrain, was a minister, four served as important secretaries of state. All these counselors reflected the attitude of the king himself: they worked extremely hard; they proffered advice but were under no illusions about the danger of arguing once Louis had made up his mind; and they favoured a protectionist, paternalist policy, whether in the organization of industry, the administration of the colonies, or the building up of the navy. Only toward the end of the reign, with the establishment of the Council of Commerce in 1700, did a less regulatory policy show signs of emerging.

To carry out the decisions reached in his intimate and secret High Council, Louis relied chiefly on his provincial intendants. Stationed in the capital cities of France's 30-odd *généralités*, or administrative districts, the intendants were, like the ministers, appointed by the king. In the provinces they could exercise powers of police; raise military forces; regulate industrial, commercial, and agricultural matters; enforce censorship; administer the financial affairs of various communities; assign and collect taxes; and wield considerable judicial authority in civil and criminal affairs. Inevitably, these agents of the central government created considerable friction and hostility. These new men, with no local roots, answerable only to the king and acting almost invariably in an authoritarian context, were deeply resented by older royal officials, by municipal authorities and guilds, and by local *parlements* and estates—all of whom operated through well-established channels and according

to traditional local privileges. The use of intendants, who held neither venal nor hereditary office, was one way in which the limiting effect of the sale of office on royal policies could be circumvented. The authoritarian element of Louis XIV's reign is undeniable: he was determined that no institution or social class would escape the supervision of the crown and its ministers. Thus, the power of patronage, which had been exercised for generations in provincial noble households, began to lose its political significance as the king's ministers built up their own alternative administrative clienteles.

In particular, because the Fronde had remained a painful memory from his childhood, the king never allowed the great nobles a similar opportunity for revolt. Versailles became a place of surveillance for pensioned noblemen and their families whose only serious occupation was the traditional one of arms, and Louis provided ample opportunities for this pursuit. Provincial nobles were drawn into cooperation with the royal administration and shared in the profits made from exploiting the system. The second rebellious group in the Fronde, the members of the Parlement of Paris, were likewise subjected to stringent controls. In 1673 Louis produced regulations stipulating that the court's remonstrances against royal enactments sent to it could in future be made only after the laws concerned had been registered. By this device the king effectively muzzled the magistrates' criticisms of royal policy. It was equally his intention to overcome the delaying tactics of the provincial courts, especially those situated close to vulnerable frontiers.

LOUIS'S RELIGIOUS POLICY

Louis was also on his guard against religious dissent. Like most of his contemporaries, he believed that toleration was no virtue and that unity in the state was extremely difficult to maintain where two or more churches were tolerated. The same fervour that had contributed to the revival of Catholic devotion after 1600 led church spokesmen to urge the king to promote conversions and to end the scandal of legal protection for heretics. By 1678 Louis, persuaded that most Protestants had already returned to the true faith, intensified the persecution of Protestants; churches were destroyed, certain professions were put out of reach of the Huguenots, and Protestant children were taken away from their parents and brought up as Roman Catholics. The notorious practice of dragonnades, the billeting of soldiers in Protestant homes with permission to behave as brutally as they wished, was introduced. Finally, in 1685, the Edict of Nantes was revoked so that Louis could claim that he had succeeded where Emperor Leopold I had failed—that is, in extirpating Protestantism from his realm.

French Catholics welcomed the revocation of the Edict of Nantes, but the decision angered Protestant Europe at a time when Louis's European designs were beginning to meet serious resistance. The revocation deprived France of a number of gifted craftsmen, sailors, and soldiers. At least 600 officers, including Marshal Frederick, Herzog (duke) von Schomberg, and Henri de Massue, marquis de Ruvigny (later the earl of Galway), joined William of Orange, the leader of the Grand Alliance against Louis. Research, however, has reversed the earlier view that the decay of French industry at the end of Louis's reign was the direct result of the expulsion of Huguenot mercantile talent.

The same zeal for uniformity made Louis attack the Jansenists. The theological position of the Jansenists is difficult to define; but Louis, who was no theologian, was content with the simple fact that these zealous Catholics had taken up an unorthodox position that threatened the unity of the state. The movement had begun over the perennial issue of grace and free will as it was propounded in the *Augustinus* of Bishop Cornelius Otto Jansen, published in 1640. In 1653 Pope Innocent X condemned five propositions from Jansen's doctrine, but the movement grew in strength with notable adherents, including Jean-François-Paul de Gondi, cardinal de Retz, and the great mathematician Blaise Pascal. In 1705 Pope Clement XI published the bull *Vineam Domini* ("Vineyard of the Lord"), which further condemned the writings of Jansen; but the archbishop of Paris, Louis-Antoine, cardinal de Noailles, appeared ready to lead the Jansenist forces in opposition to the pope. Under the influence of his confessor, Père Michel Le Tellier, Louis decided to ask the pope for another formal condemnation of the creed. Finally, in 1713, the famous bull *Unigenitus* ("Only Begotten Son") was promulgated but, far from ending Jansenism, drove it into a disruptive alliance with Gallicanism during the following reign. Louis's real attitude in this situation is not entirely clear: certainly his policy was in keeping with his authoritarian insistence upon unity. He was suspicious of religious innovation, and his action was consistent with the increasingly orthodox and rigid mood of his last years. Yet, in seeking the pope's support in this matter, he was reversing years of bitter hostility toward Rome—years when, like many of his predecessors, including Francis I and Henry IV, he had leaned heavily upon the traditional Gallican doctrine.

According to that doctrine, the French king possessed the right of temporal and spiritual *régale*—that is, the right to nominate new bishops and to administer and draw the revenue from bishoprics while they remained vacant. In 1673, despite papal opposition, Louis extended this right to the whole of the French kingdom, which had been enlarged in the recent War of Devolution (1667–68). Eventually, in 1682, the Four Gallican Articles were published as a law of the French state, asserting that the king was in no way subject to the pope in temporal matters and could not be excommunicated and reaffirming the independence of the French church from Rome. The mutual animosity of king and pope ended only in 1693, when Louis agreed to suspend the edict of 1682; but it was a suspension only, not a recantation. The tradition of Gallican independence remained.

ABSOLUTISM OF LOUIS

Thus, in religious matters (except where Jansenism was concerned), in his dealings with the nobility and the Parlement, in his attitude toward the economy, and in his manner of governing the country, Louis revealed a desire to exercise a paternal control of affairs that might suggest a modern dictator rather than a 17th-century king. Though such a comparison has been made, it is most misleading; neither in theoretical nor in practical terms could Louis XIV be thought of as all-powerful. First of all, the legitimacy of his position under the law—the ancient fundamental law of succession—made him the interpreter of the law and the fount of justice in the state, not a capricious autocrat. Similarly, his kingship bestowed upon him a quasi-spiritual role, symbolized by his consecration with holy oil at his coronation, which obliged him to govern justly in accordance with the laws of God and Christian morality. He was also bound by the need to take counsel; and, though he always made up his own mind, he insisted on receiving advice on all important matters of state, which further restricted any arbitrary instincts. Next, there was the essentially federal nature of the country, with its collection of such peripheral provinces as Brittany,

Normandy, and Provence, all retaining their own Estates and customs. Within both these *pays d'état* and *pays d'élection* (where the Estates no longer met) there was a variety of groups and corporations, not to mention individuals, with their own legally held rights, privileges, and exemptions, such as the nobility, the clergy, the towns, and the king's officers. To impose rigid uniformity in such a situation was both impossible and undreamed of by contemporaries. On the contrary, one of the king's prime obligations was to uphold and respect the myriad different rights to which his subjects laid claim.

Perhaps most of all, the king was limited by financial stringency. Louis could and often did try to persuade the cities and provincial Estates to raise their contributions and the clergy to increase the size of their *don gratuit* ("free gift"); he also created more offices and annuities. But these were mere palliatives, and the king was forced on two occasions to introduce novel measures: in 1695 he levied a capitation, or head tax, applicable to all French laymen, even to the princes of the blood, and in 1710 a *dixième* (the tithe, or tenth) that similarly went against the interests of the privileged classes, including the clergy, by requiring one-tenth to be paid to the state from all incomes. Significantly, however, Louis made it perfectly clear on both occasions that he recognized the extraordinary and temporary nature of these impositions, made necessary by the pressures of war. It was impossible to be a despot while financial resources were so precarious,

while no nationwide police force existed, and while the state of communications remained so poor. All these factors make it clear that a situation simply did not exist in which totalitarian government, at least by 20th-century standards, could have had any meaning.

The financial difficulties that limited Louis XIV's ambitions were due in part to the problems plaguing France's economy. Unfavourable climatic conditions—the so-called Little Ice Age of the 17th century—resulted in frequent crop failures; in 1693–94 and 1709–10, much of the country suffered food shortages that left the population vulnerable to epidemics. The heavy taxes required to pay for the king's wars were an additional hindrance to economic growth, and frequent warring kept France from gaining a larger share of the lucrative overseas trade that was enriching its rivals, England and the Netherlands.

Finally, Louis XIV remained the prisoner of France's social structure. It is sometimes alleged that the king ruled through the bourgeoisie, but, while a number of the most distinguished families of the reign were not of ancient nobility, their faithful and effective service to the king was rewarded in an entirely traditional way—by social elevation. Colbert's father was an unsuccessful merchant; however, all his granddaughters married dukes. In other words, the opportunity to enter the highest ranks of the nobility, which had long been available in France, was simply emphasized by Louis XIV. As the greatest nobleman in France, he had no doubt that he must retain the prestige and privileges of the nobility; but he knew equally well that the nobility should not become a caste closed to ambitious and able men. He thus maintained the tradition of royal patronage, which helped to defuse social conflict.

FOREIGN AFFAIRS

From the beginning of his reign, Louis pursued a vigorous foreign policy. Historical opinion has traditionally held that Louis sought to dominate Europe, only to meet his just deserts at the end of his reign. More recently another interpretation has emerged that argues that Louis pursued consistent and for the most part moderate aims and pursued them successfully up to and including the Treaty of Utrecht (1713). The starting point for the more recent interpretation is the ambiguous Peace of Münster (1648), forming part of the great European settlement of Westphalia, the terms of which subsequently became a bone of contention between Bourbon and Habsburg rulers. One of the critical issues of the treaty was the fate of the three bishoprics of Metz, Toul, and Verdun on the northeast frontier of France. These bishoprics, occupied by the French since 1552, were formally acquired in 1648 together with a number of towns in nearby Alsace. One of the main Habsburg aims both in the War of the League of Augsburg (1689–97; also called the War of the Grand Alliance) and in the War of the Spanish Succession (1701–14) was the restoration

of the three bishoprics and the province of Franche-Comté, also on the eastern frontier of France, connecting Burgundy with Alsace, which Louis had acquired through the Treaties of Nijmegen (1678–79) that concluded the Dutch War (1672–78). Louis, however, was determined to hold onto the gains in Alsace, however ambiguously acquired; he also hoped to add Lorraine, to the north of Franche-Comté, to consolidate further this least-secure French frontier area.

Louis's policy in the northeast was constant and understandable. Franche-Comté was one entry into France previously exploited by its enemies that Louis succeeded in closing in 1678. He had already closed another, the port of Dunkirk, by purchasing it from Charles II of England in 1662; a third gateway, from the southern Netherlands, was effectively barred by the military fortifications erected by his great military engineer, Sébastien Le Prestre de Vauban, in the 1680s. The capture of Lorraine would have bolted yet one more dangerous entry. Of course, the situation looked quite different from the Habsburg point of view, especially after Louis's seizure of the key city of Strassburg (French Strasbourg) in 1681, an episode that goes to the heart of the controversial matter of his reunion policy. Following the successful Treaties of Nijmegen, Louis began to employ his own judicial courts to claim sovereignty over all the dependencies of territories that he already possessed in Alsace, Franche-Comté, Metz, Toul, and Verdun. The maneuver enabled him

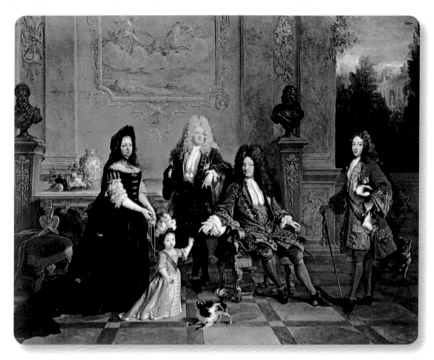

Louis XIV and His Family, *oil painting by Nicolas de Largillière, 1711; in the Wallace Collection, London*. Reproduced by permission of the trustees of the Wallace Collection, London; photograph, J.R. Freeman & Co. Ltd.

to consolidate his control, especially over Alsace and Franche-Comté, though the legality of the claims to some of the alleged "dependencies" was extremely dubious. There was no legal justification whatever for Louis's greatest coup in the area—the seizure in September 1681 of the independent city of Strassburg. To Louis this key city, the door through which imperial armies could pass (and three times in the recently concluded war had passed) into Alsace, represented a serious threat, for Strassburg was within easy reach of the Danube valley and Vienna. His fears about French vulnerability in this region may best be illustrated by his offer during the War of the League of Augsburg to

waive his claim to the Spanish succession on condition that Nijmegen be respected, that Lorraine be absorbed into France (with proper compensations elsewhere), and that the Spanish and Austrian lands not be united under one ruler. The Holy Roman emperor Leopold I immediately rejected these proposals. When the final climactic conflict of his reign, the War of the Spanish Succession, was proceeding badly, Louis offered to relinquish all the gains he had made from the Spanish inheritance; but he desperately hoped to hold on to Metz, Toul, Verdun, Alsace, and Franche-Comté.

Louis's attitude toward the Dutch was less moderate and more bullying. His

LOUIS XIV STYLE

Louis XIV style is a term applied to the visual arts produced in France during the reign of Louis XIV (1638–1715). The man most influential in French painting of the period was Nicolas Poussin. Although Poussin himself lived in Italy for most of his adult life, his Parisian friends commissioned works through which his classicism was made known to French painters. In 1648 the painter Charles Le Brun, assisted by the king, founded the Royal Academy of Painting and Sculpture, an organization that dictated style to such a degree that it virtually controlled the fortunes of all French artists for the remainder of the reign. French sculpture reached a new zenith at this time, after the mediocrity of the first half of the century. François Girardon was a favourite of the king and did several portrait sculptures of him, as well as the tomb of the cardinal de Richelieu. Antoine Coysevox also received royal commissions, including the tomb of Cardinal Mazarin, while Pierre Puget, whose work showed strong Italian Baroque influences, was not so well favoured at court.

At the Gobelins factory, founded by Louis for the production of *meubles de luxe* and furnishings for the royal palaces and the public buildings, a national decorative arts style evolved that soon spread its influence into neighbouring countries. Furniture, for example, was veneered with tortoise shell or foreign woods, inlaid with brass, pewter, and ivory, or heavily gilded all over; heavy gilt bronze mounts protected the corners and other parts from friction and rough handling and provided further ornament. The name of André-Charles Boulle is particularly associated with this style of furniture design. Common decorative motifs of the period include shells, satyrs, cherubs, festoons and garlands, mythological themes, cartouches (ornamental frames), foliated scrolls, and dolphins.

The ability of the king to form a strong "national" style was exhibited particularly in the field of architecture. The year 1665 was crucial for the history of French art, for it was in that year that Gian Lorenzo Bernini arrived in Paris to design a new facade for the Louvre. It was decided, however, that the Italian Baroque style was incompatible with the French temperament, and the Louvre was completed according to the new tenets of French classicism.

The Louvre was the project of Louis's minister Colbert; the king's interest lay at Versailles, where in the 1660s he began to renovate an ancient hunting lodge, and the resultant palace dazzled the world. Never before had a single man attempted any architectural plan on such a large scale. The result is a masterpiece of formal grandeur, and, because the arts were all under the rigid control of the state, each element at Versailles was overseen and designed to be in keeping with the whole. Versailles, though usually thought of by the French as Classical, can be considered the ultimate Baroque composition, in which motion is always present but always contained.

Not the least important element at Versailles was the landscaping. André Le Nôtre, the greatest artist in the history of European landscape architecture, worked with the king, designing vistas, fountains, and many other outdoor arrangements. Versailles had an enormous impact on the rest of Europe, both artistic and psychological, but the whole complex was so large that even the extremely long life of Louis XIV did not hold enough years to see it completed.

invasion of the Spanish Netherlands in 1667 and the ensuing War of Devolution frightened the Dutch into the Triple Alliance with England and Sweden, which led to the Treaty of Aix-la-Chapelle (1668). Then, in the Dutch War that followed shortly afterward (1672–78), Louis intended to warn the Dutch that France was a serious commercial competitor and to force the Dutch to give him a free hand in the Spanish Netherlands when the issue of the Spanish succession came to the fore. He learned from that war that he could never hope to incorporate a large part of the Netherlands into France against Dutch opposition; but he also continued to fear the manner in which the Dutch might try to influence the government of the Spanish Netherlands for their own economic benefit. Here again was an example of mutual hostility and suspicion in which interpretations of motives in Versailles and in The Hague were diametrically opposed. At the Treaty of Rijswijk (1697) the Dutch gained the right to keep a series of Dutch barrier fortresses within the southern Netherlands as a check against French aggression; it was Louis's seizure of these fortresses in 1701 that precipitated the War of the Spanish Succession (1701–14).

That war has usually been depicted as the most significant element in an assessment of Louis's total foreign policy: for some historians, all his relations with the rest of Europe were geared to this great issue; for others, it was the final misjudgment born of overconfidence, provoked by his own ambitious miscalculations, and destined to ruin France. It is certainly true that the approaching end of the direct ruling line in Spain had interested European rulers for many years, and the Bourbon claim to a share in that rich inheritance—deriving from Louis's marriage to Marie-Thérèse, elder daughter of King Philip IV of Spain—was accepted as a key factor in the situation. In 1668 Louis and Emperor Leopold I had gone so far as to sign a partition treaty, more than 30 years before the death of the last Spanish Habsburg, Charles II. No European statesman was surprised, therefore, at Louis's later concern when, after the signature of the Treaty of Rijswijk in 1697, he undertook negotiations with the English king William III out of which two further partition treaties emerged. The crucial moment came when Charles II's last will was published, offering the Spanish crown, in opposition to the second partition treaty, to Louis's grandson Philip, duc d'Anjou (later Philip V). Louis's decision to accept did not in itself provoke war. Besides, if Louis had snubbed the Spanish offer, it would have been made to Austria, and the spectre of the restoration of Charles V's empire—probably coupled with French losses on the northeastern frontiers—was intolerable. In addition, Louis had recently made peace after the War of the Grand Alliance, the hardest conflict in which he had so far been engaged, and thus had no illusions about the difficulty of overcoming another coalition under William III's leadership. One may conclude that he did not seek war. But he did make decisions that made war likely, including his recognition of the Old Pretender as James III of England, his unexplained decision to protect his grandson's right to the French throne (he was envisaging not a single, united realm of France and Spain but two Bourbon kingdoms, with the senior heir succeeding in France), his occupation of the barrier fortresses, and his seizure of the monopoly of the Spanish-American trade.

When peace was signed at Utrecht in 1713, Louis, despite the disasters of the intervening years, succeeded in holding onto the gains in Europe that he had considered vital throughout his reign, including Alsace and Strasbourg. In addition, his grandson remained king of Spain, despite all the efforts of the Grand Alliance to replace him with their candidate, the Austrian archduke Charles (as Charles III). It is true that in the darkest time of the war, during 1708–10, when the kingdom was in the grip of famine and the royal treasury on the brink of bankruptcy, the desperate king was ready to give up these precious gains and was prevented only by the intransigence of his opponents with their impossible demand that he should himself assist in driving his grandson from the throne of Spain. Likewise, a fortuitous change of government in England in 1710, which ushered in the Tory peace ministry, and the elevation of the Austrian archduke to the imperial title as Charles VI in 1711 weakened the unity of purpose of the Grand Alliance and enabled Louis's most effective soldier, Claude-Louis-Hector,

duc de Villars, to stage a military revival. Therefore, the relatively successful conclusion of the war from France's point of view was not entirely of Louis's own fashioning. Had events forced Louis to accept a total surrender, it would have been even more tempting for historians to blame the defeat upon the excessive ambitions of an arrogant man.

It cannot be denied that Louis was arrogant and that his arrogance aroused fear and resentment in his neighbours. Equally, he was intolerant, like most of his contemporaries, and feared by Protestant powers as the leader of a new and vengeful Counter-Reformation, an irony in view of his secret encouragement of the Turks in order to weaken the emperor. Both facets of the great king need to be borne in mind when assessing his overall foreign policy, and they help to counter any tendency to overestimate the defensive nature of his strategy. That defensive element, however, is of significance and has been largely lost sight of, especially in assessments of the reign written in English. Louis frightened Europe with his quest for *la gloire*, by which he meant the favourable verdict of history on his contribution to French security and territorial integrity but which his enemies interpreted more narrowly as a preoccupation with military triumphs and vainglorious display. That contemporary interpretation, still widely accepted nearly three centuries later, does less than justice to Louis's shrewd appreciation of political realities and of France's long-term interests.

FRENCH CULTURE IN THE 17TH CENTURY

If historians are not yet agreed on the political motives of Louis XIV, they all accept, however, the cultural and artistic significance of the epoch over which he and his two 17th-century predecessors reigned. In their different ways—Henry IV's interest lay in town planning, Louis XIII's in the visual arts, and Louis XIV's in the theatre and in landscape gardening—they all actively stimulated the emergence of great talents and were aided by such royal ministers as Richelieu and Mazarin, who were considered patrons in their own right.

From Henry IV's reign dates the rebuilding of Paris as a tasteful, ordered city, with the extensions to the Louvre, the building of the Pont Neuf and the Place Dauphine, and, outside the capital, the renovations and extensions at Fontainebleau and Saint-Germain-en-Laye. Henry succeeded in making Paris what it had never been before—the centre of polite society—and, though he was not personally interested in such matters, he must therefore be given some credit for the atmosphere that later led to the establishment of the famous salon of Catherine de Vivonne, marquise de Rambouillet, which flourished from 1617 until 1665. There men of letters mingled with the great nobility to the mutual advantage of both. The guests at her salon included the statesmen Richelieu and the Great Condé; the epigrammatist the duc de La Rochefoucauld; the letter writer Marie de Rabutin-Chantal, marquise de Sévigné, and Mme de La Fayette; the novelist Madeleine de Scudéry; the poet François de Malherbe; and the dramatist Pierre Corneille.

Richelieu also was a key figure in the artistic and architectural development of Paris during his years in power. He was fortunate to employ the great architect Jacques Lemercier, who built for him, close to the Louvre, the Palais-Cardinal, later the Palais-Royal; it contained two theatres and a gallery for the cardinal's objets d'art. Under the same patron, Lemercier also built the church of the Sorbonne, where Richelieu is buried. In the world of painting, the cardinal supported Simon Vouet, who decorated the Palais-Cardinal, and Philippe de Champaigne, whose surviving portraits include famous representations of Richelieu himself. The cardinal's most notable contribution, however, was in the field of letters, with the establishment in 1634 of the Académie Française to regulate and maintain the standards of the French language. One of its first tasks was the production of a standard dictionary, a massive work published in four volumes in 1694. The Académie succeeded over the years in making the pursuit of letters socially acceptable, though still inferior to the pursuit of arms. Richelieu's great interest in the theatre persuaded him to patronize a number of dramatists, including Corneille and Jean de Rotrou.

Richelieu's patronage of the arts was taken over by his great pupil Mazarin, who collected some 500 paintings. In

1648 Mazarin established the Académie Royale de Peinture et de Sculpture, which encouraged artists to follow the examples of Nicolas Poussin, the greatest French exponent of the Classical style, and of the landscape artist Claude Lorrain. Mazarin housed his own art collection in the Palais Mazarin (now the Institut de France and home of the Académie Française), which itself was enlarged for Mazarin by the architect François Mansart. Mazarin also commissioned Louis Le Vau to rebuild part of the medieval castle of Vincennes, thus setting him off on his successful career.

Louis XIV's patronage centred on Versailles, the great palace that also played such an important part in the political life of 17th-century France. There André Le Nôtre designed the formal gardens, which still attract a multitude of admiring visitors, as they did when they were first completed. There Jules Hardouin-Mansart added the long, familiar garden facade, and, with unforgettable magnificence, Charles Le Brun decorated the Galerie des Glaces (Hall of Mirrors) and the adjoining Salon de la Paix (Salon of Peace) and Salon de la Guerre (Salon of War).

At Versailles the composer Jean-Baptiste Lully devised and directed a number of musical entertainments with such success that Louis granted him noble status and the office of a royal secretary. There, too, the comic genius Molière was encouraged by the king's support; after the dramatist's death, Louis was directly responsible for the establishment, in 1680, of the Comédie-Française.

There, finally, Louis recognized the genius of Jean Racine, whose great tragedies, from *Bérénice* (1670) to *Iphigénie* (1675), earned him membership in the Académie Française and a noble office, that of *trésorier de France* (treasurer of France), from the king.

This blossoming of the arts was aided though not inspired by the patronage of kings and ministers. The artistic creations evince a strong element of order and simplicity, culminating in the Classical grandeur of Racine's plays and the facade of Versailles. Thus, they might seem to reflect the growth of political stability and order over which Louis XIV presided. The monarchy continued to expand its support for culture during his reign. In 1663 the Académie des Inscriptions et Belles-Lettres was founded; originally intended to compose inscriptions for royal medals and monuments, it eventually became a centre for historical research. Three years later Louis XIV sponsored the creation of the Académie des Sciences and a training centre for French artists in Rome. The Académie d'Architecture and the Académie Royale de Musique began in 1671. It is, however, dangerous to tie creative achievements in the arts and sciences too closely to their political environment. Moreover, there are significant counterpoints to the theme of Classical order. The philosopher René Descartes's doubting, rationalist approach to the fundamental questions of God's existence and man's relationship to God undermined the rigid adherence to revealed truths propounded by religious orthodoxy. The Jansenist Blaise Pascal, one of the most versatile geniuses of the century, represented and defended a minority religious movement that Louis XIV believed dangerously subversive. Toward the end of his long reign, Louis encountered the fierce social criticism of Jean de La Bruyère and the skepticism of the exiled Huguenot Pierre Bayle, whose *Dictionnaire historique et critique* (1697; "Historical and Critical Dictionary") raised questions about the sacred status of the Bible and foreshadowed the secularism of the Enlightenment. These discordant elements draw attention to the fact that the absolute state which Versailles was intended to represent concealed tensions that would surface after the king's death. Nonetheless, the splendour of Versailles and the Classical simplicity of Racine's tragedies represent a high point in creative human achievement, and it is to the king's credit that he chose to be identified with them.

PRELUDE TO REVOLUTION

The year 1789 is the great dividing line in the history of modern France. The fall of the Bastille, a medieval fortress used as a state prison, on July 14, 1789, symbolizes for France, as well as for other nations, the end of the premodern era characterized by an organicist and religiously sanctioned traditionalism. With the French Revolution began the institutionalization of secularized individualism in both social life and politics; individualism and rationality found expression in parliamentary government and written constitutionalism. Obviously, the English and American revolutions of 1688 and 1776 prefigure these changes, but it was the more universalist French Revolution that placed individualism and rationality squarely at the centre of human concerns.

Because the revolutionary events had such earthshaking power, the history of France in the century preceding 1789 has until recently been seen as a long prologue to the coming drama, a period marked by the decay of the *ancien régime* ("old regime"), a locution created during the Revolution. Some contemporary historians, however, reject this view and present 18th-century France as a society undergoing rapid but manageable social, economic, and cultural change. They perceive the French Revolution as a political event that could have been avoided if the French monarchy had been more consistent in its effort to modify political institutions in order to keep up with the new needs of its people.

THE SOCIAL AND POLITICAL HERITAGE

To attempt to understand the developments of the 18th century and to follow the scholarly debates associated with them, one is well served by beginning with a definition of the ancien régime. Its essence lay in the interweaving of the state's social, political, and economic forms; the term itself, though primarily a political concept, has also always had a clear social and economic resonance.

THE SOCIAL ORDER OF
THE ANCIEN RÉGIME

In the society of the ancien régime, all men and women were, by birth, subjects of the king of France. In theory always and in practice often, the lives of French men and women of all ranks and estates took shape within a number of overlapping institutions, each with rules that entitled its members to enjoy particular privileges (a term derived from the Latin words for "private law"). Rights and status flowed as a rule from the group to the individual rather than from individuals to the group, as was true after 1789.

France itself can be conceived of as an aggregate of differentiated groups or communities (villages, parishes, or guilds), all of them theoretically comparable but all of them different. In many respects the kingdom was an assembly of varying provinces, a number of them endowed with vestigial representative institutions. In some important ways France was not truly a unit of government. Unlike England, for example, France was not a single customs union; more tariffs had to be paid by shippers on brandy floated down the Garonne to Bordeaux than on wine shipped from France to Britain.

The concept of national citizenship was not unknown in France under the ancien régime, existing in the sense that all Frenchmen, regardless of their rank and privileges, had certain legal rights denied to all foreigners. There was, however, no French nation whose citizens taken one by one were equal before man-made law, as was true after 1789. Laws were in the main inherited, not made.

This is not to say that France, though structured around the "premodern" concept of the guild, or group, or corps, was a static or, materially speaking, a stable society. For many artisans, peregrination was a way of life, and many years of their young manhood were spent on a *tour de France*, which took them from city to city in order to learn their trade. Serfdom was practically unknown (only 140,000 serfs remained in France in 1789, none of them on crown lands, where Jacques Necker, the comptroller general, had abolished serfdom in 1779), and peasants were free to move as they wished from one village to the next. Indeed, such large numbers of people were moving around that the fear of unattached vagrants was strong in prerevolutionary France.

MONARCHY AND CHURCH

In the 18th century, justifications of royal authority drew on many traditions. The king still claimed the status of a feudal suzerain of his subjects. Familial imagery was an important component of royal rhetoric; the king of France was father of his subjects. His right to reign echoed all husbands' right to rule over their wives and all fathers' right to rule over their children. His messages, however draconian and confiscatory they might be, were invariably couched in a rhetoric of religious and paternal solicitude.

The king, moreover, was a Christian monarch and as such was endowed with quasi-priestly functions. He was anointed at his coronation with holy chrism said to have been brought from heaven by a dove. It was thought that, as evidence of his special status, he could cure scrofula by his touch. The relationship of church and state was complex. Oftentimes the king did not hesitate to exploit the church, over which he held extensive power by virtue of the still-valid Concordat of Bologna of 1516. Monarchs used their right to appoint bishops and abbots to secure the loyalty of impoverished or ambitious nobles. The crown asserted its right to regulate church policies, limit the authority of the pope over French Catholics, and abolish or consolidate monastic orders.

Nonetheless, until 1788 the Roman Catholic Church retained in France unusually broad doctrinal rights and social prestige, even by the standards prevailing in central or southern Europe, not to speak of what held true in the far more tolerant countries of northern Europe (Prussia, Holland, and Britain). French Protestants were denied religious toleration until 1787. Jews were tolerated only as quasi-foreigners until 1791. Of considerable symbolic importance was the fact that before 1789 it was the church that kept the registers of births and deaths that marked the beginning and end of each person's earthly existence. The church, the police, and the courts collaborated closely to maintain the prestige of religion; until at least the 1780s the church severely condemned licentious or irreligious books such as Rousseau's *Émile*, which was burned in 1762 by order of the Parlement of Paris, a measure that did little to stop its circulation.

The monarchy basically respected the various rights of the church accrued by tradition, as it did the civil and property rights, or "liberties," of its subjects generally. Continuity ordinarily seemed to be the first principle of the French state, and it was inherent in the concept of king itself: the king was held to have two bodies, a physical one, which necessarily decayed, and a spiritual one, which never died. In this view, the main purpose of the French state was to defend vested interests—i.e., to maintain continuity rather than to change the existing order.

COMMITMENT TO MODERNIZATION

The great peculiarity of the ancien régime was that a system committed to preserving tradition also contained within it powerful forces for change. The absolute monarchy developed between 1624 and 1642 by Richelieu and later by Mazarin, Colbert, Louvois, and Louis XIV was guided by a modern raison d'état, in which the state was eager to further changes of all kinds for its own purposes. Administratively, its absolutist will, formulated at Versailles in a complex array of governmental councils, was enforced in the provinces by the intendants and their subordinates. The monarchy favoured modern manufacturing and, more desultorily, modern finance. It protected and firmly guided intellectuals through the Académie Française. With greater hesitation, the monarchy also promoted France's drive to obtain economic and military supremacy not just in Europe but overseas as well, in North America, India, Africa, and the Caribbean.

Divided in its goals, some of them traditional and others modern, the state was also ideologically double-minded. In the 17th century many intellectuals (some of them clerics such as Bishop Jacques-Bénigne Bossuet [1627–1704]) developed a Hobbesian justification of absolutist rule, which was renewed throughout the 18th century. Religion and tradition went hand in hand, but absolutist theoreticians went further. They justified the state's right not only to legislate and tax more or less at will but also to imprison arbitrarily without due process of law. The lettres de cachet, which allowed the king to have individuals committed to the Bastille and to other prisons forever and without any kind of trial, were seldom given out, usually to fathers who wished to correct their wayward children. But they did exist, as liberal or scurrilous propagandists knew full well, sometimes firsthand: about one-fourth of the 5,279 people imprisoned in the Bastille between 1660 and 1790 were connected with the world of the book. Royal proclamations often stressed, however, the king's obligation to govern in the interests of his people. The parlements, frequent critics of arbitrary rule, spread the notion that subjects' rights were protected by a fixed, if ill-defined, constitution that could not be altered without the consent of their representatives.

CONTINUITY AND CHANGE

The political history of 18th-century France can be conceptualized in terms of the double heritage and the problems it entailed. The discussion may be linked to two issues: first, the economic transformation of a traditional and essentially agricultural society by both commerce and ideas; and, second, the state's efforts (and eventual inability) to modernize and unify its structure and purpose to encompass the changed economic and cultural expectations of the nation's elites.

In contrast to the France of Louis XIV's grand siècle ("great century"), beset by economic stagnation and periodic food shortages, 18th-century France enjoyed a climate of growing prosperity, fueled in part by a sustained rise in population. The kingdom's population, which had barely grown at all during the years 1500 to 1700, increased from approximately 20 million at the end of Louis XIV's reign to about 28 million by 1789. Better preventive medicine, a decline in infant mortality, and the near disappearance of widespread famine after 1709 all served to increase the population. Birth rates continued to be very high, despite both a traditional pattern of late marriage (men on the average at age 27, women at 24 or 25) and the beginnings of the practice of birth control, the effect of which was to become evident only after the Revolution. The yearly number of deaths per 10,000 fell from about 400 in 1750 to 350 in 1775, 328 in 1790, and 298 in 1800. The increased population meant more mouths to feed but also more consumers, more workers seeking employment, and more opportunities for investment; in short, every aspect of French life was affected.

AGRICULTURAL PATTERNS

In its basic organization, French agriculture continued its age-old patterns. This contrasted starkly with England, where new agricultural techniques as well as major changes in the control of land—convertible husbandry (a progressive form of land use that did away with the wasteful fallowing of land every two or three years) and the enclosure movement (which made possible the consolidation of small parcels of land into large farms fenced off from use by the rest of the community)—were beginning to cause an agricultural revolution. In France there was no significant enclosure movement, despite enabling legislation that allowed the division of some common lands in 1767 and again in 1773. Communal patterns of planting—very common in northern France, where a three-field system ordinarily prevailed—were not suspended. Modest improvements in farming techniques and the introduction of new crops such as corn (maize) and potatoes allowed French farms to feed the country's growing population. The increased number of peasants led to further subdivision of land and greater competition for leases; the economic benefits of agricultural growth went mostly to landlords and the small minority of prosperous peasants. In fact, the economic status of many peasants deteriorated markedly in the 18th century; perhaps as many as one-third of them were sporadically indigent, though there was no decline in the peasants' share of the land. In 1789 French peasants still owned about one-third of the arable land, most of it in small plots of less than 10 acres (4 hectares); nobles owned about one-fifth of the land, the church one-sixth, and bourgeois landlords about one-third.

INDUSTRIAL PRODUCTION

After 1740 industrial production in France rose annually by about 2 percent overall and even more in some sectors. During the later decades of the 18th century, French industrial production grew rapidly, although not on the same scale as in Britain, whose industrial development had begun 60 years before that of the French. Coal mining was a major industry by 1789, its production nearly 6 percent higher in the 1780s than in the preceding decade. Mining attracted vast amounts of capital, some of it from the aristocracy. In 1789 the Mines d'Anzin near the Belgian border already employed thousands of workers. In textiles, entrepreneurs such as the Swiss Protestant Guillaume-Philippe Oberkampf created new manufactories that permitted better regulation and control of production. Most production continued to be centred in small artisanal workshops, however, and power-driven machinery remained a rarity.

Although transportation difficulties and internal customs barriers meant

Rousseau, drawing in pastels by Maurice-Quentin de La Tour, 1753. In the Musée d'Art et d'Histoire, Geneva. Courtesy of the Musée d'Art et d'Histoire, Geneva; photograph, Jean Arlaud

that France on the eve of the Revolution was not yet a unified national market (as Britain had long since been), price discrepancies from province to province, as well as between northern and southern France, were less significant than before. Throughout the country the demand rose for urban manufactured goods and for those luxury items (textiles, porcelains, furniture, *articles de Paris*) that the French excelled in producing before 1800. French engineers and artisans were highly skilled. French ship design, for example, was superior to that of the English, who routinely copied captured French men-of-war. George Washington, the president of the United States, wishing to buy the best watch available anywhere, turned to the American minister in Paris because the world's most accurate timepieces were still made in France.

COMMERCE

Commerce, especially with the colonies, was an important area of change as well. France's first colonial empire, essentially located in North America, was a source of great wealth. Even though France lost both Canada and India during the Seven Years' War (1756–63), the Caribbean sugar islands continued to be the most lucrative source of French colonial activity in the last 100 years of the ancien régime. The French shared the West Indies with Spain and England: Cuba, Puerto Rico, and the eastern half of Hispaniola belonged to Spain; Jamaica belonged to England;

but Guadeloupe, Martinique, and Saint-Domingue (Haiti)—the richest of all nonwhite 18th-century colonies in the world—were French. In Saint-Domingue 30,000 whites stood an uneasy watch over a black slave population that grew to more than 400,000 by 1789. In the islands, the slaves produced sugarcane and coffee, which were refined in France at Nantes, Rochefort, and Bordeaux and often reexported to central and northern Europe. This triangular trade grew 10-fold between 1715 and 1789, and the value of international exports in the 1780s amounted to nearly one-fourth of national income. The sugar trade enriched the planters, the bankers in Paris who had acted as brokers for import and reexport, and the manufacturers of luxury goods that were shipped from France to the Caribbean. Not surprisingly, the French colonial trade was a closely watched process, governed by mercantilist protective tariffs and rules.

Indirectly millions of Frenchmen were affected by the accelerating tempo of economic life. The circulation of gold specie in the kingdom as a whole rose from 731 million livres in 1715 to some 2 billion livres in 1788. Domestic commerce also expanded in the 18th century. The urban population and even prosperous peasants began to acquire a taste for new luxuries. Estate inventories show that even modest households were buying more varied clothing, a wider range of furniture, kitchen articles, books, and other items their ancestors could not have afforded. By the early 1780s more than 40 regional newspapers with advertising, or *affiches*, had been founded, a clear sign that France was becoming a consumer society.

CITIES

Commerce rather than industry buoyed up French cities, especially the Atlantic seaports. In 1789, 15 percent of Frenchmen lived in cities with more than 2,000 inhabitants. Still, Paris, a city of about 600,000 inhabitants, was only half the size of London, the world's largest seaport. But, regardless of their size, French cities were centres of intellectual transformation. It was there, in the Sociétés de Pensées, Masonic lodges, and some 32 provincial academies, that writers found their public. There also took place the cultural revolution that inspired the writers in turn and the economic changes that gave momentum to the cultural upheaval.

THE ENLIGHTENMENT

The industrial and commercial developments, already significant by themselves, were the cause, and perhaps also the effect, of a wider and still more momentous change preceding the Revolution— the Enlightenment. Today the Enlightenment can be understood as the conscious formulation of a profound cultural transformation. Epistemologically, the French Enlightenment relied on three sources: rationalism, which had in France a strong tradition dating to Descartes; empiricism, which was borrowed from English thought and which in France underpinned the work of such writers as Claude-Adrien Helvétius (1715–71), Paul-Henri Dietrich, baron d'Holbach (1723–89), Étienne Bonnot de Condillac (1715–80), and Julien Offroy de La Mettrie (1709–51), the author of a book eloquently entitled *L'Homme machine* (1747; *Man a Machine*); and an amorphous concept of nature that was particularly strong in the immensely popular and important work of Jean-Jacques Rousseau (1712–78) and, in the 1780s, in the works of widely read pre-Romantic writers such as Jacques-Henri Bernardin de Saint-Pierre (1737–1814). The relationship between these intellectual developments and the Revolution of 1789 remains a subject of dispute among historians, but there is no doubt that Enlightenment critiques undermined belief in the traditional institutions that the Revolutionary movement was to destroy.

Though far apart from one another in a strict philosophical sense, these sources of inspiration generated a number of shared beliefs that were of obvious political consequence. The enlightened subjects of Louis XV and Louis XVI were increasingly convinced that French institutions of government and justice could be radically improved. Tradition seemed to them an increasingly inadequate principle to follow in such matters. Meliorism, gauged especially by the progress of the sciences, was one of the cardinal beliefs of the age.

PHILOSOPHE

Inspired by the philosophic thought of René Descartes, the skepticism of the Libertins, or free-thinkers, and the popularization of science by Bernard de Fontenelle, the philosophes expressed support for social, economic, and political reforms, occasioned by sectarian dissensions within the church, the weakening of the absolute monarchy, and the ruinous wars that had occurred toward the end of Louis XIV's reign. In the early part of the 18th century the movement was dominated by Voltaire and Montesquieu, but that restrained phase became more volatile in the second half of the century. Denis Diderot, Jean-Jacques Rousseau, Georges-Louis Leclerc de Buffon, Étienne Bonnot de Condillac, Anne-Robert-Jacques Turgot, and the Marquis de Condorcet were among the philosophes who devoted their energies to compiling the *Encyclopédie*, one of the great intellectual achievements of the century. In spite of divergent personal views, the philosophes were united in their conviction of the supremacy and efficacy of human reason.

Regarding the economy, physiocrats such as the king's own doctor, François Quesnay (1694–1774), praised the virtue of free-market economics and, as they put it, of "laissez-faire, laissez-aller" ("allow to do, allow to go"). The Encyclopédistes—the contributors to the great *Encyclopédie* edited by Denis Diderot (1713–84)—spread the idea that agricultural and manufacturing processes could be rationally analyzed and improved; the work also criticized religious and political orthodoxy. Voltaire (1694–1778), the most celebrated French Enlightenment author, used his sharp wit to skewer the absurdities of absolutism and intolerance. His eloquent defense of the Protestant merchant Jean Calas, broken on the wheel in 1762 for the supposed murder of his suicidal son, made him the model of the engaged intellectual, rallying public opinion against injustice.

THE INFLUENCE OF MONTESQUIEU AND ROUSSEAU

Two Enlightenment authors who had an especially profound impact on the future revolutionaries were Charles-Louis de Secondat, baron de La Brède et de Montesquieu (1689–1755), and Jean-Jacques Rousseau (1712–78). In his *Lettres persanes* (1721; *Persian Letters*), Montesquieu, a wealthy aristocratic member of the Parlement of Bordeaux, used the device of a foreign visitor to highlight the contradictions of the government shortly after the death of Louis XIV. His daring jabs at the pope, "an ancient idol, worshiped now from habit," and at Catholic doctrine brought down the wrath of the authorities but did nothing to stop the book's success. Written in an entertaining and accessible style, the *Persian Letters* did not present a clear set of doctrines: instead, readers were drawn into a process of dialogue and critique modeled by the novel's characters. In his masterwork, *De l'esprit des loix* (1748; *The Spirit of the Laws*), Montesquieu presented a survey of political institutions throughout the world. Drawing on both the rationalist and empiricist traditions, he analyzed politics in purely secular terms, arguing that each country's laws developed in response to its climate and the nature of its customs. His comparative approach made it clear that, in his view, no political system could claim divine sanction. His personal sympathies lay with mixed forms of government, in which a separation of powers protected individual liberties; his description of the English constitution, in which the king shared power with Parliament, strongly influenced French political thinking. A former *parlementaire* himself, Montesquieu argued that the aristocratic courts were "intermediary bodies" whose resistance to royal authority prevented abuses. Although he was himself no revolutionary, his ideas had great influence at the beginning of the Revolutionary movement in 1789; in the Revolution's early phase, he was cited more often than any other authority.

A generation younger than Montesquieu, Rousseau raised profound questions about both private and public life. According to Rousseau, the self becomes empowered in private union with the beloved other, as portrayed in his immensely popular novel *Julie; ou, la nouvelle Héloïse* (1761; *Julie; or, The New Eloise*), or in public union with one's fraternally minded fellow citizens, as explained in *Du contrat social* (1762; *The Social Contract*), a work less widely read before 1789 but even more symptomatic of change.

Rousseau argued for a reconstruction of private and domestic as well as public life, to make both more in accord with human nature. Women, he claimed, have a natural vocation to be wives and mothers; they are to leave public affairs to men. He put forward the harmonious domestic family as a new cultural ideal and stigmatized ancien régime society, with its emphasis on fashion and its influential "public women," such as royal mistresses and the salon hostesses who played a critical role in promoting the Enlightenment. Rousseau's insistence that mothers should breast-feed their children clashed with the realities of French life, where the employment of wet nurses was more common than in any other European country, and symbolized his program for a more "natural" style of life.

Rousseau's second best-selling novel, *Émile; ou, de l'éducation* (1762; *Émile; or, On Education*), illustrated how children could be educated to lead a "natural" life. Its most controversial chapter, the "Profession of Faith of a Savoyard Vicar," suggested that nature alone provided humanity with the religious knowledge it needed; this dismissal of the church and the Bible naturally led to the book's condemnation. Rousseau's concern for education was part of a wider movement.

The French administrator, reformer, and economist Anne-Robert-Jacques

Turgot, baron de l'Aulne (1712–81), expressed the new sensibility when he wrote that the education of children was the basis of national unity and mores.

In 1763 a prominent *parlementaire* named La Chalotais even put forward a scheme for lay and national primary education. An important landmark in this respect was the expulsion from France in 1764 of the Jesuits, who had theretofore dominated French secondary education. Increasingly, the French language was substituted for Latin in the secondary schools, or *collèges* (the forerunners of today's lycées). Rhetoric gave way to an emphasis on more "natural" manners and modes of expression. History was raised to the level of a serious discipline; with Voltaire's *Le Siècle de Louis XIV* (1751; *The Age of Louis XIV*), modern French historiography began, and there were echoes of this new attitude in the programs of the secondary schools, which added mathematics, physics, and geography to their curriculum.

Rousseau developed the political consequences of his thought in his *Social Contract* (1762). Because men are by nature free, Rousseau argued, the only natural and legitimate polity is one in which all members are citizens with equal rights and have the ability to participate in making the laws under which they live. Like Montesquieu, Rousseau himself was no revolutionary; he expressed a deep pessimism about the chances of freeing humanity from the corrupting institutions that were in place. Although his theories did influence critics of the French monarchy even before 1789, they achieved an unanticipated relevance during the Revolution, especially during its radical phase when Rousseau was read as an advocate of Jacobin-style democracy.

Exposure to such writers as Diderot, Guillaume-Thomas, abbé de Raynal (1713–96), author of the anticolonialist *Histoire des deux Indes* (1770; *History of the Two Indies*), and Jean-Jacques Barthélemy (1716–95); to such painters as Jacques-Louis David (1748–1825) and Joseph-Marie Vien (1716–1809); to such musicians as Christoph Gluck (1714–87); and to such visionary architects as Claude-Nicolas Ledoux (1736–1806) and Étienne-Louis Boullée (1728–99) enabled the educated public of the 1770s and '80s to pursue and sharpen their new insights. It allowed them to explore the limits of the private domain as well as to clarify their new understanding of the public good. These radical ideas had transforming power. Rousseau's message especially appealed to the deeper instincts of his contemporaries, inspiring them with a quasi-utopian view of what might be done in this world.

The ideological or cultural transformation was in some ways limited to a narrow segment of society. In 1789 only one-third of the population, living for the most part in northern and eastern France, could both read and write French. (Outside the aristocracy and upper bourgeoisie, literacy for women was considerably below that of men.) About one-third of the king's subjects could not even speak French.

Nonetheless, even though probably not much more than half a million people were directly involved in the cultural upheaval, their influence was decisive.

The concerns of the new "high culture" were intensely personal and, for that reason, deeply felt, even by people who did not participate in it directly. Readers of sentimental prose might after all also be employers, husbands, and fathers, who would treat their dependents differently. Printed materials were certainly more widely available in the 18th century than ever before, and new ideas reached a wide public, even if often only in watered-down form. Newspapers, some of them from abroad, were widely read (and manipulated by the royal government to influence opinion). Many pamphleteers were ready to be hired by whoever had money to pay for their services. Lawyers published their briefs. Theatrical performances, such as Pierre-Augustin Caron de Beaumarchais's comedy *Le Mariage de Figaro* (1784; *The Marriage of Figaro*), which openly exposed aristocratic privilege, were widely publicized events. In the 1780s censorship was increasingly desultory. Public opinion, whose verdict was identified by the middle class not with the expression of its own particular desires but as the voice of universal common sense and reason, became a tribunal of ideological appeal, an intellectual court of last resort, to which even the monarchy instinctively appealed.

These sweeping changes had created a country that by 1788 was deeply divided ideologically and economically. The salons of Paris, many of them directed by women, were the worldwide focus of a rationalist and Deist Enlightenment; both Catherine the Great and Thomas Jefferson, though far removed from each other in most respects, shared an abiding interest in the latest intellectual fashions from Paris. But, whatever held true for influential circles, most Frenchmen in these same years remained deeply religious, certainly in the provinces but possibly in Paris as well. Most of the books and pictures Parisians bought on the eve of the Revolution were still related to religious themes. The country was also divided economically; whereas France's foreign trade was very lively, most of the rural communities were, by English standards, unproductive and immobile villages.

THE POLITICAL RESPONSE

In broad terms, 18th-century French politics could be defined as the response of the monarchic state to the emergence of the new cultural and economic configurations that had transformed the lives and especially the imaginations of French men and women. The question was whether the Bourbon monarchy could rationalize its administration and find a way to adapt itself in the 1770s and '80s to the new perception of the relationship between citizen and state as it had come to be defined by the changes that characterized the period.

THE HISTORICAL DEBATE

On the issue of political mutation, historical opinion is divided. One set of discussions revolves around the issue of whether the monarchy's efforts at reform were sufficient; whereas some historians believe that the ancien régime almost succeeded, first in the 1770s and once again in the early 1780s, others argue more pessimistically that the efforts of the monarchy were insubstantial. A more radical view, by contrast, holds that the extent of reform was irrelevant because no monarch, however brilliant, could have met the rising liberal and nationalist expectations of tens of thousands of dissatisfied and vocal people, steeped in Enlightenment thought, who were committed to becoming the empowered citizens of a fraternal state.

The weight of evidence appears to be that the monarchy was by the late 1780s doomed to destruction, both from its inability to carry on the absolutist, administrative work formerly accomplished by such men as Colbert and by the nature of its critics' desires; the gap separating the traditionalism of the monarchy and the ambitions of nascent public opinion was too wide.

FOREIGN POLICY AND FINANCIAL CRISIS

The 18th-century French monarchy lacked both the ambition and the means to pursue a foreign policy as far-reaching as that of Louis XIV. From the time of the War of the Spanish Succession (1701–14), when France had been invaded and nearly beaten, French statesmen pursued a double goal—the preservation of the balance of power in Europe and, in the world at large, the expansion of the French colonial empire and the containment of England. In the first decades after Louis XIV's death, French leaders sought to avoid a renewal of large-scale conflict. After 1740, when Prussia's aggressive monarch Frederick II (the Great) attacked Austria, France was drawn into a war against its traditional Habsburg foe and Vienna's ally, Britain. The end of this War of the Austrian Succession (1740–48) brought France little. By 1754 France was again fighting Britain in North America. On the Continent, Prussia's rapprochement with the British drove Louis XV to break tradition and ally with the Austrians in the "diplomatic revolution" of 1756, leading to the Seven Years' War. Frederick the Great's army inflicted humiliating defeats on the poorly led French armies, while the British captured French possessions in Canada, the Caribbean, and India. After the peace settlement of 1763, the foreign minister, Étienne-François, duc de Choiseul, began military reforms that laid the basis for French successes in the Revolutionary era, but France was unable to stop its Continental rivals Prussia, Austria, and Russia from seizing territory from its traditional client Poland in the First Partition of 1772.

The one French success in the century-long competition with Britain was the support given to the rebellious North

American colonies in the American Revolution (1775–83). French military officers, most notably the young marquis de Lafayette, fought with the American forces, and for a short while the French navy had control of the high seas. The real victor of the Siege of Yorktown, Virginia (1781), in which the British were defeated, was less General George Washington than Admiral François-Joseph-Paul, comte de Grasse (1722–88), whose fleet had entered Chesapeake Bay. The American victory enhanced French prestige but failed to bring any territorial gains or economic advantages.

Regardless of defeat or victory, colonial and naval wars were problematic because of their prohibitive cost. In Bourbon France (as in Hanoverian England and the Prussia of the Fredericks) a high percentage of the governmental income was earmarked for war. Navies were a particularly costly commodity. The crown's inability to manage the ever-swelling deficit finally forced it to ask the country's elites for help, which, for reasons unrelated to the various wars and conflicts, they were unwilling to extend unconditionally. Money thus was a large factor in the collapse of the monarchy in 1789.

Ultimately, to be sure, it was not the crown's inability to pay for wars that caused its downfall. Rather, the crown's extreme financial difficulties could have led to reforms; the need for funds might have galvanized the energies of the monarchy to carry forward the task of administrative reordering begun during the reigns of Louis XIII and Louis XIV. A more determined king might have availed himself of the problems raised by the deficit in order to overwhelm the defenders of traditionalism. In so doing, the monarchy might have satisfied enough of the desires of the Enlightenment elite to defuse the tense political situation of the late 1770s and the '80s. Although in 1789 a program of "reform from above" was no longer possible, it might well have succeeded in the early 1770s.

DOMESTIC POLICY AND REFORM EFFORTS

As stated above, in the context of 17th-century absolutism, Louis XIV had already initiated many rationalizing reforms. This statist and anticorporatist program was now embraced, but in a more liberal register, by the Enlightenment partisans of meritocratic individualism. Though Montesquieu had defended intermediary bodies such as guilds as guarantees of civic liberty, thinkers of the Enlightenment attacked them in the name of public utility and of what would later be called the rights of man. In an article written for the *Encyclopédie*, Turgot denied the sanctity of what he called foundations: "Public utility is the supreme law, and cannot be countervailed by a superstitious respect for what has been called the intents of the founders." Most foundations, he thought, had as their only purpose the satisfaction of frivolous vanity. At the other end of the social spectrum, the Protestant

Rabaut Saint-Étienne, later president of the National Assembly (Assemblée Nationale), argued that "every time one creates a corporate body with privileges one creates a public enemy because a special interest is nothing else than this." No distinction was made between private interest and factional selfishness; in 1786 the future Girondin leader Jacques-Pierre Brissot was expressing what had become a commonplace when he wrote that "the history of all intermediary bodies proves, in all evidence, that to bring men and to bind men together is to develop their vices and diminish their virtues." Private benevolence applied to public purpose was loudly praised in the 1780s, and Louis XVI's finance minister, Jacques Necker (1732–1804), did a great deal for his reputation by endowing a hospital for sick children, which stands to this day. By 1789 public and charitable concern had become the themes of countless didactic works of literature and painting.

Many of the monarchy's efforts to institutionalize this new sensibility were often significant. The crown encouraged not only agriculture but also manufacturing and commerce. It allowed tax exemptions for newly cultivated land. It subsidized the slave trade, on which much of the prosperity of the Atlantic seaports was based. It improved communications and in 1747 founded the School of Bridges and Roads to train civil engineers for the royal engineering service that had existed since 1599. In the provinces, many intendants took an active role in road building and in the modernization of urban space.

The crown's administrators also gave sustained thought to the abolition of internal customs and to the creation of what would have been the largest free-trade zone in Europe at the time. Social mobility was made possible; after 1750 many successful merchants and bankers were ennobled.

These were important steps. But the royal bureaucrats tried to go much further in regard to both the rationalization of the state's financial machine and the meritocratic individuation of social and economic forms.

TAX REFORM

In 1749–51 Jean-Baptiste de Machault d'Arnouville, then comptroller general of finances, tried to deal with the debts resulting from the just-concluded War of the Austrian Succession by proposing a partial reform of the tax system, his particular concern being to restrict the financial immunities of the church. In 1764 and 1765 another comptroller general, François de L'Averdy, attempted a reform of municipal representation and administration. All royal officials understood the need to reform and rationalize both the imposition and the collection of taxes; many nobles were exempted from taxation, especially in northern France, and many taxes were inefficiently collected by private tax-farmers.

The country's overall fiscal structure was highly irrational, as it had been developed by fits and starts under the goad of immediate need. There were direct taxes, some of which were collected directly by the state: the taille (a personal tax), the capitation, and the *vingtième* (a form of income tax from which the nobles and officials were usually exempt). There were also indirect taxes that everyone paid: the salt tax, or gabelle, which represented nearly one-tenth of royal revenue; the *traites*, or customs duty, internal and external; and the *aides*, or excise taxes, levied on the sale of items as diverse as wine, tobacco, and iron. All the indirect taxes were extremely unpopular and had much to do with the state's inability to rally the rural masses to its side in 1789. In the 1740s attempts had been made to amend this system but had foundered on the *parlements'* opposition to a more equitable distribution of taxation. By 1770 the swelling debt made it obvious that something should be done. Unpopular measures, such as forced loans, were put into effect. Joseph-Marie Terray, Louis XV's comptroller general of finances, repudiated a part of the debt.

Some observers, partisans of enlightened despotism—such as Voltaire, who defended it indirectly in his play of 1773 titled *Les Lois de Minos* (*The Laws of Minos*)—argued that the French monarchy stood in this particular instance for administrative rationalization and progress. But the current of opinion was already moving against the crown. Many writers saw in Terray a tool of royal despotism, plain and simple, and his ministerial colleague René-Nicolas-Charles-Augustin de Maupeou (1714–92) was even more detested for

his destruction of the *parlements*, which had become the bastion of conservative opposition to royal reform.

PARLEMENTS

The 13 parlements (that of Paris being by far the most important) were by their origins law courts. Although their apologists claimed in 1732 that the *parlements* had emerged from the ancient *judicium Francorum* of the Frankish tribes, they had in fact been created by the king in the Middle Ages to dispense justice in his name. With the atrophy of the Estates-General, which had not met since 1614, the *parlements* now claimed to represent the Estates when those were not in session. In 1752 a Jansenist *parlementaire*, Louis-Adrien Le Paige, developed the idea that the various *parlements* should be thought of as the "classes" or parts of a larger and single "Parlement de France."

This was a politically significant claim because these courts had taken on many other quasi-administrative functions that were related to charity, education, the supervision of the police, and even ecclesiastical discipline. Royal decrees were not binding, claimed the *parlementaires*, unless the *parlements* had registered them as laws. Although the *parlementaires* admitted that the king might force them to register his decrees by staging a *lit-de-justice* (i.e., by appearing in person at their session), they also knew that the public deplored such maneuvers, which manifestly went against the grain of the monarch's supposed Christian and paternalist solicitude for the well-being of his subjects.

Various social, cultural, and institutional developments had served to turn the *parlements* into strongholds of resistance to reforms that increased the crown's powers. Since the 17th century the monarchy's need for money and the ensuing venality of offices had enabled the *parlementaires* to purchase their positions and to become a small and self-conscious elite, a new "nobility of the robe." In 1604 the creation of the *paulette* tax had enabled the *parlementaires* to make their offices a part of their family patrimony, even if the value of their offices fell somewhat during the course of the 18th century. They had gained status by intermarrying with the older chivalric nobility of the sword. By 1700 the *parlementaires* had become a hereditary and rich landowning elite. (Near Bordeaux, for example, the best vineyards were theirs.) The interregnum of the regency after the death of Louis XIV (1715–23) had given them a chance to recapture some of the ground they had lost during Louis's reign; the value of their offices, however, fell again somewhat in the course of the 18th century. The *parlementaires*' Jansenist leanings and their recent espousal of antiabsolutism—expressed in the work of Montesquieu, himself a baron and a *parlementaire*—gave this elite ideological consistency.

In 1764 the Jansenist *parlementaires*, as ideological "progressives," secured the expulsion of the Jesuits from France. Incidents such as the death sentence administered by the Parlement of Paris in 1766 against the 18-year-old chevalier de la Barre, accused of mutilating a crucifix and owning a copy of Voltaire's *Dictionnaire philosophique* (1764; *Philosophical Dictionary*), showed, however, that the courts were not entirely on the side of the Enlightenment. In 1768–69 the Parlement of Brittany, in an antiabsolutist stance, forced the resignation of an appointed royal official, the duc d'Aiguillon, who had boldly tried to limit the power of the local nobility, with whom the Parlement was now in close alliance.

KING AND *PARLEMENTS*

In 1770 the conflict with the *parlements* had reached such a level that Louis XV was finally goaded into a burst of absolutist energy. The Paris Parlements, which had dared to attack Terray's financial reform, were dissolved on January 19, 1771. Maupeou was then authorized to create an altogether different set of *parlements* with appointed judges shorn of administrative and political power.

In time, opinion might well have accepted Terray's and Maupeou's reforms, despite the outcry raised by the *parlements*' supporters, who argued that the arbitrary uprooting of these centuries-old institutions threatened to turn France into a "ministerial despotism." France might then, like Prussia, have avoided revolution from below through the practice of a revolution from above. But the death of Louis XV in 1774 put an end to the experiment. His 20-year-old successor, Louis XVI (reigned 1774–92), unsure of himself and eager to please, recalled the *parlements* and forced Maupeou into retirement.

In late 1774 Louis XVI appointed Turgot, a former intendant, comptroller general. Perhaps because he thought that the success of his reforms would guarantee their acceptance, perhaps also because he thought it vain to attack the Parlement directly so soon after Maupeou's dismissal, Turgot carried through his measures without first destroying the institutional bases of privileged conservatism. He left the Parlement alone and attempted instead to reduce government expenditures and to alter the methods of tax collecting. In accordance with his physiocratic laissez-faire principles, he freed the grain trade from restraint; suppressed the corvée, or forced labour service, exacted from the peasants; and abolished the guilds, which had limited both access to artisanal professions and the competition within them. Finally, he suggested that Protestants should be given freedom of conscience. In short, Turgot attempted to rationalize the administrative practices of the French state and to individuate French social and economic life. The solution to the financial crisis, he thought, would come not through the state's appropriation of a larger share of extant resources but from the expansion of the nation's ability to produce and pay. The strength of creative individualism, he thought, would break the political impasse.

In May 1776, however, Turgot was dismissed. Opposition to his measures had come from all sides: a poor harvest had sparked peasant disturbances, the clericalists were antagonized by Turgot's philosophical friends (his greatest and most loyal disciple was Marie-Jean-Antoine-Nicolas de Caritat, marquis de Condorcet, the future Girondin), and, when the Parlement of Paris once again refused to register the new edicts, Louis abandoned Turgot as he had dismissed Maupeou. Thenceforth, the state carried through only minor reforms, none of them on a scale commensurate with the needs felt by the Enlightenment bourgeoisie and notables of the cities and towns. The vestiges of serfdom were suppressed in 1779, and in 1780 torture was abolished. In 1784 the king's use of lettres de cachet for purposes of arbitrary imprisonment without trial was considerably curtailed. But these were minor adjustments. Nothing was done to solve the fundamental problems of the organization of society and of the state in a manner that would be acceptable to progressive public opinion.

The issue of fundamental reform came to the fore again in 1786, when the loans floated to pay for the American war began to come due, and the controller general, Charles-Alexandre de Calonne (1734–1802), had to tell the king that they could not be repaid. "The only way to bring real order into the finances is to revitalize the entire state by reforming all that is defective in its constitution," Calonne told his sovereign.

Although Louis XVI accepted Calonne's proposal to convene an Assembly of Notables, chosen from the country's elites, and to seek their endorsement for a comprehensive reform program, the monarchy had already frittered away the prestige and authority that might have allowed this gamble to succeed. Repeated changes of policy in the previous decades had made the public wary of royal initiatives. Louis XV's sexual adventures, especially his public liaison with Mme du Barry, widely rumoured to have once been a prostitute, had severely damaged the monarchy's image. Louis XVI's embarrassing inability to consummate his marriage with Marie-Antoinette for seven years also undermined respect for the throne, which suffered a further blow from the Affair of the Diamond Necklace of 1785–86, in which a high-ranking prelate was accused of having tried to seduce the queen.

The Assembly of Notables that Calonne had suggested met in February 1787. The minister presented a program that offered the country's upper classes some voice in lawmaking in exchange for their consent to the abolition of many traditional privileges, particularly the nobility's immunity to taxes. Although he did not suggest the creation of a national parliament, Calonne's plan involved the establishment of provincial assemblies that would oversee the use of public money. Even though Calonne's proposals were a major step in the direction of representative government and the abolition of special privileges, the notables refused to accept proposals put forward by a minister who they held responsible for previously worsening the deficit.

Desperate to obtain badly needed new revenues, Louis XVI replaced Calonne with Loménie de Brienne, archbishop of Toulouse, who had been one of Calonne's strongest critics in the Assembly of Notables. Almost at once Loménie reversed himself and came to Calonne's conclusion: the state could not go on as it had. The notables, however, refused to be more amenable to Loménie than they had been to Calonne. Despairing of securing the consent of the privileged orders, Loménie dismissed the assembly in May of 1787, and in August the Paris Parlement was exiled to Troyes.

But these measures were desperate, and already the monarchy was beginning to lose control of the political process. Indeed, for the next two years it floundered from one scheme to another in the impossible hope of squaring the circle of modernistic reform, popular hostility, respect of privilege, and the preservation of royal absolutism. Essentially unwilling to force the privileged notables to yield their corporate rights, the crown was unable to assert any coherent policy. The Parlement was therefore recalled from Troyes in September 1787, again dismissed in May 1788, and, in the face of a beginning of a breakdown of law and order and of the inability of officials to collect taxes, once more recalled to Paris by the crown in August 1788.

By this time, the government had already announced the summoning of a national representative assembly, the Estates-General. All the king's subjects would be allowed to participate in

choosing representatives and in drafting lists of grievances, called *cahiers
de doléances*, in which they could voice
their opinions about the problems facing the kingdom. When the just-restored
Parlement of Paris, concerned to prevent
ministerial manipulation of the Estates-
General, rushed to declare that it should
be structured "according to the forms
of 1614," with the two privileged orders
(the clergy and the nobility) having
separate chambers and a veto on all legislation, the judges quickly lost most of
their popularity. Leadership of the movement for political reform passed to new
men who had no stake in preserving old
institutions.

Self-proclaimed "patriot" pamphleteers such as the abbé Emmanuel-Joseph
Sieyès, whose pamphlet *Qu'est-ce que
le tiers état?* (1789; *What Is the Third
Estate?*) was one of the most widely read
of the thousands of tracts published as
the royal censorship system ceased to
function, demanded that the upcoming
assembly be structured so that the Third
Estate of commoners, the vast majority of the population, could prevent the
privileged orders from paralyzing its
deliberations. In a last and fitful assertion of authority, at the behest of Necker,
recalled as minister when Loménie was
dismissed in August 1788, the crown
decided on December 27 to overrule the
Paris Parlement. The Estates, it resolved,
would meet separately, but the Third
Estate would have as many deputies as
the other two orders combined. The stage
was set for the coming Revolution.

THE CAUSES OF THE FRENCH REVOLUTION

In an immediate sense, what brought
down the ancien régime was its own
inability to change or, more simply, to
pay its way. The deeper causes for its
collapse are more difficult to establish.
One school of interpretation maintains
that French society under the ancien
régime was rent by class war. This position implies that the French Revolution
revolved around issues of class; it has led
to the class analysis of prerevolutionary
society as well as to the class analysis of
the opposing Revolutionary factions of
Girondins and Montagnards and, more
generally, to what the historian Alfred
Cobban called "the social interpretation
of the French Revolution."

In keeping with this interpretation,
Marxist historians from the 1930s to the
'70s emphasized that the French 18th-cen-
tury bourgeoisie had assumed a distinct
position in French society in that it was in
control of commerce, banking, and industry. Revisionist historians in the 1980s,
however, responded that the bourgeoisie
had no monopoly in these sectors; nobles
were also heavily involved in foreign
trade, in banking, and in some of the most
modern industries, such as coal mining
and chemicals.

Most historians today argue that, on
balance, it was becoming increasingly
difficult to distinguish clearly between
the nobility and the bourgeoisie. Like
most nobles, wealthy French non-nobles
were landlords and even owners of

seigneuries, which were bought and sold before 1789 like any other commodity. Although one can speak of a secularized "bourgeois" ethic of thrift and prudence that had come into its own, supporters of this ethic, as of the Enlightenment ethic, were both noble and non-noble.

There were two areas, however, in which the nobility enjoyed important institutional privileges: the upper ranks of the army and the clergy were, in the main, aristocratic preserves and had become more so in the 1780s. Henri de Boulainvilliers, in his posthumous essays of 1732 on the nobility of France, had even developed a wholly fraudulent but widely praised theory of noble racial superiority. Thus, there were some issues on which all the bourgeoisie might unite against most of the nobility. But such issues, it is now claimed, were relatively unimportant.

Proponents of a social explanation of the Revolution have also emphasized the role of the lower classes. As population increased during the 18th century, peasant landholdings tended to become smaller, and the gap between rich and poor grew. Although the general trend after 1715 had been one of greater overall prosperity, the 20 years before 1789 were a time of economic difficulties. The months leading up to the convening of the Estates-General coincided with the worst subsistence crisis France had suffered in many years; a spring drought was followed by a devastating hailstorm that ruined crops in much of the northern half of the country in July 1788.

Distressed peasants were thus eager to take advantage of a situation in which the privileges of their landlords seemed vulnerable to attack. Urban workers, who suffered acutely when bread prices rose, as they had after Turgot's reforms in 1775 and again after the 1788 hailstorm, also had social grievances. Some felt menaced by the development of large-scale manufacturing enterprises; others resented the regulations that, for example, prevented journeymen from setting up their own shops in competition with privileged guild masters. The process of elections to the Estates-General gave both rural and urban populations an unprecedented opportunity to articulate grievances against elite privileges that had been endemic under the ancien régime but that had not been openly voiced.

Contemporary historiography has refocused the discussion regarding the causes for the Revolution. Studying the representation of politics, the shape of revolutionary festivals, and the revolutionary cults of sacrifice and heroism, scholars have come to place the transformation of culture at the core of their discussion. What really mattered was the desanctifying of the monarchy, the new understanding of the self and the public good, and the belief that thinking individuals might seize the state and fundamentally reshape it. Other historians, by contrast, have emphasized the persistent liabilities that French political culture carried through the Enlightenment, such as the suspicion of dissent and the readiness to rely on force to subvert it.

From either of these two perspectives, it follows that the prospects of the monarchy's survival were dim in 1788. Many government officials, it is true, were finely attuned to public opinion. The vast neorepublican canvases of Jacques-Louis David (1748–1845), such as his *Oath of the Horatii* (1784), glorifying traditional republicanism, were commissioned by the king's dispenser of patronage, the marquis d'Angivillers, a friend of Turgot. Visionary architects, developing a style of Revolutionary Neoclassicism, similarly received royal commissions for new public works. Chrétien Guillaume de Lamoignon de Malesherbes (1721–94), another friend of Turgot and, like him, a minister of the crown, protected the Encyclopédistes. On balance, however, it is hard to see how the monarchy, even if it had resolved its financial problems, which

THE BASTILLE

The Bastille was a medieval fortress on the east side of Paris that became, in the 17th and 18th centuries, a French state prison and a place of detention for important persons charged with various offenses. Stormed by an armed mob of Parisians in the opening days of the French Revolution, it was a symbol of the despotism of the ruling Bourbon monarchy and held an important place in the ideology of the Revolution.

With its eight towers, 100 feet (30 metres) high, linked by walls of equal height and surrounded by a moat more than 80 feet (24 metres) wide, the Bastille dominated Paris. The first stone was laid on April 22, 1370, on the orders of Charles V of France, who had it built as a *bastide*, or fortification (the name Bastille is a corruption of *bastide*), to protect his wall around Paris against English attack. The Bastille, in fact, was originally a fortified gate, but Charles VI turned it into an independent stronghold by walling up the openings. In 1557 its defensive system was completed on the eastern flank by the erection of a bastion. In the 17th century a transverse block was built, dividing the inner court into unequal parts.

Cardinal de Richelieu was the first to use the Bastille as a state prison, in the 17th century; the yearly average number of prisoners was 40, interned by lettre de cachet, a direct order of the king, from which there was no recourse. Prisoners included political troublemakers and individuals held at the request of their families, often to coerce a young member into obedience or to prevent a disreputable member from marring the family's name. Under Louis XIV the Bastille became a place of judicial detention in which the *lieutenant de police* could hold prisoners; under the regency of Philippe II, duc d'Orléans, persons being tried by the Parlement were also detained there. Imprisonment by lettre de cachet remained, however, in force, and prohibited books were also placed in the Bastille. The high cost of maintaining the building prompted talk of demolition in 1784.

On the morning of July 14, 1789, when only seven prisoners were confined in the building, a crowd advanced on the Bastille with the intention of asking the prison governor, Bernard Jordan, marquis de Launay, to release the arms and munitions stored there. Angered by Launay's evasiveness, the people stormed and captured the place; this dramatic action came to symbolize the end of the ancien régime. The Bastille was subsequently demolished by order of the Revolutionary government.

Bastille Day, celebrated annually on July 14, was chosen as a French national holiday in 1880.

it was very far from doing, could have extended this ecumenism from art to politics and social life. To do so, it would have had to transform its institutions in keeping with new conceptions regarding men's public and private affairs and to commit itself to the rejection of the corporatist ethic in economic life. Thus, the monarchy seemed fated to failure and the stage set for revolution.

THE END OF THE ANCIEN RÉGIME, THE FRENCH REVOLUTION, AND THE NAPOLEONIC ERA

A seismic shift was occurring in elite public opinion. What began in 1787–88 as a conflict between royal authority and traditional aristocratic groups had become a triangular struggle, with "the people" opposing both absolutism and privilege. A new kind of political discourse was emerging, and within a year it was to produce an entirely new concept of sovereignty with extremely far-reaching implications.

THE CONVERGENCE OF REVOLUTIONS, 1789

Louis XVI's decision to convene the Estates-General in May 1789 became a turning point in French history. When he invited his subjects to express their opinions and grievances in preparation for this event—unprecedented in living memory—hundreds responded with pamphlets in which the liberal ideology of 1789 gradually began to take shape. Exactly how the Estates-General should deliberate proved to be the pivotal consciousness-raising issue. Each of the three Estates could vote separately (by order) as they had in the distant past, or they could vote jointly (by head). Because the Third Estate was to have twice as many deputies as the others, only voting by head would assure its preponderant influence. If the estates voted by order, the clergy and nobility would effectively exercise a veto power over important decisions. Most pamphleteers of 1789 considered themselves "patriots," or reformers, and (though some were nobles themselves) identified the excessive influence of "aristocrats" as a chief obstacle to reform. In his influential tract *Qu'est-ce que le tiers état?* (1789; *What Is the Third Estate?*) the constitutional theorist Emmanuel-Joseph Sieyès asserted that the Third Estate really was the French nation. While commoners did all the truly laborious and productive work of society, he claimed with some exaggeration, the nobility monopolized its lucrative sinecures and honours. As a condition of genuine reform, the Estates-General would have to change that situation.

THE JURIDICAL REVOLUTION

Patriots were driven to increasingly bold positions in part by the resistance and bad faith of royal and aristocratic forces. It is not surprising that some of the Third Estate's most radical deputies came from Brittany, whose nobility was so hostile to change that it finally boycotted the Estates-General altogether. Hoping that the king would take the lead of the patriot cause, liberals were disappointed at the irresolute, business-as-usual attitude of the monarchy when the Estates opened at Versailles in May 1789. While the nobility organized itself into a separate chamber (by a vote of 141 to 47), as did the clergy (133 to 114), the Third Estate refused to do so. After pleading repeatedly for compromise and debating their course of action in the face of this deadlock, the Third Estate's deputies finally acted decisively. On June 17 they proclaimed that they were not simply the Third Estate of the Estates-General but a National Assembly (Assemblée Nationale), which the other deputies were invited to join. A week later 150 deputies of the clergy did indeed join the National Assembly, but the nobility protested that the whole notion was illegal.

Now the king had to clarify his position. He began by closing the hall assigned to the Third Estate and ordering all deputies to hear a royal address on June 23. The deputies, however, adjourned to an indoor tennis court on the 20th and there swore a solemn oath to continue meeting until they had provided France with a constitution. Two days later they listened to the king's program for reform. In the "royal session" of June 23, the king pledged to honour civil liberties, agreed to fiscal equality (already conceded by the nobility in its *cahiers*, or grievance petitions), and promised that the Estates-General would meet regularly in the future. But, he declared, they would deliberate separately by order. France was to become a constitutional monarchy, but one in which "the ancient distinction of the three orders will be conserved in its entirety." In effect the king was forging an alliance with the nobility, whose most articulate members—the judges of the parlements—only a year before had sought to hobble him. For the patriots this was too little and too late.

In a scene of high drama, the deputies refused to adjourn to their own hall. When ordered to do so by the king's chamberlain, the Assembly's president, astronomer Jean-Sylvain Bailly (1736–93), responded—to the official's amazement—that "the assembled nation cannot receive orders." Such defiance unnerved the king. Backing down, he directed the nobles several days later to join a National Assembly whose existence he had just denied. Thus, the Third Estate, with its allies in the clergy and nobility, had apparently effected a successful nonviolent revolution from above. Having been elected in the bailliages (the monarchy's judicial districts, which served as electoral circumscriptions) to represent particular constituents to their king, the deputies had transformed themselves into representatives of the entire nation. Deeming the nation alone to be sovereign, they, as its representatives, claimed sole authority to exercise that sovereignty. This was the juridical revolution of 1789.

PARISIAN REVOLT

In fact, the king had by no means reconciled himself to this revolutionary act. His concession was a strategic retreat until he could muster the military power to subdue the patriots. Between June 27 and July 1 he ordered 20,000 royal troops into the Paris region, ostensibly to protect the assembly and to prevent disorder in the restive capital. The assembly's pleas to the king to withdraw these menacing and unnecessary troops fell on deaf ears. For all of their moral force, the deputies utterly lacked material force to counter the king's obvious intentions. The assembly was saved from likely dissolution only by a massive popular mobilization.

During the momentous political events of 1788–89, much of the country lay in the grip of a classic subsistence crisis. Bad weather had reduced the grain crops that year by almost one-quarter the normal yield. An unusually cold winter compounded the problem, as frozen rivers halted the transport and milling of flour in many localities. Amid fears of hoarding and profiteering, grain and flour reserves dwindled. In Paris the price of the four-pound loaf of bread—the standard item of consumption accounting for most of the population's calories and nutrition—rose from its usual 8 sous to 14 sous by January 1789. This intolerable trend set off traditional forms of popular protest. If royal officials did not assure basic food supplies at affordable prices, then people would act directly to seize food. During the winter and spring of 1789, urban consumers and peasants rioted at bakeries and markets and attacked millers and grain convoys. Then, in July, this anxiety merged with the looming political crisis at Versailles. Parisians believed that food shortages and royal troops would be used in tandem to starve the people and overwhelm them into submission. They feared an "aristocratic plot" to throttle the patriot cause.

When the king dismissed the still-popular finance minister Necker on July 11, Parisians correctly read this as a signal that the counterrevolution was about to begin. Instead of yielding, however, they rose in rebellion. Street-corner orators such as Camille Desmoulins stirred their compatriots to resist. Confronting royal troops in the streets, they won some soldiers to their side and induced officers to confine other potentially unreliable units to their barracks. On July 13, bands of Parisians ransacked armourers' shops in a frantic search for weapons. The next day a large crowd invaded the Hôtel des Invalides and seized thousands of rifles without resistance. Then they moved to the Bastille, an old fortress commanding the Faubourg Saint-Antoine, which had served as a notorious royal prison earlier in the century but was now scheduled for demolition. Believing that gunpowder was stored there, the crowd laid siege to the Bastille. Unlike the troops at the Invalides, the Bastille's tiny garrison resisted, a fierce battle erupted, and dozens of Parisians were killed. When the garrison finally capitulated, the irate crowd massacred several of the soldiers.

In another part of town two leading royal officials were lynched for their presumed role in the plot against the people. Meanwhile, the electors of Paris, who had continued to meet after choosing their deputies to the Estates-General, ousted the royal officials of the city government, formed a revolutionary municipality, and organized a citizens' militia, or national guard, to patrol the streets. Similar municipal revolutions occurred in 26 of the 30 largest French cities, thus assuring that the capital's defiance would not be an isolated act.

By any standard, the fall of the Bastille to the Parisian crowd was a spectacular symbolic event—a seemingly miraculous triumph of the people against the power of royal arms. The heroism of the crowd and the blood of its martyrs—ordinary Parisian artisans, tradesmen, and workers—sanctified the patriot cause. Most important, the elites and the people of Paris had made common cause, despite the inherent distrust and social distance between them. The mythic unity of the Third Estate—endlessly invoked by patriot writers and orators—seemed actually to exist, if only momentarily. Before this awesome material and moral force, Louis XVI capitulated. He did not want civil war in the streets. The Parisian insurrection of July 14 not only saved the National Assembly from dissolution but altered the course of the Revolution by giving it a far more active, popular, and violent dimension. On July 17 the king traveled to Paris, where he publicly donned a cockade bearing a new combination of colours: white for the Bourbons and blue and red for the city of Paris. This tricolour was to become the new national flag.

PEASANT INSURGENCIES

Peasants in the countryside, meanwhile, carried on their own kind of rebellion, which combined traditional aspirations and anxieties with support of the patriot cause. The peasant revolt was autonomous, yet it reinforced the urban uprising to the benefit of the National Assembly.

Competition over the ownership and use of land had intensified in many regions. Peasants owned only about 40 percent of the land, leasing or sharecropping the rest from the nobility, the urban middle class, and the church. Population growth and subdivision of the land from generation to generation was reducing the margin of subsistence for many families. Innovations in estate management—the grouping of leaseholds, conversion of arable land to pasture, enclosure of open fields, division of common land at the lord's initiative, discovery of new seigneurial dues or arrears in old ones—exasperated peasant tenants and smallholders. Historians debate whether these were capitalistic innovations or traditional varieties of seigneurial extraction, but in either case the countryside was boiling with discontent over these trends as well as over oppressive royal taxes and food shortages. Peasants were poised between great hopes for the future raised by the calling of the Estates-General and extreme anxiety—fear of losing land, fear of hunger (especially after the catastrophic harvest of 1788), and fear of a vengeful aristocracy.

In July peasants in several regions sacked the castles of nobles and burned the documents that recorded their feudal obligations. This peasant insurgency eventually merged into the movement known as the Great Fear. Rumours abounded that these vagrants were actually brigands in the pay of nobles, who were marching on villages to destroy the new harvest and coerce the peasants into submission. The fear was baseless, but hundreds of false alarms and panics stirred up hatred and suspicion of nobles, led peasants to arm themselves as best they could, and set off widespread attacks on châteaus and feudal documents. The peasant revolt suggested that the unity of the Third Estate against "aristocrats" extended from Paris to villages across the country. The Third Estate truly seemed invincible.

THE ABOLITION OF FEUDALISM

Of course the violence of peasant insurgency worried the deputies of the National Assembly; to some it seemed as if the countryside were being engulfed by anarchy that threatened all property. But the majority were unwilling to turn against the rebellious peasants. Instead of denouncing the violence, they tried to appease peasant opinion. Liberal nobles and clergy began the session of August 4 by renouncing their ancient feudal privileges. Within hours the Assembly was propelled into decreeing "the abolition of feudalism" as well as the church tithe, venality of office, regional privilege, and fiscal privilege. A few days later, to be sure, the Assembly clarified the August 4 decree to assure that "legitimate" seigneurial property rights were maintained. While personal feudal servitudes such as hunting rights, seigneurial justice, and labour services were suppressed outright, most seigneurial dues were to be abolished only if the peasants paid compensation to their lords, set at 20 to 25 times the annual value of the obligation. The vast majority of peasants rejected that requirement by passive resistance, until pressure built in 1792–93 for the complete abolition of all seigneurial dues without compensation.

The abolition of feudalism was crucial to the evolution of a modern, contractual notion of property and to the development of an unimpeded market in land. But it did not directly affect the ownership of land or the level of ordinary rents and leases. Seigneurs lost certain kinds of traditional income, but they remained landowners and landlords. While all peasants gained in dignity and status, only the landowning peasants came out substantially ahead economically. Tenant farmers found that what they had once paid for the tithe was added on to their rent. And the Assembly did virtually nothing to assure better lease terms for renters and sharecroppers, let alone their acquisition of the land they tilled.

THE NEW REGIME

By sweeping away the old web of privileges, the August 4 decree permitted the Assembly to construct a new regime. Since it would take months to draft a constitution, the Assembly on August 27 promulgated its basic principles in a Declaration of the Rights of Man and of the Citizen. A rallying point for the future, the declaration also stood as the death certificate of the ancien régime. The declaration's authors believed it to have universal significance. "In the new hemisphere, the brave inhabitants of Philadelphia have given the example of a people who reestablished their liberty," conceded one deputy, but "France would give that example to the rest of the world." At the same time, the declaration responded to particular circumstances and was thus a calculated mixture of general principles and specific concerns. Its concept of natural rights meant that the Revolution would not be bound by history and tradition but could reshape the contours of society according to reason—a position vehemently denounced by Edmund Burke in England.

The very first article of the declaration resoundingly challenged Europe's old order by affirming that "men are born and remain free and equal in rights. Social distinctions may be based only on common utility." Most of its articles concerned individual liberty, but the declaration's emphasis fell equally on the prerogatives of the state as expressed through law. (Considering how drastically the erstwhile delegates to the Estates-General had exceeded their mandates, they certainly needed to underscore the legitimacy of their new government and its laws.) The declaration, and subsequent Revolutionary constitutions, channeled the sovereignty of the nation into representative government, thereby negating claims by parlements, provincial estates, or divine-right monarchs as well as any conception of direct democracy. Though the declaration affirmed the separation of powers, by making no provision for a supreme court, it effectively left the French legislature as the ultimate judge of its own actions. The declaration defined liberty as "the ability to do whatever does not harm another... whose limits can only be determined by law." The same limitation by positive law was attached to specific liberties, such as freedom from arbitrary arrest, freedom of expression, and freedom of religious conscience. The men of 1789 believed deeply in these liberties, yet they did not establish them in autonomous, absolute terms that would ensure their sanctity under any circumstances.

RESTRUCTURING FRANCE

From 1789 to 1791 the National Assembly acted as a constituent assembly, drafting a constitution for the new regime while also governing from day to day. The constitution established a limited monarchy, with a clear separation of powers in which the king was to name and dismiss his ministers. But sovereignty effectively resided in the legislative branch, to consist of a single house, the Legislative Assembly, elected by a system of indirect voting. ("The people or the nation can have only one voice, that of the national legislature," wrote Sieyès. "The people can speak and act only through its representatives.") Besides failing to win a bicameral system, the moderate Anglophile, or *monarchien*, faction lost a bitter debate on the king's veto power: the Assembly granted the king only a suspensive or delaying veto over legislation; if a bill passed the Legislative Assembly in three successive sessions, it would become law even without royal approval.

Dismayed at what he deemed the ill-considered radicalism of such decisions, Jean-Joseph Mounier, a leading patriot deputy in the summer of 1789 and author of the Tennis Court Oath, resigned from the Assembly in October. In a similar vein, some late-20th-century historians (notably François Furet) suggested that the Assembly's integral concept of national sovereignty and legislative supremacy effectively reestablished absolutism in a new guise, providing the new government with inherently unlimited powers. Nor, they believed, is it surprising that the revolutionaries abused those powers as their pursuit of utopian goals encountered resistance. In theory this may well be true, but it must be balanced against the actual institutions created to implement those powers and the spirit in which they were used. With a few exceptions—notably the religious issue—the National Assembly acted in a liberal spirit, more pragmatic than utopian, and was decidedly more constructive than repressive.

The revolutionaries took civil equality seriously but created a limited definition of political rights. They effectively transferred political power from the monarchy and the privileged estates to the general body of propertied citizens. Nobles lost their privileges in 1789 and their titles in 1790, but, as propertied individuals, they could readily join the new political elite. The constitution restricted the franchise to "active" citizens who paid a minimal sum in taxes, with higher property qualifications for eligibility for public office (a direct-tax payment equivalent to 3 days' wages for voters and 10 days' wages for electors and officeholders). Under this system about two-thirds of adult males had the right to vote for electors and to choose certain local officials directly. Although it favoured wealthier citizens, the system was vastly more democratic than Britain's.

Predictably, the franchise did not extend to women, despite delegations and pamphlets advocating women's rights. The Assembly responded brusquely that, because women were too emotional and easily misled, they must be kept out of public life and devote themselves to their nurturing and maternal roles. But the formal exclusion of women from politics did not keep them on the sidelines. Women were active combatants in local conflicts that soon erupted over religious policy, and they agitated over subsistence issues—Parisian women, for example, made a mass march to Versailles in October that forced the king to move back to the capital. In the towns, they formed auxiliaries to local Jacobin clubs and even a handful of independent women's clubs, participated in civic festivals, and did public relief work.

The Assembly's design for local government and administration proved to be one of the Revolution's most durable legacies. Obliterating the political identity of France's historic provinces, the deputies redivided the nation's territory into 83 *départements* of roughly equal size. Unlike the old provinces, each *département* would have exactly the same institutions; *départements* were in turn subdivided into districts, cantons, and communes (the common designation for a village or town). On the one hand, this administrative transformation promoted decentralization and local autonomy: citizens of each *département*, district, and commune elected their own local officials. On the other hand, these local governments were subordinated to the national legislature and ministries in Paris. The *départements* therefore became instruments of national uniformity and integration, which is to say, centralization. This ambiguity the legislators fully appreciated, assuming that a healthy equilibrium could be maintained between the two tendencies. That the Revolutionary government of 1793 and Napoleon would later use these structures to concentrate power from the centre was not something they could anticipate.

The new administrative map also created the parameters for judicial reform. Sweeping away the entire judicial system of the ancien régime, the revolutionaries established a civil court in each district and a criminal court in each *département*. At the grass roots they replaced seigneurial justice with a justice of the peace in each canton. Judges on all of these tribunals were to be elected. While rejecting the use of juries in civil cases, the Assembly decreed that felonies would be tried by juries; if a jury convicted, judges would merely apply the mandatory sentences set out in the Assembly's tough new penal code of 1791. Criminal defendants also gained the right to counsel, which had been denied them under the jurisprudence of the ancien régime. In civil law, the Assembly encouraged arbitration and mediation to avoid the time-consuming and costly processes of formal litigation. In general, the revolutionaries hoped to make the administration of justice more accessible and expeditious.

Guided by laissez-faire doctrine and its hostility to privileged corporations, the Assembly sought to open up economic life to unimpeded individual initiative and competition. Besides proclaiming the right of all citizens to enter any trade and conduct it as they saw fit, the Assembly dismantled internal tariffs and chartered trading monopolies and abolished the guilds of merchants and artisans. Insisting that workers must bargain in the economic marketplace as individuals, the Le Chapelier Law of June 1791 (named after reformer Jean Le Chapelier) banned workers' associations and strikes. The precepts of economic individualism extended to rural life as well. In theory, peasants and landlords were now free to cultivate their fields as they wished, regardless of traditional collective routines and constraints. In practice, however, communal restraints proved to be deep-rooted and resistant to legal abolition.

SALE OF NATIONAL LANDS

The Assembly had not lost sight of the financial crisis that precipitated the collapse of absolutism in the first place. Creating an entirely new option for its solution, the Assembly voted to place church property—about 10 percent of the land in France—"at the disposition of the nation." This property was designated as biens nationaux, or national lands. The government then issued large-denomination notes called assignats, underwritten and guaranteed by the value of that land. It intended to sell national lands to the public, which would pay for it in assignats that would then be retired. Thus, church property would in effect pay off the national debt and obviate the need for further loans. Unfortunately, the temptation to print additional assignats proved too great. Within a year the assignat evolved into a paper currency in small and large denominations, with sharp inflationary effects.

As the national lands went on sale, fiscal needs took priority over social policy. Sales were arranged in large lots and at auction in the district capitals—procedures that favoured wealthier buyers. True, for about a year in 1793–94, after émigré property was added to the biens nationaux, large lots were divided into small parcels. In addition, small-scale peasants acquired some of this land through resale by the original buyers. But overall the urban middle classes and large-scale peasants emerged with the bulk of this land, to the intense frustration of small-scale peasants. The French historian Georges Lefebvre's study of the Nord département, for example, found that 7,500 bourgeois purchased 48 percent of the land, while 20,300 peasants bought 52 percent. But the top 10 percent of these peasant purchasers accounted for 60 percent of the peasants' total. Whatever the social origins of the buyers, however, they were likely to be reliable supporters of the Revolution if only to guarantee the security of their new acquisitions.

SEEDS OF DISCORD

Security could not be taken for granted, however, because the Revolution progressively alienated or disappointed important elements of French society. Among the elites, opposition began almost immediately when some of the king's close relatives left the country in disgust after July 14, thus becoming the first émigrés. Each turning point in the Revolution touched off new waves of emigration, especially among the nobility. By 1792 an estimated two-thirds of the royal officer corps had resigned their commissions, and most had left the country. A contentious royalist press bitterly denounced the policies of the Assembly as spoliation and the Revolutionary atmosphere as a form of anarchy. Abroad, widespread enthusiasm for the events in France among the general public from London to Vienna was matched by intense hostility in ruling circles fearful of revolutionary contagion within their own borders.

After the first months of solidarity, long-standing urban-rural tensions took on new force. Though peasants might vote in large numbers, the urban middle classes predictably emerged with the lion's share of the new district and *département* offices after the first elections of 1790. Administrative and judicial reform gave these local officials more powers for intrusion into rural society than royal officials ever had, with battalions of armed national guards to back them up. Peasants might easily view urban revolutionary elites as battening on political power and national lands. And, while the Assembly made the tax system more uniform and equitable, direct taxes remained heavy and actually rose in formerly privileged regions, while nothing was done to relieve the plight of tenant farmers. Later, when the Revolutionary government sought to draft young men into the army, another grievance was added to the list.

RELIGIOUS TENSIONS

It was religious policy that most divided French society and generated opposition to the Revolution. Most priests had initially hoped that sweeping reform might return Roman Catholicism to its basic ideals, shorn of aristocratic trappings and superfluous privileges, but they assumed that the church itself would collaborate in the process. In the Assembly's view, however, nationalization of church property gave the state responsibility for regulating the church's temporal affairs, such as salaries, jurisdictional boundaries, and modes of clerical appointment. On its own authority the Assembly reduced the number of dioceses and realigned their boundaries to coincide with the new *départements*, while requesting local authorities to redraw parish boundaries in conformity with population patterns. Under the Assembly's Civil Constitution of the Clergy (July 1790), bishops were to be elected by *départements*' electoral assemblies, while parish priests were to be chosen by electors in the districts. Clerical spokesmen deplored the notion of lay authority in such matters and insisted that the Assembly must negotiate reforms with a national church council.

In November 1790 the Assembly forced the issue by requiring all sitting bishops and priests to take an oath of submission. Those who refused would lose their posts, be pensioned off, and be replaced by the prescribed procedures. Throughout France a mere seven bishops complied, while only 54 percent of the parish clergy took the oath. Contrary to the Assembly's hopes, the clergy had split in two, with "constitutional" priests on one side and "refractory" priests on the other. Regional patterns accentuated this division: in the west of France, where clerical density was unusually high, only 15 percent of the clergy complied.

The schism quickly engulfed the laity. As refractories and constitutionals vied for popular support against their rivals, parishioners could not remain neutral. Intense local discord erupted over the implementation of the Civil Constitution of the Clergy. District administrations backed by urban national guards intervened to install "outsiders" chosen to replace familiar or even beloved refractory priests in many parishes; villagers responded by badgering or boycotting the hapless priests who took the oath. Opinion on both sides tended to fateful extremes, linking either the Revolution with impiety or the Roman Catholic Church with counterrevolution.

POLITICAL TENSIONS

The political life of the new regime was also proving more contentious than the revolutionaries had anticipated. With courage and consistency, the Assembly had provided that officials of all kinds be elected. But it was uncertain whether these officials, once the ballots were cast, could do their duty free from public pressure and agitation. Nor was it clear what the role of "public opinion" and the mechanisms for its expression would be. The spectacular development of a free press and political clubs provided an answer. Fearful that these extra-parliamentary institutions could be abused by demagogues, the Assembly tried to curb them from time to time but to no avail. Freed entirely from royal censorship, writers and publishers rushed to satisfy the appetite for news and political opinion. The first journalists included deputies reporting to their constituents by means of a newspaper. Paris, which had only 4 quasi-official newspapers at the start of 1789, saw more than 130 new periodicals by the end of the year, most admittedly short-lived, including 20 dailies. As the journalist Jacques-Pierre Brissot put it, newspapers are "the only way of educating a large nation unaccustomed to freedom or to reading, yet looking to free itself from ignorance." Provincial publishers were as quick to found new periodicals in the larger towns. Bordeaux, for example, had only 1 newspaper in 1789, but 16 appeared within the next two years. While some papers remained bland and politically neutral, many had strong political opinions.

Like the National Assembly, revolutionary clubs also began at Versailles, when patriot deputies rallied to a caucus of outspoken Third Estate deputies from Brittany. Thus began the Club Breton—complete with bylaws, minutes, committees, correspondence, and membership requirements—which later reorganized as the Society of the Friends of the Constitution. Soon it was known as the Jacobin Club, after the Dominican convent where the club met when the assembly transferred to Paris in October. Most prominent revolutionaries belonged to the Jacobin Club, from constitutional royalists such as the comte de Mirabeau, the marquis de Lafayette, and the comte de Barnave to radicals such as Brissot, Alexandre Sabès Pétion, and Maximilien Robespierre. By mid-1791, however, moderates became uncomfortable with the Jacobin Club, where Robespierre was emerging as a dominant figure.

The Jacobin Club was pushed from the left by the Club of the Cordeliers, one of the neighbourhood clubs in the capital. The Cordeliers militants rejected the Assembly's concept of representation as the exclusive expression of popular sovereignty. They held to a more direct vision of popular sovereignty as relentless vigilance and participation by citizens through demonstrations, petitions, deputations, and, if necessary, insurrection. In his newspaper *L'Ami du peuple* ("The Friend of the People") Jean-Paul Marat injected an extreme rhetoric about alleged conspiracies and the need for violence against counterrevolutionaries that exceeded anything heard in the Assembly's political discourse.

Like the press, clubs quickly spread in the provinces. Building, no doubt, on old-regime patterns of sociability—reading clubs, Freemasonry, or confraternities—political clubs became a prime vehicle for participation in the Revolution. More than 300 towns had clubs by the end of 1790 and 900 by mid-1791. Later clubs spread to the villages as well: a study has counted 5,000 localities that had clubs at one time or another between 1790 and 1795. Many clubs affiliated with the Paris Jacobin Club, the "mother club," in an informal nationwide network. Most began with membership limited to the middle class and a sprinkling of liberal nobles, but gradually artisans, shopkeepers, and peasants joined the rolls. Initially the clubs promoted civic education and publicized the Assembly's reforms. But some became more activist, seeking to influence political decisions with petitions, to exercise surveillance over constituted authorities, and to denounce those they deemed remiss.

By 1791 the Assembly found itself in a cross fire between the machinations of counterrevolutionaries—émigrés, royalist newspapers, refractory clergy—and the denunciations of radicals. Its ability to steer a stable course depended in part on the cooperation of the king. Publicly Louis XVI distanced himself from his émigré relatives, but privately he was in league with them and secretly corresponded with the royal houses of Spain and Austria to enlist their support. On June 21, 1791, the royal family attempted to flee its "captivity" in the Tuileries Palace and escape across the Belgian border. Rashly, Louis left behind a letter revealing his utter hostility to the Revolution. At the last minute, however, the king was recognized at the town of Varennes near the border, and the royal party was forcibly returned to Paris.

A great crisis for the Revolution ensued. While the Assembly reinforced the frontiers by calling for 100,000 volunteers from the national guard, its moderate leaders hoped that this fiasco would end Louis's opposition once and for all. To preserve their constitutional compromise, they turned a blind eye to the king's manifest treason by inventing the fiction that he had been kidnapped. As Antoine Barnave put it, "Are we or are we not going to terminate the Revolution? Or are we going to start it all over again?" Outside the Assembly, however, Jacobins and Cordeliers launched a petition campaign against reinstating the king. A mass demonstration on July 17 at the Champ de Mars against the king ended in a bloody riot, as the authorities called out the national guard under Lafayette's command to disperse the demonstrators. This precipitated vehement recriminations in the Jacobin Club, which finally split apart under the pressure. The mass of moderate deputies abandoned the club to a rump of radicals and formed a new association called the Club of the Feuillants. Under the leadership of Robespierre and

Jérôme Pétion (who later became mortal enemies), the purged Jacobin Club rallied most provincial clubs and emerged from the crisis with a more unified, radical point of view. For the time being, however, the moderates prevailed in the Assembly. They completed the Constitution of 1791, and on the last day of September 1791 the National Assembly dissolved itself, having previously decreed the ineligibility of its members for the new Legislative Assembly.

When the newly elected Legislative Assembly convened in October, the question of counterrevolution dominated its proceedings. Such Jacobin deputies as Brissot argued that only war against the émigré army gathering at Coblenz across the Rhine could end the threat: "Do you wish at one blow to destroy the aristocracy, the refractory priests, and the malcontents: then destroy Coblenz." Whereas the Feuillants opposed this war fever, Lafayette saw a successful military campaign as a way to gain power, while the king's circle believed that war would bring military defeat to France and a restoration of royal authority. On the other side, the Habsburg monarch, Leopold II, had resisted the pleas of his sister Marie-Antoinette and opposed intervention against France, but his death in March 1792 brought his bellicose son Francis II to the throne, and the stage was set for war.

In April 1792 France went to war against a coalition of Austria, Prussia, and the émigrés. Each camp expected rapid victory, but both were disappointed. The allies repulsed a French offensive and soon invaded French territory. The Legislative Assembly called for a new levy of 100,000 military volunteers, but, when it voted to incarcerate refractory clergy, the king vetoed the decree. Though many Frenchmen remained respectful of the king, the most vocal elements of public opinion denounced Louis and demonstrated against him; but the Legislative Assembly refused to act. As Prussian forces drove toward Paris, their commander, the duke of Brunswick, proclaimed his aim of restoring the full authority of the monarchy and warned that any action against the king would bring down "exemplary and memorable vengeance" against the capital. Far from terrifying the Parisians, the Brunswick Manifesto enraged them and drove them into decisive action.

Militants in the Paris Commune, the Revolutionary government of Paris set up by the capital's 48 wards, or sections, gave the Legislative Assembly a deadline in which to suspend the king. When it passed unheeded, they organized an insurrection. On August 10, 1792, a huge crowd of armed Parisians stormed the royal palace after a fierce battle with the garrison. The Legislative Assembly then had no choice but to declare the king suspended. That night more than half the deputies themselves fled Paris, for the Legislative Assembly, too, had lost its mandate. Those who remained ordered the election by universal male suffrage of a National Convention. It would judge the king, draft a new republican constitution, and govern France

during the emergency. The constitution of 1791 had lasted less than a year, and the second revolution dreaded by the Feuillants had begun.

THE FIRST FRENCH REPUBLIC

The insurrection of August 10, 1792, did not, of course, stop the Prussian advance on the capital. As enthusiastic contingents of volunteers left for the front, fear of counterrevolutionary plots gripped the capital. Journalists such as Jean-Paul Marat pointed to the prisons bursting with vagrants and criminals as well as refractory clergy and royalists and asked what would happen if traitors forced open the jails and released these hordes of fanatics and brigands. In response, Parisians took the law into their own hands with an orgy of mass lynching.

THE SECOND REVOLUTION

On their own initiative, citizens entered the prisons, set up "popular tribunals" to hold perfunctory trials, and summarily executed between 1,100 and 1,400 prisoners out of a total of 2,800, stabbing and hacking them to death with any instruments at hand. These prison massacres were no momentary fit of frenzy but went on for four days. At the time, no one in authority dared try to stop the slaughter. Officials of the provisional government and the Paris Commune "drew a veil" over this appalling event as it ran its course, though soon political rivals were accusing each other of instigating the massacres. In a different vein, Robespierre among others concluded that popular demands for vengeance and terror had to be channeled into legal forms; to prevent such anarchy, the state itself must become the orderly instrument of the people's punitive will.

The next two weeks brought this period of extreme uncertainty to a close. On September 20 the French army turned back the invaders at the Battle of Valmy, and in November at the Battle of Jemappes it won control of the Austrian Netherlands (now Belgium). On September 21 the National Convention convened, ending the vacuum of authority that had followed the August 10 insurrection. Its first major task was to decide the fate of the ex-king. The Convention's trial of Louis became an educational experience for the French people in which the institution of monarchy was to be completely desacralized.

Hard evidence of Louis's treason produced a unanimous guilty verdict, but the issue of punishment divided the deputies sharply. In a painstaking and solemn debate each deputy cast his vote individually and explained it. At the end the Convention voted the death sentence, 387 to 334. A motion for reprieve was defeated (380 to 310), and one to submit the verdict to a national referendum was rejected (425 to 286). This ill-considered proposal left the impression that certain deputies were frantic to save the king's life, and their Jacobin opponents were quick to raise vague accusations of treasonous intent against them. In any event,

the former king Louis XVI, now known simply as "Citizen Capet," was executed on January 21, 1793, in an act of immense symbolic importance. For the deputies to the National Convention, now regicides, there could be no turning back. Laws to deport the refractory clergy, to bar the émigrés forever upon pain of death, and to confiscate their property rounded out the Convention's program for eliminating the Revolution's most determined enemies.

A REPUBLIC IN CRISIS

By the spring of 1793, however, the republic was beleaguered. In the second round of the war, the coalition—now reinforced by Spain, Piedmont, and Britain—routed French forces in the Austrian Netherlands and the Rhineland and breached the Pyrenees. Fighting on five different fronts and bereft of effective leadership, French armies seemed to be losing everywhere. Even General Charles-François du Périer Dumouriez, the hero of the first Netherlands campaign, had gone over to the enemy in April after quarreling with the Convention. Meanwhile, civil war had broken out within France. Rural disaffection in western France, especially over the religious question referred to earlier, had been building steadily, leaving republicans in the region's cities and small towns an unpopular and vulnerable minority. Rural rage finally erupted into armed rebellion in March 1793 when the Convention decreed that each *département* must produce

GUILLOTINE

The guillotine is an instrument for inflicting capital punishment by decapitation, introduced into France in 1792 during the Revolution. It consists of two upright posts surmounted by a crossbeam and grooved so as to guide an oblique-edged knife, the back of which is heavily weighted to make it fall forcefully upon (and slice through) the neck of a prone victim.

Previous to the French Revolution, similar devices were in use in Scotland, England, and various other European countries—often for the execution of criminals of noble birth.

A French physician, Joseph-Ignace Guillotin, who was born at Saintes in 1738 and elected to the National Assembly in 1789, was instrumental in having a law passed requiring all sentences of death to be carried out by "means of a machine." This was done so that the privilege of execution by decapitation would no longer be confined to the nobles and the process of execution would be as painless as possible. After the machine had been used in several satisfactory experiments on dead bodies in the hospital of Bicêtre, it was erected on the Place de Grève for the execution of a highwayman on April 25, 1792. At first the machine was called Louisette, or Louison, but soon became known as *la guillotine*. Later the French underworld dubbed it "the widow." Use of the guillotine continued in France well into the 20th century, diminishing during the 1960s and '70s, with only eight executions occurring between 1965 and the last one in 1977. In September 1981 France outlawed capital punishment and abandoned the use of the guillotine.

a quota of citizens for the army. In four *départements* south of the Loire River, the Vendée rebellion began with assaults on the towns and the massacre of patriots. Gradually, royalist nobles assumed the leadership of the peasants and weavers who had risen on their own initiative. Forging them into a "Catholic and Royalist Army," they hoped to overthrow the republic and restore the Bourbons.

The Convention could take no comfort from the economic situation either. An accelerating depreciation of the assignats compounded severe shortages of grain and flour in 1793. Inflation, scarcity, and hoarding made life unbearable for the urban masses and hampered efforts

to provision the republic's armies. In reaction to such economic hardships and to the advance of antirepublican forces at the frontiers and within France, Parisian radicals clamoured relentlessly for decisive action such as price controls and the repression of counterrevolutionaries.

GIRONDINS AND MONTAGNARDS

The Convention was bitterly divided almost to the point of paralysis. From the opening day, two outspoken groups of deputies vied for the support of their less factional colleagues. The roots of this rivalry lay in a conflict between Robespierre and Brissot for leadership of the Jacobin Club in the spring and summer of 1792. At that time Robespierre had argued almost alone against the war that Brissot passionately advocated. Later, when the war went badly and the Brissotins, anxious to wield executive power, acted equivocally in their relations with the king, the Jacobins turned on them. Brissot was formally expelled from the club in October, but his expulsion merely formalized a division that had already crystallized during the elections to the Convention in the previous month.

The Paris electoral assembly sent Robespierre, Marat, Georges Danton, and other stalwarts of the Paris Commune and the Jacobin Club to the Convention, while systematically rejecting Brissot and his allies such as the former mayor of Paris, Pétion. The Parisian deputies and their provincial supporters, numbering between 200 and 300 (depending on which historian's taxonomy one accepts), took seats on the Convention's upper benches and came to be known as the Montagnards.

Supported by a network of journalists and by politicians such as Interior Minister Jean-Marie Roland, however, the Brissotins retained their popularity in the provinces and were returned as deputies by other *départements*. In the Convention the Brissotin group included most deputies from the *département* of the Gironde, and the group came to be known by their opponents as the Girondins. The inner core of this loose faction, who often socialized in Roland's salon, numbered about 60 or, with their supporters, perhaps 150 to 175.

At bottom the Girondin-Montagnard conflict stemmed from a clash of personalities and ambitions. Over the years, historians have made the case for each side by arguing that their opponents constituted the truly aggressive or obstructive minority seeking to dominate the Convention. Clearly most deputies were put off by the bitter personal attacks that regularly intruded on their deliberations. The two factions differed most over the role of Paris and the best way to deal with popular demands. Though of a middle-class background similar to that of their rivals, the Montagnards sympathized more readily with the sans-culottes (the local activists) of the capital and proved temperamentally bolder in their response to economic, military, and political problems. United by an extreme hostility to Parisian militance, the Girondins never forgave the Paris Commune for its inquisitorial activity after August 10. Indeed, some Girondins did not feel physically secure in the capital. They also appeared more committed to political and economic liberties and therefore less willing to adopt extreme revolutionary measures no matter how dire the circumstances. Ready to set aside similar constitutional scruples, the Montagnards tailored their policies to the imperatives of "revolutionary necessity" and unity.

While the Girondins repeatedly attacked Parisian militants—at one point demanding the dissolution of the Paris Commune and the arrest of its leaders—the Montagnards gradually forged an informal alliance with the sans-culottes. Similarly, the Montagnards supported deputies sent "on mission" to the *départements* when they clashed with locally elected officials, while the Girondins tended to back the officials. The Montagnards therefore alienated many moderate republicans in the provinces. As deputies of the centre, or "Plain," such as Bertrand Barère, vainly tried to mediate between the two sides, the Convention navigated through this factionalism as best it could and impro-vised new responses to the crisis: a Revolutionary Tribunal to try political crimes; local surveillance committees to seek out subversives; and a Committee of Public Safety to coordinate measures of revolutionary defense. By the end of May 1793 a majority seemed ready to support the Montagnards.

Believing that the Girondins had betrayed and endangered the republic, the Paris sections (with the connivance of the Montagnards and the Paris Jacobin Club) demanded in petitions that the Convention expel the "perfidious depu-ties." On May 31 they mounted a mass demonstration, and on June 2 they forced a showdown by deploying armed national guards around the convention's hall. Backed by a huge crowd of unarmed men and women, their solid phalanx of fixed bayonets made it impossible for the deputies to leave without risking seri-ous violence. Inside, the Montagnards applauded this insurrection as an expres-sion of popular sovereignty, akin to that of July 14 or August 10. When the people thus spoke directly, they argued, the deputies had no choice but to com-ply. Centrists did everything they could to avoid a purge but in the end decided that only this fateful act could preserve the Revolution's unity. Barère composed a report to the French people justifying the expulsion of 29 Girondins. Later 120 deputies who signed a protest against the purge were themselves suspended from the Convention, and in October the original Girondins stood trial before the Revolutionary Tribunal, which sentenced them to death. The Montagnard ascen-dancy had begun.

Though the deadlock in the Convention was now broken, the bal-ance of forces in the country was by no means clear. The Parisian sansculottes might well have continued to intimi-date the Convention and emerge as the dominant partner in their alliance with the Montagnards—just as Girondin ora-tors had warned. Conversely, provincial opinion might have rebelled against this mutilation of the National Convention by Paris and its Montagnard partisans. Purged of the Girondins, the Convention itself was able to reach consensus more readily, but the nation as a whole was more divided than ever.

At first it seemed as if the expulsion of the Girondins would indeed backfire. More than half of the departmental direc-tories protested against the purge. But, faced with pleas for unity and threats from the Convention, most of this opposition subsided quickly. Only 13 *départements* continued their defiant stance, and only

6 of these passed into overt armed rebellion against the Convention's authority. Still, this was a serious threat in a country already beleaguered by civil war and military reversals. The Jacobins stigmatized this new opposition as the heresy of federalism—implying that the "federalists" no longer believed in a unified republic. Jacobin propaganda depicted the federalists as counterrevolutionaries. In fact, most were moderate republicans hostile to the royalists and committed to constitutional liberties. They did not intend to overthrow the republic or separate from it. Rather they hoped to wrest power back from what they deemed the tyrannical alliance of Montagnards and Parisian sansculottes.

In Lyon, Marseille, Toulon, and Bordeaux, bitter conflicts between local moderates and Jacobins contributed decisively to the rebellion. Uprisings in Lyon and Marseille (France's second and third largest cities, respectively) began in late May when moderates seized power from local Jacobin authorities who had threatened their lives and property—Jacobins such as the firebrand Marie-Joseph Chalier in Lyon, who was supported by Montagnard representatives-on-mission. The expulsion of the Girondins was merely the last straw. Whatever its causes, however, "federalist" rebellion did threaten national unity and the Convention's sovereign authority. Royalists, moreover, did gain control of the movement in Toulon and opened that port to the British. Holding out no offer of negotiation, the Convention organized military force to crush the rebellions and promised the leaders exemplary punishment. "Lyon has made war against liberty," declared the Convention, "Lyon no longer exists." When the republic's forces recaptured the city in October, they changed its name to "Liberated City," demolished the houses of the wealthy, and summarily executed more than 2,000 Lyonnais, including many wealthy merchants.

THE REIGN OF TERROR

After their victory in expelling the Girondins, Parisian militants "regenerated" their own sectional assemblies by purging local moderates, while radicals such as Jacques-René Hébert and Pierre-Gaspard Chaumette tightened their grip on the Paris Commune. On September 5, 1793, they mounted another mass demonstration to demand that the Convention assure food at affordable prices and "place terror on the order of the day." Led by its Committee of Public Safety, the Convention placated the popular movement with decisive actions. It proclaimed the need for terror against the Revolution's enemies, made economic crimes such as hoarding into capital offenses, and decreed a system of price and wage controls known as the Maximum. The Law of Suspects empowered local revolutionary committees to arrest "those who by their conduct, relations or language spoken or written, have shown themselves partisans of tyranny or federalism and enemies of liberty." In 1793–94 well over 200,000 citizens were detained under this law; though most of them never stood trial, they languished in pestiferous jails, where an estimated 10,000 perished. About 17,000 death sentences were handed down by the military commissions and revolutionary tribunals of the Terror, 72 percent for charges of armed rebellion in the two major zones of civil war—the federalist southeast and the western Vendée region. One-third of the *départements*, however, had fewer than 10 death sentences passed on their inhabitants and were relatively tranquil.

To help police the Maximum and requisition grain in the countryside, as well as to carry out arrest warrants and guard political prisoners, the Convention authorized local authorities to create paramilitary forces. About 50 such *armées révolutionnaires* came into being as ambulatory instruments of the Terror in the provinces. Fraternizing with peasants and artisans in the hinterland, these forces helped raise revolutionary enthusiasm but ultimately left such village sansculottes vulnerable to the wrath of the wealthy citizens whom they harassed.

Back in June the Convention had quickly drafted a new democratic constitution, incorporating such popular demands as universal male suffrage, the right to subsistence, and the right to free public education. In a referendum this Jacobin constitution of 1793 was approved virtually without dissent by about two million voters. Because of the emergency, however, the Convention placed the new constitution on the shelf in October and declared that "the provisional government of France is revolutionary until the peace." There would be no elections, no local autonomy, no guarantees of individual liberties for the duration of the emergency. The Convention would rule with a sovereignty more absolute than the old monarchy had ever claimed. Nor would serious popular protest be tolerated any longer, now that the Jacobins had used such intervention to secure power. The balance in the alliance between Montagnards and sansculottes gradually shifted from the streets of Paris to the halls and committee rooms of the Convention.

From the beginning a popular terrorist mentality had helped shape the Revolution. Peasants and townspeople alike had been galvanized by fear and rage over "aristocratic plots" in 1789. Lynchings of "enemies of the people" punctuated the Revolution, culminating in the September massacres, which reflected an extreme fear of betrayal and an unbridled punitive will. Now the Revolution's leaders were preempting this punitive will in order to control it: they conceived of terror as rational rather than emotional and as organized rather than instinctive. Paradoxically they were trying to render terror lawful—legality being an article of faith among most revolutionaries—but without the procedural safeguards that accompanied the regular criminal code of 1791.

For the more pragmatic Montagnards that deviation was justified by the unparalleled emergency situation confronting

France in 1793: before the benefits of the Revolution could be enjoyed, they must be secured against their enemies by force. ("Terror is nothing other than justice, prompt, severe, inflexible....Is force made only to protect crime?" declared Robespierre.) For the more ideologically exalted Jacobins such as Robespierre and Louis de Saint-Just, however, the Terror would also regenerate the nation by promoting equality and the public interest. In their minds a link existed between terror and virtue: "virtue, without which terror is fatal; terror, without which virtue is powerless." Whoever could claim to speak for the interests of the people held the mantle of virtue and the power of revolutionary terror.

THE JACOBIN DICTATORSHIP

One of the changes affected by the Convention was the creation of the French republican calendar to replace the Gregorian calendar, which was viewed as nonscientific and tainted with religious associations. The Revolutionary calendar was proclaimed on 14 Vendémiaire, year II (October 5, 1793), but its starting point was set to be about a year prior, on 1 Vendémiaire, year I (September 22, 1792). The new calendar featured a 10-day week called the *décade*, designed to swallow up the Christian Sunday in a new cycle of work and recreation. Three *décades* formed a month of 30 days, and 12 months formed a year, with 5 to 6 additional days at the end of each year.

The Convention consolidated its revolutionary government in the Law of 14 Frimaire, year II (December 4, 1793). To organize the Revolution, to promote confidence and compliance, efficiency and control, this law centralized authority in a parliamentary dictatorship, with the Committee of Public Safety at the helm. The committee already controlled military policy and patronage; henceforth local administrators (renamed national agents), tribunals, and revolutionary committees also came under its scrutiny and control. The network of Jacobin clubs was enlisted to monitor local officials, nominate new appointees, and in general serve as "arsenals of public opinion."

Opposed to "ultrarevolutionary" behaviour and uncoordinated actions even by its own deputies-on-mission, the committee tried to stop the de-Christianization campaigns that had erupted during the anarchic phase of the Terror in the fall of 1793. Usually instigated by radical deputies, the de-Christianizers vandalized churches or closed them down altogether, intimidated constitutional priests into resigning their vocation, and often pressured them into marrying to demonstrate the sincerity of their conversion. Favouring a deistic form of civil religion, Robespierre implied that the atheism displayed by some de-Christianizers was a variant of counterrevolution. He insisted that citizens must be left free to practice the Roman Catholic religion, though for the time being most priests were not holding services.

The committee also felt strong enough a few months later to curb the activism of the Paris sections, dissolve the *armées révolutionnaires*, and purge the Paris Commune—ironically what the Girondins had hoped to do months before. But in this atmosphere no serious dissent to official policy was tolerated. The once vibrant free press had been muzzled after the purge of the Girondins. In March 1794 Hébert and other "ultrarevolutionaries" were arrested, sent to the Revolutionary Tribunal, and guillotined. A month later Danton and other so-called "indulgents" met the same fate for seeking to end the Terror—prematurely in the eyes of the committee. Then the Convention passed the infamous law of 22 Prairial, year II (June 10, 1794), to streamline revolutionary justice, denying the accused any effective right to self-defense and eliminating all sentences other than acquittal or death. Indictments by the public prosecutor, now virtually tantamount to a death sentence, multiplied rapidly.

The Terror was being escalated just when danger no longer threatened the republic—after French armies had prevailed against Austria at the decisive Battle of Fleurus on 8 Messidor (June 26) and long after rebel forces in the Vendée, Lyon, and elsewhere had been vanquished. By that time the Jacobin dictatorship had forged an effective government and had mobilized the nation's resources, thereby mastering the crisis that had brought it into being. Yet, on 8 Thermidor (July 26), Robespierre took the rostrum to proclaim his own probity and to denounce yet another unnamed group as traitors hatching "a conspiracy against liberty." Robespierre had clearly

lost his grip on reality in his obsession with national unity and virtue. An awkward coalition of moderates, Jacobin pragmatists, rival deputies, and extremists who rightly felt threatened by the "Incorruptible" (as he was known) finally combined to topple Robespierre and his closest followers. On 9 Thermidor, year II (July 27, 1794), the Convention ordered the arrest of Robespierre and Saint-Just, and, after a failed resistance by loyalists in the Paris Commune, they were guillotined without trial the following day. The Terror was over.

THE ARMY OF THE REPUBLIC

The Jacobin dictatorship had been an unstable blend of exalted patriotism, resolute political leadership, ideological fanaticism, and populist initiatives. The rhetoric and symbolism of democracy constituted a new civic pedagogy, matched by bold egalitarian policies. The army was a primary focal point of this democratic impetus. In 1790 the National Assembly had opted for a small military of long-term professionals. One-year volunteers bolstered the line army after the outbreak of war, and in March 1793 the Convention called for an additional 300,000 soldiers, with quotas to be provided by each *département*. Finally, in August 1793 it decreed the *levée en masse*—a "requisition" of all able-bodied, unmarried men between the ages of 18 and 25. Despite massive draft evasion and desertion, within a year almost three-quarters of a million men were under arms, the citizen-soldiers merged with line-army troops in new units called demibrigades. This huge popular mobilization reinforced the Revolution's militant spirit. The citizen-soldiers risking their lives at the front had to be supported by any and all means back home, including forced loans on the rich and punitive vigilance against those suspected of disloyalty.

Within the constraints of military discipline, the army became a model of democratic practice. Both noncommissioned and commissioned officers were chosen by a combination of election and appointment, in which seniority received some consideration, but demonstrated talent on the battlefield brought the most rapid promotion. The republic insisted that officers be respectful toward their men and share their privations. Jacobin military prosecutors enforced the laws against insubordination and desertion but took great pains to explain them to the soldiers and to make allowances for momentary weakness in deciding cases. Soldiers received revolutionary newspapers and sang revolutionary songs, exalting the citizen-soldier as the model sansculotte. Meanwhile, needy parents, wives, or dependents of soldiers at the front received subsidies, while common soldiers seriously wounded in action earned extremely generous veterans' benefits.

The Revolution's egalitarian promise never involved an assault on private property, but its concept of "social limitations" on property made it possible for the Convention to abolish all seigneurial dues without compensation, abolish slavery in the colonies (where slave rebellions had already achieved that result in practice), endorse the idea of progressive taxation, and temporarily regulate the economy in favour of consumers. In 1793–94 the Convention enacted an unprecedented national system of public assistance entitlements, with one program allocating small pensions to poor families with dependent children and another providing pensions to aged and indigent farm workers, artisans, and rural widows—the neediest of the needy. "We must put an end to the servitude of the most basic needs, the slavery of misery, that most hideous of inequalities," declared Barère of the Committee of Public Safety. The Convention also implemented the Revolution's long-standing commitment to primary education with a system of free public primary schooling for both boys and girls. The Lakanal Law of November 1794 authorized public schools in every commune with more than 1,000 inhabitants, the teachers to be selected by examination and paid fixed salaries by the government.

THE THERMIDORIAN REACTION

With control passing from the Montagnards after Robespierre's fall, moderates in the Convention hoped to put the Terror and sansculotte militance behind them while standing fast against counterrevolution and rallying all patriots around the original principles of the Revolution. But far from stabilizing the Revolution, the fall of "the tyrant" on 9 Thermidor set in motion a brutal struggle for power. Those who had suffered under the Terror now clamoured for retribution, and moderation quickly gave way to reaction. As federalists were released, Jacobins were arrested; as the suspended Girondins were reinstated, Montagnards were purged; as moderates could feel safe, Jacobins and sansculottes were threatened. Like the Terror, the Thermidorian Reaction had an uncontrollable momentum of its own. Antiterrorism—in the press, the theatre, the streets—degenerated into a "white terror" against the men of year II. In the south, especially in Provence and the Rhône valley, the frontier between private feuds and political reaction blurred as law and order broke down. Accounts were settled by lynchings, murder gangs, and prison massacres of arrested sansculottes.

In addition to these political consequences, the Thermidorian Reaction set off a new economic and monetary crisis. Committed to free-trade principles, the Thermidorians dismantled the economic regulation and price controls of year II, along with the apparatus of the Terror that had put teeth into that system. The depreciation of the assignats, which the Terror had halted, quickly resumed. By 1795 the cities were desperately short of grain and flour, while meat, fuel, dairy products,

and soap were entirely beyond the reach of ordinary consumers. By the spring of 1795 scarcity was turning into famine for working people of the capital and other cities. Surviving cadres of sansculottes in the Paris sections mobilized to halt the reaction and the economic catastrophe it had unleashed. After trying petitions and demonstrations, a crowd of sansculottes invaded the Convention on 1 Prairial, year III (May 20, 1795), in the last popular uprising of the French Revolution. "Bread is the goal of their insurrection, physically speaking," reported a police observer, "but the Constitution of 1793 is its soul." This rearguard rebellion of despair was doomed to fail, despite the support of a few remaining Montagnard deputies, whose fraternization with the demonstrators was to cost them their lives after the insurgents were routed the following day.

Instead of implementing the democratic Constitution of 1793, the Thermidorian Convention was preparing a new, more conservative charter. Anti-Jacobin and antiroyalist, the Thermidorians clung to the elusive centre of the political spectrum. Their constitution of year III (1795) established a liberal republic with a franchise based on the payment of taxes similar to that of 1791, a two-house legislature to slow down the legislative process, and a five-man executive Directory to be chosen by the legislature. Within a liberal framework, the central government retained great power, including emergency powers to curb freedom of the press and freedom of association. Departmental and municipal administrators were to be elected but could be removed by the Directory, and commissioners appointed by the Directory were to monitor them and report on their compliance with the laws.

THE DIRECTORY

The new regime, referred to as the Directory, began auspiciously in October 1795 with a successful constitutional plebiscite and a general amnesty for political prisoners. But as one of its final acts the Convention added the "Two-thirds Decree" to the package, requiring for the sake of continuity that two-thirds of its deputies must sit by right in the new legislature regardless of voting in the *départements*. This outraged conservatives and royalists hoping to regain power legally, but their armed uprising in Paris was easily suppressed by the army. The Directory also weathered a conspiracy on the far left by a cabal of unreconciled militants organized around a program of communistic equality and revolutionary dictatorship. The Babeuf plot was exposed in May 1796 by a police spy, and a lengthy trial ensued in which François-Noël ("Gracchus") Babeuf, the self-styled "Tribune of the People," was sentenced to death.

Apart from these conspiracies, the political life of the Directory revolved around annual elections to replace one-third of the deputies and local administrators. The spirit of the Two-thirds Decree haunted this process, however, since the directors believed that stability required their continuation in power and the exclusion of royalists or Jacobins. The Directory would tolerate no organized opposition. During or immediately after each election, the government in effect violated the constitution in order to save it, whenever the right or the left seemed to be gaining ground.

As a legacy of the nation's revolutionary upheavals, elections under the Directory displayed an unhealthy combination of massive apathy and rancorous partisanship by small minorities. When the elections of 1797 produced a royalist resurgence, the government responded with the coup of Fructidor, year V (September 1797), ousting two of the current directors, arresting leading royalist politicians, annulling the elections in 49 *départements*, shutting down the royalist press, and resuming the vigorous pursuit of returned émigrés and refractory clergy. This heartened the Neo-Jacobins, who organized new clubs called "constitutional circles" to emphasize their adherence to the regime. But this independent political activism on the left raised the spectre of 1793 for the Directory, and in turn it closed down the Neo-Jacobin clubs and newspapers, warned citizens against voting for "anarchists" in the elections of 1798, and promoted schisms in electoral assemblies when voters spurned this advice. When democrats (or Neo-Jacobins) prevailed nonetheless, the Directory organized another purge in the coup of Floréal, year VI (May 1798), by annulling all or some elections in 29 *départements*. Ambivalent and fainthearted in its republican commitment, the Directory was eroding political liberty from within. But as long as the Constitution of 1795 endured, it remained possible that political liberty and free elections might one day take root.

SISTER REPUBLICS

Meanwhile the Directory regime successfully exported revolution abroad by helping to create "sister republics" in western Europe. During the Revolution's most radical phase, in 1793–94, French expansion had stopped more or less at the nation's self-proclaimed "natural frontiers"—the Rhine, Alps, and Pyrenees. The Austrian Netherlands (now Belgium) and the left bank of the Rhine had been major battlefields in the war against the coalition, and French victories in those sectors were followed by military occupation, requisitions, and taxation but also by the abolition of feudalism and similar reforms. In 1795 Belgium was annexed to France and divided into departments, which would henceforth be treated like other French *départements*.

Strategic considerations and French national interest were the main engines of French foreign policy in the Revolutionary decade but not the only ones. Elsewhere in Europe, native patriots invited French support against their own ruling princes or oligarchies. Europe was divided not simply by a conflict between Revolutionary France and other states but by conflicts within various states between revolutionary or democratic forces and conservative or traditional forces. Indeed, abortive revolutionary movements had already occurred in the Austrian Netherlands and in the United Provinces (Dutch Netherlands). When French troops occupied their country in 1795, Dutch "Patriots" set up the Batavian Republic, the first of what became a belt of "sister republics" along France's borders.

By 1797 Prussia and Spain had made peace with France, but Austria and Britain continued the struggle. In 1796 the French had launched an attack across the Alps aimed at Habsburg Lombardy, from which they hoped to drive north toward Vienna. Commanded by General Napoleon Bonaparte, this campaign succeeded beyond expectations. In the process, northern Italy was liberated from Austria, and the Habsburgs were driven to the peace table, where they signed the Treaty of Campo Formio on 26 Vendémiaire, year VI (October 17, 1797). Italian revolutionaries under French protection proclaimed the Cisalpine Republic in northern Italy, later joined by the Helvetic Republic in Switzerland, and two very shaky republics—the Roman Republic in central Italy and the Parthenopean Republic in the south around Naples. All these republics were exploited financially by the French, but then again their survival depended on the costly presence of French troops. The French interfered in their internal politics, but this was no more than the Directory was doing at home. Because these republics could not defend themselves in isolation, they acted like sponges on French resources as much as they provided treasure or other benefits to France. France's extended lines of occupation made it extremely vulnerable to attack when Britain organized a second coalition in 1798 that included Russia and Austria. But when the battles were over, Switzerland, northern Italy, and the Netherlands remained in the French sphere of influence.

The treasure coming from the sister republics was desperately needed in Paris since French finances were in total disarray. The collapse of the assignats and the hyperinflation of 1795–96 not only destroyed such social programs as public assistance pensions and free public schooling but also strained the regime's capacity to keep its basic institutions running. In 1797 the government finally engineered a painful return to hard currency and in effect wrote down the accumulated national debt by two-thirds of its value in exchange for guaranteeing the integrity of the remaining third.

ALIENATION AND COUPS

After the Fructidor coup of 1797 the Directory imprudently resumed the republic's assault on the Roman Catholic religion. Besides prohibiting the outward signs of Catholicism, such as the ringing of church bells or the display of crosses, the government revived the Revolutionary calendar, which had fallen into disuse after the Thermidorian Reaction. The Directory ordered in 1798 that *décadi* (the final day of the 10-day week, or *décade*) be treated as the official day of rest for workers and businesses as well as public employees and schoolchildren. Forbidding organized recreation on Sundays, the regime also pressured Catholic priests to celebrate mass on *décadis* rather than on ex-Sundays. This aggressive confrontation with the habits and beliefs of most French citizens sapped whatever shreds of popularity the regime still had.

French citizens were already alienated by the Directory's foreign policy and its new conscription law. Conscription became a permanent obligation of young men between the ages of 20 and 25 under the Jourdan Law of 19 Fructidor, year VI (September 5, 1798), named for its sponsor, the comte de Jourdan. To fight the War of the Second Coalition that began in 1799, the Directory mobilized three "classes," or age cohorts, of young men but encountered massive draft resistance and desertion in many regions. Meanwhile, retreating armies in the field lacked rations and supplies because, it was alleged, corrupt military contractors operated in collusion with government officials. This war crisis prompted the legislature to oust four of the directors in the coup on 30 Prairial, year VII (June 18, 1799), and allowed a brief resurgence of Neo-Jacobin agitation for drastic emergency measures.

In reality the balance of power was swinging toward a group of disaffected conservatives. Led by Sieyès, one of the new directors, these "revisionists" wished to escape from the instability of the Directory regime, especially its tumultuous annual elections and its cumbersome separation of powers. They wanted a more reliable structure of political power, which would allow the new elite to govern securely and thereby guarantee the basic reforms and property rights of 1789. Ironically, the Neo-Jacobins stood as the constitution's most ardent defenders against the maneuvers of these "oligarchs."

Using mendacious allegations about Neo-Jacobin plots as a cover, the revisionists prepared a parliamentary coup to jettison the constitution. To provide the necessary military insurance, the plotters sought a leading general. Though he was not their first choice, they eventually enlisted Napoleon—recently returned from his Egyptian campaign, about whose disasters the public knew almost nothing. Given a central role in the coup, which occurred on 18 Brumaire, year VIII (November 9, 1799), General Bonaparte addressed the legislature, and, when some deputies balked at his call for scrapping the constitution, his troopers cleared the hall. A rump of each house then convened to draft a new constitution, and during these deliberations Napoleon shouldered aside Sieyès and emerged as the dominant figure in the new regime. The Brumaire event was not really a military coup and did not at first produce a dictatorship. It was a parliamentary coup to create a new constitution and was welcomed by people of differing opinions who saw in it what they wished to see. The image of an energetic military hero impatient with the abuses of the past must have seemed reassuring.

THE RISE AND FALL OF NAPOLEON

The revisionists who engineered the Brumaire coup intended to create a strong, elitist government that would curb the republic's political turmoil and guarantee the conquests of 1789. They had in mind what might be called a senatorial oligarchy rather than a personal dictatorship. General Bonaparte, however, advocated a more drastic concentration of power. Within days of the coup, Napoleon emerged as the dominant figure, an insistent and persuasive presence who inspired confidence. Clearly outmaneuvered, Sieyès soon withdrew from the scene, taking with him his complex notions of checks and balances. While the regime, known as the Consulate, maintained a republican form, Napoleon became from its inception a new kind of authoritarian leader.

THE CONSULATE

Approved almost unanimously in a plebiscite by 3,000,000 votes (of which half may have been manufactured out of thin air), the Constitution of the year VIII created an executive consisting of three consuls, but the first consul wielded all real power. That office was, of course, vested in Napoleon. In 1802, after a string of military and diplomatic victories, another plebiscite endowed him with the position for life. By 1804 Napoleon's grip on power was complete, and belief in his indispensability was pervasive in the governing class. In April 1804 various government bodies agreed "that Napoleon Bonaparte be declared Emperor and that the imperial dignity be declared hereditary in his family." The constitution of the year XII (May 1804), establishing the empire, was approved in a plebiscite by more than 3,500,000 votes against about 2,500. (After this point General Bonaparte was known officially as Emperor Napoleon I.)

The constitution of 1791, the Convention, and the Directory alike had been organized around representation and legislative supremacy, the fundamental political principles first proclaimed in June 1789 by the National Assembly. This tradition came to an end with the Consulate. Its new bicameral legislature lost the power to initiate legislation; now the executive branch drafted new laws. One house (the Tribunate) debated such proposals, either endorsed or opposed them, and then sent deputies to present its opinion to the other house, the Corps Législatif, which also heard from government spokesmen. Without the right to debate, the Corps Législatif then voted on whether to enact the bill. Even these limited powers were rarely used independently, since both houses were appointed in the first instance by the government and later renewed by co-option. When certain tribunes such as Benjamin Constant did manifest a critical spirit, they were eventually purged, and in 1807 the Tribunate was suppressed altogether. On the whole, then, the legislative branch of government became little more than a rubber stamp.

After the Brumaire coup, Sieyès had envisaged an independent institution called the Senate to conserve the constitution by interpreting it in the light of changing circumstances. In practice, the Senate became the handmaiden of Napoleon's expanding authority, sanctioning changes such as the life consulship, the purge of the Tribunate, and Napoleon's elevation to the rank of hereditary emperor. For creating "legislation above the laws" at Napoleon's behest, its 80 handpicked members were opulently rewarded with money and honours. As power shifted decisively to the executive branch, Napoleon enlisted a new institution called the Conseil d'État (Council of State) to formulate policy, draft legislation, and supervise the ministries. Appointed by the first consul, this body of experienced jurists and legislators was drawn from across the former political spectrum. Talent and loyalty to the new government were the relevant criteria for these coveted posts.

The Consulate did not entirely eliminate the electoral principle from the new regime, but voters were left with no real power, and elections became an elaborate charade. Citizens voted only for electoral colleges, which in turn created lists of candidates from which the government might fill occasional vacancies in the Conseil d'État or Senate. In the event, the primary assemblies of voters were rarely convened, and membership in the electoral colleges became a kind of honorific lifetime position. The judiciary, too, lost its elective status. In the hope of creating a more professional and compliant judiciary, the Consulate's sweeping judicial reform provided for lifetime appointments of judges—which did not prevent Napoleon from purging the judiciary in 1808. Napoleon was also disposed to eliminate criminal juries as well, but the Conseil d'État prevailed on him to maintain them.

Successive Revolutionary regimes had always balanced local elections with central control, but the Consulate destroyed that balance completely. The Local Government Act of February 1800 eliminated elections for local office entirely and organized local administration from the top down. To run each *département*, the Consulate appointed a prefect, reminiscent of the old royal intendants, who was assisted by subprefects on the level of the arrondissements (subdistricts of the *départements*) and by appointed mayors in each commune. The original Revolutionary commitment to local autonomy gave way before the rival principles of centralization and uniformity. The prefect became the cornerstone of the Napoleonic dictatorship, supervising local government at all levels, keeping careful watch over his *département's* "public spirit," and above all assuring that taxes and conscripts flowed in smoothly. While even the most trivial local matter had to be referred to the prefect, all major decisions taken by the prefect had in turn to be sanctioned by the interior ministry in Paris.

LOSS OF POLITICAL FREEDOM

Politics during the Directory had been marked by an unwholesome combination of ferocious partisanship and massive apathy. Weary of political turmoil and disillusioned by politicians of all kinds, most Frenchmen now accepted the disappearance of political freedom and participation with equanimity. The few who still cared passionately enough to resist collided with the apparatus of a police state. A regime that entirely avoided genuine elections would scarcely permit open political dissent. Where the Directory had been ambivalent about freedom of association, for example, the Consulate simply banned political clubs outright and placed Jacobin and royalist cadres under surveillance by the police ministry. In 1801, blaming democratic militants for a botched attempt to assassinate him with a bomb as his carriage drove down the rue Saint-Nicaise—a plot actually hatched by fanatical royalists—Napoleon ordered the arrest and deportation to Guiana of about 100 former Jacobin and sansculotte militants. In

1804 he had the duc d'Enghien, a member of the Bourbon family, abducted from abroad, convicted of conspiracy by a court-martial, and executed.

Outspoken liberals also felt the lash of Napoleon's intolerance for any kind of opposition. After he purged the Tribunate, the consul registered his displeasure with the salon politics of liberal intellectuals by dissolving the Class of Moral and Political Science of the National Institute in 1803. One of the most principled liberals, Madame de Staël, chose to go into exile rather than exercise the self-censorship demanded by the regime. Meanwhile, the only newspapers tolerated were heavily censored. Paris, for example, had more than 70 newspapers at the time of the Brumaire coup; by 1811 only 4 quasi-official newspapers survived, ironically the same number as had existed before 1789. In the provinces each *département* had at most 1 newspaper, likewise of quasi-official character. The reimposition of censorship was matched by Napoleon's astute management of news and propaganda.

SOCIETY IN NAPOLEONIC FRANCE

Napoleonic reforms gave permanence to the great gains of the Revolution: individual liberty, freedom of work, freedom of conscience, the lay character of the state, and equality before the law. Yet, at the same time, they protected landed property, gave greater liberty to employers, and showed little concern for employees. The reforms also maintained divorce but granted only limited legal rights to women. Education was transformed into a major public service; secondary education was given a semimilitary organization, and the university faculties were reestablished. Primary education, however, was still neglected.

RELIGIOUS POLICY

If the Consulate's motto was "Authority from above, confidence from below," Napoleon's religious policy helped secure that confidence. The concordat negotiated with the papacy in 1802 reintegrated the Roman Catholic church into French society and ended the cycle of bare toleration and persecution that had begun in 1792. Having immediately halted the campaign to enforce the republican calendar (which was quietly abolished on January 1, 1806), the Consulate then extended an olive branch to the refractory clergy. The state continued to respect the religious freedom of non-Catholics, but the concordat recognized Catholicism as "the preferred religion" of France—in effect, though not in name, the nation's established religion. Upkeep of the church became a significant item in local budgets, and the clergy regained de facto control over primary education. The state, however, retained the upper hand in church-state relations. By signing the concordat, the pope accepted the nationalization of church property in France and its sale as *biens nationaux*. Bishops, though again consecrated by Rome, were named by the head of state, and the government retained the right to police public worship.

The most conservative Catholics looked askance at the concordat, which in their eyes promoted an excessively national or Gallican church rather than a truly Roman Catholic Church. They correctly suspected that Napoleon—personally a religious skeptic—would use it as a tool of his own ambitions. Indeed, he claimed that the clergy would become his "moral prefects," propagating traditional values and obedience to authority. Later, for example, the clergy was asked to teach an imperial catechism, which would "bind the consciences of the young to the august person of the Emperor."

The Napoleonic regime also organized France's approximately 1,000,000 Calvinists into hierarchical "consistories" subject to oversight by the state. Protestant pastors, paid by the state, were designated by the elders who led local congregations and consistories; the more democratic tendencies of Calvinism were thus weakened in exchange for official recognition. France's 60,000 Jews, residing mainly in Alsace and Lorraine, were also organized into consistories. Like priests and pastors, their rabbis were enlisted to promote obedience to the laws, though they were not salaried by the state. Napoleon's convocation in 1807 of a "Grand Sanhedrin" of Jewish religious authorities to reconcile French and Jewish law attracted widespread attention. Official recognition, however, did not prevent discriminatory measures against Jews. A law of 1808, ostensibly for "the social reformation of the Jews," appeased peasant debtors in Alsace by canceling their debts to Jewish moneylenders.

NAPOLEONIC NOBILITY

Napoleon cultivated the loyalty of the nation's wealthy landed proprietors by a system of patronage and honours. He thereby facilitated the emergence of a ruling class drawn from both the middle classes and the nobility of the old regime, which had been divided by the artificial barriers of old-regime estates and privileges. The principal artifacts of Napoleon's social policy were the lists he ordered of the 600 highest-paid taxpayers in each *département*, most having incomes of at least 3,000 livres a year. Inclusion on these lists became an insignia of one's informal status as a notable. Members of the electoral colleges and departmental advisory councils were drawn from these lists. Although such honorific positions had little power and no privileges, the designees were effectively co-opted into the regime. Napoleon's Legion of Honour, meanwhile, conferred recognition on men who served the state, primarily military officers who largely stood outside the ranks of the landed notables. By 1814 the Legion had 32,000 members, of whom only 1,500 were civilians.

After Napoleon had himself crowned emperor in 1804, he felt the need for a court aristocracy that would lend lustre and credibility to his new image. He also reasoned that only by creating a new nobility based on merit could he displace and absorb the old nobility, which had lost its titles in 1790 but not its pretensions. By 1808 a new hierarchy of titles had been created, which were to be hereditary provided that a family could support its title with a large annual income—30,000 livres, for example, in the case of a count of the empire. To facilitate this, the emperor bestowed huge landed estates and pensions on his highest dignitaries. The Napoleonic nobility, in other words, would be a veritable upper class based on a combination of service and wealth. Predictably, the new nobility was top-heavy with generals (59 percent altogether), but it also included many senators, archbishops, and members of the Conseil d'État; 23 percent of the Napoleonic nobility were former nobles of the ancien régime. These social innovations endured after Napoleon's fall—the Bourbons adopted the system of high-status electoral colleges, maintained the Legion of Honour, and even allowed the Napoleonic nobles to retain their titles alongside the restored old-regime nobility.

THE CIVIL CODE

The Napoleonic Code had a far greater impact on postrevolutionary society than did the social innovations. This ambitious work of legal codification, perhaps the crowning glory of the Conseil d'État, consolidated certain basic principles established in 1789: civil equality and equality before the law; the abolition of feudalism in favour of modern contractual forms of property; and the secularization of civil relations. Codification also made it easier to export those principles beyond the borders of France. In the area of family relations, however, the Napoleonic Code was less a codification of Revolutionary innovations than a reaction against them. By reverting to patriarchal standards that strengthened the prerogatives of the husband and father, it wiped out important gains that women had made during the Revolution. The code's spirit on this subject was summed up in its statement that "a husband owes protection to his wife; a wife owes obedience to her husband." Wives were again barred from signing contracts without their husbands' consent, and a wife's portion of the family's community property fell completely under her husband's control during his lifetime. The code also curbed the right of equal inheritance, which the Revolution had extended even to illegitimate children, and increased the father's disciplinary control over his children.

The code also rolled back the Revolution's extremely liberal divorce legislation. When marriage became a civil rite rather than an obligatory religious sacrament in 1792, divorce became possible for the first time. Divorce could be obtained by mutual consent but also for a range of causes including desertion and simple incompatibility. Under the Napoleonic Code, contested divorce was possible only for unusually cruel treatment resulting in grave injury and for adultery on the part of the wife. Faced with an unfaithful husband, however, "the wife may demand divorce on the ground of adultery by her husband [only] when he shall have brought his concubine into their common residence."

Napoleonic policy frequently reacted against the Revolution's liberal individualism. While the regime did not restore the guilds outright, for example, it reimposed restrictive or even monopolistic state regulation on such occupational groups as publishers and booksellers, the Parisian building trades, attorneys, barristers, notaries, and doctors. Napoleon wished to strengthen the ties that bound individuals together, which derived from religion, the family, and state authority. Napoleon's domestic innovations—the prefectorial system, with its extreme centralization of administrative authority; the university, a centralized educational bureaucracy that scrutinized all types of teachers; the concordat with the Vatican that reversed the secularizing tendencies of the Revolution; the civil code, which strengthened property rights and patriarchal authority; and the Legion of Honour, which rewarded service to the state—all endured in the 19th century despite a succession of political upheavals. Historians who admire Napoleon consider these innovations the "granite masses" on which modern French society developed.

CAMPAIGNS AND CONQUESTS, 1797–1807

Napoleon's sway over France depended from the start on his success in war.

After his conquest of northern Italy in 1797 and the dissolution of the first coalition, the Directory intended to invade Britain, France's century-long rival and the last remaining belligerent. Concluding that French naval power could not sustain a seaborne invasion, however, the government sent Napoleon on a military expedition to Egypt instead, hoping to choke off the main route to Britain's Indian empire. When the expedition bogged down in disease and military stalemate, its commander quietly slipped past a British naval blockade to return to France, where (in the absence of accurate news from Egypt) he was received as the nation's leading military hero.

At the time of the Brumaire coup, the republic's armies had been driven from Italy by a second coalition, but they had halted a multifront assault on France by the armies of Russia, Austria, and Britain. The republic, in other words, was no longer in imminent military danger, but the prospect of an interminable war loomed on the horizon. After Brumaire the nation expected its new leader to achieve peace through decisive military victory. This promise Napoleon fulfilled, once again leading French armies into northern Italy and defeating Austria at the Battle of Marengo in June 1800. Subsequent defeats in Germany drove Austria to sign the peace treaty of Lunéville in February 1801. Deprived of its Continental allies for the second time, a war-weary Britain finally decided to negotiate. In March 1802 France and

Britain signed the Treaty of Amiens, and for the first time in 10 years Europe was at peace.

Within two years, however, the two rivals were again in a state of war. Most historians agree that neither imperial power was solely responsible for the breakdown of this peace, since neither would renounce its ambitions for supremacy. Napoleon repeatedly violated the treaty's spirit—by annexing Piedmont, occupying the Batavian Republic, and assuming the presidency of the Cisalpine Republic. To Britain, the balance of power in Europe required an independent Italy and Dutch Netherlands. Britain violated the letter of the treaty, however, by failing to evacuate the island of Malta as it had promised.

Once again, British naval power frustrated Napoleon's attempt to take the war directly to British soil, and there was little actual fighting until Britain was able to form a new Continental coalition in 1805. At the Battle of Trafalgar (October 21, 1805), British naval gunners decimated the French and Spanish fleets, ending all thought of a cross-Channel invasion. Napoleon turned instead against Britain's Austrian and Russian allies. He surprised the Austrians at Ulm and then smashed them decisively at the Battle of Austerlitz (December 2, 1805), probably his most brilliant tactical feat. Under the Treaty of Pressburg (criticized by the French foreign minister Charles-Maurice de Talleyrand as entirely too harsh), Austria paid a heavy indemnity, ceded its provinces of Venetia and Tyrol, and allowed Napoleon to abolish the Holy Roman Empire. Prussia, kept neutral for a time by vague promises of sovereignty over Hanover, finally mobilized against France, only to suffer humiliating defeats at the Battles of Jena and Auerstädt in October 1806. The French occupied Berlin, levied a huge indemnity on Prussia, seized various provinces, and turned northern Germany into a French sphere of influence. The ensuing campaign against Russia's army in Europe resulted in a bloody stalemate at the Battle of Eylau (February 8, 1807), leaving Napoleon in precarious straits with extremely vulnerable lines of supply. But, when fighting resumed that spring, the French prevailed at the Battle of Friedland (June 14, 1807), and Tsar Alexander I sued for peace. The Treaty of Tilsit, negotiated by the two emperors, divided Europe into two zones of influence, with Napoleon pledging to aid the Russians against their Ottoman rivals and Alexander promising to cooperate against Britain.

THE GRAND EMPIRE

Napoleon now had a free hand to reorganize Europe and numerous relatives to install on the thrones of his satellite kingdoms. The result was known as the Grand Empire. Having annexed Tuscany, Piedmont, Genoa, and the Rhineland directly into France, Napoleon placed the Kingdom of Holland (which until 1806 was the Batavian Commonwealth) under his brother Louis, the Kingdom of Westphalia under his brother Jérôme, the Kingdom of Italy under his stepson

Eugène as his viceroy, the Kingdom of Spain under his brother Joseph, and the Grand Duchy of Warsaw (carved out of Prussian Poland) under the nominal sovereignty of his ally the king of Saxony, Frederick Augustus I. To link his allied states in northern and southern Germany, Napoleon created the Confederation of the Rhine. Even Austria seemed to fall into Napoleon's sphere of influence, with his marriage to Archduchess Marie-Louise in 1810. (Since the emperor had no natural heirs from his marriage to Joséphine Beauharnais, he reluctantly divorced her and in 1810 married the Austrian princess, who duly bore him a son the following year.)

THE CONTINENTAL SYSTEM

Britain, however, was insulated from French military power; only an indirect strategy of economic warfare remained possible. Thus far Britain had driven most French merchant shipping from the high seas, and in desperation French merchants sold most of their ships to neutrals, allowing the United States to surpass France in the size of its merchant fleet. But after his string of military victories, Napoleon believed that he could choke off British commerce by closing the Continent to its ships and products. With limited opportunities to sell its manufactured goods, he believed, the British economy would suffer from overproduction and unemployment, while the lack of foreign gold in payment for British exports would bankrupt the treasury. As France moved into Britain's foreign markets, Britain's economic crisis would drive its government to seek peace. Accordingly, Napoleon launched the "Continental System": in the Berlin Decree of November 1806, he prohibited British trade with all countries under French influence, including British products carried by neutral shipping. When the British retaliated by requiring all neutral ships to stop at British ports for inspection and licenses, Napoleon

BATTLE OF WATERLOO

The Battle of Waterloo (June 18, 1815) represented Napoleon's final defeat, ending 23 years of recurrent warfare between France and the other powers of Europe. It was fought during the Hundred Days of Napoleon's restoration, 3 miles (5 km) south of Waterloo village (which is 9 miles [14.5 km] south of Brussels), between Napoleon's 72,000 troops and the combined forces of the Duke of Wellington's Allied army of 68,000 (with British, Dutch, Belgian, and German units) and about 45,000 Prussians, the main force of Gebhard Leberecht von Blücher's command. After defeating the Prussians at Ligny and holding Wellington at Quatre-Bras in secondary battles south of Waterloo on June 16, Napoleon's marshals,

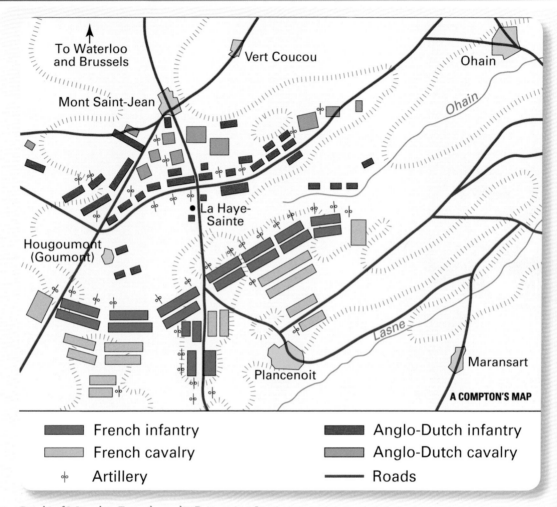

Battle of Waterloo. Encyclopædia Britannica, Inc.

Michel Ney and Emmanuel de Grouchy, failed to attack and annihilate either enemy while their armies were separated. Grouchy, with 33,000 men, nearly one-third of Napoleon's total strength of 105,000, led a dilatory pursuit of Blücher. On the 18th he was tied down at Wavre by 17,000 troops of Blücher's rear guard, while Blücher's main force escaped him, rejoined Wellington, and turned the tide of battle at Waterloo, 8 miles (13 km) to the south-west. At Waterloo, Napoleon made a major blunder in delaying the opening of his attack on Wellington from morning until midday, to allow the ground to dry; this delay gave Blücher's troops exactly the time they needed to reach Waterloo and support Wellington.

The four main French attacks against Wellington's army prior to 6:00 PM on June 18 all failed in their object—to decisively weaken the Allied centre to permit a French breakthrough—because they all lacked coordination between infantry and cavalry. Meanwhile, a secondary

British army resisting a charge by the French cavalry, Battle of Waterloo, 1815. © Photos.com/ Thinkstock

battle developed, in which the French were on the defensive against the 30,000 Prussian troops of Karl von Bülow's corps of Blücher's army. The Prussians arrived at Waterloo gradually and put pressure on Napoleon's eastern flank. To prevent the Prussians from advancing into his rear, Napoleon was forced to shift a corps under Georges Mouton, Count de Lobau, and to move several Imperial Guard battalions from his main battle against Wellington.

Finally, at 6:00 PM, Ney employed his infantry, cavalry, and artillery in a coordinated attack and captured La Haye Sainte, a farmhouse in the centre of the Allied line. The French artillery then began blasting holes in the Allied centre. The decisive hour had arrived: Wellington's heavy losses left him vulnerable to any intensification of the French attack. But Ney's request for infantry reinforcements was refused because Napoleon was preoccupied with the Prussian flank attack. Only after 7:00 PM, with his flank secured, did he release several battalions of the Imperial Guard to Ney; but by then Wellington had reorganized his defenses, aided by the arrival of a Prussian corps under H.E.K. von Zieten. Ney led part of the guard and other units in the final assault on the Allies. The firepower of the Allied infantry shattered the tightly packed guard infantry. The repulse of the guard

Napoleon I fleeing the battlefield of Waterloo, engraving, 1817. © Photos.com/Thinkstock

at 8:00 PM, followed in 15 minutes by the beginning of the general Allied advance and further Prussian attacks in the east, threw the French army into a panic; a disorganized retreat began. The pursuit of the French was taken up by the Prussians. Napoleon lost 25,000 men killed and wounded and 9,000 captured. Wellington's casualties were 15,000 and Blücher's were about 8,000. Four days later Napoleon abdicated for the second time.

threatened to seize any ship stopping at English ports. Thus, a total naval war against neutrals erupted.

Economic warfare took its toll on all sides. While France did make inroads in cotton manufacturing in the absence of British competition, France and especially its allies suffered terribly from the British blockade, in particular from a dearth of colonial raw materials. The great Atlantic ports of Nantes, Bordeaux, and Amsterdam never recovered, as ancillary industries such as shipbuilding and sugar refining collapsed. The axis of European trade shifted decisively inland. The Continental System did strain the British economy, driving down exports and gold reserves in 1810, but the blockade was extremely porous. Because Europeans liked British goods, smugglers had incentive to evade the restrictions in such places as Spain and Portugal. By 1811, moreover, a restive Tsar Alexander withdrew from the Continental System. Thus, the most dire effect of the Continental System was the stimulus it gave Napoleon for a new round of aggression against Portugal, Spain, and Russia.

By 1810 almost 300,000 imperial troops were bogged down in Iberia, struggling against a surprisingly vigorous Spanish resistance and a British expeditionary force. Then, in 1812, Napoleon embarked on his most quixotic aggression—an invasion of Russia designed to humble "the colossus of Northern barbarism" and exclude Russia from any influence in Europe. The Grand Army of 600,000 men that crossed into Russia reached Moscow without inflicting a decisive defeat on the Russian armies. By the time Napoleon on October 19 belatedly ordered a retreat from Moscow, which had been burned to the ground and was unfit for winter quarters, he had lost two-thirds of his troops from disease, battle casualties, cold, and hunger. The punishing retreat through the Russian winter killed most of the others. Yet this unparalleled disaster did not humble or discourage the emperor. Napoleon believed that he could hold his empire together and defeat yet another anti-French coalition that was forming. He correctly assumed that he could still rely on his well-honed administrative bureaucracy to replace the decimated Grand Army.

CONSCRIPTION

Building on the Directory's conscription law of September 1798, the Napoleonic regime, after considerable trial and error, had created the mechanisms for imposing on the citizens of France and the annexed territories the distasteful obligation of military service. Each year the Ministry of War Administration assigned a quota of conscripts for every *département*. Using communal birth registers, the mayor of each commune compiled a list of men reaching the age of 19 that year. After a preliminary examination to screen out the manifestly unfit and those below the minimum height of 5 feet 1 inch (1.5 metres), the young men drew numbers in a lottery at the cantonal seat. Doctors in the departmental capitals later ruled on other claims for medical exemptions, and in all about a third of the youths avoided military service legally as physically unfit. Though married men were not exempt from the draft, two other means of avoiding induction remained, apart from drawing a high number: the wealthy could purchase a replacement, and the poor could flee.

For Napoleon's prefects, the annual conscription levy was the top priority and draft evasion the number-one problem in most *départements*. Persistence, routine stepped-up policing, and coercion gradually overcame the chronic resistance. Napoleon had begun by drafting 60,000 Frenchmen annually, but by 1810 the quota hit 120,000, and the first of many "supplementary levies" was decreed to call up men from earlier classes who had drawn high numbers. In January 1813, after the Russian disaster, Napoleon replenished his armies by calling up the class of 1814 a year early and by repeated supplementary levies. Because he could still rely on his conscription machine, Napoleon consistently rebuffed offers by the allies to negotiate peace. Only after he lost the decisive Battle of Leipzig in October 1813 and was driven back across the Rhine did the machine break down. His call of November 1813 for 300,000 more men went largely unfilled. With the troops at his disposal, the emperor fought the Battle of France skillfully, but he could not stop the allies. Shortly after Paris fell, he abdicated, on April 6, 1814, and departed for the island of Elba. France was reduced to its 1792 borders, and the Bourbons returned to the throne. Altogether—along with large levies of Italians, Germans, and other foreigners from the annexed

territories and satellite states—nearly 2,500,000 Frenchmen had been drafted by Napoleon, and at least 1,000,000 of these conscripts never returned, roughly half that number being casualties and the other half imprisoned or missing.

The most sympathetic explanation for Napoleon's relentless aggression holds that he was responding to the irreducible antagonism of Britain: French power and glory were the only antidotes to John Bull's arrogance. Others have argued that Napoleon's vendetta against Britain was merely a rationalization for a mad 10-year chase across Europe to establish a new version of Charlemagne's empire. This "imperial design" thesis, however, makes sense only in 1810, as a way Napoleon might have organized his conquests and not as the motivation for them. (Only retrospectively did Napoleon write, "There will be no repose for Europe until she is under only one Head...an Emperor who should distribute kingdoms among his lieutenants.") In the end, one is thrown back on the explanation of temperament. In his combination of pragmatism and insatiable ambition, this world-historic figure remains an enigma. Increasingly "aristocratic" at home and "imperial" abroad, Napoleon was obviously something more than the "general of the Revolution." And yet, with civil code in one hand and sabre in the other, Napoleon could still be seen by Europeans as a personification on both counts of the French Revolution's explosive force.

NAPOLEON AND THE REVOLUTION

The Revolutionary legacy for Napoleon consisted above all in the abolition of the ancien régime's most archaic features—"feudalism," seigneurialism, legal privileges, and provincial liberties. No matter how aristocratic his style became, he had no use for the ineffective institutions and abuses of the ancien régime. Napoleon was "modern" in temperament as well as destructively aggressive. But in either guise he was an authoritarian, with little patience for argument, who profited from the Revolution's clearing operations to construct and mobilize in his own fashion. His concept of reform exaggerated the Revolution's emphasis on uniformity and centralization. Napoleon also accepted the Revolutionary principles of civil equality and equality of opportunity, meaning the recognition of merit. Other rights and liberties did not seem essential. Unlike others before him who had tried and failed, Napoleon terminated the Revolution, but at the price of suppressing the electoral process and partisan politics altogether. Toward the end of the empire, his centralizing vision took over completely, reinforcing his personal will to power. France was merely a launching pad for Napoleon's boundless military and imperial ambition, its prime function being to raise men and money for war. In utter contrast to the Revolution, then, militarism became the defining quality of the Napoleonic regime.

Napoleon's ambiguous legacy helps explain the dizzying events that shook France in 1814 and 1815. Even before Napoleon's abdication, the Imperial Senate, led by the former foreign minister Talleyrand, had begun negotiations with the allies to ensure a transition to a regime that would protect the positions of those who had gained from the Revolution and the Napoleonic period. Louis XVI's long-exiled brother was allowed to return as King Louis XVIII, but he had to agree to rule under a constitution (called the Charter) that provided for legislative control over budgets and taxes and guaranteed basic liberties. However, the Bourbons alienated the officer corps by retiring many at half pay and frightened many citizens by not making clear how much of their property and power the church and émigrés would regain. As the anti-Napoleonic allies argued among themselves about the spoils of war, Napoleon slipped back to France for a last adventure, believing that he could reach Paris without firing a shot. At various points along the way, troops disobeyed royalist officers and rallied to the emperor, while Louis fled the country. Between March and June 1815—a period known as the Hundred Days—Napoleon again ruled France. Contrary to his expectation, however, the allies patched up their differences and were determined to rout "the usurper." At the Battle of Waterloo (June 18, 1815) British and Prussian forces defeated Napoleon's army decisively, and he abdicated again a few days later. Placed on the remote island of St. Helena in the South Atlantic, he died in 1821. The "Napoleonic legend"—the retrospective version of events created by Napoleon during his exile—burnished his image in France for decades to come. But in the final analysis Napoleon's impact on future generations was not nearly as powerful as the legacy of the French Revolution itself.

CHAPTER 9

RESTORATION, REPUBLICANISM, THE GREAT WAR, WORLD WAR II, AND BEYOND

Despite political conflict and instability during the 19th and early 20th centuries, France enjoyed great economic progress, and its cultural prestige was at its zenith. Agricultural production increased greatly after the Revolution broke up the great estates and put small holdings into the hands of industrious farm families. After the monarchy's arbitrary regulations of manufacturing and trade were swept away, enterprising French manufacturers began to compete favorably with British factories. French companies stressed quality and elegance in their wares and found a market for them abroad.

THE RESTORATION AND CONSTITUTIONAL MONARCHY

The Napoleonic wars left France devastated, and the country was slow in accustoming itself to the new order. The allies avenged themselves for the Hundred Days by writing a new and more severe Treaty of Paris. France lost several frontier territories, notably the Saar basin and Savoy (Savoie), that had been annexed in 1789–92; a war indemnity of 700 million francs was imposed; and, pending full payment, eastern France was to be occupied by allied troops at French expense.

LOUIS XVIII, 1815–24

King Louis XVIII's second return from exile was far from glorious. Neither the victorious powers nor Louis's French subjects viewed his restoration with much enthusiasm, yet there seemed to be no ready alternative to Bourbon rule.

Within France, political tensions were exacerbated by Napoleon's mad gamble and by the mistakes committed during the first restoration. The problem facing the Bourbons would have been difficult enough without these tensions—namely, how to arrive at a stable compromise between those Frenchmen who saw the Revolutionary changes as irreversible and those who were determined to resurrect the ancien régime. The reactionary element, labeled ultraroyalists (or simply "ultras"), was now more intransigent than ever and set out to purge the country of all those who had betrayed the dynasty. A brief period of "white terror" in the south claimed some 300 victims; in Paris, many high officials who had rallied to Napoleon were dismissed, and a few eminent figures, notably Marshal Michel Ney, were tried and shot. The king refused, however, to scrap the Charter of 1814, in spite of ultra pressure. When a new Chamber of Deputies was elected in August 1815, the ultras scored a sweeping victory; the surprised king, who had feared a surge of antimonarchical sentiment, greeted the legislature as *la chambre introuvable* ("the incomparable chamber"). But the political honeymoon was short-lived. Louis was shrewd enough, or cautious enough, to realize that ultra policies would divide the country and might in the end destroy the dynasty. He chose as ministers, therefore, such moderate royalists

as Armand-Emmanuel du Plessis, duc de Richelieu, and Élie Decazes—men who knew the nation would not tolerate an attempt to resurrect the 18th century.

There followed a year of sharp friction between these moderate ministers and the ultra-dominated Chamber—friction and unrest that made Europe increasingly nervous about the viability of the restored monarchy. Representatives of the occupying powers began to express their concern to the king. At last, in September 1816, his ministers persuaded him to dissolve the Chamber and order new elections, and the moderate royalists emerged with a clear majority. In spite of ultra fury, several years of relative stability ensued. Richelieu and Decazes, with solid support in the Chamber, could proceed with their attempt to pursue a moderate course. By 1818 they were able, thanks to loans from English and Dutch bankers, to pay off the war indemnity and thus to end the allied occupation; at the Congress of Aix-la-Chapelle, France was welcomed back into the Concert of Europe. In domestic politics there were some signs that France might be moving toward a British-style parliamentary monarchy, even though the Charter had carefully avoided making the king's ministers responsible to the Chamber of Deputies. In the Chamber something anticipating a party system also began to emerge: ultras on the right, independents (or liberals) on the left, constitutionalists (or moderates) in the centre. None of these factions yet possessed the real attributes of a party—disciplined organization and doctrinal coherence. The most heterogeneous of all was the independent group—an uneasy coalition of republicans, Bonapartists, and constitutional monarchists brought together by their common hostility to the Bourbons and their common determination to preserve or restore many of the Revolutionary reforms.

The era of moderate rule (1816–20) was marked by a slow but steady advance of the liberal left. Each year one-fifth of the Chamber faced reelection, and each year more independents won seats, despite the narrowly restricted suffrage. The ultras, in real or simulated panic, predicted disaster for the regime and the nation; but the king clung stubbornly to his favourite, Decazes, who by now was head of the government in all but name, and Decazes, in turn, clung to his middle way.

The uneasy balance was wrecked in February 1820 by the assassination of the king's nephew, Charles-Ferdinand de Bourbon, duc de Berry. The assassin, a fanatic Bonapartist, proudly announced his purpose: to extinguish the royal line by destroying the last Bourbon still young enough to produce a male heir. In this aim he failed, for Marie-Caroline de Bourbon-Sicile, duchesse de Berry, seven months later bore a son, whom the royalists hailed as "the miracle child." But the assassin did bring to an end the period of moderate rule and returned the ultras to power. In the wave of emotion that followed, the king dismissed Decazes and

manipulated the elections in favour of the ultras, who regained control of the Chamber and dominated the new cabinet headed by one of their leaders, Joseph, comte de Villèle.

This swing toward reaction goaded some segments of the liberal left into conspiratorial activity. A newly formed secret society called the Charbonnerie, which borrowed its name and ritual from the Italian Carbonari, laid plans for an armed insurrection, but their rising in 1822 was easily crushed. One group of conspirators—"the four sergeants of La Rochelle"—became heroic martyrs in the popular mythology of the French left. Subversion gave the government an excuse for intensified repression: the press was placed under more rigid censorship and the school system subjected to the clergy.

Meanwhile, the ultras were winning public support through a more assertive foreign policy. Spain had been in a state of quasi-civil war since 1820, when a revolt by the so-called liberal faction in the army had forced King Ferdinand VII to grant a constitution and to authorize the election of a parliament. The European powers, disturbed at the state of semianarchy in Spain, accepted a French offer to restore Ferdinand's authority by forcible intervention. In 1823 French troops crossed the Pyrenees and, despite predictions of disaster from the liberal left, easily took Madrid and reestablished the king's untrammeled power. This successful adventure strengthened the ultra politicians and discredited their critics. In the elections of 1824 the ultras increased their grip on the Chamber and won a further victory in September 1824 when the aged Louis XVIII died, leaving the throne to a new king who was the very embodiment of the ultra spirit.

CHARLES X, 1824–30

Charles X, the younger brother of Louis XVIII, had spent the Revolutionary years in exile and had returned embittered rather than chastened by the experience. What France needed, in his view, was a return to the unsullied principle of divine right, buttressed by the restored authority of the established church. The new king and his cabinet—still headed by Villèle—promptly pushed through the Chamber a series of laws of sharply partisan character. The most bitterly debated of these laws was the one that indemnified the émigrés for the loss of their property during the Revolution. The cost of the operation—almost one billion francs—was borne by government bondholders, whose bonds were arbitrarily converted to a lower interest rate. A severe press law hamstrung the publishers of newspapers and pamphlets; another established the death penalty for sacrilegious acts committed in churches.

Along with these signs of reaction went a vigorous campaign to reassert the authority of the Roman Catholic Church, which had been undermined by Enlightenment skepticism and by the Revolutionary upheaval. The Concordat of 1802 had allowed the beginning of a religious revival, which gained strength after 1814. The best-selling *Le Génie du christianisme* (1802; *Genius of Christianity*), by the Romantic writer François-Auguste-René, vicomte de Chateaubriand, marked a change in public attitudes toward belief; Chateaubriand rejected Enlightenment rationalism and argued that only religion could satisfy human emotional needs. Under the Bourbons several new missionary orders and lay organizations were founded in an effort to revive the faith and to engage in good works. Catholic seminaries began to draw increasing numbers of students away from the state lycées. Charles X threw himself enthusiastically into the campaign for Catholic revival. The anticlericals of the liberal left were outraged, and even many moderates of Gallican sympathies were perturbed. Rumours spread that the king had secretly become a Jesuit and was planning to turn the country over to "the men in black."

King Charles and his ultra ministers might nevertheless have remained in solid control if they had been shrewd and sensitive men, aware of the rise of public discontent and flexible enough to appease it. Instead, they forged stubbornly ahead on the road to disaster. Villèle, though a talented administrator, lacked creative imagination and charismatic appeal. As the years passed, his leadership was increasingly challenged even within his own ultra majority. A bitter personal feud between Villèle and Chateaubriand, who had entered politics after 1814 and had become the most colourful of the ultra politicians, undermined both the ministry and the dynasty. The liberal campaign organization "Aide-toi, le ciel t'aidera" ("God helps those who help themselves") coordinated the opposition's preparations for the elections of 1827, which brought a sharp resurgence of liberal and moderate strength and led to Villèle's downfall. The king patched together a disparate ministry of moderates and ultras headed by an obscure official, Jean-Baptiste-Sylvère Gay, vicomte de Martignac. But Martignac lacked Charles's confidence and failed to win the support of the more moderate leftists in the Chamber. In 1829 the king brusquely dismissed him and restored the ultras to power.

The delayed consequences of this act were to be fatal to the dynasty. The king, instead of entrusting power to an able ultra such as Villèle or a popular one such as Chateaubriand, chose a personal favourite, Jules-Auguste-Armand-Marie, prince de Polignac, a fanatic reactionary. The makeup of the cabinet, which included several members of the most bigoted faction of "ultra-ultras," seemed to indicate the king's determination to polarize politics. That, in any case, was the immediate result. On the left the mood turned aggressively hostile; the republicans of Paris began to organize; an Orleanist faction emerged, looking to a constitutional monarchy headed by the king's cousin, Louis-Philippe-Joseph, duc d'Orléans. The liberal banker Jacques Laffitte supplied funds for a new opposition daily, *Le National*, edited by a young and vigorous team whose most notable member was Adolphe Thiers. A confrontation of some sort seemed inevitable.

Some of Polignac's ministers urged a royal coup d'état at once, before the rejuvenated opposition could grow too strong. Instead, the king procrastinated for several months, offering no clear lead or firm policy. When the Chamber met at last in March 1830, its majority promptly voted an address to the throne denouncing the ministry. The king retaliated by dissolving the Chamber and ordering new elections in July. Both Charles and Polignac hoped that pressure on the electors, plus foreign policy successes, might shape the outcome. Such a success was won at just the opportune moment: news came that Algiers had fallen to a French expeditionary force sent to punish the bey for assorted transgressions. But even this brilliant victory could not divert the fury of the king's critics. The opposition won 274 seats, the ministry 143. When Charles chose not to substitute a moderate for Polignac and accept the role of constitutional monarch, the risk was great that a royal coup d'état would leave the Charter of 1814 in tatters. King and ministers prepared a set of decrees that dissolved the newly elected Chamber, further restricted the already narrow suffrage, and stripped away the remaining liberty of the press. These July Ordinances, made public on the 26th, completed the polarization process and ensured that the confrontation would be violent.

THE REVOLUTION OF 1830

The July Revolution was a monument to the ineptitude of Charles X and his advisers. At the outset, few of the king's critics imagined it possible to overthrow the regime; they hoped merely to get rid of Polignac. As for the king, he naively ignored the possibility of serious trouble. No steps were taken to reinforce the army garrison in Paris; no contingency plans were prepared. Instead, Charles went off to the country to hunt, leaving the capital weakly defended. During the three days known to Frenchmen as les Trois Glorieuses (July 27–29), protest was rapidly transmuted into insurrection; barricades went up in the streets, manned by workers, students, and petty bourgeois citizens (some of them former members of the National Guard, which Charles, in pique, had disbanded in 1827). On July 29 some army units began to fraternize with the insurgents. The king, on July 30, consented at last to dismiss Polignac and to annul the July Ordinances; but the gesture came too late. Paris was in the hands of the rebels, and plans for a new regime were crystallizing rapidly.

As the insurrection developed, two rival factions had emerged. The republicans—mainly workers and students—gained control of the streets and took over the Hôtel de Ville, where on July 29 they set up a municipal commission. They looked to the venerable General Lafayette, commander of the National Guard, as their symbolic leader. The constitutional monarchists had their headquarters at the newspaper *Le National*; their candidate for the throne was Louis-Philippe. He was at first reluctant to take the risk, fearing failure and renewed exile; Adolphe Thiers undertook the task of persuading him and succeeded. On July 31 Louis-Philippe made his way through a largely hostile crowd to the Hôtel de Ville and confronted the republicans. His cause was won by Lafayette, who found a constitutional monarchy safer than the risks of Jacobin rule; Lafayette appeared on the balcony with Louis-Philippe and, wrapped in a tricolour flag, embraced the duke as the crowd cheered. Two days later Charles X abdicated at last, though on condition that the throne pass to his grandson, "the miracle child." But the parliament, meeting on August 7, declared the throne vacant and on August 9 proclaimed Louis-Philippe "king of the French by the grace of God and the will of the nation."

THE JULY MONARCHY

The renovated regime (often called the July Monarchy or the bourgeois monarchy) rested on an altered political theory and a broadened social base. Divine right gave way to popular sovereignty; the social centre of gravity shifted from the landowning aristocracy to the wealthy bourgeoisie. The Charter of 1814 was retained but no longer as a royal gift to the nation; it was revised by the Chamber of Deputies and in its new form imposed on the king. Censorship was abolished;

the Tricolor was restored as the national flag, and the National Guard was resuscitated. Roman Catholicism was declared to be simply the religion "of the majority of Frenchmen," the voting age was lowered to 25, and the property qualification was reduced to include all who paid a direct tax of 200 (formerly 300) francs. The suffrage was thus doubled, from about 90,000 to almost 200,000.

The new king seemed admirably suited to this new constitutional system. The "Citizen King" was reputed to be a liberal whose tastes and sympathies coincided with those of the upper bourgeoisie. He had spent the Revolutionary years in exile but was out of sympathy with the irreconcilable émigrés; and since his return, his house in Paris had been a gathering place for the opposition. Yet, in spite of appearances, Louis-Philippe was not prepared to accept the strictly symbolic role of a monarch who (in Thiers's phrase) "reigns but does not govern." His authority, he believed, rested on heredity and not merely on the will of the Chamber; his proper function was to participate actively in decision making and not merely to appoint ministers who would govern in his name. As time went by, he was increasingly inclined to choose ministers who shared his view of the royal power. The Orleanist system thus rested on a basic ambiguity about the real locus of authority.

In the Chamber two major factions emerged, known by the rather imprecise labels right-centre and left-centre. The former group, led by the historian François Guizot, shared the king's political doctrines; it saw the revised Charter of 1814 as an adequate instrument of government that needed no further change. The left-centre, whose ablest spokesman was the kingmaker Adolphe Thiers, saw 1830 as the beginning rather than the culmination of a process of change. It favoured restricting the king's active role and broadening the suffrage to include the middle strata of the bourgeoisie. These differences of viewpoint, combined with the king's tendency to intrigue, contributed to chronic political instability during the 1830s.

The decade of the 1830s was marked also by repeated challenges to the regime by its enemies on the right and the left and by a series of attempts to assassinate the king. Both the ultras (who now came to be called Legitimists) and the republicans refused to forgive "the usurper" of 1830. In 1832 the duchesse de Berry, mother of "the miracle child," landed clandestinely in southern France in an effort to spark a general uprising; but the scheme collapsed, and most Legitimists withdrew into sullen opposition. More serious was the agitation in the cities. Economic distress led to the November 1831 insurrection in Lyon, in which armed workers seized control of the city for a week. In June 1832 a republican demonstration in Paris drew 100,000 participants. Again in 1834 there were serious disturbances in Lyon and Paris that had to be put down by the army. In 1836 it was the turn of the Bonapartist pretender to challenge the regime. Since Napoleon's death in 1821, a legend had taken shape around his name. No longer detested as a ruthless autocrat who had sacrificed a generation of young Frenchmen on the battlefield, he became transmuted into the Little Corporal who had risen to the heights by his own talents and had died a victim of British jealousy. The emperor's nephew Louis-Napoléon Bonaparte presented himself as the true heir; he crossed the frontier in 1836 and called on French troops in Strasbourg to join his cause. The venture failed ignominiously, as did also a second attempt on the Channel coast in 1840. Louis-Napoléon was condemned to prison for life but managed in 1846 to escape to England. Interspersed with these attempts at political risings were individual attacks on the king's person; the most elaborate of these plots was the one organized by a Corsican named Giuseppe Fieschi in 1835.

By 1840, however, the enemies of the regime had evidently become discouraged, and a period of remarkable stability followed. François Guizot emerged as the key figure in the ministry; he retained that role from 1840 to 1848. One of the first Protestants to attain high office in France, Guizot possessed many of the moral and intellectual qualities that marked the small but influential Protestant minority. Hardworking and intelligent, Guizot was devoted to the service of the king and to the defense of the status quo. He was convinced that the wealthy governing class was an ideal natural elite to which any Frenchman might have access through talent and effort. To those who complained at being excluded by the property qualification for voting and seeking office, Guizot's simple reply was "Enrichissez-vous!" ("Get rich!"). His government encouraged the process by granting railway and mining concessions to its bourgeois supporters and by contributing part of the development costs. High protective tariffs continued to shelter French entrepreneurs against foreign competition. The result was an economic boom during the 1840s, beginning the transformation of France from a largely rural society into an industrial one.

Guizot shared with Louis-Philippe a strong preference for a safe and sane foreign policy. The king, from the beginning of his reign, had cautiously avoided risks and confrontations and had especially sought friendly relations with Britain. In 1830, when the revolution in Paris inspired the Belgians to break away from Dutch rule, Louis-Philippe avoided the temptation of seeking to annex Belgium or of placing one of his sons on the Belgian throne. Again in 1840, when a crisis flared up in the Middle East and Thiers (then head of the government) took an aggressive stance that threatened to coalesce all of Europe against France, the king had found an excuse to replace his firebrand minister. Guizot continued this cautious line through the 1840s, with the single exception of an episode in Spain. A long contest involving rival suitors for the Spanish queen's hand finally tempted Guizot, in 1846, to try for a cheap diplomatic victory; it infuriated the British and helped to destroy the Anglo-French entente. One problem Guizot inherited from his predecessors was that of Algeria. Since 1830 the French had maintained an uneasy presence there, wavering between total withdrawal and expanded conquest. The decision to remain had been made in the mid-1830s; during the Guizot era, General Thomas-Robert Bugeaud used brutal methods to break Algerian resistance, pushed the native population back into the mountains, and began the process of colonizing the rich coastal plain.

THE SECOND REPUBLIC AND SECOND EMPIRE

After 1840 the regime settled into a kind of torpid stability, but it had provided the nation with peace and relative prosperity. Louis-Philippe and his ministers had prided themselves on their moderation, their respect for the ideal of cautious balance embodied in the concept of *juste-milieu*. France seemed to be arriving at last at a working compromise that blended traditional ways with the reforms of the Revolutionary era. There were, nevertheless, persistent signs of discontent.

THE REVOLUTION OF 1848

The overthrow of the constitutional monarchy in February 1848 still seems, in retrospect, a puzzling event. The revolution has been called a result without a cause; more properly, it might be called a result out of proportion to its cause. The republicans had never forgiven Louis-Philippe for "confiscating" their revolution in 1830. The urban workers, moved by their misery and by the powerful social myths engendered by the Revolution of 1789, remained unreconciled. For a decade or more they had been increasingly drawn toward socialism in its various utopian forms. An unprecedented flowering of socialist thought marked the years 1830–48 in France: this was the generation of the Saint-Simonians (followers of utopian thinker Henri de Saint-Simon [1760–1825]) and of Charles Fourier, Auguste Blanqui, Louis Blanc, Pierre-Joseph Proudhon, Étienne Cabet, and many others. Most of these system builders preached persuasion rather than violence, but they stimulated the hopes of the common man for an imminent transformation of society. Women also began to question existing social arrangements; the first French feminist groups grew out of the Saint-Simonian movement in 1831–32. Within the bourgeoisie as well, there was strong and vocal pressure for change in the form of a broadening of the political elite. Bills to extend the suffrage (and the right to hold office) to the middle bourgeoisie were repeatedly introduced in parliament but were stubbornly opposed by Guizot. Even the National Guard, that honour society of the lesser bourgeoisie, became infected with this mood of dissatisfaction.

Other factors, too, contributed to this mood. In 1846 a crop failure quickly developed into a full-scale economic crisis: food became scarce and expensive; many businesses went bankrupt; unemployment rose. Within the governing elite itself there were signs of a moral crisis: scandals that implicated some high officials of the regime and growing dissension among the notables. Along with this went a serious alienation of many intellectuals. Novelists such as Victor Hugo, George Sand, and Eugène Sue glorified the common man; the caricaturist Honoré Daumier exposed the foibles of the nation's leaders; and historians such as Jules Michelet and Alphonse de Lamartine wrote with romantic passion about the heroic episodes of the Great Revolution.

Beginning in 1847, the leaders of the opposition set out to take advantage of this restless mood and to force the regime to grant liberal reforms. Since public political meetings were illegal, they undertook a series of political "banquets" to mobilize the forces of discontent. This campaign was to be climaxed by a mammoth banquet in Paris on February 22, 1848. But the government, fearing violence, ordered the affair canceled. On the 22nd, crowds of protesting students and workers gathered in the streets and began to clash with the police. The king and Guizot expected no serious trouble: the weather was bad, and a large army garrison was available in case of need. But the disorders continued to spread, and the loyalty of the National Guard began to seem dubious. Toward the end of two days of rioting, Louis-Philippe faced a painful choice: unleash the army (which would mean a bloodbath) or appease the demonstrators. Reluctantly, he chose the second course

and announced that he would replace the hated Guizot as his chief minister. But the concession came too late. That evening, an army unit guarding Guizot's official residence clashed with a mob of demonstrators, some 40 of whom died in the fusillade. By the morning of February 24, the angry crowd was threatening the royal palace. Louis-Philippe, confronted by the prospect of civil war, hesitated and then retreated once more; he announced his abdication in favour of his nine-year-old grandson and fled to England.

THE SECOND REPUBLIC, 1848–52

The succession to the throne was not to be decided so easily, however. The Chamber of Deputies, invaded by a crowd that demanded a republic, set up a provisional government whose members ranged from constitutional monarchists to one radical deputy, Alexandre-Auguste Ledru-Rollin. Led by the poet-deputy de Lamartine, the members of the government proceeded to the Hôtel de Ville, where the radical republican leaders had begun to organize their own regime. After considerable palaver, the provisional government co-opted four of the radical leaders, including the socialist theoretician Blanc and a workingman who called himself Albert. Under heavy pressure from the crowd surrounding the Hôtel de Ville, the government proclaimed the republic. During the next few days, continuing pressure from the social reformers pushed the government further than its bourgeois members really wanted to go. The government issued a right-to-work declaration, obligating the state to provide jobs for all citizens. To meet the immediate need, an emergency-relief agency called the *ateliers nationaux* (national workshops) was established. A kind of economic and social council called the Luxembourg Commission was created to study programs of social reform; Blanc was named its president. The principle of universal manhood suffrage was proclaimed—a return to the precedent of 1792 that increased the electorate at a stroke from 200,000 to 9,000,000. In matters of foreign policy, on the other hand, Foreign Minister Lamartine resisted radical demands. The radicals were eager for an ideological crusade on behalf of all peoples who were thirsting for freedom: Poles, Italians, Hungarians, and Germans had launched their own revolutions and needed help. Lamartine preferred to confine himself to lip-service support, since he was aware that an armed crusade would quickly inspire an anti-French coalition of the major powers.

By April 23, when Frenchmen went to the polls to elect their constituent assembly, the initial mood of brotherhood and goodwill had been largely dissipated. Paris had become a cauldron of political activism; dozens of clubs and scores of newspapers had sprung up after the revolution. Severe tension developed between moderates and radicals both within and outside the government and led to a number of violent street demonstrations that were controlled with difficulty. The *ateliers nationaux* satisfied no one: for the radicals they were a mere caricature of social reform, whereas for the moderates they were a wasteful and dangerous experiment that attracted thousands of unemployed to Paris from every corner of France. Financial problems plagued the government, which sought a solution by imposing a special 45-centime surtax on each franc of direct property taxes; this burden weighed most heavily on the peasantry and was bitterly resented in the countryside. The radicals, fearing that universal suffrage under these conditions might produce unpleasant results, vainly urged postponement of the elections until the new voters could be "educated" as to the virtues of a social republic.

The election returns confirmed the radicals' fears: the country voted massively for moderate or conservative candidates. Radicals or socialists won only about 80 of the 880 seats; the rest were bourgeois republicans (500) or constitutional monarchists (300). Lamartine led the popularity parade, being elected in 10 districts. When the assembly convened in May, the new majority showed little patience or caution; it was determined to cut costs and end risky experiments. In spite of Lamartine's efforts to maintain broad republican unity and avert a sharp turn to the right, the assembly abolished the Luxembourg Commission and the *ateliers nationaux* and refused to substitute a more useful program of public works to provide for the unemployed.

The immediate consequence was a brief and bloody civil war in Paris—the so-called June Days (June 23–26, 1848). Thousands of workers suddenly cut off the state payroll were joined by sympathizers—students, artisans, employed workers—in a spontaneous protest movement. Barricades went up in many working-class sections. The assembly turned to General Louis-Eugène Cavaignac as a saviour. Cavaignac had made his mark in repressing Algerian rebel tribes and was entrusted with full powers to do the same in Paris. He gave the workers time to dig themselves in, then brought up artillery against their barricades. At least 1,500 rebels were killed; 12,000 were arrested, and many were subsequently exiled to Algeria. The radical movement was decapitated; the workers withdrew into silent and bitter opposition.

Social conflict now gave way to political maneuvering and constitution making. Cavaignac was retained in office as temporary executive, while the assembly turned to its central task. After six months of discussion, it produced a constitution that appeared to be the most democratic in Europe. The president of the republic would be chosen for a four-year term by universal male suffrage; a one-house legislative assembly would be elected for three years by the same suffrage. What remained unclear was the relationship between president and assembly and the way out of a potential deadlock between them.

This problem might not have been fatal if the right kind of president had been available in 1848. Instead, the voters chose Louis-Napoléon Bonaparte, who had returned from British exile in September after having successfully stood for the constituent assembly in a by-election. He had made a poor initial impression; indeed, some politicians, such as Thiers, backed him for the presidency because they thought him too stupid to rule and thus soon to be shunted aside for an Orleanist monarch. What he possessed, however, was a name—a name that Frenchmen knew and that conveyed an aura of glory, power, and public order. In December Louis-Napoléon won by a landslide, polling 5.5 million votes against 2 million for all other candidates combined. In May 1849 the election of the legislative assembly produced an equal surprise. The two extremes—the radical left and the monarchist right—made impressive gains, whereas the moderate republicans, who had shaped the new system, were almost wiped out. The moderates emerged with only 80 seats, the radicals with 200, the monarchists with almost 500. But the monarchist majority lacked coherence, being split into legitimist and Orleanist factions that distrusted each other and differed on political principles.

During the next two years, President Bonaparte played his cards carefully, avoiding conflict with the monarchist assembly. He pleased Roman Catholics by restoring the pope to his temporal throne in Rome, from which he had been driven by Roman republicans. At home he accepted without protest a series of conservative measures adopted by the assembly: these laws deprived one-third of all Frenchmen of the right to vote, restricted the press and public assemblage, and gave the church a firm grip on public as well as private education. Yet there was some reason to doubt that Louis-Napoléon really welcomed this trend toward conservatism. His writings of the 1840s had been marked by a kind of technocratic outlook, in the tradition of Saint-Simonian socialism. His effort to please the assembly probably derived from his hope that the assembly would reciprocate: he wanted funds from the treasury to pay his personal debts and run his household, along with a constitutional amendment that would allow him to run for a second term.

By 1851 it was clear that the majority was not ready to give the president what he wanted. His alternatives were to step down in 1852, bereft of income and power, or to prepare a coup d'état. Some members of his entourage had long urged the latter course; Louis-Napoléon now concurred, with some reluctance.

On the early morning of December 2, 1851, some 70 leading politicians were arrested, and the outlines of a new constitution were proclaimed to the nation. It restored manhood suffrage, sharply reduced the assembly's powers, and extended the president's term to 10 years. Although the coup went off smoothly, it was followed by several days of agitation. Barricades went up in the streets, crowds clashed with troops and police in Paris and in the provinces, several hundred demonstrators were killed, and 27,000 were arrested. A widespread peasant revolt in southeastern France showed that republican convictions were much stronger by 1851 than they had been in 1848. Once the resistance was broken, Louis-Napoléon proceeded with his announced plebiscite on the new constitution and was gratified to receive the approval of 92 percent of those who voted. But the authoritarian republic was only a stopgap. Officially inspired petitions for a restoration of the empire began to flow to Paris; the Senate responded to what it described as the nation's desires, and on December 2, 1852, Louis-Napoléon was proclaimed emperor of the French as Napoleon III. This time there was no open protest; and the voters, in a new plebiscite, accorded Napoleon a handsome majority of 97 percent.

THE SECOND EMPIRE, 1852–70

Posterity's image of Napoleon III and his regime has not been uniform. Some historians have seen him as a shallow opportunist whose only asset was a glorious name. Others have described him as a visionary reformer and patron of progress, a man who successfully attempted to reconcile liberty and authority, national prestige and European cooperation. The emperor's enigmatic character and the contradictions built into his regime make it possible to argue either case.

THE AUTHORITARIAN YEARS

From 1852 to 1859 the empire was authoritarian in tone. Civil liberties were narrowly circumscribed; vocal opponents of the regime remained in exile or were constrained to silence; parliament's wings were clipped; elections to the Corps Législatif (the lower house of the parliament) were spaced at six-year intervals and were "managed" by Napoleon's prefects, who sponsored official candidates. An illusion of popular control was created by the use of the plebiscite to ratify decisions already made. The emperor and his ministers (members of his personal entourage or former Orleanist politicians) rested their authority on the peasant masses, the business class, the church, and those local notables who were willing to cooperate. Little attempt was made to install a new power elite or to create an organized Bonapartist party. Policy during the 1850s was consistently conservative; defense of the social order took precedence over reform.

The most striking achievements of these authoritarian years were in economic growth and foreign policy. The economic crisis of the late 1840s had been prolonged by political instability after the revolution; the restoration of order set off a vigorous economic expansion. During the Second Empire industrial production doubled, foreign trade tripled, the use of steam power increased fivefold, and railway mileage grew sixfold. The first great investment banks were founded (e.g., the Péreire brothers' Crédit Mobilier) and the first department store (the Bon Marché in Paris). The surge of French enterprise transcended frontiers: French capital and engineers built bridges, railways, docks, and sewerage systems throughout much of Continental Europe.

In part, this burst of energy had its source in favourable world conditions: the availability of more rapid steam transportation, an influx of new gold from overseas, general recovery from the slump of 1846–51. But to some degree Napoleon's government could claim credit, too—not so much by direct intervention in economic life as by creating a favourable climate for private enterprise. Many Frenchmen took advantage of the opportunities offered; they accumulated sizable fortunes and founded enterprises that still exist today. Among these entrepreneurs, however, there was a disproportionate number of "outsiders"— notably men of Protestant or Jewish origin or former disciples of Henri de Saint-Simon. Alongside these dynamic newcomers, the older business and banking leaders continued to operate on more cautious traditional lines. From the Second Empire onward, the French economy would combine these two contrasting sectors: a dynamic modernized element superimposed upon a largely static traditional kind of enterprise.

Napoleon's foreign policy at the outset was cautious; "the empire means peace," he assured his countrymen and the nervous powers of Europe. Yet, for a ruler who bore the name Napoleon, the prudent and colourless policy of a

Louis-Philippe seemed hardly appropriate. Besides, the emperor was eager to achieve recognition from the other European monarchs, who regarded him as an upstart. It was for these reasons rather than because of urgent national interest that he became involved in the Crimean War in 1854. Britain and Russia were engaged in a contest for influence in the crumbling Turkish empire. A dispute over the holy places in Palestine gave Napoleon an excuse to offer the British his support and thus to restore the Franco-British entente. Although the Crimean campaign was on the whole a fiasco for all the participating armies, the French forces came off less ingloriously than the others and could with some justice pose as victors. Napoleon served as host for the Paris peace conference that ended the war in 1856. Midway through the conference, the birth of a male heir to the emperor and his empress, Eugénie, seemed to assure the permanence of the dynasty.

THE LIBERAL YEARS

The empire thus appeared to have compiled a record of unbroken successes and to be beyond challenge by its domestic critics. Perhaps it was this stability and self-confidence that led Napoleon, beginning in 1859, to turn in the direction of liberalizing the empire. The immediate impulse for this dramatic reversal was the attempted assassination of the emperor in January 1858 by an Italian patriot, Felice Orsini, who sought thus to draw public attention to the frustrated hopes of Italian nationalists. Napoleon, shaken by the episode and by the reminder that in his youth he, too, had fought for Italian independence, met secretly in July 1858 with the conte di Cavour, premier of Piedmont; the two men laid plans designed to evict Austria from northern Italy and to convert Italy into a confederation of states headed by the pope. In return, France was promised Nice and Savoy (Savoie). The new allies provoked the Austrians into a declaration of war in April 1859, and Napoleon led his armies across the Alps. French victories at Magenta and Solferino were followed by a somewhat premature settlement in which the Austrians turned over the province of Lombardy to the Piedmontese. The campaign had aroused the passions of Italian nationalists up and down the peninsula; revolutions broke out in some of the smaller Italian states, and in 1860 the colourful guerrilla leader Giuseppe Garibaldi set forth from Piedmont to conquer Sicily and Naples.

These repercussions of Napoleon's new foreign policy stirred up bitter controversy in France. Conservatives were outraged and feared that the pope would be deposed as temporal ruler of Rome by the Italian nationalists. On the other hand, the long-silent liberal and radical opposition voiced reluctant approval. It is likely that Napoleon, whose bent toward Saint-Simonian reform ideas was strong, had never been very comfortable in his alliance with the conservatives and welcomed a chance to indulge his deeper instincts. At any rate, late in 1859 he announced the first hesitant steps toward a liberal empire. Political exiles were amnestied, press controls were relaxed, and the Corps Législatif was given slightly increased authority. An even more dramatic turn toward economic liberalism soon followed; in January 1860 Napoleon negotiated a low-tariff treaty with Britain, ending the long tradition of protectionism that had insulated French producers. With this move, however, the emperor alienated the businessmen, who until now had been his strong supporters.

Some of the emperor's advisers had sharply opposed the turn toward liberalism. Events during the next decade seemed to confirm their warnings; for the empire now ran into increasingly stormy weather. The political opposition, stifled since 1851, showed little gratitude to its benefactor and took every opportunity to harass the government. In the 1863 elections, opposition candidates polled two million votes, and 35 of them were elected to the Corps Législatif—including such effective spokesmen as the Orleanist Thiers and the republican Jules Favre. A downward turn in the economy played into the hands of the opposition. Foreign policy errors added to the regime's embarrassment: Napoleon's ill-conceived intervention in Mexico, where he hoped to establish a client empire under Maximilian of Austria, proved costly and futile and seemed to threaten a conflict with the United States. And from the mid-1860s a new threat began to loom across the Rhine: the burgeoning power of Prussia, under the guidance of Otto von Bismarck.

Despite these evil portents, Napoleon clung doggedly to his liberalization venture; additional reforms were granted throughout the decade. He expressed sympathy with the workers, granted them a kind of extralegal right to form trade unions and to strike, and helped them organize mutual-aid societies. His minister of education, Victor Duruy, carried out an enlightened program of broadened public education, including the establishment of the first secondary education for girls. In 1867 the emperor restored quite considerable freedom of the press and of public assembly and further broadened the powers of the Corps Législatif. Yet the response of the voters to these concessions caused some dismay; in the elections of 1869 the opposition vote rose to 3.3 million, and the number of seats held by oppositionists more than doubled.

The emperor now faced a momentous choice: a still further dose of liberalism or a brusque return to the authoritarian empire. He chose the former alternative; in January 1870 he asked the leader of the liberal opposition, Émile Ollivier, to form a government. Ollivier supervised the drafting of a new constitution, which, though hybrid in nature, converted the empire into a quasi-parliamentary regime. The ministers were declared to be "responsible," and their powers (as well as those of the Corps Législatif) were increased. At the same time, the emperor retained most of his existing prerogatives, so that the real locus of power in case of a conflict was unclear. Nevertheless, the voters, when consulted by referendum (May 8, 1870), gave the new system a massive vote of confidence: 7 million in favour and only 1.5 million against. Outwardly, at least, it appeared that the emperor had found a widely accepted solution. But war and defeat only four months later were to prevent a fair test of the liberal empire in its final form.

THE FRANCO-GERMAN WAR

Napoleon, meanwhile, had become uncomfortably involved in a diplomatic poker game with Bismarck. Prussian victories over Denmark (1864) and Austria (1866) indicated a serious shift in the European balance of power. Napoleon, aware that he faced a severe challenge, set out to strengthen his armed forces; he proposed a tighter conscription law that would increase the size of the standing army but had to retreat in the face of public and parliamentary hostility. The crisis that finally erupted in July 1870 over the succession to the Spanish throne was clumsily handled by French officials. The French successfully blocked the accession of a Hohenzollern prince in Spain, then demanded further guarantees for the future; they thus provided Bismarck with an easy opportunity to arouse German opinion and to goad France into declaring war on July 19.

Few French or foreign observers anticipated the military disaster that followed. The French armies, sunk in routine and slow to mobilize, were not yet ready to fight when the Prussian forces under Helmuth von Moltke crossed into France. One French army, under Achille-François Bazaine, was bottled up in Metz; another, under Patrice de Mac-Mahon, was cornered at Sedan. There, on September 1, the Prussians won a clear-cut victory; Napoleon himself was taken prisoner. The regime could not survive such a humiliation. When the news reached Paris on September 4, crowds filled the streets and converged on the Corps Législatif, demanding the proclamation of a republic. The imperial officials put up no serious resistance; the revolution of September 4 was the most bloodless in French history.

THE THIRD REPUBLIC

A provisional government of national defense was set up in 1870 and took as its first task the continuation of the war against the invaders. Composed of the deputies representing Paris and formally headed by General Louis-Jules Trochu, the new government's most forceful member was Léon Gambetta, hero of the radical republicans. Gambetta, a young Parisian lawyer of provincial origin, had been elected to the Corps Législatif in 1869 and had already made his mark through his energy and eloquence. As minister of the interior and, some weeks later, minister of war as well, he threw himself into the task of improvising military resistance. His task was complicated by the advance of the Prussian forces, which, by September 23, surrounded and besieged Paris. Gambetta shortly left the city by balloon to join several members of the government at Tours. During the next four months, Gambetta's makeshift armies fought a series of indecisive battles with the Prussians in the Loire valley and eastern France. But his attempt to send a force northward to relieve Paris from siege was frustrated by Moltke and by the poor quality of the scratch French forces. Adolphe Thiers had been sent meanwhile to tour the capitals of Europe in search of support from the powers; but he returned empty-handed. By January 1871 it was clear that further armed resistance would be futile. Over Gambetta's angry protests, an armistice was signed with the Prussians on January 28, 1871.

One provision of the armistice called for the prompt election of a National Assembly with authority to negotiate a definitive treaty of peace. That election, held on February 8, produced an assembly dominated by monarchists—more than 400 of them, compared with only 200 republicans and a few Bonapartists. The decisive issue for the voters, however, had not been the nature of the future regime but simply war or peace. Most of the monarchists had campaigned for peace; the republicans had insisted on a last-ditch fight. Most Frenchmen opted for peace, though Paris and certain provinces, such as Alsace, voted heavily for republicans. When the National Assembly convened in Bordeaux on February 13, it chose the aging Orleanist Adolphe Thiers as "chief

of the executive power of the French republic." Thiers had been the most outspoken critic of Napoleon III's foreign policy and had repeatedly warned the country of the Prussian danger. He set out at once to negotiate a settlement with Bismarck; on March 1 the Treaty of Frankfurt was ratified by a large majority of the assembly. The terms were severe: France was charged a war indemnity of five billion francs plus the cost of maintaining a German occupation army in eastern France until the indemnity was paid. Alsace and half of Lorraine were annexed to the new German Empire. The German army was authorized to stage a victory march through the Arc de Triomphe in Paris. After the assembly ratified the treaty, the deputies of the lost provinces (Léon Gambetta, too) resigned their seats in protest.

THE COMMUNE OF PARIS

A few days later, the assembly transferred the seat of government from Bordeaux to Versailles. Immediately after, it was confronted by a major civil war—the rebellion of the Commune of Paris. This event, complex in itself, has been made even more difficult to understand by the mythology that later grew up around it. Karl Marx, who promptly hailed the Commune as the first great uprising of the proletariat against its bourgeois oppressors, was partly responsible for inspiring imaginative but misleading misrepresentations. There was undoubtedly a class-struggle element in the episode, but this was not the central thread. Parisians, tense and irritable after the long strain of the siege, were outraged by the action of rural France in electing a monarchist assembly committed to what they regarded as a dishonourable peace. They were further angered by the assembly's subsequent acts, notably those that ended the wartime moratorium on debts and rents, cut off further wage payments to the National Guard (which had been resuscitated in Paris after the empire fell), and transferred the capital to Versailles rather than to Paris.

Thiers, aware that Paris was in an ugly mood, thought it prudent to disarm the National Guard, which heavily outnumbered the regular army units at the government's disposition. Before dawn on March 18 he sent troops to confiscate the National Guard cannon on the butte of Montmartre. A crowd gathered; a bloody encounter ensued; two generals were caught and lynched by the mob. As violence spread through the city, Thiers hastily withdrew all troops and government offices from Paris and went to Versailles to plan his strategy. He appealed successfully to Bismarck to release French prisoners of war in order to form a siege army that could eventually force Paris to capitulate. During the next two months, this governmental force was slowly assembled. Within Paris, meanwhile, initial chaos gradually gave way to an improvised experiment in

municipal self-government. On March 26, Parisians elected a council that promptly adopted the traditional label Commune of Paris. Its membership ranged from radical republicans of the Jacobin and Blanquist variety to socialists of several different sorts—notably disciples of Proudhon, who favoured a decentralized federation of self-governing communes throughout France. These internal divisions prevented any vigorous or coherent experiments in social reform and also interfered with the Commune's efforts to organize an effective armed force. Communes on the Paris model were set up briefly in several other cities (Lyon, Marseille, Toulouse) but were quickly suppressed.

By May 21 Thiers's forces were ready to strike. In the course of "Bloody Week" (May 21–28), the Communards resisted, street by street, but were pushed back steadily to the heart of Paris. In their desperation, they executed a number of hostages (including the archbishop of Paris) and in the last days set fire to many public buildings, including the Tuileries Palace and the Hôtel de Ville. A final stand was made in Père-Lachaise Cemetery, where the last resisters were shot down against the Federalists' Wall (Mur des Fédérés)— ever since, a place of pilgrimage for the French left. Thiers's government took a terrible vengeance. Twenty thousand Communards were killed in the fighting or executed on the spot; thousands of survivors were deported to the penal islands, while others escaped into exile.

THE FORMATIVE YEARS
(1871–1905)

The repression of the Commune of Paris left its mark on the emerging republic. The various socialist factions and the newly organized labour movement were left leaderless; the resultant vacuum eventually opened the way to Marxist activists in the 1880s. Much of the working class became more deeply alienated than before, but, among moderate and conservative elements, Thiers gained added stature as the preserver of law and order against "the reds." His ruthless action probably hastened the conversion of many rural and small-town Frenchmen to the idea of a republic, because the regime had proved its toughness in handling subversion. A large number of by-elections to the assembly in July 1871 brought startling gains to the republicans: they won 99 of 114 vacancies. The voters were clearly willing to accept a republic so long as it was run by such a man as Thiers.

ATTEMPTS AT A RESTORATION

The monarchists, however, still held a comfortable majority in the assembly and continued to hope and plan for a restoration. Legitimists and Orleanists remained at odds, but a compromise seemed possible. The Bourbon pretender, the comte de Chambord ("the miracle child" of 1820), was old and childless; the Orleanist pretender, Philippe d'Orléans, comte de Paris, was young and prolific. The natural solution was to restore Chambord, with the comte de Paris as his successor. Chambord, however, refused to accept the throne except on his own terms, which implied a return to the principle of absolute royal authority, unchecked by constitutional limitations. The Orleanists and even some Legitimists found this too much to swallow. For the time being, they, too, settled for Thiers's presidential rule.

During the next two years, Thiers's position was beyond challenge, and he gave the republic vigorous and efficient leadership. He reorganized the army and worked to restore national morale; he successfully floated two bond issues that permitted the war indemnity to be paid off in 1873, thus ending the German occupation ahead of schedule. Late in 1872, however, Thiers abjured his long-held Orleanist faith and publicly announced his conversion to republicanism. The monarchists, outraged and seeing their majority in the assembly dwindling because of by-elections, found an excuse to force Thiers's resignation as provisional president (May 1873) and hastily substituted the commander of the army, Marshal Patrice de Mac-Mahon. Behind the scenes, monarchist politicians again set out to arrange an agreement between the two pretenders. Their hopes were once more sabotaged by Chambord, who again announced that he would return only on his own terms and under the fleur-de-lis flag of the old regime. The disheartened monarchists fell back on waiting for the Bourbon line to die out. But when Chambord passed from the scene in 1883, it was too late for a restoration.

THE CONSTITUTION OF THE THIRD REPUBLIC

Meanwhile, the task of writing a constitution for the republic could no longer be postponed. The assembly began its deliberations in 1873; in 1875 it adopted a series of fundamental laws, which, taken collectively, came to be known as the constitution of the Third Republic. A patchwork compromise, it established a two-house legislature (with an indirectly elected Senate as a conservative check on the Chamber of Deputies); a Council of Ministers (cabinet), responsible to the Chamber; and a president, elected for seven years by the two houses, with powers resembling those of a constitutional monarch. The label *republic* was approved by a single-vote margin. Monarchists believed that this system could be easily converted to their purposes once the right monarch was available. The constitution left untouched many aspects of the French governmental structure, notably the centralized administrative system inherited from Napoleon I, the hierarchy of courts and judges, and the Concordat of 1801, governing church-state relations. At the end of 1875 the National Assembly at last dissolved itself, and the provisional phase of the Third Republic came to an end.

The new Senate, which heavily over-represented rural France, was safely monarchist from the outset; and the term of President Mac-Mahon, a loyal monarchist, ran until 1880. But when the first Chamber of Deputies was elected in 1876, the republicans won more than two-thirds of the seats. A period of severe friction between Mac-Mahon and the Chamber followed, and a crisis in May 1877 produced a total deadlock. Mac-Mahon dissolved the Chamber and called on the voters' support, but again they opted for the republic, by a narrower but clear-cut margin. Léon Gambetta, who had returned to political life and had led the republicans during the campaign, called on Mac-Mahon to "give in or get out." The president gave in, naming a premier acceptable to the republican majority. Two years later partial elections gave the republicans control of the Senate, and Mac-Mahon shortly found an excuse to resign. He was replaced by a colourless republican, Jules Grévy, who was believed to favour a reduced role for the president.

REPUBLICAN FACTIONS

With the republican regime apparently safe from outside attack, rival factions developed among the republicans. During the 1880s the labels Radical and Opportunist began to be attached to the two wings of the republican movement. On the left, the Radicals saw themselves as heirs to the Jacobin tradition: they stood for a strong centralized regime, intransigent anticlericalism, an assertive nationalism in foreign policy, a revision of the constitution to prune out its monarchical aspects, and such social reforms as labour laws and a graduated income tax; their most colourful spokesman was Georges Clemenceau, a ferocious debater and duelist who specialized in overthrowing cabinets. The Opportunists (so named by a satiric journalist because of their penchant for compromises and postponements) occupied the centre seats in the Chamber: their stance was more cautious and their techniques gradualist; they were content to work within the system, and they aimed to restrict governmental interference in the affairs of private citizens. Only on the issue of the church's role in politics and education were the two factions in general agreement.

OPPORTUNIST CONTROL

Between 1879 and 1899 the Opportunists, with only brief interruptions, controlled the machinery of government. Gambetta, their most dynamic leader, had begun his career as an outspoken Radical, but in time his political instincts had prevailed. The other Opportunist leaders—men such as President Grévy and Jules Ferry—disliked Gambetta's flamboyance, however, and feared his alleged dictatorial ambitions; they kept him out of the premiership save for a brief interlude in 1881–82, shortly before his death. Ferry served as premier or in other key cabinet posts during most of the period from 1880 to 1885 and left his mark on two institutions: the public school system and the colonial empire. His school laws made primary education free, compulsory, and secular, with religious teaching in the public schools replaced by "civic education"; a strong anticlerical bias thenceforth marked French public education. Ferry's support of various colonial expeditions—sometimes behind the back of the Chamber—gave France protectorates over Tunisia and in Vietnam (Annam and Tonkin), a large new colony in the Congo basin, and an initial foothold in Madagascar. This expansionist policy, unpopular at the time, led later generations to call Ferry the founder of the French empire.

In the 1885 elections the monarchists, Bonapartists, and Radicals all made significant gains, partly because of boredom with the Opportunists, Catholic resentment over the school laws, and revived agitation by socialist organizers. The Opportunists, lacking a clear majority in the Chamber, sought Radical support to form a cabinet; the Radicals insisted on the inclusion of General Georges Boulanger as minister of war. Within a few weeks Boulanger was the most talked-about man in France. He restored the tradition of military parades and rode at their head; he instituted popular reforms in the army; and he spoke out in chauvinistic fashion against the Germans, thus reviving the memory of 1871 and the lost provinces. The unnerved Opportunist leadership dropped him from the cabinet and sent him in 1887 to an obscure provincial command. But Boulanger's backers urged him to plunge into politics and began to enter his name in by-elections. Privately, monarchist and Bonapartist agents also made contact with Boulanger, promising financial support and hoping to use him for their cause.

By 1889 the Boulanger movement had become a major threat to the regime. The government had placed him on the retired list, but this merely freed him to run openly for office on a vague program of constitutional revision. He triumphed in a series of by-elections, but his goal was the parliamentary election of 1889, which he hoped to turn into a kind of national plebiscite. Just prior to the election, however, believing that he was about to be arrested for subversive activities, Boulanger took flight to Brussels. His movement gradually disintegrated; word leaked out of his dealings with the monarchists, and his supporters fell away. The Opportunists' hold on the republic was strengthened by the discomfiture of those on both right and left who had been taken in by this adventurer.

A new crisis soon arose for the regime: the Panama Scandal. Ferdinand, vicomte de Lesseps, the noted French engineer who had built the Suez Canal, had organized a joint-stock company to cut a canal across the Isthmus of Panama. The venture proved difficult and costly; in 1889 the company collapsed, and large numbers of shareholders were stripped of their savings. Demands for a parliamentary investigation proved ineffective until 1892, when a muckraking journalist named Édouard Drumont obtained evidence that agents of the company had bribed a large number of politicians and journalists in a desperate effort to get funds to keep the company afloat. The directors of the company and several deputies and senators were brought to trial in 1893, but the outcome was on the whole a whitewash. The regime survived the scandal, but the effects were more serious than first appeared to be the case. Cynicism about the honesty of the republic's political leadership bolstered the rising socialist movement; in 1893 almost 50 socialists won seats in the Chamber. Clemenceau, unjustly accused of involvement in the scandal, was defeated; and many prominent Opportunists, tainted by the affair, withdrew and were replaced by such younger men as Raymond Poincaré and Louis Barthou, who thenceforth preferred to call themselves Progressists or Moderates.

The dramatic socialist gains in 1893 resulted only partly from the Panama Scandal. For more than a decade socialism had been gaining strength among the increasingly class-conscious urban workers. The movement was weakened, however, by multiple splits into antagonistic factions. The Marxist party created by Jules Guesde in 1880 broke up two years later into Guesdists and followers of Paul Brousse—the latter group popularly called Possibilists because of their gradualist temper. In 1890 a third faction broke away, headed by Jean Allemane and limited to simon-pure proletarian members. Alongside these Marxist sects there were the Blanquistes (disciples of Auguste Blanqui [1805–81]), the anarchists (whose terrorist campaign in the early 1890s earned them wide notoriety), and a considerable scattering of independent socialists (mainly intellectuals, notably Jean Jaurès). By 1900 the parties had been reduced to the two led by Guesde and Jaurès, which merged in 1905 to form the French Section of the Workers' International (Section Française de l'Internationale Ouvrière; SFIO), known as the Socialist Party.

The trade union movement, however, refused to join forces with the socialists. Trade unions were finally legalized in 1884 and joined together to form a national General Labour Confederation (Confédération Générale du Travail; CGT) in 1895. CGT leaders rejected political action in favour of direct action—sabotage, boycotts, strikes, and especially the general strike, which they saw as the ultimate weapon that would transform France into a workers' state. This doctrine, known as revolutionary syndicalism, made the French trade union movement appear to be one of the most radical in Europe. In practice, however, the trade union rank and file was less revolutionary than its leadership.

THE DREYFUS AFFAIR

The 1890s also saw the Third Republic's greatest political and moral crisis—the Dreyfus Affair. In 1894 Captain Alfred Dreyfus, a career army officer of Jewish origin, was charged with selling military secrets to the Germans. He was tried and convicted by a court-martial and sentenced to life imprisonment on Devil's Island off the South American coast. Efforts by the Dreyfus family to reopen the case were frustrated by the general belief that justice had been done. But secrets continued to leak to the German embassy in Paris, and a second officer, Major Marie-Charles-Ferdinand Esterhazy, became suspect. The chief of army counterintelligence, Colonel Georges Picquart, eventually concluded that Esterhazy and not Dreyfus had been guilty of the original offense, but his superior officers refused to reopen the case. Rumours and scraps of evidence soon began to appear in the press; and a few politicians, notably Clemenceau, took up Dreyfus's cause. But the army high command refused to discuss the affair, although army officers leaked documents to the press in an effort to discredit the critics. Each leak aroused new controversy, and by 1898 the case had become a violently divisive issue. Intellectuals of the left led the fight for Dreyfus, while right-wing politicians and many Roman Catholic periodicals defended the honour of the army. The socialists were split: Jaurès insisted that no socialist could remain aloof on such a moral issue, while Guesde called the conflict a bourgeois squabble. In 1898 some of the army's most persuasive documents against Dreyfus were discovered to be forgeries. Esterhazy promptly fled to England. In a second court-martial, late

Parade celebrating Bastille Day and the end of World War I, Paris, July 14, 1919. Encyclopædia Britannica, Inc.

in 1899, Dreyfus was again found guilty but with extenuating circumstances; he received a presidential pardon and was later (1906) vindicated by a civilian court.

For a generation the affair left deep scars on French political and intellectual life. The Moderates, who had tried to avoid involvement in the affair and in the end had split into two warring factions, lost control to the Radicals. A coalition cabinet headed by René Waldeck-Rousseau, a pro-Dreyfus Moderate, took office in June 1899; the Radicals dominated the coalition, and even the socialists supported it. From then until the end of the Third Republic, the Radical Party (thenceforth called Radical-Socialist) remained the fulcrum of French political life. Both the army and the church were seriously hurt by their role in the affair; republicans of the left were more convinced than ever that both institutions were antirepublican and hostile to the rights of man enunciated during the Revolution. The new left majority retaliated by bringing the army under more rigorous civilian control and by embarking on a new wave of anticlerical legislation. Most religious orders were dissolved and exiled, and in 1905 a new law separated church and state, thus liquidating the Concordat of 1801.

FOREIGN POLICY

Meanwhile, some important successes were being scored in the field of foreign policy. For two decades after 1871 France had remained diplomatically isolated in Europe. Bismarck, to ward off potential French ideas of revenge, had shrewdly encouraged the republic's governments to embark on colonial conquest overseas and had negotiated alliances with all those European powers the French might otherwise have courted. He thus kept Austria-Hungary, Russia, and Italy in tow, while Britain chose to remain aloof in "splendid isolation." Upon Bismarck's fall in 1890, the German emperor William II (Kaiser Wilhelm) terminated the secret treaty between Germany and Russia. The Russians began to cast about for friends and looked with some distaste toward Paris. French policy makers encouraged French bankers to make loans to the Russian government and opened negotiations for an entente. In 1891 a loose agreement provided for mutual consultation in crisis; in 1894 this was broadened into a military alliance by whose terms each partner promised to aid the other in case of attack by Germany or Germany's allies.

For a decade the Franco-Russian alliance had little practical effect (though French loans did continue to flow to Russia). French diplomats turned to winning the Italians away from the Triple Alliance, and a Franco-Italian secret agreement in 1902 substantially weakened the commitment Italy had made to Germany and Austria-Hungary in 1882. Of more central importance throughout the 1890s was recurrent tension between France and Britain, who had been at odds in various parts of the world and whose colonial competition at times seemed to threaten war. Britain's South African (Boer) War added further ill feeling, and some British leaders began to urge an end to "splendid isolation" in favour of an entente with a Continental power—most probably Germany, which was seen as part of an Anglo-Saxon racial bloc. But the German government responded coolly to overtures in this direction, thus feeding the fears of British leaders who saw Germany as a threat to British interests. The British turned to France instead and found a willing partner in the foreign minister Théophile Delcassé. A visit to Paris by King Edward VII in 1903 helped pave the way to the Anglo-French Entente Cordiale of 1904, which resolved all outstanding colonial conflicts between the two powers but stopped short of military alliance. The new entente was consolidated a year later, when French moves to take over Morocco as a protectorate were resented by the Germans, who thought they saw an opportunity to break up the new entente. Kaiser Wilhelm offered Germany's support to the sultan of Morocco; this action irritated the

British and led them to promise France strong support. In the conference of powers that followed at Algeciras, Spain, in 1906, France had to be content with special privileges rather than a protectorate in Morocco; but the Entente Cordiale was reinforced, and it was Germany that thenceforth began to complain of isolation.

THE PREWAR YEARS

From 1899 to 1905 a fairly coherent coalition of left-wing and centre parties (the so-called Bloc Républicain) provided France with stable government. The cabinets headed by Waldeck-Rousseau in 1899–1902 and Émile Combes in 1902–05 managed to liquidate the Dreyfus Affair and to carry through the anticlerical reforms that culminated in the separation of church and state. The Entente Cordiale and the Russian alliance ensured France a more influential voice in European affairs. France possessed a colonial empire second only to Britain's in size. A new period of economic growth set in after the mid-1890s. Not surprisingly, later generations were to look back on the pre-1914 decade as *la belle époque* ("the beautiful age").

Still, some sources of sharp dissatisfaction and conflict remained. Many Roman Catholics were outraged by the triumph of the anticlericals, and they responded to the Vatican's urging to sabotage the new system. They resisted (sometimes violently) the transfer of church property to state ownership and refused to establish lay associations to govern the church. By 1907, however, resistance was clearly futile, and they began to accept the separation law as an accomplished fact. A difficult period followed for the church. The recruitment of priests fell off sharply, and many Catholic schools were closed for lack of funds. In the long run, however, the separation law reduced the intensity of conflict between Catholics and anticlericals. There was less reason for republicans to suspect and denounce a disestablished church.

A vocal minority on the right remained unreconciled to the radical republic and rallied round the banner of the Action Française ("French Action"), headed by Charles Maurras. This organization had developed at the height of the Dreyfus Affair as a focal point for intellectuals who opposed a new trial for Dreyfus. Maurras, an aspiring young writer from the south, quickly emerged as its theorist and leader. In his view, France had gone astray in 1789 and had since been dominated by the "four alien nations"—Jews, Freemasons, Protestants, and *métèques* ("aliens"). He preached a return to stable institutions and an organic society, in which the monarchy and the church would be essential pillars. Maurras appealed to many traditionalists, professional men, churchmen, and army officers. Action Française readily resorted to both verbal and physical violence, and its organized bands, the Camelots du Roi, anticipated the tactics of later fascist movements. By 1914 Maurras's movement, though still relatively small, was the most coherent and influential enemy of the republic.

Equally serious was the alienation of much of the working class. The main labour-union federation, CGT, remained officially committed to revolutionary syndicalism; it rejected political action as a useless diversion of the proletariat's energies and exalted the idea of the general strike as the proper weapon to destroy bourgeois society. Although the CGT attracted only about 10 percent of French workers (most workers stubbornly refused to join any union), it was aggressive enough to cause sporadic turmoil during 1906–10. Several major strikes were broken by forcible repression; the government either called out troops or mobilized the strikers (who were also reservists) into the army. Proposals for labour-reform legislation drew little support in a parliament dominated by representatives of the bourgeoisie and the peasantry.

Despite the CGT, most workers by now were voting for the new unified Socialist Party. But the SFIO refused to permit its deputies to participate in or support bourgeois cabinets (a policy dictated to the French party in 1904 by the Second International, dominated by the German socialists) and thus condemned itself to an oppositionist stance in parliament. This destroyed the left-wing coalition that had given France stable cabinets from 1899 to 1905. Socialist strength continued to rise, and by 1914 the party was second only to the Radicals in the Chamber of Deputies. Although

its doctrine remained rigorously Marxist, in deference to the instructions of the International, the party's conduct was much more flexible. Jaurès, whose "humanitarian" socialism was in large part derived from an older French heritage of left-wing thought, guided the Socialists in parliament toward informal cooperation with the bourgeois left in an effort to achieve domestic social reforms and an internationalist, antimilitarist foreign policy. Jaurès's central concern during the pre-1914 decade was to avert the general war that he saw looming ahead in Europe.

The Socialist withdrawal from the Bloc Républicain in 1905 forced the Radicals to look to the other centre parties as coalition partners. Until 1914—and, indeed, most of the time until 1940—France was governed by heterogeneous centre coalitions in which the Radicals most often held the key posts. In 1906 the Radical Georges Clemenceau began a three-year premiership. He proposed a long list of social reforms, including the eight-hour day and an income tax, but parliament blocked virtually all of them. More surprising was Clemenceau's ruthless suppression of strikes and his vigorous, nationalistic foreign policy. In 1907 his government sponsored a rapprochement between Britain and Russia that completed the triangle of understandings thenceforth called the Triple Entente. But Clemenceau refused to risk war through all-out support of his Russian ally during the Bosnian crisis of 1908. When his cabinet fell in 1909,

Clemenceau had effectively alienated his own Radical Party and seemed unlikely ever to return to high office.

Clemenceau's successors, Aristide Briand and Joseph Caillaux, undertook a policy of détente in European affairs. Briand, like Clemenceau, belied his left-wing origins by forcibly repressing a major strike in 1910; in foreign affairs, however, he preferred a policy of coexistence with Germany. Caillaux pushed this latter experiment even further. In 1911 he had to deal with a new crisis in Morocco, where the French were again driving toward a protectorate against German objections. When the Germans sent a gunboat to Morocco, Caillaux made an effort at appeasement, handing over to Germany a slice of the Congo region as compensation. French patriots were outraged; the Caillaux cabinet was overthrown and replaced in January 1912 by one headed by Raymond Poincaré.

There were signs of a changing intellectual mood in the country, especially among young Frenchmen. A nationalist revival affected many Frenchmen who for a decade had grown increasingly anxious about what they regarded as the puzzling and threatening attitude of Germany's post-Bismarckian leadership; they looked once more to the army as the nation's bulwark, and its prestige was on the rise. These nationalist tendencies found their embodiment in Poincaré, whose intransigent patriotism and determination to stand up to Germany were beyond doubt. As premier in 1912–13 Poincaré

devoted himself to strengthening the armed forces and to reinvigorating France's alliance system. An agreement with the British provided for a new sharing of naval responsibilities: the French concentrating in the Mediterranean, the British in the North Sea. Poincaré made a state visit to Russia to revive the sagging Franco-Russian alliance. In January 1913 he was elected to the presidency of the republic, where, he believed, he could ensure continuity of policy during his seven-year term. In 1913 the size of the standing army was increased by lengthening the conscription period from two to three years.

Poincaré found bitter opposition on the left. The socialists were strongly antimilitarist and hoped for an eventual reconciliation with Germany via collaboration between the two socialist parties. They clung to the belief that the working class everywhere could block war by resorting to a general strike. A large segment of the Radical Party followed the Caillaux line, favouring Franco-German collaboration through such ventures as banking consortia for joint investment abroad. Much of rural France also lacked enthusiasm for the new nationalistic mood. The combined strength of this opposition was revealed in the parliamentary elections of 1914, when the parties of the left won a narrow victory.

WORLD WAR I

Before a change in policy could be imposed, however, a new crisis in the

Balkans threatened a general war. The assassination of the Austrian archduke Francis Ferdinand in Sarajevo (now in Bosnia and Herzegovina) on June 28, 1914, inaugurated five weeks of feverish negotiations, in which France's role has been much debated. Some historians have accused Poincaré and his supporters of a willingness to go to the brink of war rather than seek a negotiated settlement or use restraint on the Serbs and Russians; Poincaré's state visit to St. Petersburg at the height of the crisis has been seen as an occasion for a French promise of full support to Russia. A more judicious view is that many French statesmen had long seen the possibility and even the likelihood of a general war, and they suspected that the German government desired such a war; the Poincaré group believed that under these circumstances France could not risk the loss of its allies. French support of the Serbs and the Russians, according to this view, was thus inspired by a calculated judgment regarding French security.

Germany's declaration of war against France on August 3 produced a spontaneous outburst of patriotic sentiment. Trade-union and socialist leaders, some of whom had been on a governmental list of dangerous subversives to be arrested in case of war, rallied to the colours. A national union cabinet was formed. Parliament, after voting war credits, went into an extended recess, handing over the conduct of the war to the cabinet and the high command. During the initial months the high command made most of the crucial decisions; the cabinet accorded almost unlimited freedom of action to the commander in chief, General Joseph Joffre, assuming that the war would last only a few weeks and that civilian interference would only prolong hostilities.

Joffre's war plans for an immediate advance across the frontier into the lost provinces of Alsace and Lorraine were suspended when German forces struck through Belgium and threatened late in August to envelop Paris. Joffre managed to blunt the German attack and force the Germans to more defensible positions. The rival armies dug into trench positions that remained largely static until 1918. Meanwhile, the French high command continued to believe that the fate of France would be decided on the Western Front. In 1916 a powerful German artillery attack on the French fortress positions surrounding Verdun lasted from February to June and resulted in 380,000 French casualties (162,000 dead) and 330,000 German casualties (143,000 dead). For the French, the hero of Verdun was the sector commander, General Philippe Pétain.

Joffre was by now under heavy criticism in Paris. Both the cabinet and the Chamber were determined to assert greater control over the war effort, so that the high command's authority was steadily whittled away. Joffre was finally replaced in late 1916 by General Robert Nivelle. All through 1917, rival factions in the Chamber debated the conduct of the war, backing different generals and threatening cabinet crises. Worse still, morale among the troops reached a dangerous low point in 1917, culminating in serious mutinies that affected 54 French divisions. Pétain, who replaced Nivelle in May, managed to achieve stability by a judicious combination of severity and concessions.

Nevertheless, by autumn 1917 there was widespread defeatism in France and much talk of a "white peace." The Radical leader Caillaux was prepared to try for negotiations with the Germans; but his chance never came. When the cabinet of Premier Paul Painlevé was overthrown in November 1917, President Poincaré recalled Clemenceau to the premiership. Clemenceau stood for a fight to the finish. At age 76 he still had enormous energy and doggedness, and he infused a new spirit into the country. In March 1918, when the Germans launched a last major offensive in the West, Clemenceau replaced the cautious and pessimistic Pétain with a more attack-minded general, Ferdinand Foch, and persuaded the British as well to accept him as supreme commander. The German drive was checked. On November 11 an armistice was signed in Foch's railway car near Compiègne.

The victory was won at enormous cost for France. Of the 8 million Frenchmen mobilized, 1.3 million had been killed and almost 1 million crippled. Large parts of northeastern France, the nation's most advanced industrial and agricultural area, were devastated. Industrial production had fallen to 60 percent of the prewar level; economic growth had been set back by a decade. The enormous cost of the war seriously undermined the franc and foreshadowed many years of currency fluctuation. Even deeper, though largely hidden, were the psychological lesions caused by the strain of protracted warfare and by the sentiment that France could not again endure such a test.

At the Paris Peace Conference in 1919, Clemenceau, as the principal French negotiator, declared that his goal was to ensure the nation's security against renewed German aggression. He sought, therefore, to reduce Germany's power in every possible fashion and to surround Germany with strong barrier nations. He knew, however, that France could not dictate the peace terms and that he would have to compromise with the Americans and British, to whom he looked for aid in case of German resurgence. His stubborn advocacy of French demands irritated France's wartime allies; but his willingness to compromise in the end alienated many Frenchmen, who charged him with sacrificing the nation's security. The critics—who included Poincaré and Foch—were particularly outraged when Clemenceau abandoned his initial demand that Germany give up all territory west of the Rhine and that the Saar basin be annexed to France. These and other concessions led many right-wing deputies to oppose the Treaty of Versailles when it was presented for ratification in the autumn of 1919. Joining the opposition were the Socialists, who argued that the treaty was too harsh and that democratic Germany should not be punished for the sins of the kaiser. A

MAGINOT LINE

The fact that certain modern fortresses had held out against German artillery during World War I, as well as the admitted saving in military manpower, induced France to build the celebrated Maginot Line as a permanent defense against German attack. The elaborate defensive barrier in northeast France was constructed in the 1930s and named after its principal creator, André Maginot, who was France's minister of war in 1929–31. This ultramodern defensive fortification showed traces of the old circular system of fortifications, but its dominant feature was linear. The Maginot Line was, from the standpoint of the troops, a tremendous advance over previous fortifications. Its concrete was thicker than anything theretofore known and its guns heavier. In addition, there were air-conditioned areas for the troops, and the line was usually referred to as being more comfortable than a modern city. There were recreation areas, living quarters, supply storehouses, and underground rail lines connecting various portions of the line. Strongpoints had been established in depth, capable of being supported by troops moved underground by rail.

Unfortunately, the line covered the French–German frontier, but not the French–Belgian. Thus the Germans in May 1940 outflanked the line. They invaded Belgium on May 10, continued their march through Belgium, crossed the Somme River, and on May 12 struck at Sedan at the northern end of the Maginot Line. Having made a breakthrough with their tanks and planes, they continued around to the rear of the line, making it useless.

majority of the Chamber, however, reluctantly ratified Versailles and vowed to assure its enforcement to the letter.

THE INTERWAR YEARS

Frenchmen concentrated much of their energy during the early 1920s on recovering from the war. The government undertook a vast program of reconstructing the devastated areas and had largely completed that task by 1925. To compensate for manpower losses, immigration barriers were lowered, and two million foreign workers flooded into the country. Underlying all other concerns, however, was anxiety about the nation's security and about financing the costs of war and reconstruction. The peace settlement, in the eyes of many Frenchmen, had not provided adequate guarantees; and, except among Socialists and Radicals, there was little confidence in the League of Nations. American and British promises to aid France in case of future attack had been written into the treaty, but they became meaningless when the U.S. Senate rejected Versailles.

GERMAN REPARATIONS

The general elections of November 1919 resulted in a massive majority for the right-wing coalition called the Bloc National. The new Chamber set out to enforce the Treaty of Versailles to the letter; it also sought traditional security guarantees, maintaining the largest standing army in Europe and attempting to encircle Germany with a ring of military allies (Belgium and Poland in 1920-21; Czechoslovakia, Romania, and Yugoslavia in 1924–27). But the central issue was that of German reparations. A clause in the treaty had ascribed war guilt to the Germans and their allies and had obligated Germany to make reparations; the total sum due was calculated in 1921 at $33 billion, but the French were aware that the British hoped to see this total reduced. By the end of 1921 the British clearly favoured a reduction of the burden in order to get Germany back on its feet; this issue caused increasing strain between the British and French governments. Premier Briand, who seemed willing to compromise, was overthrown by the Chamber and replaced by the more intransigent Poincaré. Repeated German defaults on reparations deliveries led Poincaré in January 1923 to send French troops and engineers (supported by a token force of Belgians) into the Ruhr valley to force German compliance or, if necessary, to collect reparations by direct seizure. The German government attempted passive resistance but finally had to comply. Germany agreed in 1924 to a revised reparations settlement, the Dawes Plan, and the French occupation forces were withdrawn. The plan enabled the Germans to meet their obligations on schedule during the rest of the decade with the help of large American loans. In 1926 France and the United States finally reached agreement on another nagging problem—the repayment of French war debts for wartime deliveries of American munitions and other supplies.

FINANCIAL CRISIS

The aftermath of the Ruhr occupation was to cast doubt on its apparent success. The German republic was weakened by the runaway inflation of 1923, and its future clouded. The occupation had embittered Britain and the United States. Even among Frenchmen the victory had left a sour aftertaste, because the costs of the occupation forced an increase in French taxes. In the elections of 1924, Poincaré's Bloc National was beaten by a coalition of the left, the Cartel des Gauches, and the Radicals were returned to power. But their triumph was brief; they were confronted by the nation's worst financial crisis since the war. The shaky franc went into rapid decline until there seemed to be danger of complete financial collapse. Seven Cartel cabinets in 1924–26 wrestled ineffectively with the problem; at last the Cartel gave up, and Poincaré returned. The latter's reputation for decisive character and conservative views enabled him to win the bankers' support and to embark on such measures as slashing government expenses and increasing taxes. The franc began to rise, and it finally stabilized at about one-fifth of its 1914 value. Poincaré was hailed as "saviour of the franc," and, when he resigned in 1929 for reasons of health, he was acclaimed as one of the Third Republic's outstanding statesmen.

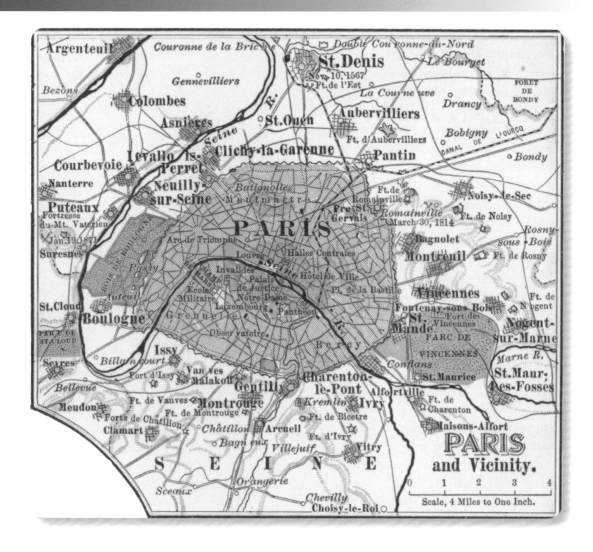

Map of Paris, *c.* 1900, from the 10th edition of *Encyclopædia Britannica.*

COLLECTIVE SECURITY

Poincaré, in his final term of office (1926–29), retained as foreign minister Aristide Briand, who had been named to that post by the Cartel in 1925 and who was to remain there for seven years almost without interruption. Briand sensed a change in the public mood after the Ruhr episode and proclaimed himself "the pilgrim of peace"; he formulated a policy that he called *apaisement.* His goal was to work for collective security through the League of Nations, for disarmament, and for a reconciliation with those Germans who favoured peaceful and cooperative methods. Briand found a ready partner in Gustav Stresemann, the German foreign minister. By the Pact of Locarno (1925), the French and German governments bound themselves not to use force to alter the existing Franco-German frontier. In subsequent years, France sponsored Germany's entry into the League of Nations and made a series of concessions softening various aspects of the Treaty of Versailles. A revised reparations agreement in 1929 (the Young Plan) further eased Germany's obligations, and in 1930 the French ended their occupation of the German Rhineland five years ahead of schedule.

INTERNAL CONFLICT ON THE LEFT

Throughout the 1920s, much of the working class remained alienated from a regime that showed little concern for social reform. The CGT had emerged from the war with redoubled strength and energy, its membership swelled by the workers who had poured into new war industries in the Paris region. The Clemenceau government had rewarded labour for its war effort by legislating the eight-hour workday in 1919; but when the unions pushed for more reforms, a deadlock ensued. An attempted general strike in May 1920 was easily broken, and thousands of discouraged and embittered workers abandoned the CGT. Labour's strength was further dissipated by the formation of rival Catholic and communist trade-union federations in 1919 and 1921.

The political influence of the workers was further impaired by a split in the Socialist Party in 1920. During the war, Socialist opposition to the slaughter had become increasingly vocal. The Bolshevik Revolution in Russia had reinforced this trend and offered a model that attracted many French Socialists. From 1918 onward, conflict intensified among Socialists over the possibility of joining Lenin's Comintern (Third International). At the party's annual congress in Tours in December 1920, Lenin's partisans carried the day by a large majority and shortly renamed their organization the French Communist Party. The minority, headed by Jaurès's disciple Léon Blum, walked out of the congress and retained the traditional name SFIO. Throughout the 1920s, antagonisms between these two Marxist factions hampered the left and prevented workable coalitions. Neither the Socialists nor the Communists would enter bourgeois-dominated cabinets; the Communists refused even to make electoral agreements in support of a single left-wing candidate. The trend through the 1920s was favourable to the Socialists, while the Communists steadily lost influence and members; in 1928 the Socialists won 107 seats in the Chamber, the Communists only 11. Many French Communists resented dictation from Moscow, and the decade saw a long series of resignations and purges; by 1930 the remnant had been thoroughly "bolshevized" on the pattern of Lenin's own party.

THE GREAT DEPRESSION AND POLITICAL CRISES

France at the end of the 1920s had apparently recovered its prewar stability, prosperity, and self-confidence. For a time it even seemed immune to the economic crisis that spread through Europe beginning in 1929; France went serenely on behind its high-tariff barrier, a healthy island in a chaotic world. By 1931, however, France in its turn succumbed to the effects of the Great Depression, and the impact was no less severe than elsewhere.

In 1932 the right-wing parties lost control of the Chamber to the Radicals and Socialists. The Radical leader Édouard Herriot returned to the premiership, with Socialist support but not participation. During the next two years Herriot and a series of successors groped for a solution to the deepening crisis. French nervousness was increased by the surge of Nazi power across the Rhine, culminating in Adolf Hitler's accession to the chancellorship in January 1933. Right-wing movements in France—some openly fascist, others advocating a more traditional authoritarianism—grew in size and activity. By 1934 the shaky coalition was at the mercy of an incident—the Stavisky scandal, a sordid affair that tarnished the reputations of several leading Radicals. Antiparliamentary groups of the far right seized the occasion to demonstrate against the regime; on February 6 a huge rally near the Chamber of Deputies degenerated into a bloody battle with armed police, during which 15 rioters were killed and 1,500 injured. Premier Édouard Daladier, confronted by a threat of civil war, resigned in favour of a national union cabinet under former president Gaston Doumergue. The regime survived the crisis, but serious stress persisted. Right-wing agitation was countered by unity of action on the left, grouping all the left-wing parties and the CGT; even the Communists participated in this effort, which culminated in 1935 in the formation of the Popular Front.

Doumergue's government had meanwhile disintegrated when Radical ministers resigned over the premier's increasingly authoritarian tone. Doumergue was soon replaced by Pierre Laval, a former socialist who had migrated toward the right. Laval embarked on a vigorous but unpopular attempt to combat the Depression through traditional techniques: sharp cuts in government spending and increased taxes. These policies wrecked his cabinet early in 1936 and became campaign issues in the parliamentary election that spring. That election, probably the most bitterly contested since 1877, gave the Popular Front a narrow majority of the popular vote and a large majority in the Chamber. The Socialists for the first time became the largest party; but the greatest proportional gain went to the Communists, who jumped from 10 to 72 seats.

Blum, the Socialist leader, became premier. An intellectual, Blum was the first French premier of Jewish origin. His ministers were mostly Socialists and Radicals; the Communists refused his urgent invitation to participate. At the very outset, a wave of sit-down strikes spread throughout the country, expressing workers' pent-up resentment toward past governments and their determination to get what they considered to be justice. Blum persuaded industrial leaders to grant immediate wage increases, which ended the strike. Then he pushed additional reforms through parliament: the 40-hour workweek, paid vacations, collective bargaining, and the seminationalization of the Bank of France. Many other reform bills, however, were stalled in committee or in the Senate, which remained much more conservative than the Chamber.

Blum's social reforms were costly and controversial and were not buttressed by a program of economic reforms that might have stimulated production and restored confidence. Production surged briefly, then lagged again; unemployment remained high, rising prices offset wage gains, a flight of capital set in. When Blum attempted to impose exchange controls, the Senate rebelled and overthrew his cabinet (June 1937). The Popular Front held together for another year, but the Socialists and Radicals were irretrievably divided on economic policy. In April 1938 France returned once more to the usual pattern of unstable centre coalitions, with the Socialists in opposition. The Radical Daladier served as premier in 1938–40; his finance minister, Paul

Women in the Garden, *oil on canvas by Claude Monet, 1866–67; in the Louvre, Paris.* Giraudon/ Art Resource, New York

Reynaud, suspended most of the Popular Front reforms and sought economic recovery through more orthodox policies favoured by business.

GERMAN AGGRESSIONS

Meanwhile, Hitler's accession had placed French governments in an increasingly grave foreign-policy dilemma. By 1934 many French leaders believed that a return of "Poincarism" was in order, and

Doumergue's foreign minister, Louis Barthou, set out to reinforce and extend France's alliance system. He reaffirmed French ties with Poland and the "Little Entente" countries and sought new understandings with both Italy and the Soviet Union. Barthou's assassination in late 1934 weakened the new alliance policy, though Laval in 1935 paid visits to both Rome and Moscow and actually signed a mutual assistance treaty with the U.S.S.R.

Mussolini's invasion of Ethiopia in late 1935 and Hitler's military reoccupation of the Rhineland in March 1936 were serious blows to French policy. After consulting the British, the French cabinet decided not to risk a confrontation with Hitler, who thus won a major diplomatic victory. Hitler promptly fortified the Rhine frontier, so that French guarantees of military aid to eastern European allies lost much credibility. Furthermore, Hitler and Mussolini joined forces against the status quo powers. With Italy lost, Frenchmen of the centre and right grew cool toward closer ties with the Soviet Union; they had counted on Italy to counterbalance Soviet influence. France found itself dangerously isolated, dependent on the small eastern European countries and on the uncertain prospect of British military support in crisis. Not surprisingly, French policy after 1936 showed signs of weakness and drift.

The outbreak of the Spanish Civil War in July 1936 posed a severe problem of conscience for Blum's Popular Front government: whether to send aid to the Spanish republic, the only other Popular Front regime in Europe. Reluctantly, Blum remained aloof; his Radical allies strongly opposed intervention and threatened to bring down the cabinet.

A new crisis developed in March 1938, when Hitler's troops for the first time crossed a frontier—into Austria. The French and British confined themselves to formal protests. German pressure on Czechoslovakia followed. Although France was formally committed to aid Czechoslovakia in case of aggression, Premier Daladier succumbed to British pressure to appease Hitler by a compromise settlement. The Munich Agreement of September 30 provided a breathing space but caused sharp dissension and self-doubt in France. When Hitler occupied what was left of Czechoslovakia in March 1939, it appeared to be too late for successful diplomatic or military resistance to Hitler, yet a failure to resist would hand over the Continent to German domination. From April until August the French and British sought to bring the Soviet Union into a joint pact against Hitler, with the French pressing the reluctant British to take the risks involved. A Soviet decision to break off negotiations and to sign a pact with Hitler instead was the last in a long chain of disasters for France. On September 3, two days after Germany invaded Poland, the French and British governments reluctantly declared war on Germany.

French and British attempts to aid the Poles would have been ineffective even if tried. Hitler's offer of peace immediately after Poland fell was rejected by the Western Allies. The German armies smashed through the Netherlands and Belgium on May 10, 1940, and soon broke the French defensive lines near Sedan. The German blitz brought chaos all along the Allied front. In Paris, Premier Paul Reynaud (who had replaced Daladier in March) pleaded for emergency aid from Britain and the United States; the British sent some additional air units but were unwilling to denude their island of all air defense; U.S. President Franklin D. Roosevelt offered moral encouragement but not open intervention.

On June 10, with the Germans approaching Paris, the government departed for Tours and declared Paris an open city. British Prime Minister Winston Churchill twice flew to Tours in an effort to keep France in the war. But Reynaud, who favoured continued resistance (from North Africa, if necessary), rapidly lost ground to the defeatists in his cabinet, headed by Pétain. On June 14 the cabinet left Tours for Bordeaux. Churchill, in a last desperate effort, proposed a pact of "indissoluble union" that would merge France and Britain as a single nation. By the time the proposal reached Bordeaux on June 16, however, the Pétain faction had gained control of the cabinet. Reynaud resigned that evening; Pétain was appointed in his place and asked Germany for surrender terms. On June 22 an armistice was signed with the Germans, near Compiègne, in the same railway car that had been the scene of Foch's triumph in 1918. The armistice provided for the maintenance of a quasi-sovereign French state and for the division of the country into an occupied zone (northern France plus the western coast) and an unoccupied southern zone. France was made responsible for the German army's occupation costs. The French army was reduced to 100,000 men and the navy disarmed in its home ports.

SOCIETY AND CULTURE UNDER THE THIRD REPUBLIC

Under the Third Republic the middle and lower sectors of society came to share political and social dominance with the rich notables. Universal suffrage gave them a new political weapon; France's peculiar socioeconomic structure gave them political weight.

ECONOMY

Republican France remained a nation of small producers, traders, and consumers. The surge of industrialization that marked the era of Napoleon III had stopped short of a full-scale industrial revolution. The new dynamic sector of the economy was far outweighed by a static or slowly changing sector. The bulk of industry remained smaller and more dispersed than in other industrializing countries. As late as the decade before 1914, 90 percent of France's industrial enterprises employed fewer than five workers each; in the extensive textile and clothing trades, more than half of the employees still worked at home rather than in factories. Commerce and trade followed the same pattern, with small shops and banks surviving in profusion. Similarly, rural France was dominated by small, subsistence family farms. The proportion of farmers in the total active population, which stood at 52 percent in 1870, was about 45 percent in 1914 and 35 percent in 1930. When grouped together, the small independent producers, traders, and farmers far outnumbered any other segment of society, including the proletariat.

The reasons given for this slow pace of socioeconomic change are varied: shortages of basic natural resources, a tradition of specialization in luxury items, a code of mores that emphasized prudent management rather than risky experiment and that regarded as ideal the "family firm," small enough to be financed and managed by the owners alone. In any case, French industrialization took a different form from that of England or Germany. An initial burst of growth in the 1850s was followed by several decades of much more gradual expansion, which did not threaten the existing structure of society and the underlying value system. Most segments of society were reasonably satisfied and felt no threat to their way of life (only the members of the working class, both urban and agricultural, considered themselves outsiders and victims rather than participants); thus, the stability of the system was ensured. Not until well into the 20th century, and especially after 1918, did this state of affairs begin to change.

The governments of the Third Republic were representative of the small independents and responsive to their interests. Most of the bourgeoisie and the peasantry wanted a laissez-faire policy: low taxes, hands off the affairs of private citizens. There was little popular enthusiasm for costly ventures in foreign policy or expensive social reforms; the major exception—the conquest of colonial empire—had to be accomplished somewhat secretively and with limited resources. Only in tariff policy was laissez-faire flagrantly violated by the government, with the active consent of its bourgeois supporters. When the low-tariff treaties of Napoleon III expired in 1877, the government promptly returned to protectionism. Much of French agriculture and industry was thereby protected against more efficient foreign producers and insulated against the need for modernization. The short-range interests of the small independent producer were thus guaranteed; the prospect of harm to his longer-range interests—as well as to those of the nation as a whole—was not yet clear.

From 1873 to the mid-1890s the French economy experienced a period of slackness. This trend reflected a condition affecting most of Europe, although France suffered a special blow when an epidemic of phylloxera in 1875–87 destroyed one-third of the nation's vineyards. From 1896 to 1914 industrial output rose impressively, exports increased by 75 percent, and prices returned to the pre-slump level. This upturn was also generally Europe-wide rather than peculiar to France; but some special factors, such as the opening of a vast new iron-ore field in French Lorraine, did increase the French rate of industrial expansion. By 1914 French Lorraine had become the major centre of French iron and steel production, and France had become the world's largest exporter of raw iron ore (primarily to Germany). Yet the French were being outpaced by rivals. In 1870 France had still ranked as the world's second industrial and trading nation; by 1914 it had fallen to a poor fourth. Much of the liquid capital that might have been used for business expansion at home was being siphoned off into foreign investment; by 1914 almost one-third of such available French capital had been placed abroad—one-fourth of that sum in Russia and only one-tenth in the French colonies. Yet few Frenchmen had serious doubts about the course of economic policy under the Third Republic.

Only after World War I, and particularly after 1930, were such doubts widely shared. The disruptive impact of the war exceeded the understanding not only of most citizens but also of most political leaders. Efforts to return to normality were futile because the postwar world and France had changed vastly. The enormous cost of a four-year mobilization, of reconstruction, and of war debts had to be borne. By the time of the Great Depression, the government had been forced to write off a large share of war costs by devaluing the franc (1928) to one-fifth of its old value, costing many Frenchmen on fixed incomes much of their savings and shaking their confidence in the future. Still, no large group of embittered déclassés was created, ripe for the appeals of a demagogue. And after 1926 there was a brief resurgence of prosperity, so that by the end of the decade the indexes of industrial production, foreign trade, and living standards had risen well above the 1914 peak. Some illusions about the future and hopes of a happy return to prewar stability could therefore be retained.

But by 1935 industrial production had fallen to 79 percent of the 1928 level and exports to 55 percent. Registered unemployment hovered at less than 500,000, but this figure concealed the fact that many urban workers were subsisting on family farms owned by relatives. Besides, the French exported much of their unemployment; thousands of immigrant workers lost their work permits and had to return home. Not until 1938–39 did a measure of recovery set in, thanks to Reynaud's business-oriented policies plus the stimulus of rearmament. By the time war broke out again, France had barely returned to the pre-Depression level.

The workers, always outside the bourgeois consensus, were by now largely hostile to the system; most of the gains they had finally achieved in 1936 had quickly been snatched away again. But in addition many bourgeois Frenchmen now questioned the virtues of the traditional system. The 1930s therefore brought an intense fermentation of political and social thought; dozens of study groups and movements sprang up in Paris, seeking or preaching doctrines of drastic renovation and structures of government that might carry them out.

CULTURAL AND SCIENTIFIC ATTAINMENTS

The cultural climate of the later 19th century in France, as in the Atlantic world generally, was strongly marked by the current called positivism. The post-1848 generation looked with contempt on what it considered the excesses and the bad taste of the preceding Romantic era. A new interest in science and a new vogue of realism in literature and the arts prevailed during the Second Empire; it was best embodied in the novels of Gustave Flaubert and the paintings of Gustave Courbet. By the 1870s this mood had formed into what its advocates regarded as a coherent philosophical system, the content and label of which they borrowed from the French thinker Auguste Comte. These self-styled positivists placed their faith in science and reason as the path to inevitable progress, with only the remnants of superstition (surviving mainly in the church) still blocking the hopeful future. The positivist temper is manifest in the novels of Émile Zola and the paintings of Impressionists such as Édouard Manet, Claude Monet, Edgar Degas, and Pierre-Auguste Renoir.

The French also showed great creativity in pure science and made major discoveries in a wide variety of fields. Among the most notable figures were Louis Pasteur in medicine, Pierre and Marie Curie in physics, Marcelin Berthelot in chemistry, Henri Poincaré in mathematics, and Jean-Martin Charcot in psychopathology. In the social sciences the work of Gustave Le Bon and Émile Durkheim had a broad and enduring impact.

Although the positivist mood prevailed at least until World War I, it was contested by a rival current of thought that from the 1890s onward began to assert itself. To some sensitive people of artistic temperament, the positivist outlook seemed arid and narrow, neglecting the emotional side of man. This was the view of the school of poets, including Paul Verlaine and Stéphane Mallarmé, who called themselves Symbolists. A remarkable group of composers carried the upstart Neoromantic mood into music: mainstream works by composers such as Jules Massenet, Georges Bizet, and Camille Saint-Saëns were followed by the more experimental compositions of Claude Debussy and Maurice Ravel.

Of equal significance was the growing influence after 1890 of such writers and thinkers as Paul Bourget, Maurice Barrès, and Henri Bergson. Bourget's novels challenged what he called "brutal positivism" and asserted such traditional values as authority, the family, and the established order. Barrès preached what

Charles Maurras had defined as "integral nationalism"; Barrès called for a return to "the sources of national energy," which he found in historic institutions, the soil of the fatherland, and the solidarity between the living and the dead. The philosopher Bergson attacked scientific dogmatism and exalted humankind's nonrational drives—notably a creative force that he called élan vital, which he held distinguishes heroic individuals and nations from the plodding herd.

This new spirit had its parallel in political thought and action as well: in the syndicalist doctrines of Georges Sorel, in the activism of a minority in the labour movement, and in the resurgent nationalism that strongly affected many French young people in the years just before 1914. It also brought a return to the church and to an emotional patriotism. In the fine arts a new generation of painters abandoned both realism and Impressionism. These so-called Post-Impressionists were moved by an intense subjectivism, an urge to express in various ways the artist's inner vision and deeper emotions. The changed mood was best-embodied in the work of Paul Cézanne, Paul Gauguin, and the Dutch immigrant Vincent van Gogh.

The terrible strain and disillusionment of World War I weighed heavily on French cultural life during the interwar era, leading to the development of the literary and artistic movement called Dadaism. Its program of calculated nonsense was inspired by a deep revulsion against the insanity of war and the positivist view that the world had sense and meaning. Dadaism soon gave way, though, to the more durable Surrealist movement, whose principal theorist and founder was the poet André Breton. The declared goal of Surrealist writers and artists was to free man's unconscious impulses from the distorting controls of rational reflection; creativity, they said, came from deep nonrational drives.

A number of France's most notable writers, however, remained within the older humanistic tradition; yet they likewise reflected the doubts and neuroses of an age of crisis. Marcel Proust, whose massive multivolume novel *À la recherche du temps perdu* (*Remembrance of Things Past*) began to appear in 1913, used the stream-of-consciousness technique to probe, in minutely introspective fashion, into the recesses of his own mind and memory. André Gide, in similarly sensitive and introspective fashion, wrestled with the psychological difficulties arising from the conflict between a bourgeois society's values and the individual's instinctive drives.

As the mood of crisis deepened in the 1930s, so did the intensity of the challenge to old values, bringing forth men of frankly fascist temper, such as Robert Brasillach, and brutally nihilistic literary experimenters, such as Louis-Ferdinand Céline. Other writers continued to create works in the older tradition, including the supple, sensual explorations of (Sidonie-Gabrielle) Colette; the social commentary of Roger Martin du Gard, Georges Duhamel, Jules Romains, and

François Mauriac; the Neoromantic novels of André Malraux, preaching a modern gospel of heroic activism; the first writings of Jean-Paul Sartre; and the essays of Emmanuel Mounier, who was to inspire the new Catholic left after World War II.

WORLD WAR II AND THE FIFTH REPUBLIC

Although the German occupation would result in the demise of the Third Republic, the war would also provide the elements from which the republic's successors would be forged. Members of the Resistance were instrumental not only in the liberation of the country but also in the establishment of the postwar government. The most prominent among them, Charles de Gaulle, emerged as the architect of France's Fifth Republic.

WARTIME FRANCE

The German victory left the French groping for a new policy and new leadership. Some 30 prominent politicians—among them Édouard Daladier and Pierre Mendès-France—left for North Africa to set up a government-in-exile there; but Pétain blocked that enterprise by ordering their arrest on arrival in Morocco. The undersecretary of war in the fallen Reynaud cabinet, General Charles de Gaulle, had already flown to London and in a radio appeal on June 18, 1940, summoned French patriots to continue the fight; but few heard or heeded his

call in the first weeks. It was to Pétain, rather, that most of the nation looked for salvation.

THE VICHY GOVERNMENT

Parliament met at Vichy on July 9–10 to consider France's future. The session was dominated by Pierre Laval, Pétain's vice premier, who was already emerging as the strongman of the government. Laval, convinced that Germany had won the war and would thenceforth control the Continent, saw it as his duty to adapt France to the new authoritarian age. By skillful manipulation, he persuaded parliament to vote itself and the Third Republic out of existence. The vote (569 to 80) authorized Pétain to draft a new constitution. The draft was never completed, but Pétain and his advisers did embark on a series of piecemeal reforms, which they labeled the National Revolution. Soon the elements of a corporative state began to emerge, and steps were taken to decentralize France by reviving the old provinces. In the early stages of Vichy, Pétain's inner circle—except for Laval and a few others—was made up of right-wing traditionalists and authoritarians. The real pro-fascists, such as Jacques Doriot and Marcel Déat, who wanted a system modeled frankly on those of Hitler and Mussolini, soon left Vichy and settled in Paris, where they accepted German subsidies and intrigued against Pétain.

In December 1940 Pétain dismissed Laval and placed him briefly under house arrest. Laval had offended Pétain and his

ALGERIAN WAR

The movement for Algerian independence began during World War I (1914–18) and gained momentum after French promises of greater self-rule in Algeria went unfulfilled after World War II (1939–45). In 1954 the National Liberation Front (FLN) began a guerrilla war against France and sought diplomatic recognition at the UN to establish a sovereign Algerian state. Although Algerian fighters operated in the countryside—particularly along the country's borders—the most serious fighting took place in and around Algiers, where FLN fighters launched a series of violent urban attacks that came to be known as the Battle of Algiers (1956–57). French forces (which increased to 500,000 troops) managed to regain control but only through brutal measures, and the ferocity of the fighting sapped the political will of the French to continue the conflict. In 1959 Charles de Gaulle declared that the Algerians had the right to determine their own future. Despite terrorist acts by French Algerians opposed to independence and an attempted coup in France by elements of the French army, an agreement was signed in 1962, and Algeria became independent.

followers by his arrogance and his obvious taste for intrigue. His critics charged him also with attempting to bring Vichy France back into the war in alliance with the Germans. Both Laval and Pétain had accepted Hitler's invitation to a meeting at Montoire on October 24, 1940, and, during the weeks that followed, the French leaders had publicly advocated Franco-German "collaboration." Whether Laval hoped for a real Franco-German alliance remains somewhat controversial. If so, it was a futile effort because Hitler had no interest in accepting France as a trusted partner; "collaboration" remained a French and not a German slogan. Hitler tolerated the temporary existence of a quasi-independent Vichy state as a useful device to help police the country and to collect the enormously inflated occupation costs imposed by the armistice.

Laval was succeeded by another pre-war politician, Pierre-Étienne Flandin, and he, in turn, by Admiral François Darlan, who was intensely anti-British and an intriguer by nature who followed a devious path that involved continuing efforts at active collaboration with the Germans. Hitler, meanwhile, concentrated on draining France of raw materials and foodstuffs that were useful for the conduct of the war.

In April 1942 Pétain restored Laval to power, partly under German pressure. Laval retained that post until the collapse of Vichy in 1944. His role was increasingly difficult because the terrible drain of the war in the Soviet Union caused the Germans to increase their exactions. The Germans were short of manpower for their factories, and Laval, under heavy pressure, agreed to the conscription of able-bodied French workers, allegedly in return for the release of some French prisoners of war. He also assumed the task of repressing the French underground movement, whose activities hampered the delivery of supplies and men to Germany. After the war, Laval and his friends were to argue that he had played a "double game" of limited collaboration to protect France against a worse fate.

Most of Vichy's remaining autonomy and authority was destroyed in November 1942, in direct consequence of the Anglo-American landings in North Africa. Vichy troops in Morocco and Algeria briefly resisted the American invasion, then capitulated when Admiral Darlan, who happened to be visiting Algiers at the time, negotiated an armistice. On November 11 Hitler ordered his troops in the occupied zone to cross the demarcation line and to take over all of France. The Vichy government survived, but only on German sufferance—a shadowy regime with little power and declining prestige.

THE RESISTANCE

Vichy's decline was paralleled by the rise of the anti-German underground. Within weeks of the 1940 collapse, tiny groups of men and women had begun to resist. Some collected military intelligence for transmission to London; some organized escape routes for British airmen who had been shot down; some circulated anti-German leaflets; some engaged in sabotage of railways and German installations.

The Resistance movement received an important infusion of strength in June 1941, when Hitler's attack on the Soviet Union brought the French Communist Party into active participation in the anti-German struggle. It was further reinforced by the German decision to conscript French workers; many draftees took to the hills and joined guerrilla bands that took the name Maquis (meaning "underbrush"). A kind of national unity was finally achieved in May 1943, when de Gaulle's personal representative, Jean Moulin, succeeded in establishing a National Resistance Council (Conseil National de la Résistance) that joined all the major movements into one federation.

De Gaulle's original call for resistance had attracted only a handful of French citizens who happened to be in Britain at the time. But, as the British continued to fight, a trickle of volunteers from France began to find its way to his headquarters in London. De Gaulle promptly established an organization called Free France and in 1941 capped it with a body called the French National Committee (Comité National Français), for which he boldly claimed the status of a legal government-in-exile. During the next three years, first in London and then (after 1943) in Algiers, he insisted on his right to speak for France and on France's right to be heard as a Great Power in the councils of the Allies. His demands and his manner irked Churchill and Roosevelt and caused persistent tension. The U.S. government unsuccessfully attempted in 1942 to side-track him in favour of General Henri Giraud, who immediately after the Allied landings in North Africa was brought out of France to command the French armies in liberated North Africa and to assume a political role as well. De Gaulle arrived in Algiers in May 1943 and joined Giraud as copresident of a new French Committee of National Liberation. By the end of the year he had outmaneuvered Giraud and emerged as the unchallenged spokesman for French resisters everywhere. Even the Communists in 1943 grudgingly accepted his leadership.

LIBERATION

When the Allied forces landed in Normandy on June 6, 1944, the armed underground units had grown large enough to play a prominent role in the battles that followed—harassing the German forces and sabotaging railways and bridges. As the Germans gradually fell back, local Resistance organizations took over town halls and prefectures from Vichy incumbents. De Gaulle's provisional government immediately sent its own delegates into the liberated areas to ensure an orderly transfer of power. On August 19 Resistance forces in Paris launched an insurrection against the German occupiers, and on August 25 Free French units under General Jacques Leclerc entered the city. De Gaulle himself arrived later that day, and on the next he headed a triumphal parade down the Champs-Élysées. Most high-ranking Vichy officials (including Pétain and Laval) had moved eastward with the Germans; at the castle of Sigmaringen in Germany they adopted the posture of a government-in-exile.

De Gaulle's provisional government, formally recognized in October 1944 by the U.S., British, and Soviet governments, enjoyed unchallenged authority in liberated France. But the country had been stripped of raw materials and food by the Germans; the transportation system was severely disrupted by air bombardment and sabotage; 2.5 million French prisoners of war, conscripted workers, and deportees were still in German camps; and the task of liquidating the Vichy heritage threatened to cause grave domestic stress. An informal and spontaneous purge of Vichy officials or supporters had already begun in the summer of 1944; summary executions by Resistance bands appear to have exceeded 10,000.

A more systematic retribution followed. Special courts set up to try citizens accused of collaboration heard 125,000 cases during the next two years. Some 50,000 offenders were punished by "national degradation" (loss of civic rights for a period of years), almost 40,000 received prison terms, and between 700 and 800 were executed.

THE FOURTH REPUBLIC

Shortly after his return to Paris, de Gaulle announced that the citizens of France would determine their future governmental system as soon as the absent prisoners and deportees could be repatriated. That process was largely completed by midsummer 1945, soon after Germany's defeat, whereupon de Gaulle scheduled a combined referendum and election for October. Women, for the first time in French history, were granted suffrage. By an overwhelming majority (96 percent of the votes cast), the nation rejected a return to the prewar regime. The mood of the liberation era was marked by a thirst for renovation and for change.

New men of the Resistance movement dominated the constituent assembly, and the centre of gravity was heavily to the left: three-fourths of the deputies were Communists, Socialists, or Christian Democrats who had adhered to the new party of the Catholic left—the Popular Republican Movement (Mouvement Républicain Populaire).

CONSTITUTION OF THE FOURTH REPUBLIC

It soon became clear that the apparent unity forged in the Resistance was superficial and that the new political elite was sharply divided over the form of the new republic. Some urged the need for greater stability through a strong executive; others, notably the Communists, favoured concentrating power in a one-house legislature subject to grassroots control by the voters. De Gaulle remained aloof from this controversy, though it was obvious that he favoured a strong presidency. In January 1946 de Gaulle suddenly resigned his post as provisional president, apparently expecting that a wave of public support would bring him back to power with a mandate to impose his constitutional ideas. Instead, the public was stunned and confused, and it failed to react. The assembly promptly chose the Socialist Félix Gouin to replace him, and the embittered de Gaulle retired to his country estate.

The assembly's constitutional draft, submitted to a popular referendum in May 1946, was rejected by the voters. A new assembly was quickly elected to prepare a revised draft, which in October was narrowly approved by the voters. De Gaulle actively intervened in the campaign for the second referendum, denouncing the proposed system as unworkable and urging the need for a stronger executive. His ideas anticipated the system that later was to be embodied in the constitution of the Fifth Republic (1958).

POLITICAL AND SOCIAL CHANGES

The structure of the Fourth Republic seemed remarkably like that of the Third; in actual operation it seemed even more familiar. The lower house of parliament (now renamed the National Assembly) was once more the locus of power; shaky coalition cabinets again succeeded one another at brief intervals, and the lack of a clear-cut majority in the country or in parliament hampered vigorous or coherent action.

Many politicians from the prewar period turned up once again in cabinet posts.

Yet outside the realm of political structure and parliamentary gamesmanship there were real and fundamental changes. The long sequence of crises that had shaken the nation since 1930 had left a deep imprint on French attitudes. There was much less public complacency; both the routines and the values of the French people had been shaken up and subjected to challenge by a generation of upheaval. Many of the new men who had emerged from the Resistance movement into political life, business posts, or the state bureaucracy retained a strong urge toward renovation as well as to a reassertion of France's lost greatness.

This altered mood helps to explain the economic growth that marked the later years of the Fourth Republic. The painful convalescence from the ravages of war was speeded by massive aid from the United States and by the gentle persuasion (and ample credits) of Jean Monnet's Planning Commissariat (Commissariat Général du Plan), adopted in 1947. A burst of industrial expansion in most branches of the economy began in the mid-1950s, unmatched in any decade of French history since the 1850s. The rate of growth for a time rivaled that of Germany and exceeded that of most other European countries. The only serious flaw in the boom was a nagging inflationary trend that weakened the franc. Short-lived coalition cabinets were incapable of taking the painful measures needed to check this trend.

COLONIAL INDEPENDENCE MOVEMENTS

A less fortunate aspect of the national urge to reassert France's stature in the world was the Fourth Republic's costly effort to hold the colonial empire. France's colonies had provided de Gaulle with his first important base of support as leader of Free France, and, as the war continued, they had furnished valuable resources and manpower. The colonial peoples, therefore, now felt justified in demanding a new relationship with France, and French leaders recognized the need to grant concessions. But most of these leaders, including de Gaulle, were not prepared to permit any infringement on French sovereignty, either immediately or in the foreseeable future. For a nation seeking to rebuild its self-respect, the prospect of a loss of empire seemed unacceptable; most of the French, moreover, were convinced that the native peoples overseas lacked the necessary training for self-government and that a relaxation of the French grip would merely open the way to domination by another imperial power. The constitution of 1946 therefore introduced only mild reforms: the empire was renamed the French Union, within which the colonial peoples would enjoy a narrowly limited local autonomy plus some representation in the French parliament.

This cautious reform came too late to win acceptance in many parts of the empire. The situation was most serious in Southeast Asia, where the Japanese had displaced the French during World War II. Japan's defeat in 1945 enabled the French to regain control of southern Indochina, but the northern half was promptly taken over by a Vietnamese nationalist movement headed by the communist Ho Chi Minh. French efforts to negotiate a compromise with Ho's regime broke down in December 1946, and a bloody eight-year war followed. In the end, the financial and psychological strain proved too great for France to bear, and, after the capture of the French stronghold of Dien Bien Phu in 1954 by the Vietnamese, the French sought a face-saving solution. A conference of interested powers at Geneva that year ended the war by establishing what was intended as a temporary division of Vietnam into independent northern and southern states. Two other segments of Indochina, the former protectorates of Laos and Cambodia, had earlier been converted by the French into independent monarchies to preserve some French influence there.

On the night of October 31, 1954, barely six months after the fighting in Indochina ended, Algerian nationalists raised the standard of rebellion. By 1958 more than a half million French soldiers had been sent to Algeria—the largest overseas expeditionary force in French history. France's determination to hold Algeria stemmed from a number of factors: the presence of almost a million European settlers, the legal fiction that Algeria was an integral part of

France, and the recent discovery of oil in the southern desert. Fears that the rebellion might spread to Tunisia and Morocco led the French to make drastic concessions there; in 1956 both of these protectorates became sovereign states.

The long and brutal struggle in Algeria gravely affected the political life of the Fourth Republic and ended by destroying it. A vocal minority in France openly favoured a negotiated settlement, though no political leader dared take so unpopular a position. Right-wing activists, outraged at what they saw as the spread of defeatism, turned to conspiracy; both in Paris and in Algiers, extremist groups began to plot the replacement of the Fourth Republic by a tougher regime, headed by army officers or perhaps by General de Gaulle.

These plans had not yet matured when a cabinet crisis in April–May 1958 gave the conspirators a chance to strike. On May 13, when a new cabinet was scheduled to present its program to the National Assembly, activist groups in Algiers went into the streets in an effort to influence parliament's vote. By nightfall they were in control of the city and set up an emergency government with local army support. De Gaulle on May 15 announced that he was prepared to take power if called to do so by his fellow citizens. Two weeks of negotiations followed, interspersed with threats of violent action by the Algiers rebels. Most of the Fourth Republic's political leaders reluctantly concluded that de Gaulle's return was the only alternative to an army coup that might lead to civil war. On June 1, therefore, the National Assembly voted de Gaulle full powers for six months, thus putting a de facto end to the Fourth Republic.

THE FIFTH REPUBLIC

During his years of self-imposed exile, de Gaulle had scorned and derided the Fourth Republic and its leaders. He had briefly sought to oppose the regime by organizing a Gaullist party, but he had soon abandoned this venture as futile. Back in power, he adopted a more conciliatory line; he invited a number of old politicians to join his cabinet, but, by naming his disciple Michel Debré head of a commission to draft a new constitution, de Gaulle made sure that his own ideas would shape the future. This draft, approved in a referendum in September by 79 percent of the valid votes cast, embodied de Gaulle's conceptions of how France should be governed. Executive power was considerably increased at the expense of the National Assembly. The president of the republic was given much broader authority; he would henceforth be chosen by an electorate of local notables rather than by parliament, and he would select the premier (renamed prime minister), who would continue to be responsible to the National Assembly but would be less subject to its whims. In the new National Assembly, elected in November, the largest block of seats

was won by a newly organized Gaullist party, the Union for the New Republic (Union pour la Nouvelle République; UNR); the parties of the left suffered serious losses. In December de Gaulle was elected president for a seven-year term, and he appointed Debré as his first prime minister. The Fifth Republic came into operation on January 8, 1959, when de Gaulle assumed his presidential functions and appointed a new government.

The new president's most immediate problems were the Algerian conflict and the inflation caused by the war. He attacked the latter, with considerable success, by introducing a program of deflation and austerity. As for Algeria, he seemed at first to share the views of those whose slogan was "Algérie française"; but, as time went by, it became clear that he was seeking a compromise that would keep an autonomous Algeria loosely linked with France. The Algerian nationalist leaders, however, were not interested in compromise, while the die-hard French colonists looked increasingly to the army for support against what they began to call de Gaulle's betrayal. Open sedition followed in 1961, when a group of high army officers headed by General Raoul Salan formed the Secret Army Organization (Organisation de l'Armée Secrète; OAS) and attempted to stage a coup in Algiers. When the insurrection failed, the OAS turned to terrorism; there were several attempts on de Gaulle's life. The president pushed ahead nevertheless with his search for a settlement with the Algerians that would combine independence with guarantees for the safety of French colonists and their property. Such a settlement was finally worked out, and in a referendum (April 1962) more than 90 percent of the war-weary French voters approved the agreement. An exodus of European settlers ensued; 750,000 refugees flooded into France. The burden of absorbing them was heavy, but the prosperous French economy was able to finance the process despite some psychological strains.

The Algerian crisis sped the process of decolonization in the rest of the empire. Some concessions to local nationalist sentiment had already been made during the 1950s, and de Gaulle's new constitution had authorized increased self-rule. But the urge for independence was irresistible, and by 1961 virtually all the French territories in Africa had demanded and achieved it. De Gaulle's government reacted shrewdly by embarking on a program of military support and economic aid to the former colonies; most of France's foreign-aid money went to them. This encouraged the emergence of a French-speaking bloc of nations, which gave greater resonance to France's role in world affairs.

The Algerian settlement brought France a respite after 16 years of almost unbroken colonial wars. Prime Minister Debré resigned in 1962 and was replaced by one of de Gaulle's closest aides, Georges Pompidou. The party leaders now began to talk of amending the constitution to restore the powers of the National Assembly. Faced by this prospect, de Gaulle seized the initiative by proposing his own constitutional amendment; it provided for direct popular election of the president, thus further increasing his authority. When his critics denounced the project as unconstitutional, de Gaulle retaliated by dissolving the assembly and proceeding with his constitutional referendum. On October 28, 62 percent of those voting gave their approval, and in the subsequent elections (November) the Gaullist UNR won a clear majority in the assembly. Pompidou was reappointed prime minister.

When de Gaulle's presidential term ended in 1965, he announced his candidacy for reelection. For the first time since 1848 the voting was to be by direct popular suffrage. De Gaulle's challengers forced de Gaulle into a runoff, and his victory over the moderate leftist François Mitterrand in the second round by a 55–45 margin was closer than had been predicted but sufficed to assure him of seven more years in power. Although de Gaulle's leadership had not ended political division in France, his compatriots could not ignore the achievements of his first term. Not only had he disengaged France from Algeria without producing a civil war at home, but he could also point to continuing economic growth, a solid currency, and a stability of government that was greater than any living French citizen had known.

The mid-1960s were the golden years of the Gaullist era, with the president playing the role of elected monarch and respected world statesman. France had adjusted well to the loss of empire and to membership in the European Common Market (later the European Community), which brought the country more benefits than costs. De Gaulle could now embark on an assertive foreign policy, designed to restore what he called France's grandeur; he could indulge in such luxuries as blocking Britain's entry into the Common Market, ejecting North Atlantic Treaty Organization (NATO) forces from France, lecturing the Americans on their involvement in Vietnam, and traveling to Canada to call for a "free Quebec." He continued the Fourth Republic's initiative in developing both nuclear power and nuclear weapons—the so-called *force de frappe*. His foreign policy enjoyed broad domestic support, and the French people also seemed content with the prosperity and order that accompanied his paternalistic rule.

Beneath the surface, however, basic discontent persisted and was startlingly revealed by the crisis that erupted in May 1968. Student disorders in the universities of the Paris region had been sporadic for some time; they exploded on May 3, when a rally of student radicals at the Sorbonne became violent and was broken up by the police. This minor incident quickly became a major confrontation: barricades went up in the Latin Quarter, street fighting broke out, and the Sorbonne was occupied by student rebels, who converted it into a huge commune. The unrest spread to other universities and then to the factories as well; a wave of wildcat strikes rolled across France, eventually involving several million workers and virtually paralyzing the nation. Prime Minister Pompidou ordered the police to evacuate the Latin Quarter and concentrated on negotiations with the labour union leaders. An agreement calling for improved wages and working conditions was hammered out, but it collapsed when the rank-and-file workers refused to end their strike.

By the end of May various radical factions no longer concealed their intent to carry out a true revolution that would bring down the Fifth Republic. De Gaulle seemed incapable of grappling with the crisis or of even understanding its nature. The Communist and trade union leaders, however, provided him with breathing space; they opposed further upheaval, evidently fearing the loss of their followers to their more extremist and anarchist rivals. In addition, many middle-class citizens who had initially enjoyed the excitement lost their enthusiasm as they saw established institutions disintegrating before their eyes.

De Gaulle, sensing the opportune moment, suddenly left Paris by helicopter on May 29. Rumours spread that he was about to resign. Instead, he returned the next day with a promise of armed support, if needed, from the commanders of the French occupation troops in Germany. In a dramatic four-minute radio address, he appealed to the partisans of law and order and presented himself as the only barrier to anarchy or Communist rule. Loyal Gaullists and nervous citizens rallied round him; the activist factions were isolated when the Communists refused to join them in a resort to force. The confrontation moved from the streets to the polls. De Gaulle dissolved the National Assembly, and on June 23 and 30 the Gaullists won a landslide victory. The Gaullist Union of Democrats for the Republic (Union des Démocrates pour la République [UDR]; the former UNR), with its allies, emerged with three-fourths of the seats.

The repercussions of the May crisis were considerable. The government, shocked by the depth and extent of discontent, made a series of concessions to the protesting groups. Workers were granted higher wages and improved working conditions; the assembly adopted a university reform bill intended to modernize higher education and to give teachers and students a voice in running their institutions. De Gaulle took the occasion to shake up his cabinet; Pompidou was replaced by Maurice Couve de Murville. De Gaulle evidently sensed the emergence of Pompidou as a serious rival, for the prime minister had shown toughness and nerve during the crisis, while the president had temporarily lost his bearings. The economy also suffered from the upheaval; austerity measures were needed to stabilize things once more.

Although normalcy gradually returned, de Gaulle remained baffled and irritated by what the French called *les événements de mai* ("the events of May"). Perhaps it was to reaffirm his leadership that he proposed another test at the polls: a pair of constitutional amendments to be voted on by referendum. Their content was of secondary importance, yet de Gaulle threw his prestige into the balance, announcing that he would resign if the amendments failed to be approved. Every opposition faction seized upon the chance to challenge the president. On April 27, 1969, the amendments were defeated by a 53 to 47 percent margin, and that night de Gaulle silently abandoned his office. He returned to the obscurity of his country estate and turned once more to the writing of his memoirs. In 1970, just before his 80th birthday, he died of a massive stroke. His passing inspired an almost worldwide chorus of praise, even from those who up to then had been his most persistent critics.

FRANCE AFTER DE GAULLE

De Gaulle's departure from the scene provoked some early speculation about the survival of the Fifth Republic and of the Gaullist party (the UDR); both, after all, had been tailored to the general's measure. But both proved to be durable, although his successors gave the system a somewhat different tone. Pompidou won the presidency in June 1969 over several left and centre rivals. He adopted a less assertive foreign policy stance and in domestic affairs showed a preference for classic laissez-faire, reflecting his connections with the business community.

The turn toward a more conservative, business-oriented line contributed to a revival of the political left, which had been decimated by the aftershocks of the events of May 1968. Mitterrand, leader of a small left-centre party, took advantage of the change in political climate. In 1971 he engineered a merger of several minor factions with the almost moribund Socialist Party and won election as leader of the reinvigorated party. He then persuaded the Communists to join the Socialists in drafting what was called the Common Program, which was a plan to combine forces in future elections and in an eventual coalition government.

Unexpectedly, in April 1974 President Pompidou died of cancer. Mitterrand declared his candidacy as representative of the united left, while the conservatives failed to agree on a candidate. The Gaullists nominated Prime Minister Jacques Chaban-Delmas, but a sizable minority of the UDR broke ranks and instead declared support for a non-Gaullist, Valéry Giscard d'Estaing, who was the leader of a business party, the Independent Republicans (Républicains Indépendants). Giscard won over Chaban-Delmas in the first

round and narrowly defeated Mitterrand in the runoff.

Despite his conservative connections, the new president declared his goal to be the transformation of France into "an advanced liberal society." He chose as prime minister the young and forceful Jacques Chirac, leader of the Gaullist minority that had bolted the UDR in Giscard's favour. The new leadership pushed through a reform program designed to attract young voters: it reduced the voting age to 18, legalized abortion within certain limits, and instituted measures to protect the environment. But the course of reform was stalled by the oil crisis of 1973, brought on by events in the Middle East. Industrial production slowed, unemployment rose, and inflation threatened.

As discontent grew, Giscard's leadership was challenged by his ambitious prime minister, Chirac. Open rivalry between the two men led Giscard to dismiss Chirac in favour of Raymond Barre, a professional economist. Chirac retaliated by persuading the divided and disheartened Gaullists to transform the UDR into a new party, the Rally for the Republic (Rassemblement pour la République; RPR), with himself as its head. He also gained an additional power base by standing successfully for election to the revived post of mayor of Paris.

These factional conflicts on the right opened new prospects for the coalition of the rejuvenated left and seemed to assure its victory in the 1978 parliamentary elections. But at that point the Socialist-Communist alliance fell apart. The Socialists had made dramatic gains at Communist expense since the Common Program had been adopted, and the Communists decided it was safer to scuttle the agreement. The collapse of leftist unity alienated a large number of left voters and enabled the conservatives to retain control of the National Assembly in the 1978 elections.

FRANCE UNDER A SOCIALIST PRESIDENCY

When Giscard's presidential term ended in May 1981, opinion polls seemed to indicate that he would be elected to a second term. He overcame a vigorous challenge by Chirac in the first round of voting and seemed well placed to defeat the Socialist Mitterrand in the runoff. But Mitterrand surprised the pollsters by scoring a slim victory—the first major victory for the left in three decades. Profiting from the wave of euphoria that followed, Mitterrand dissolved the National Assembly and, calling for elections, succeeded once again. The Socialists won a clear majority of seats (269 of the total 491) and seemed in a position to transform France into a social democratic state.

MITTERRAND'S FIRST TERM

Mitterrand moved at once to carry out what appeared to be the voters' mandate. He named as prime minister a longtime Socialist militant, Pierre Mauroy, whose cabinet was almost solidly Socialist except for four Communists. Major reforms followed quickly. A broad sector of the economy was nationalized (including 11 large industrial conglomerates and most private banks); a considerable degree of administrative decentralization shifted part of the state's authority to regional and local councils; social benefits were expanded and factory layoffs made subject to state controls; tax rates were increased at the upper levels; and a special wealth tax was imposed on large fortunes.

The Socialists hoped that other industrial countries would adopt similar measures and that this joint effort would stimulate a broad recovery from the post-1973 recession. Instead, most of the other Western nations took the opposite course, turning toward conservative retrenchment. Isolated in an unsympathetic world and hampered by angry opposition at home, the Socialist experiment sputtered: exports declined, the value of the franc fell, unemployment continued to rise, and capital fled to safe havens abroad. The government was soon forced to retreat. Mauroy was replaced by a young Socialist technocrat, Laurent Fabius, who announced a turn from ideology to efficiency, with modernization the new keynote.

Many leftist voters were disillusioned by the frustration of their hopes. Discontent also emerged on the political margins. On the far left the Communists withdrew their ministers from the cabinet. On the far right a new focus of discontent emerged in Jean-Marie Le Pen's National Front (Front National), which scored successes with its campaign to expel immigrant workers. To nobody's surprise, the Socialists lost control of the National Assembly in the March 1986 elections; they and their allies retained only 215 seats, while the rightist coalition rose to 291.

Mitterrand's presidential term still had two years to run. But the Fifth Republic now faced a long-debated test: Could the system function when parliament and president were at odds? Mitterrand sidestepped the dilemma by choosing the path of prudent retreat. He named as prime minister the conservatives' strongest leader, Chirac of the Gaullist RPR, and abandoned to him most governmental decisions (except on foreign and defense policy, which de Gaulle himself had reserved for the president). This uneasy relationship was promptly labeled "cohabitation"; it lasted two years and in the end worked in Mitterrand's rather than Chirac's favour.

Chirac acted at once to reverse many of the Socialists' reforms. He began the complex process of privatizing the nationalized enterprises, reduced income tax rates at the upper levels and abolished the wealth tax, and removed some of the regulatory controls on industry. These moves brought Chirac praise but also criticism. His popularity suffered in addition from a series of threats to public order—notably a long transport strike and a wave of terrorist attacks on the streets of Paris—that cast some doubt on the government's promise to ensure law and order. As Chirac's approval ratings fell, Mitterrand's recovered. Cohabitation enabled him to avoid making sensitive decisions, and voters gave him credit for faithfully respecting his constitutional limitations.

MITTERRAND'S SECOND TERM

Restraint paid dividends when Mitterrand ran, against Chirac, for a second term in April–May 1988 and scored a clear victory (54 to 46 percent). The resurgent president chose the Socialist Michel Rocard as prime minister and once again dissolved the National Assembly in the hope that the voters would give him a parliamentary majority. That hope was only partially realized this time; the Socialists and their allies won 279 seats, but they fell short of a clear majority.

Mitterrand's choice of Rocard as prime minister caused some surprise, for the two men had headed rival factions within the Socialist Party, and they were temperamentally alien. Rocard was a brilliant financial expert and an advocate of government by consensus of the left and centre, while Mitterrand was considered a master of political gamesmanship. The uneasy relationship lasted three years, and Rocard was successful enough in managing the economy to maintain his high approval rating in the polls until the end.

Mitterrand's decision to replace Rocard in 1991 with France's first woman prime minister, Edith Cresson, provoked serious controversy. Cresson, a Mitterrand loyalist, had held a variety of cabinet posts during the 1980s and was seen as an able but tough and abrasive politician. Brash public statements by Cresson affected her ability to rule, the Socialists suffered disastrous losses in regional elections (March 1992), and Mitterrand replaced Cresson in April 1992 with a different sort of Socialist, Pierre Bérégovoy.

"Béré" (as he was familiarly known) was a rare example of a proletarian who had risen through trade union ranks to political eminence. The son of an immigrant Ukrainian blue-collar worker, he had earned a reputation as an expert on public finance and as an incorruptible politician. His promise to end the plague of financial scandals that had beset recent Socialist governments won applause but left him vulnerable when he, in turn, was accused of misconduct: he had accepted, from a wealthy businessman under investigation for insider trading, a large loan to finance the purchase of a Paris apartment. Although no illegality was involved, Bérégovoy's reputation for integrity suffered. In the parliamentary elections that took place in March 1993, the Socialists suffered a crushing defeat; they retained only 67 seats compared with 486 for the right-wing coalition (RPR and UDR). Bérégovoy resigned as prime minister and a few weeks later shocked the country by committing suicide.

Although the triumphant conservatives called on Mitterrand also to resign, he refused; his presidential term still had two years to run. But he had to face cohabitation again, this time with another Gaullist, Édouard Balladur. Chirac preferred to avoid the risks of active decision making while he was preparing his own campaign for the presidency.

Mitterrand entered his second cohabitation experience with his prestige damaged by his party's recent misfortunes. He had also lost stature by a mistaken judgment in his own "reserved" sector of foreign policy. Mitterrand had been a leading drafter of the Maastricht Treaty (1991), designed to strengthen the institutional structures of the European Community. When the treaty encountered hostile criticism, he gambled on a popular referendum in France to bolster support. The outcome was a bare 51 percent approval by the French voters, and, although it was enough to put Maastricht into effect, the evidence of deep division in France further reduced the president's prestige. Still another embarrassment was the revelation in 1994 that Mitterrand had accepted a bureaucratic post in Pétain's Vichy regime in 1942–43. There were cries of outrage, yet the shock and fury quickly faded. In some circles he was credited with throwing his critics off balance by his clever management of the news. Prior to his death in January 1996, Mitterrand left his mark culturally on Paris as well, where grandiose architecture projects such as the Opéra de la Bastille, the expanded Louvre, the towering Grande Arche de la Défense, and the new Bibliothèque Nationale de France kept his name alive.

Mitterrand's second venture into cohabitation (1993–95) had proved more helpful to Prime Minister Balladur than to the president. It also had proved deeply disappointing to Chirac, who had engineered Balladur's appointment on the assumption that he would stand in for Chirac and step aside in his favour when the presidential election approached. Chirac had failed to see that his stylish and courteous stand-in might develop into his own most serious rival.

FRANCE UNDER CONSERVATIVE PRESIDENCIES

By 1995 Balladur was the clear frontrunner and announced his presidential candidacy against his own party leader, Chirac. Meanwhile, the Socialists, after some initial scrambling to find a viable candidate, ended by choosing party official Lionel Jospin, who led the field in the first round of voting on April 23. Chirac, a vigorous campaigner, outpaced Balladur, and in the runoff he won again, this time against Jospin. His victory brought to an end the 14-year Socialist presidency.

THE CHIRAC ADMINISTRATION

The right-of-centre triumph of 1995 did not last. In the anticipated elections that Chirac called in 1997, a Socialist majority swept back to power, and Jospin returned to head a coalition of Socialists, Communists, and Greens. Whereas the policies of Mitterrand's second term had made concessions to the free market, Chirac's moderate prime minister, Alain Juppé (1995–97), made serious concessions to the welfare state. Under Jospin, as under Juppé, pragmatic cohabitation struggled to maintain both economic growth and the social safety net. Privatization proceeded apace, inflation remained under control, and the introduction of the euro (the single European currency) in January 1999 boosted competition and investment. Yet unemployment stubbornly hovered around 12 percent in the last decade of the century, casting doubt on Jospin's hope that growth and social progress would be reconciled.

When France hosted and won the football (soccer) World Cup in 1998, however, it was a triumph not only for national sporting pride but for cohabitation at the highest levels, as it showcased multiracial cooperation on a winning squad made up of Arabs, Africans, and Europeans, reflecting France's increasingly diverse society.

In 2002 the RPR merged with other parties to create the centre-right Union for the Presidential Majority—later renamed the Union for a Popular

Movement (Union pour un Mouvement Populaire; UMP)—which succeeded in securing Chirac's reelection that year. Chirac easily defeated the extremist Le Pen, whose surprisingly strong showing in the first round of voting led Jospin to announce his resignation. No longer having to share power with the Socialists, Chirac named fellow Gaullist Jean-Pierre Raffarin to replace Jospin as prime minister. This socioeconomic balancing act remained in place, though, pitting the popularity of progressive social legislation against the difficulties of high taxes, restrictive social security demands on employers, and precarious funding for health and welfare projects.

France took the world spotlight in 2003, when the Chirac administration—believing the regime of Iraqi leader Saddam Hussein to be cooperating with United Nations inspectors searching for weapons of mass destruction—led several members of the UN Security Council in effectively blocking authorization of the use of force against Iraq. Although the French public largely agreed with Chirac on Iraq, the UMP suffered losses in both regional and European Parliament elections in 2004. The following year Chirac experienced a further loss of prestige when French voters rejected the ratification of a new European Union constitution, which he had strongly supported. In the aftermath of the failed vote, the president named his protégé Dominique de Villepin to replace Raffarin as prime minister. He selected Villepin over his longtime rival Nicolas Sarkozy, who then added the duties of interior minister to his job as head of the UMP.

Later in 2005, French pride in the country's diversity wavered when the accidental deaths of two immigrant teenagers sparked violence in Paris that spread rapidly to other parts of the country. Nearly 9,000 cars were torched and nearly 3,000 arrests made during the autumn riots, which were fueled by high unemployment, discrimination, and lack of opportunity within the primarily North African immigrant community. In 2006, in a further illustration of widespread dissatisfaction with the government, more than a million people gathered around the country to protest a law that would have facilitated the dismissal of young employees. Chirac, already suffering a sharp decline in popularity, was forced to suspend the law.

THE SARKOZY ADMINISTRATION

Although he was constitutionally eligible, Chirac chose not to run for president again in 2007. Echoing the public's desire for change, the country's two main political parties nominated a pair of relative newcomers to replace him. The Socialist Party selected Ségolène Royal, a former adviser to Mitterrand, while Chirac's rival Sarkozy easily won the nomination of the centre-right UMP. Both advanced to the second round of elections (Royal was the first woman ever to do so), in which Sarkozy won a decisive victory. Although Socialists disparagingly likened Sarkozy to an American neoconservative, his supporters welcomed his promises to reduce unemployment, cut taxes, simplify the public sector, and toughen immigration and sentencing laws.

By 2010, however, high unemployment and economic uncertainty had contributed to growing dissatisfaction with Sarkozy and the UMP. Having fared poorly in French regional elections that March, the UMP retained control of only 1 of 22 régions, while the Socialists and their allies captured the remainder. That summer the French government's proposed austerity measures, particularly a plan to raise the retirement age, prompted a nationwide strike and other protests; further strikes in the fall brought hundreds of thousands of people to the streets and wreaked chaos in the country's transportation networks. Sarkozy drew additional criticism, notably from the European Union, for the deportation of hundreds of Romanians and Bulgarians, most of whom were Roma (Gypsies) living in illegal camps.

In September 2010, following a July vote by the lower house of the French parliament, the Senate overwhelmingly approved legislation to outlaw face-concealing garments in public places. The ban did not explicitly refer to Islamic dress but was widely understood to target veils that fully covered a woman's face. The law took effect in April 2011, with violators facing fines of €150.

French foreign and domestic policy throughout 2011 focused on the ongoing euro zone debt crisis, while support began to coalesce around a small group of candidates who were likely to contest the 2012 presidential race. Marine Le Pen was chosen to succeed her father as the leader of the National Front, and her populist appeal quickly made her a factor in the contest. Dominique Strauss-Kahn, the director of the International Monetary Fund, who was presumed by many to be the likely Socialist candidate, was dramatically removed from contention after he was arrested on sexual assault charges in New York City in May 2011. Although the charges were dropped several months later, the Socialists had already found a new candidate in former party leader François Hollande. Sarkozy, for his part, spent much of his time on international issues, acting as president of the Group of Eight and the Group of 20, as well as teaming with German Chancellor Angela Merkel to try to halt the financial contagion that was spreading throughout Europe.

Sarkozy's domestic economic policies contributed to a steady erosion of his support, as he proposed a series of austerity measures that were intended to reduce France's budget deficit. Hollande secured his position as the Socialist candidate in France's first-ever open primary in October 2011, and he went on to top a field of 10 candidates in the first round of the presidential election in April 2012. In that contest Le Pen led the National Front to its best-ever performance in a presidential election, capturing more than 18 percent of the vote for a strong third-place finish. Sarkozy, who finished second, qualified for a runoff against Hollande, and he spent the next two weeks courting the National Front voters who represented his best chance at victory. On May 6, 2012, Hollande defeated Sarkozy, capturing almost 52 percent of the vote and becoming the first Socialist to win a presidential election since Mitterrand bested Chirac in 1988. One month later the sweep was made complete when the Socialist bloc captured 314 seats in the National Assembly, giving it a clear majority in the lower house. Although Marine Le Pen narrowly lost her bid for a seat in the legislature, two other National Front candidates were victorious, and the party returned to parliament for the first time since 1997.

CONCLUSION

While the French people look to the state as the primary guardian of liberty, this centralist tendency is often at odds with another long-standing theme of the French nation: the insistence on the supremacy of the individual. On this matter historian Jules Michelet remarked, "England is an empire, Germany is a nation, a race, France is a person." Statesman Charles de Gaulle, too, famously complained, "Only peril can bring the French together. One can't impose unity out of the blue on a country that has 265 kinds of cheese."

This tendency toward individualism joins with a pluralist outlook and a great interest in the larger world. Even though its imperialist stage was driven by the impulse to civilize that world according to French standards (*la mission civilisatrice*), the French still note approvingly the words of writer Gustave Flaubert:

> *I am no more modern than I am ancient, no more French than Chinese; and the idea of la patrie, the fatherland—that is, the obligation to live on a bit of earth coloured red or blue on a map, and to detest the other bits coloured green or black—has always seemed to me narrow, restricted, and ferociously stupid.*

At once universal and particular, French culture has spread far and greatly influenced the development of art and science, particularly anthropology, philosophy, and sociology. The country has been influential in the spread of democratic ideals throughout the world, with the Enlightenment and the French Revolution inspiring political movements for centuries. In October 2012, the Norwegian Nobel Committee awarded its peace prize to the European Union for the ongoing contributions and cooperation of its members, including France.

GLOSSARY

ABSOLUTISM A political theory that absolute power should be vested in one or more rulers.

ARCHBISHOP A bishop at the head of an ecclesiastical province or one of equivalent honorary rank.

ARISTOCRACY Government by the best individuals or by a small privileged class.

BASTILLE A prison or jail.

BLACK DEATH A severe epidemic of plague and especially bubonic plague that occurred in Asia and Europe in the 14th century.

BOURGEOISIE Members of the middle class.

CALVINISM The theological system of John Calvin and his followers marked by strong emphasis on the sovereignty of God, the depravity of humankind, and the doctrine of predestination.

DADA A movement in art and literature based on deliberate irrationality and negation of traditional artistic values.

DUKE A sovereign male ruler of a continental European duchy.

FEDERALISM The distribution of power in an organization (as a government) between a central authority and the constituent units.

HUGUENOT A member of the French Reformed communion especially of the 16th and 17th centuries.

IMPRESSIONISM A theory or practice in painting especially among French painters of about 1870 of depicting the natural appearances of objects by means of dabs or strokes of primary unmixed colors in order to simulate actual reflected light.

MISSIONARY A person who is sent to a foreign country to do religious work (such as to convince people to join a religion or to help people who are sick, poor, etc.).

MONK A member of a religious community of men who usually promise to remain poor, unmarried, and separated from the rest of society.

POSITIVISM A theory that theology and metaphysics are earlier imperfect modes of knowledge and that positive knowledge is based on natural phenomena and their properties and relations as verified by the empirical sciences.

POST-IMPRESSIONISM A theory or practice of art originating in France in the last quarter of the 19th century that in revolt against impressionism stresses variously volume, picture structure, or expressionism.

REALISM A theory that objects of sense perception or cognition exist independently of the mind.

RENAISSANCE The transitional movement in Europe between medieval and modern times beginning in the

14th century in Italy, lasting into the 17th century, and marked by a humanistic revival of classical influence expressed in a flowering of the arts and literature and by the beginnings of modern science.

SERFDOM A member of a servile feudal class bound to the land and subject to the will of its owner.

SOCIALISM Any of various economic and political theories advocating collective or governmental ownership and administration of the means of production and distribution of goods.

SUFFRAGE The right of voting.

UTOPIAN Proposing or advocating impractically ideal social and political schemes.

BIBLIOGRAPHY

GEOGRAPHY

GENERAL WORKS

Comprehensive surveys of the country, using both descriptive and analytic approaches, include Philippe Pinchemel et al., *France: A Geographical, Social, and Economic Survey* (1987; originally published in French, 1964); Christopher Flockton and Eleonore Kofman, *France* (1989); and Xavier de Planhol, *An Historical Geography of France* (1994; originally published in French, 1988), all with important bibliographies. See also Michelin Pneu, *Michelin: Atlas Routier et Touristique*, (2003), a useful reference source with more detailed information than its title suggests.

LAND

Characteristics of major physical regions of France are provided in Clifford Embleton (ed.), *Geomorphology of Europe* (1984); and Gérard Mottet, *Géographie Physique de la France*, 3rd rev. and enlarged ed. (1999). Comité National française de Géographie, *Atlas de la France rurale: les campagnes françaises* (1984), contains maps and photographs illustrating aspects of rural France, both by type of agriculture and by region; and André Brun et al., *Le Grand Atlas de la France rurale* (1989),

provides documentation on all aspects of life from the point of view of agricultural geography. Ian Scargill, *Urban France* (1983), includes case studies of new towns.

HUMAN GEOGRAPHY

General overviews of regional planning, demography, social structure, economic conditions, culture, and politics are found in John Ardagh, *France in the New Century: Portrait of a Changing Society* (1999); and Robert Gildea, *France Since 1945* (1996, updated 2002). Urban France is discussed in Maryse Fabriès-Verfaillie, Pierre Stragiotti, and Annie Jouve, *La France des villes: le temps des métropoles*, 2nd ed. (2000). Demographic analyses are provided in Daniel Noin and Yvan Chauviré, *La Population de la France*, 5th ed., updated (1999); and Alec G. Hargreaves, *Immigration, 'Race' and Ethnicity in Contemporary France* (1995).

ECONOMY

Comprehensive surveys of modern economic conditions include John Tuppen, *The Economic Geography of France* (1983); Jean-François Eck, *La France dans la nouvelle économie mondiale*, 3rd ed. updated (1998); Marcel Baleste, *L'Économie française*, 13th ed. rev. (1995); and John Tuppen,

France Under Recession, 1981–1986 (1988). Additional surveys include Colin Gordon and Paul Kingston, *The Business Culture in France* (1996); Joseph Szarka, *Business in France: An Introduction to the Economic and Social Context* (1992); Dominique Taddei and Benjamin Coriat, *Made in France: l'industrie française dans la competition mondiale* (1993); and Jean Jacques Tur, *Géographie humaine et économique de la France* (1994). Comprehensive regional studies can be found in Marcel Baleste et al., *La France: les 22 régions*, 5th ed. (2001); and Pierre Estienne, *Les Régions françaises*, 2 vol. (1999). Current developments are brought together in *Organisation for Economic Co-operation and Development, OECD Economic Surveys: France* (annual). Studies of special features of the French economy include Dominique Gambier and Michel Vernieres, *L'Emploi en France*, new ed. (1998); Nacima Baron-Yellès, *Le Tourisme en France: territoires et stratégies* (1999); Laurence Bancel-Charensol, Jean-Claude Delaunay, and Muriel Jougleux, *Les Services dans l'economie française* (1999); and Pierre Bloc-Duraffour, *L'Industrie française* (1999).

POLITICS AND SOCIETY

Studies of political administration include Sudhir Hazareesingh, *Political Traditions in Modern France* (1994); Alistair Cole, *French Politics and Society* (1998); James F. McMillan, *Twentieth-Century France: Politics and Society 1898–1991* (1992); Nick Hewlett, *Modern French Politics: Analysing Conflict and Consensus Since 1945* (1998); and Maurice Larkin, *France Since the Popular Front: Government and People 1936–1996*, 2nd ed. (1997). Law is treated in Christian Dadomo and Susan Farran, *The French Legal System*, 2nd ed. (1996); and John Bell et al., *Principles of French Law* (1998). On the more specific question of decentralization, see Jean Marc Ohnet, *Histoire de la décentralisation française* (1996). Health care is discussed in Marc Duriez et al., *Le Système de santé en France*, 2nd updated ed. (1999). Social conditions and organizations in the social sphere are the focus of Pierre Laroque (ed.), *Les Institutions sociales de la France*, updated ed. (1963, reissued 1980). The social conditions of the 19th century are explored in Peter McPhee, *A Social History of France, 1789–1914*, 2nd ed. (2004). A general view of contemporary features of French society is given in Insee, *Données sociales: la société française* (1999), as well as *France, portrait social 1998–1999*, 2nd ed. (1999). A detailed discussion of urban policy is provided in Antoine Anderson, *Politiques de la ville* (1998).

CULTURE

The philosophical perspectives of French cultural life are examined in Alain Finkielkraut, *The Defeat of the Mind* (1995; also published as *The Undoing of Thought*, 1988; originally published in French, 1987). Robert Darnton, *The Great Cat Massacre: And Other Episodes in French Cultural History* (1984, reissued 2001), provides a lively introduction to the philosophes. Cultural policies and the interaction of politics and culture are the subject of Pascal Ory, *L'Entre-deux-mai: histoire culturelle de la France, mai 1968–mai 1981* (1983). Bernard-Henri Lévy, *Éloge des intellectuels* (1987), is an introduction to intellectual life. For literature, see Denis Hollier (ed.), *A New History of French Literature* (1989, reissued 1994). General views of French culture and society are given in Jill Forbes and Michael Kelly (eds.), *French Cultural Studies: An Introduction* (1995); Max Silverman, *Facing Postmodernity: Contemporary French Thought on Culture and Society*, (1999); Martin Cook (ed.), *French Culture Since 1945* (1993); and Alex Hughes and Keith Reader, *Encyclopedia of Contemporary French Culture* (1998, reissued 2002).

HISTORY

GENERAL WORKS

A great historian's review of the long sweep of French history, from prehistoric times to the modern era, is Fernand Braudel, *The Identity of France*, 2nd ed. (1988–90, originally published in French, 1986), and *The Identity of France: People and Production* (1990; originally published in French,

1986). Excellent thematic treatments are provided in Marc Bloch, *French Rural Society: An Essay on Its Basic Characteristics* (1966; originally published in French, 1931), a classic study; Fernand Braudel and Ernest Labrousse (eds.), *Histoire économique et sociale de la France* (1970–82); Georges Duby and Armand Wallon (eds.), *Histoire de la France rurale*, 4 vol. (1975–76, reprinted 1992); and Georges Duby (ed.), *Histoire de la France urbaine*, 5 vol. (1980–85).

GAUL

A stimulating overview of Gaul in the context of French prehistory and early history is found in J.M. Wallace-Hadrill and John McManners (eds.), *France: Government and Society*, 2nd ed. (1970). Outstanding investigations of particular sites and areas of relevance to the study of Gaul as a whole are Edith Mary Wightman, *Gallia Belgica* (1985); and A.L.F. Rivet, *Gallia Narbonensis: With a Chapter on Alpes Maritimae: Southern France in Roman Times* (1988). Life in later Roman Gaul is studied in John Matthews, *Western Aristocracies and Imperial Court, A.D. 364–425* (1975, reissued 1998); and Raymond Van Dam, *Leadership and Community in Late Antique Gaul* (1985, reissued 1992).

MEROVINGIAN AND CAROLINGIAN AGE

A comprehensive introduction to the period is found in J.M. Wallace-Hadrill,

The Barbarian West, 400–1000, 3rd rev. ed. (1998). On the Merovingians, see the engaging overview in Patrick J. Geary, *Before France and Germany* (1988), and J.M. Wallace-Hadrill, *The Long-Haired Kings and Other Studies in Frankish History* (1962, reprinted 1982). For the Carolingians, see Pierre Riché, *The Carolingians: A Family Who Forged Europe* (1993; originally published in French, 1983); and F.L. Ganshof, *The Carolingians and the Frankish Monarchy*, trans. from French and German (1971). Special studies of the civilization of the period include J.M. Wallace-Hadrill, *The Frankish Church* (1983); Pierre Riché, *Education and Culture in the Barbarian West, Sixth Through Eighth Centuries* (1976; originally published in French, 3rd ed., 1962); Suzanne Fonay Wemple, *Women in Frankish Society: Marriage and the Cloister, 500 to 900* (1981, reprinted 1985); and Georges Duby, *The Early Growth of the European Economy: Warriors and Peasants from the Seventh to the Twelfth Century* (1974, reissued 1978; originally published in French, 1973).

THE EMERGENCE OF FRANCE IN THE EARLY MIDDLE AGES, c. 850–1180

This period as a whole is well treated in Jean Dunbabin, *France in the Making, 843–1180* (1985). The political history of this and the succeeding periods is surveyed best in Elizabeth M. Hallam and Judith Everard, *Capetian France, 987–1328*, 2nd ed. (2001); but Robert Fawtier, *The Capetian Kings in France: Monarchy & Nation, 987–1328* (1960, reissued 1982; originally published in French, 1942), is still a useful classic. Social change and feudalization are studied in Marc Bloch, *Feudal Society* (1961, reprinted 1989; originally published in French, 1939–40), a seminal work. An alternative to Bloch's model has been developed by Georges Duby, *La Société aux XIe et XIIe siècles dans la région mâconnaise* (1953, reissued 1988), and *The Three Orders: Feudal Society Imagined* (1980; originally published in French, 1978). Dominique Barthelemy, *La Mutation de l'an mil, a-t-elle eu lieu?: servage et chevalerie dans la France des Xe et XIe siècles* (1997), is also important.

FRANCE IN THE LATER MIDDLE AGES, 1180–1490

For the general political history of the period, see the works of Hallam and Fawtier in the previous section. Individual reigns are studied in John W. Baldwin, *The Government of Philip Augustus: Foundations of French Royal Power in the Middle Ages* (1986); and William Chester Jordan, *Louis IX and the Challenge of the Crusade: A Study in Rulership* (1979). For economy and society, see Georges Duby, *Rural Economy and Country Life in the Medieval West* (1968, reprinted 1998; originally published in French, 1962). Social unrest is discussed in Michel Mollat and Philippe Wolff, *The Popular*

Revolutions of the Late Middle Ages (1973; originally published in French, 1970). Charles Petit-Dutaillis, *The French Communes in the Middle Ages* (1978; originally published in French, 1947), remains the standard account on the cities and towns.

FRANCE FROM 1490 TO 1715

Janine Garrisson, *History of Sixteenth-Century France* (1995; originally published in French, 1991); and Emmanuel Le Roy Ladurie, *The Royal French State, 1460–1610* (1994; originally published in 1987), offer clear summaries of French history from the Renaissance through the Wars of Religion. David Potter, *A History of Modern France, 1460–1560* (1995), is institutional rather than chronological in approach. J. Russell Major, *Representative Government in Early Modern France* (1980), and *From Renaissance Monarchy to Absolute Monarchy: French Kings, Nobles & Estates* (1994), explain the role of representative assemblies. Sarah Hanley, *The Lit de Justice of the Kings of France: Constitutional Ideology in Legend, Ritual, and Discourse* (1983), analyzes one particularly important aspect of the relationship between monarch and institutions. See also R.J. Knecht, *Renaissance Warrior and Patron: The Reign of Francis I*, rev. and expanded ed. (1994); and David Parker, *Class and State in Ancien Régime France: The Road to Modernity?* (1996). Donald

R. Kelley, *The Beginning of Ideology: Consciousness and Society in the French Reformation* (1981), is a study of political thought.

Robin Briggs, *Early Modern France, 1560–1715*, 2nd ed. (1998), is a reliable introduction to 17th-century history. On the religious wars, Mack P. Holt, *The French Wars of Religion, 1562–1629* (1995), is an able synthesis. Barbara B. Diefendorf, *Beneath the Cross* (1991), shows the social origins of the rival religious parties. Roland Mousnier, *The Assassination of Henry IV* (1973; originally published in French, 1964), is a brilliant analysis of the intersection of politics and religion at the beginning of the 17th century.

Yves-Marie Bercé, *The Birth of Absolutism: A History of France, 1598–1661* (1996; originally published in French, 1992), is an admirably clear narrative of the rise of the absolutist monarchy. James B. Collins, *The State in Early Modern France* (1995, reissued 1999), is an overview of the development of monarchical institutions from 1600 to the Revolution. David Buisseret, *Henry IV* (1984, reissued 1992); and Vincent Pitt, *Henri IV of France: His Reign and Age* (2008), offer portraits of the monarch who ended the religious wars. A. Lloyd Moote, *Louis XIII, the Just* (1989), brings Henri IV's enigmatic successor to life. A.D. Lublinskaya, *French Absolutism: The Crucial Phase, 1620–1629* (1968; originally published in Russian, 1965), discusses the economic crisis of the 17th century. Other works on the period's political developments include Joseph Bergin, *Cardinal Richelieu: Power and the Pursuit of Wealth* (1985); J.H. Shennan, *The Parlement of Paris*, rev. ed. (1998); N.M. Sutherland, *The French Secretaries of State in the Age of Catherine de Medici* (1962, reprinted 1976); Richard Bonney, *The King's Debts: Finance and Politics in France, 1589-1661* (1981), and *Society and Government in France Under Richelieu and Mazarin, 1624-61* (1988); and Sharon Kettering, *Patrons, Brokers, and Clients in Seventeenth-Century France* (1986). Yves-Marie Bercé, *History of Peasant Revolts* (1990; originally published in French, 1986), synthesizes scholarship on popular movements. Orest Ranum, *The Fronde: A French Revolution* (1993), is a concise summary of the confusion of conflicts from 1648 to 1653. A. Lloyd Moote, *The Revolt of the Judges: The Parlement of Paris and the Fronde, 1643-1652* (1971), covers one important aspect of the Fronde. Geoffrey Treasure, *Mazarin: The Crisis of Absolutism in France* (1995), is a thorough biography of the man who preserved Richelieu's handiwork and set the stage for Louis XIV's reign. Elizabeth Rapley, *The Dévotes: Women and Church in Seventeenth-Century France* (1990, reissued 1993), highlights the role of women in the period's Catholic revival.

On social conditions, see Robert Mandrou, *Classes et luttes de classes en France au début du XVIIe siècle* (1965); James R. Farr, *Hands of Honor: Artisans and Their World in Dijon, 1550-1650* (1988); and Georges Vigarello, *Concepts of Cleanliness: Changing Attitudes in France Since the Middle Ages* (1988; originally published in French, 1985).

THE AGE OF LOUIS XIV

Pierre Goubert, *Louis XIV and Twenty Million Frenchmen* (1970, originally published in French, 1966), provides a synthesis of Louis's reign; it is supplemented in such special accounts as Lionel Rothkrug, *Opposition to Louis XIV: The Political and Social Origins of the French Enlightenment* (1965); John C. Rule (ed.), *Louis XIV and the Craft of Kingship* (1969); Louis André, *Louis XIV et l'Europe* (1950), on foreign policy; and John B. Wolf, *Louis XIV* (1968). François Bluche, *Louis XIV* (1990; originally published in French, 1986); and Vincent Cronin, *Louis XIV* (2011), are two of the most recent full biographies of France's most famous king. W.H. Lewis, *The Splendid Century: Life in the France of Louis XIV* (1997), examines the political, social, and economic forces that converged under the Sun King. Daniel Dessert, *Louis XIV prend le pouvoir* (1989, reissued 2000), offers a revisionist account of the reign's beginnings. Albert N. Hamscher, *The Parlement of Paris After the Fronde, 1653-1673* (1976), and *The Conseil Privé and the Parlements in the Age of Louis XIV: A Study in French Absolutism* (1987), provide good introductions to the period. Roger Mettam, *Power and*

Faction in Louis XIV's France (1988); and Roger Mettam (ed.), *Government and Society in Louis XIV's France* (1977), analyze the political structure. William Beik, *Absolutism and Society in Seventeenth-Century France* (1985), demonstrates in detail how Louis XIV's government enlisted the collaboration of the nobility. John A. Lynn, *Giant of the Grand Siècle: The French Army 1610–1715* (1997), recounts the rise of the main tool of France's international power. Warren C. Scoville, *The Persecution of Huguenots and French Economic Development, 1680–1720* (1960), is important in assessing the effects of the revocation of the Edict of Nantes. Peter Burke, *The Fabrication of Louis XIV* (1992), shows the interconnection between politics and art under the Sun King.

FRANCE FROM 1715 TO 1789

Alexis de Tocqueville, *The Old Régime and the French Revolution* (1955, reprinted 1978; originally published in French, 1856), is still a basic source for the study of the period. Comprehensive histories include Daniel Roche, *France in the Enlightenment* (1998; originally published in French, 1993), a detailed survey of the period's society and culture; and vol. 1 of Alfred Cobban, *A History of Modern France*, 3 vol. (1969). Michel Antoine, *Louis XV* (1989), is both a biography and an exhaustive account of high politics in that monarch's reign. Guy Chaussinand-Nogaret, *The French Nobility in the Eighteenth Century* (1985; originally published in French, 1986), explains the changing nature of the country's ruling elite.

Steven Laurence Kaplan, *Provisioning Paris: Merchants and Millers in the Grain and Flour Trade During the Eighteenth Century* (1984), describes a basic feature of the period's economy. Economic histories make much use of the 18th-century travelogue of Arthur Young, *Travels During the Years 1787, 1788, & 1789: Undertaken More Particularly with a View of Ascertaining the Cultivation, Wealth, Resources, and National Prosperity of the Kingdom of France*, 2nd ed., 2 vol. (1794), available in many later editions. There are fascinating glimpses of urban life in Louis-Sébastien Mercier, *Panorama of Paris: Selections from Tableau de Paris* (1999; originally published in French, 1781); and Jacques-Louis Ménétra, *Journal of My Life* (1986; originally published in French, 1982). The culture and ideology of the period are explored in Robert Darnton, *The Forbidden Best-Sellers of Pre-Revolutionary France* (1995); Lieselotte Steinbrügge, *The Moral Sex: Woman's Nature in the French Enlightenment* (1995; originally published in German, 1992); Dena Goodman, *The Republic of Letters: A Cultural History of the French Enlightenment* (1994); and Thomas E. Crow, *Painters and Public Life in Eighteenth-Century Paris* (1985). David Bell, *The Cult of the Nation* (2001), offers an important new analysis of the growth of national identity. A classic analysis of his thought is Jean Starobinski, *Jean-Jacques Rousseau, Transparency and Obstruction* (1988; originally published in French, 1957). Keith Michael Baker, *Inventing the French Revolution* (1990); and Dale K. Van Kley, *The Religious Origins of the French Revolution* (1996), show how revolutionary ideas developed out of prerevolutionary political discourse.

FRANCE FROM 1789 TO 1815

Reliable overviews of the period include D.M.G. Sutherland, *France 1789–1815: Revolution and Counter-Revolution* (1985); William Doyle, *The Oxford History of the French Revolution* (1989); and Norman Hampson, *A Social History of the French Revolution* (1963, reissued 1995).

On the origins of the Revolution, see Jean Egret, *The French Pre-Revolution* (1977; originally published in French, 1962); and William Doyle, *Origins of the French Revolution*, 3rd ed. (1998). The best book on the Terror is still R.R. Palmer, *Twelve Who Ruled: The Year of the Terror in the French Revolution* (1941, reissued 1989). George Rudé, *Robespierre* (1967), provides excerpts from the Jacobin leader's speeches. Martyn Lyons, *France Under the Directory* (1975), surveys the Revolution's later phase. François Furet and Mona Ozouf (eds.), *A Critical Dictionary of the French Revolution* (1989; originally published in French, 1988), is an important and original collection of short essays on selected events, actors, institutions, ideas, and historians of the French Revolution. Lynn Hunt, *Politics, Culture, and Class in the French Revolution* (1984), analyzes the imagery and sociology of revolutionary politics. Notable thematic studies include Georges Lefebvre, *The Great Fear of 1789: Rural Panic in Revolutionary France* (1973, reissued 1989; originally published in French, 1932); P.M. Jones, *The Peasantry in the French Revolution* (1988); Albert Soboul, *The Parisian Sans-culottes and the French Revolution, 1793–4*, trans. from French (1964, reprinted 1979); George Rudé, *The Crowd in the French Revolution* (1959, reprinted 1986); Dominique Godineau, *The Women of Paris and Their French Revolution* (1998; originally published in French, 1988); John McManners, *The French Revolution and the Church* (1969, reprinted 1982); Jean-Paul Bertaud, *The Army of the French Revolution* (1988; originally published in French, 1979); Emmet Kennedy, *A Cultural History of the French Revolution* (1989); and Jacques Godechot, *The Counter-Revolution: Doctrine and Action, 1789–1804* (1971, reissued 1981; originally published in French, 1961). The international dimension of the Revolution is interpreted in R.R. Palmer, *The World of the French Revolution* (1971). The best biography of a revolutionary leader is Leo Gershoy, *Bertrand Barère: A Reluctant Terrorist*

(1962). John Hardman, *Louis XVI* (1993), is a life of the movement's most illustrious victim; and the reasons for his fate are explained in David Jordan, *The King's Trial* (1979, reprinted 1993). Isser Woloch, *The New Regime* (1994), shows how the Revolution's principles were institutionalized. Jeremy D. Popkin, *Revolutionary News* (1990), explains the "media revolution" that was an integral part of the upheaval after 1789.

Martyn Lyons, *Napoleon Bonaparte and the Legacy of the French Revolution* (1994), is a good overview. On Napoleon's life, see Felix Markham, *Napoleon* (1963); Jean Tulard, *Napoleon: The Myth of the Saviour* (1984; originally published in French, 1977); and Geoffrey Ellis, *Napoleon* (1997, reissued 2000). The best volume on the Napoleonic regime in France is Louis Bergeron, *France Under Napoleon* (1981; originally published in French, 1972). Owen Connelly, *Blundering to Glory: Napoleon's Military Campaigns*, rev. ed. (1999), is a critical and incisive analysis. For the views of historians across the generations, see Pieter Geyl, *Napoleon: For and Against* (1949, reissued 1976; originally published in Dutch, 1946).

FRANCE SINCE 1815

Volumes 2 and 3 of the already mentioned Alfred Cobban, *A History of Modern France*, 3 vol. (1957–62, reprinted 1969), present the period from the First Empire to the Republics in a sophisticated synthesis. Gordon Wright, *France in Modern Times: From the Enlightenment to the Present*, 5th ed. (1995); and Jeremy D. Popkin, *History of Modern France*, 2nd ed. (2001), are general surveys. Good introductions to the periods they cover are H.A.C. Collingham and R.S. Alexander, *The July Monarchy 1830–1848* (1988); Maurice Agulhon, *The Republican Experiment 1848–1852* (1983; originally published in French, 1973); Alain Plessis, *Rise and Fall of the Second Empire 1852–1871* (1985); Jean-Marie Mayeur and Madeleine Réberioux, *The Third Republic from Its Origins to the Great War 1871–1914* (1984; originally published in French, 1973); Eugen Weber, *The Hollow Years: France in the 1930s* (1994); Julian Jackson, *France: The Dark Years, 1940–1944* (2002); Jean-Pierre Rioux, *The Fourth Republic 1944–1958* (1987; originally published in French, 1980–83); and Serge Berstein, *The Republic of de Gaulle 1958–1969* (1993). Serge Berstein, *La France de l'expansion: l'apogée Pompidou 1969–1974* (1995), continues the story through the presidency of de Gaulle's successor. Annie Moulin, *Peasantry and Society in France Since 1789* (1991; originally published in French, 1988); and Gérard Noiriel, *Workers in French Society in the 19th and 20th Centuries* (1990; originally published in French, 1986), are good introductions to social history.

Surveys of special topics on all or most of the period since 1815 include René Rémond, *The Right Wing in*

France from 1815 to de Gaulle, 2nd ed. (1969; originally published in French, 1954), tracing change and continuity of the political right; Gérard Cholvy and Yves-Marie Hilaire, *Histoire religieuse de la France contemporaine*, 3 vol. (1985–88, reissued 2000), an analysis of the role of various religions; and Raoul Girardet, *La Société militaire dans la France contemporaine, 1815-1939*, updated ed. (1998), on the changing role and composition of the military corps. The role of France in world affairs is emphasized in Pierre Renouvin, *Le XIXe*, 2 vol. (1954–55), on the developments of the 19th century, part of the series *Histoire des relations internationales*. François Caron, *An Economic History of Modern France*, trans. from French (1979, reissued 1983), revises older views about France's rate of growth. Theodore Zeldin, *France, 1848-1945*, 2 vol. (1973–77), explores modern French society, stressing its complexity and continuity. Eugen Weber, *Peasants into Frenchmen: The Modernization of Rural France: 1870-1914* (1976), argues that a sense of nationhood came to rural France only in the late 19th century.

Period studies include Guillaume de Bertier de Sauvigny, *The Bourbon Restoration* (1966, originally published in French, 1955), the standard work on the period 1815–30; Claire Goldberg Moses, *French Feminism in the Nineteenth Century* (1984), which narrates the growth of women's movements; Bonnie G. Smith, *Ladies of the Leisure Class* (1981), a model study of women's lives;

David H. Pinkney, *Decisive Years in France, 1840-1847* (1986), arguing that France changed fundamentally in these years; Roger Price, *The French Second Republic: A Social History* (1972), a thoughtful reevaluation; Philip Nord, *The Republican Moment* (1995), which analyzes the rise of opposition to the Second Empire; Michael B. Miller, *The Bon Marché: Bourgeois Culture and the Department Store, 1869-1920* (1981); Michael Howard, *The Franco-Prussian War: The German Invasion of France, 1870-1871*, 2nd ed. (2001), a model study; Stewart Edwards, *The Paris Commune, 1871* (1971), a balanced reevaluation; and Eugen Weber, *France fin de siècle* (1986). Roger Shattuck, *The Banquet Years: The Origins of the Avant Garde in France, 1885 to World War I*, rev. ed. (1968, reissued 1984), is a brilliant survey of Parisian culture of the period. Charles Rearick, *Pleasures of the Belle Époque: Entertainment and Festivity in Turn-of-the-Century France* (1985), describes the high life in Montmartre. D.W. Brogan, *France Under the Republic: The Development of Modern France (1870-1939)* (1940, reprinted 1974), is a classic account. Jean-Denis Bredin, *The Affair: The Case of Alfred Dreyfus* (1986; originally published in French, 1983), provides a highly readable account of the great crisis.

For the 20th century, see Eugen Weber, *Action Française: Royalism and Reaction in Twentieth Century France* (1962), a full analysis of this right-wing movement; Zeev Sternhell,

La Droite révolutionnaire, 1885–1914: les origines françaises du fascisme, new ed., enlarged (2000), a controversial argument that fascism was born in France; Jean-Jacques Becker, *The Great War and the French People* (1985, reissued 1993; originally published in French, 1980), which shows how France endured the ordeal of total war; Robert O. Paxton, *Vichy France: Old Guard and New Order, 1940–1944* (1972, reissued 2001), a critical analysis of the Pétain regime; Jean-Baptiste Duroselle, *La Décadence, 1932–1939*, 3rd rev. ed. (1985), and *L'Abîme: 1939–1945*, 2nd rev. ed. (1986, reissued 1990), two volumes of devastating analysis of French foreign policy before and during World War II; Philippe Burrin, *France Under the Germans* (1996; originally published in French, 1995), a synthesis of research on the occupation; Charles de Gaulle, *War Memoirs*, 3 vol. (1955–60; originally published in French, 1954–60), and *Memoirs of Hope: Renewal and Endeavor* (1971; originally published in French, 2 vol., 1970–71), indispensable for an understanding of the Gaullist era; Jean Lacouture, *Charles de Gaulle*, 3 vol. (1984–86), a full and perceptive biography; Robert Gildea, *France Since 1945*, rev. ed. (2001), good on the postwar period; and Alfred Grosser, *Affaires extérieures: la politique de la France, 1944–1989* (1989), a penetrating analysis of postwar France's role in the world. Julius W. Friend, *The Long Presidency: France in the Mitterrand Years, 1981–1995* (1998), is a handy guide to the recent past. Hugh Dauncey and Geoff Hare (eds.), *France and the 1998 World Cup: The National Impact of a World Sporting Event* (1999), examines France as the host country and winner of the 1998 football (soccer) championships.
EB: Should this say François, 2e duc de Guise, or was the "2e" a slip up? It is in pageseeder as well. (Before "The wars of Religion").EB: Should this say led by Henri I de Lorraine, 3e duc de Guise, or was the "3e" a slip up? It is in pageseeder as well. 3rd sentence up.

INDEX